IET COMPUTING SERIES 21

Virtual Reality and Light Field Immersive Video Technologies for Real-World Applications

Other volumes in this series:

Virtual Reality and Light Field Immersive Video Technologies for Real-World Applications

Gauthier Lafruit and Mehrdad Teratani

The Institution of Engineering and Technology

Published by The Institution of Engineering and Technology, London, United Kingdom

The Institution of Engineering and Technology is registered as a Charity in England & Wales (no. 211014) and Scotland (no. SC038698).

The Institution of Engineering and Technology
Michael Faraday House
Six Hills Way, Stevenage
Herts, SG1 2AY, United Kingdom

www.theiet.org

British Library Cataloguing in Publication Data
A catalogue record for this product is available from the British Library

ISBN 978-1-78561-578-8 (hardback)
ISBN 978-1-78561-579-5 (PDF)

Typeset in India by MPS Limited
Printed in the UK by CPI Group (UK) Ltd, Croydon

Contents

About the authors

Gauthier Lafruit is Professor Multimedia, with a research focus on Virtual Reality and Light Field technologies at Université Libre de Bruxelles (ULB), the French wing of Brussels University, Belgium. He received his Master and PhD degrees in Electromechanical Engineering with a speciality in Electronics from the Vrije Universiteit Brussel (VUB), the Flemish wing of Brussels University, in 1989 and 1995, respectively. He has worked for 25 years in the domain of visual data analysis and compression, participating to compression standardisation committees such as CCSDS (space applications), JPEG (still picture coding) and MPEG (moving picture coding). In 2014, he joined the LISA department of ULB, Laboratory of Image Synthesis and Analysis, with a research focus on image synthesis techniques for six degrees of freedom virtual reality using real content, like in the movie Déjà-Vu where highly realistic viewpoints to a scene can be rendered without ever having captured them. This includes depth image-based rendering, immersive video and point cloud technologies. From 2014 to 2016, he was co-chair of the FTV (Free viewpoint TV) working group in the international MPEG standardisation committee. In 2018, LISA's Virtual Reality research unit (LISA-VR) has actively contributed to part of the MPEG reference software for immersive experiences that will be published by Q1-2022 as the MIV standard: 'MPEG Immersive Video'. Professor Lafruit teaches 3D graphics and virtual/augmented reality with OpenGL, as well as imaging courses with GPU programming in CUDA.

Mehrdad Teratani is Professor of Light Field Video Engineering at the Laboratory of Image Synthesis and Analysis (LISA), Université Libre de Bruxelles, Belgium. He was previously an Associate Professor at the Department of Information and Communication Engineering, Nagoya University, Japan, where he also received his PhD degree in Information Electronics, in 2004. His research interests include 3D imaging systems with a focus on 3D image processing and compression, virtual reality, 3D media integration and immersive communication, robotics, intelligent video systems and computer vision. His teaching experience includes digital image processing, visual media compression, signal processing and data analysis. Since 2009, he has been involved in the MPEG standardisation, especially the activities related to immersive video, where he served as a co-chair of the MPEG-I (immersive) Visual Ad Hoc Group from 2019 to 2021 with focus on dense light field activities. Since April 2021, he has been appointed as the chair of the Lenslet Video Coding (LVC) Ad Hoc Group. He holds 16 granted patents on the technologies related to image and video processing.

Chapter 1

Immersive video introduction

This book has been written trying to demystify virtual reality and immersive video technology. For sure there exist many books speaking about three-dimensional (3D) graphics on one hand, and 2D video, on the other hand, covering open-source libraries such as OpenGL and OpenCV, but an immersive video is something in-between, also sometimes referred to as 2.5D video.

We want to understand that new beast of 2.5D immersive video at a high level of abstraction, and interestingly, it sometimes revives old ideas published already 30 to 50 years ago. This may look surprising, but mathematically many things were already known for a long time, some of them even back to the mid-nineteenth century! In fact, what really has evolved this last decennium is the technology that can capture and render even higher resolution images than before, as well as all the computing power that has been harnessed to make all required calculations in real-time, thus providing stunning experiences. We are not pretending that mathematically or conceptually nothing has progressed in half a century, but for sure, it is the tremendous evolution in technology that has brought virtual reality (VR) to the level of quality we witness today.

This progress also comes from many open-source initiatives that have been developed since the late 1990s and early 2000s, with for instance OpenGL and OpenCV, just to name a couple of software frameworks that are game changers in 2D image and 3D graphics processing these last decades. OpenGL, which stands for Open Graphics Library, is the de facto standard for 3D graphics. It has been developed by the Khronos group, which ever since has further developed many utilities in 3D graphics, with OpenXR being one of the latest ones to date, simplifying the interfacing between the computing platforms and the VR and augmented reality (AR) head mounted devices (HMD). Its name XR stems from agglomerating VR and AR, giving mixed and eXtended Reality (XR). OpenCV, referring to Open Computer Vision, is a 20 years old (yet regularly updated) open-source library focusing on 2D imaging, including 2D projections of 3D graphics objects, as well as all related aspects of camera pose estimation.

Since the early 1990s, the MPEG standardization committee has developed compression technology to reduce the data rate for transmission of audio-visual and multimedia data, culminating in MPEG-2, MPEG-4 AVC, HEVC, EVC and VVC codecs over the last decades. Note that the last two characters 'VC' stand for video coding, developed by the Motion Picture Expert Group (MPEG), and that each codec generation has brought considerable compression gains. Today, the compression performance reaches two orders of magnitude, with video file sizes and/or transmission rates that are 200 times smaller than the original, raw video data, enabling transmission at around 10 Mbps for high and ultra-high-definition TV. Without MPEG and its compression technology, digital videos would require 2 Gbps bandwidth to the living room, for a single TV channel to transmit, which is hardly reachable with nowadays transmission network technology in the consumer market.

Now that we know the historical context, let us come back to the core technology to better understand how 2.5D video works. While the 3D graphics functionalities of OpenGL have been tremendously successful for video games –which by the way do not use video technology, but rather 3D graphics – they target mostly synthetic 3D content that has been prepared in 3D photoshop alike utilities, such as Blender, MeshLab, Unity, Unreal and the like. OpenGL was not developed with real content in mind, and that represents a serious bottleneck for authentic VR/AR experiences that virtually should teleport the user into naturally looking scenery.

To address this issue, so-called 360 video technology was developed, where the user is immersed into a panoramic scene, projected onto a sphere, with the user positioned in the very centre of it, a bit like in a sky-dome of a planetarium. The surroundings can be captured as a spherical video to give the user full immersion in a real and authentic looking scene.

A real satisfactory VR experience, however, requires that the user can navigate in a virtual scene, even turning around the objects in the scene, like it is the case with 3D synthetic content in video games. This is not an easy target to reach for real, captured content. One may think of reconstructing 3D objects from 2D pictures taken around the scene, aka photogrammetry, but this technique does not always provide satisfactory results, especially not for complex objects or animals and people; it is a technique that is mostly recommended for architectural objects. Another approach consists in using 3D scanners and depth sensors to recreate a so-called point cloud in space, which can be further filled to create 3D objects. Professional solutions can give stunning results, but consumer products may give a rather disappointing experience.

More recently, there is an increasing trend in so-called light fields, which is a rather abstract concept that may cover many different topics. Image-based rendering is one of these that is known for a long time without convincing practical implementations. It has recently got revived within the MPEG-I community, where 'I' stands for 'Immersive'. It is a technique that combines the strengths of using real images from existing scenes, like in 360 video technology, with perspective 3D rendering like in OpenGL. It supports the extraction of depth information from available images using depth estimation techniques, rather than solely relying on depth sensing devices with limited acquisition resolution. This results in depth image-based rendering (DIBR), which – if used with care and good calibration – provides authentic looking scenes, natural objects and persons in the VR experience, as well as for 3D light field displays and digital holography.

Last, but not least, many theoretical aspects that we describe have already been implemented in open-source libraries, such as OpenGL, OpenCV, OpenVG,

Open3D, OpenVR, OpenXR, OpenSLAM, OpenVSLAM, OpenMVG, VCG, CGAL, CVSBA, PCL, to name only a few. In fact, some fully functional, open-source 3D software suits have extensively used these libraries, for example, Blender, COLMAP, Meshroom, MeshLab and CloudCompare, which all are wonderful tools that are freely available on the Internet... but as for any tool, if you do not know what happens behind the scenes, you may be wondering why sometimes the tool does not react as expected. We hope that this textbook will give a glimpse of what is under the hood of such tools.

See it as if you would be driving a car, and suddenly it breaks down, you stop aside the road and you want to bring a quick fix so you can at least reach the closest garage for repair. You look under the hood and then ... surprise! You expected to see an electrical engine only, but instead, you see it is a hybrid car with an old-fashioned fuel engine recharging the battery for the electrical engine driving the wheels ... and you have no clue on how to start fixing all this mess. You are stuck there, in the middle of the desert, and you think to yourself that it would have been wiser to bring a do-it-yourself (DIY) manual with you, just in case ... Well, this book is exactly about that, but not for your car engine; rather for 2.5D video that borrows aspects of both 3D graphics and 2D video. In this sense, it is complementary to the many books about 3D graphics and computer vision, bringing another viewpoint to it ... literally.

At the end of the day, you will understand the main principles underlying the MPEG immersive video (MIV) standard that will be made publicly available beginning of 2022. In contrast to its predecessors developed for the last 30 years in 2D video coding, MIV uses a mixture of 3D graphics, computer vision and 2D video codecs, to address virtual reality applications using real scenes; not only synthetic 3D modelled content. We will not dig into the tiny details of MIV with its compression performance and bitstream syntax that are completely beyond the scope of this textbook. We rather would like to give the reader a look and feel of the – between 2D and 3D – and thus 2.5D technology that are the fundamentals of MIV, so that when you grasp an electrical cable in your hybrid car above, you at least understand whether this is to serve the electrical engine, or rather the fuel engine (the spark plugs). Once you know that, you can better act to get you out of trouble, dropping all superfluous things out of the car for the next 100 km to drive you out of hell ... sounds a bit like a Mad Max story in a post-apocalyptic world, but do not be afraid, we will gradually bring you to the destination without too many hurdles.

I know, you have by now already browsed through the book and you say: 'Oups! Are we sure that we are not stepping into the hell of mathematical formulas with all kinds of bizarre 3D projection concepts?'. Believe me, we got rid of dead weight, focusing on what is strictly needed to get you alive through the adventure. Yes, there are mathematical equations that look scary, but there are also many pictures, and once you get the mindset, you will see things get rather easy. In fact, 2.5D immersive video could have been done in full 3D graphics mode with all its horrific details, but that would have brought a lot of additional complexity for rendering photorealistic scenes. 2.5D video is rather the art of finding the good compromise between the indispensable functionalities, the superfluous functions that are perhaps nice to have but one can nevertheless get rid of, and finally, the complexity of the rendering process.

After all, 2.5D video is meant to run on a smartphone, and not only on a high-performance computing cluster to provide the service to the client. It is certainly nice to have a 3D video one could edit, change the light source colour and/or position and all these fancy things film producers need for their special effects. The question is whether the average man in the street really needs all this? Do not we just want to have the functionality to watch the video from any viewpoint along a path and/or in a viewing zone, not only from a predetermined set of camera viewpoints? Yes, that is what immersive video is all about: support free viewpoint video (within a certain extend), like in virtual reality, but without interacting with the objects and without the need for changing the scene's look and feel. Of course, if one would like to touch the objects, move them in the scene, change the light sources, ... technologically, all this can be done, but at what cost? The cost of a full 3D graphics format, which – after all – might give deceiving visual impressions, in quality and/or interactivity speed, or even the hardware cost of the compute platform that can support all these things together? So, let us keep it simple and reveal the minimum number of ingredients for 2.5D video.

We will gradually build this 2.5D immersive video story by comparing it with 3D graphics, point clouds and the well-known 360 videos, as shown in Figure 1.1. The simplest way to create 360 videos in VR is to have one video per eye, and depending on the viewer's head position, a specific viewport is extracted.

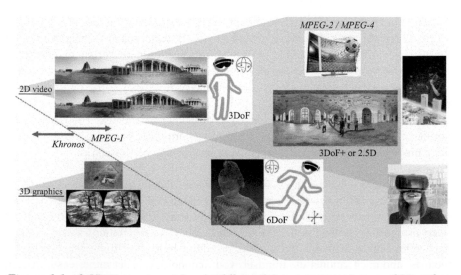

Figure 1.1   *2.5D immersive video (middle-right) is a smart mixture of 2D video and 3D graphics, as shown by the two horizontal, grey cones with their top at the left of the picture*

The evolution of the 2D video media towards stereoscopic video and later 2.5D video is given in the top part of Figure 1.1. Note that the video codec technology one finds in all TV set top boxes over the world contains MPEG technology from the Motion Picture Expert Group standardization committee, with MPEG-2 and MPEG-4 being the most prominent codecs that the committee has developed over its past 30 years of existence.

360 videos are just 2D videos that are presented to the viewer; they do not contain any geometric information such as the shape of objects or their depth. This highly simplifies the roll-out of 360 video technology, which is probably the reason for its popularity ... but be careful in using 360 videos in a VR headset: they will make you easily sick because what you see does not move in correspondence to your own body and head lateral movements. In fact, only the head's rotational movements are considered for changing the images presented to the viewer, not the lateral body movements. 360 videos therefore only present 3 degrees of freedom (3DoF) capabilities.

Complementary to 2D video, we see at the bottom of Figure 1.1, the evolution of 3D graphics that requires very explicit geometric information for synthesizing the stereoscopic image pair that is presented to the viewer. This geometric information can be a 3D model of the scene (here a house) or a point cloud representing the shape and texture of a person (bottom-centre), or even a textured 3D mesh that we will study further in the textbook. With this geometry and texture information, any viewpoint to the scene can be synthesized, like in a 3D video game. The images presented to the viewer will change according to the head and body pose changes, covering 6 degrees of freedom (6DoF) capabilities: three head rotations and three body (and head) translations. Note that 3D graphics technologies have mostly been addressed by the Khronos standardization group, shown at the bottom-left side of the dashed line in Figure 1.1.

Though 3D graphics 6DoF technology looks the most appealing for addressing VR applications, it has a high cost for rendering photo-realistic scenes, as we will see up to Chapter 7. In a nutshell, this comes from the fact that the 3D scene, its lighting, and all physical phenomena are fully simulated to render the stereoscopic image pair to the viewer. This is also the main reason for not blindly using this 3D graphics technology for immersive video.

The ideal solution for immersive video is rather to take the best of the two worlds of 2D video and 3D graphics, that is to provide photo-realistic rendering using mainly 2D images but add some geometrical information to enable the 6DoF free navigation movements. In this process, we will see that we lose the ability to edit the content or grasp objects in the scene, but that is perfectly OK for a vast majority of applications where someone wants to see the 3D scene from any viewpoint, without interacting with it. This is exactly what immersive or 2.5D video provides; nothing more, nothing less... but the technology that can make that work needs a smart mixture of 2D and 3D technology. This is what this textbook is about; it addresses the MPEG-I technology – where 'I' stands for 'Immersive' – from a high level of abstraction, without digging into the details, nevertheless providing sufficient information as to understand any other more bitstream-related syntax book on MPEG-I immersive video, abbreviated as MIV.

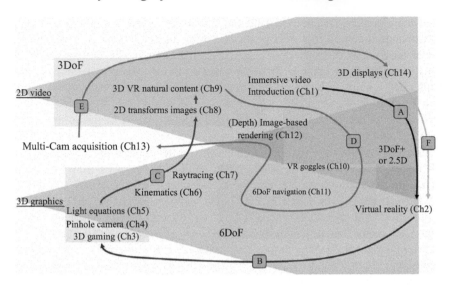

Figure 1.2   Book structure with the chapters overlaying the important subjects presented in Figure 1.1

The structure of the book is given in Figure 1.2, addressing the main topics presented in Figure 1.1 along a spiral path, with segments A to F, covering the various chapters of the textbook, indicated by ChXX within parentheses. When looping through all the chapters, we will come back to our starting point, cf. segment F along path A, closing the loop of our story.

Important topics are given in large type setting, that is virtual reality applications (Chapter 2), starting with 3D gaming technology (Chapters 3–7), gradually understanding that an alternative technology must be developed, irremediably reaching the central topic of depth image-based rendering (Chapter 12). We will then understand that multi-camera acquisitions are required (Chapter 13), and at the end of the day, this will also be useful for 3D displays (Chapter 14), besides our starting point of virtual reality (Chapter 2). In traversing this loop, we will eventually understand the need of developing 2.5D immersive video as a low-cost alternative to 6DoF free navigation with 3D graphics.

In gradually building up this storyline, we will start our adventure with an overview of OpenGL and 3D graphics technology in Chapters 3–7. We will expose the main aspects of 3D geometry and 2D textures while giving a feeling of their underlying complexity. The runtime will highly depend on the supported features such as the level of detail, the need to support collision detection or not, and the extension to raytracing or not. As told above, complexity is an important issue that will already be exposed by the structure of some mathematical formulas, but also by some concrete numerical examples. The reader will then gradually understand that supporting all these 3D graphics features is probably not the way to go for 2.5D video.

We will then show in Chapters 8 and 9 how image-based approaches can give an illusion of perspective changes by applying a mathematical transformation called homography, and how it relates to camera pose estimation and panoramic multi-images stitching that will gradually bring us to 360 videos. Wide angle fisheye lenses and their distortions are also important in the domain of virtual reality, especially to explain how VR headsets work. This will be tackled in Chapter 10. Finally, before starting the main dish of immersive video, we survey depth sensing devices that help in building up point clouds in Chapter 11, which provide 6DoF VR free navigation functionalities, but sometimes at a quite deceiving quality.

Chapter 12 further builds on depth estimation techniques, which – combined with image-based rendering – leads to the main ingredients of 2.5D immersive video, our destination. At the end of the chapter, we will have gathered all knowledge that explains how 2.5D immersive video works, as a smart mixture of all preceding 2D and 3D concepts. The multi-camera acquisition systems of Chapter 13, as well as the 3D light field displays of Chapter 14 fully comply with this framework. Finally, Chapter 15 provides an overview of how 2.5D video can be compressed and transmitted with conventional 2D video codecs, enabling end-to-end immersive video VR applications. The reader is referred to an overview paper of the compression technology of MIV [1] for more details. To be complete, MIV and point cloud coding [2] are so close to each other with respect to their bitstream syntax, that they have been brought under the same MPEG-I umbrella, called Visual Volumetric Video-based Coding (V3C), which will also be very briefly discussed in Chapter 15.

We could have continued our story beyond this point, explaining some specificities of MIV, for instance. We feel, however, that this would be a bit over the edge, exposing unnecessary details to many readers. Moreover, MIV is at the time of writing going through its last standardization stage, before open publication early 2022, so we decided to postpone this to another book, one day ... and if not us, it will be someone else who will take the challenge to explain the (for the layman) unreadable standard specification to anybody eager to really use it in the field. But that is another story ...

References

[1] J. M. Boyce, R. Doré, A. Dziembowski, *et al.* 'MPEG immersive video coding standard'. In *Proceedings of the IEEE*. doi: 10.1109/JPROC.2021.3062590

[2] S. Schwarz, M. Preda, V. Baroncini, *et al.* 'Emerging MPEG standards for point cloud compression'. In *IEEE Journal on Emerging and Selected Topics in Circuits and Systems*. 2019; 9(1): 133–148. doi: 10.1109/JETCAS.2018.2885981

Chapter 2
Virtual reality

2.1 Introduction/history

The story of virtual reality (VR) starts all back in in the late-1830s/early-1840s, with stereoscopic viewing (yes, already in that time, cf. [1,2]) and autostereoscopic photography invented by Lippman in 1908, allowing to see 3D without wearing glasses [3,4]; in a sense, the predecessor of what we now call holography, officially invented by Gabor in 1948, for which he got the Nobel prize.

Many devices have since been developed for stereoscopy, as shown in Figure 2.1, even finding its way into consumer photography [5], cinema theatres [6] and VR goggles [7], however with some concerns with respect to visual fatigue and cyber-sickness [8].

Figure 2.1 shows a couple of important steps in these 3D stereoscopic inventions: at the top-right stereoscopic VR goggles, at the bottom-right light field and holographic displays, and at the left stereo and multi-camera systems that capture sufficient information to create the light field that will be rendered. Such light fields allow to see 3D without wearing stereo glasses, and even provide a holographic vision effect where the user can decide him/herself to focus his/her eyes on the foreground or background objects at will, cf. the change in focus on the dragon in an augmented reality headset, cf. bottom-right of Figure 2.1.

The top-right of Figure 2.1 shows some stereoscopic devices, dating back from the nineteenth century. It all started with the Wheatstone and Brewster stereoscope, the former using mirrors to project left and right images to the eyes like in binoculars (using prisms), while the latter resembles much more the stereoscopic VR head mounted devices (HMD) we know today. Note that already back then, 150 years ago, stereoscopic pictures were in colour ... in fact, hand-painted to add colour (people were incredibly patient, back in that time) [1,2,9]. Half a century later, ca. 1920, the first stereo capturing camera was invented, cf. Figure 2.1-left, and around 40 years later came a big development in video VR goggles, cf. Figure 2.2, probably stimulated by the Apollo era for reaching the moon, with in its slipstream a bunch of new technological developments. In 1962, a patent was filed for a 3D wide-vision motion picture system, called Sensorama, and in 1968, Ivan Sutherland and Bob Sproull designed the first VR goggles, called the sword of Damocles, that interfaced directly with a computer, instead of getting the images from a stereo camera feed.

Indeed, back in the 1960s, close before the first man was sent to the moon, computers were in their infancy, and large computer facilities were needed to make

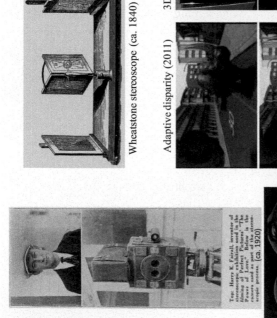

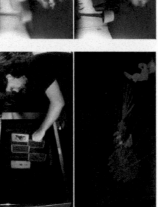

Oculus Rift (ca. 2015)

Hololens (ca. 2015)

Brewster stereoscope (ca. 1870)

Holographic stereoscope (2020)

Wheatstone stereoscope (ca. 1840)

3D Light field display (ca. 2012)

Adaptive disparity (2011)

facebook.com/OmniCamApp

© Disney Enterprises, Inc.

© Holografika

© Creal

Figure 2.1 Stereoscopic devices from the nineteenth century (top-right), adaptive stereoscopy and 3D light field/holographic display (bottom-right), and multi-camera capturing devices (left). © Disney Enterprises Inc.: Reproduced under a Creative Commons license from [10]; Brewster Stereoscope: Reproduced under a Creative Commons license from [11] and London Stereoscopic Company: Reproduced from Public Domain resources [12]

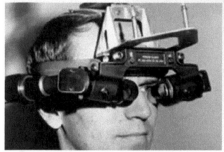

Sword of Damocles (1968)   VPL Research, Inc. (1985)

*Figure 2.2   VR headsets, inspired by NASA's Apollo program. Sensorama:
Reproduced from [13]; Sword of Damocles: Reproduced from [14];
and NASA VPL headset: Reproduced under a Creative Commons
license from [15]*

all the necessary navigational calculations in Apollo's lunar module simulators, cf.
Figure 2.3 bottom-left. Astronauts were trained using lunar maps that were put on
large spheres, and all navigational actions were mechanically moving trolleys and
cameras to create lunar flyover images from these spherical maps, instead of calculating these images on the computer by simulation. After all, by then it was an
impossible mission to synthesize images of decent quality: graphical processing
units (GPU) did not yet exist. Remember the scenes in the Apollo 13 movie, where
all computer screens were ASCII-based and even bar graphs were constructed
using Tetris-alike blocks with predefined patterns printed on screen rather than
really drawing neat lines. Other simulations like the Apollo rendezvous dockings
were also simulated opto-mechanically with camera images directly fed to the
astronaut's screen, cf. Figure 2.3 bottom-right.

Whatever the means they used, even though not fully computer-driven, the first
6DoF free navigation VR system was born; yes, half a century ago! Of course, in
the late 1960s and early 1970s, NASA used extensively such infrastructure for
lunar simulations in the Apollo program, and this has most probably inspired further VR developments, like NASA's VR headsets, cf. Figure 2.2-right.

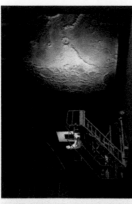

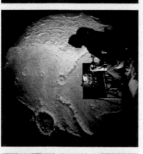

3D Lunar Orbit and Landing Approach (LOLA) simulator for Apollo astronauts training (1963)

Apollo Rendez-vous Docking simulator (1964)

Apollo Lunar Module simulators (1968)

Figure 2.3   *Flight simulator (bottom) using 3D elevation maps (top) in Apollo moon programs. Reproduced from NASA public domain*

But was there already sufficient technology available to make these lunar surface maps, in the first place? In fact, yes: during the first world war, reconnaissance squads started to show interest in stitching photographs together for making a map of the enemy's infrastructure, including some information about the ground elevation [16]. This was the first step toward so-called photogrammetry for environmental map reconstruction, with pioneering publications coming out from the mid-1970s [17], stimulated by NASA's Mars exploration program [18]. Photogrammetry has since constantly evolved, enabling today automatic 3D reconstructions from 2D images captured along the scene. Sparse Bundle Adjustment, a technique often used in 3D reconstructions, cf. Chapter 11, was already mentioned in these early publications. Of course, it has now matured to a fully automatic system that can run in a reasonable amount of time on today's computers.

And today, the big computers shown in Figure 2.3 bottom-left have become sufficiently small and cheap to enter one's living room, for all kinds of VR gaming, Google 3D map and Street View applications, and the like. And guess what: Sparse Bundle Adjustment in photogrammetry is still the favourite solution at hand. Not surprisingly, we will devote a large chapter on the subject, cf. Chapter 11. The interested reader can benefit from a multitude of open-source software tools – OpenCV being the most well-known one – but it is not our intention to go into their programming details in the current textbook; we will rather give the mathematical formalisms so that the reader can better understand how to use such tools in his/her daily applications.

Photogrammetric techniques have also been used to reconstruct 3D representations of actors in movies, but with mild success, since it remains incredibly challenging to render a real-looking human being, this way. This is called the uncanny valley effect; we will come back to this issue soon. Nevertheless, the era of '*immersive video*' has come, with technologies showing similarities with photogrammetry, though some subtle modifications have been added to provide realistic renderings of real-world scenes and human beings. Depth image-based rendering that will be tackled in Chapter 12 falls under that umbrella. Early implementations were already developed at the end of the last century, for example [19], but of course, since then, many things have evolved towards more mature and high-quality solutions that can support applications like free navigation in a soccer stadium [20] or holoportation telecollaboration [21]. Some examples of holograms synthesized with this technology will also be shown in Chapter 12.

Finally, at the time of writing (mid-2021), MPEG – the worldwide committee standardizing compression technology for more than 30 years, without which digital TV would not exist – is finalizing a new standard for immersive video, called MPEG Immersive Video (MIV) [22]. It allows the user in his/her living room to watch the scene from any chosen viewpoint; not only a viewpoint from which the scene has been captured. We return on the promises of this technology for streaming and broadcasting applications in Chapter 15.

2.2   The challenge of three to six degrees of freedom

A typical application for 2.5D immersive video is given in Figure 2.4. We see here a lady that sits on a chair, wearing VR goggles to observe a scene of the lunar module of Apollo 11 landed on the moon. Whenever the lady moves a bit left or right, the images that are projected in her VR goggles should change accordingly. Since the lady's movements are restricted – she stays on her chair – there is no real free navigation all around the scene, hence the parallax changes will remain limited. For such an application, 2.5D immersive video will perfectly fit the bill.

To better explain what happens in this application scenario, let us remind the reader about the main differences between three and six degrees of freedom (3DoF vs. 6DoF), as well as something in-between called 3DoF+, as suggested in Figure 2.5. The top row (a) shows how 6DoF is reached in 3D graphics VR gaming, row (b) corresponds to 3DoF in stereoscopic video, while row (c) gives a glimpse on 6DoF in point cloud rendering, where the content is compressed with reference views and – let us simplify – 'small differences' in an atlas (more explanations will be given in Chapter 15). Finally, row (d) shows an example of the intermediate compression format of 3DoF+ for 2.5D video, also using reference views and atlases that allow synthesizing any viewpoint to the scene within a limited volume. In this sense, 2.5D immersive video is a 6DoF technology, but since it is restricted in the freedom of movement, the MPEG-I standardization committee has named it 3DoF+, that is a bit more than 3D, but at the same time also suggesting that it is somehow a bit less than 6DoF.

Figure 2.4   2.5D immersive video with slight motion parallax while observing the scene with VR goggles. Courtesy: Lytro

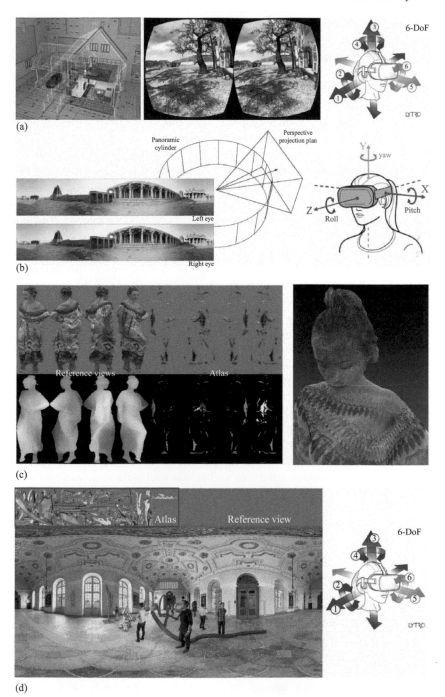

Figure 2.5   6DoF in 3D graphics VR gaming (a), 3DoF in stereoscopic video (b), and 6DoF in point cloud rendering (Courtesy: 8i) (c) have given birth to an intermediate format of 3DoF+ for 2.5D video (Courtesy: InterDigital) (d)

Of course, one may ask: 'In which applications can we use all these 3DoF, 3DoF+ and 6DoF flavours presented in Figure 2.5?'. Let us discuss some examples.

In a live concert broadcast application, for instance, various cameras capture the scene from different viewpoints, and a single 360 panoramic view of the concert is obtained by judiciously stitching the camera views together. A so-called Equirectangular Projection (ERP) video is then broadcasted, and each client may select a portion of the virtual sphere for visualization, as if he/she would have a windowed view of the concert. Most of the time the user will look to the singer, while spuriously deciding to look elsewhere, for example the cord in the background, the drummer who suddenly gets excited during a hard rock passage of the song, or even sometimes look to the public to get an even stronger impression of immersion. Each windowed view – called a viewport – is selected by the user independently from the producer's choices, which provides a feeling of freedom, so far not encountered in conventional broadcasting. Note, however, that the user has only 3DoF: the three angular movements of the head. The absence of translational movement does not present any bottleneck, since the user is most probably enjoying the experience by watching the concert through his/her large, high-definition TV screen at home, virtually looking through a window to a portion of the concert outside. As such, the user still feels to be positioned in his/her living room without the feeling of being teleported into the concert hall.

The situation, however, is quite different when wearing VR goggles for 360 immersion: the user is then literally teleported within the virtual panoramic scene, staying right in the centre of the virtual sphere on which the ERP video is projected. As long as the user only rotates his/her head (cf. the 3DoF situation above), no cognitive mismatch will occur: he/she sees a portion of the scene through a binocular window, getting a stereoscopic 3D immersed feeling. However, when the user changes position, the user will get the feeling that all static objects in that image are following him/her. Indeed, without any modifications to the ERP image accounting for perspective changes (3DoF technology does not provide this), the user gets the illusion to stay in the centre of the virtual sphere, which is hence spatially following him/her. For instance, when the user moves laterally to the left, while a statue is projected onto the virtual sphere at his/her right, he/she will get the illusion that the statue is also moving to the left, following him/her like a dog. This creates a very creepy immersive experience, worth a horror movie. To counteract this cognitive mismatch, the ERP image must be modified to visually move the statue to the right, away from the user, in accordance with his/her positional displacement toward the left. In fact, the image on the sphere should look as if the statue were looked at from a non-centred position in a non-moving spherical dome, and without any depth information about the scene, such transformation (technically referred as 'warping' or 'view synthesis') will never be correct. In Chapter 12, we will come back to this issue to enable so-called 6DoF VR experiences, supporting both the angular movements (the three rotations) and translational movements (in three dimensions).

At this point, the reader might be wondering why such 6DoF technology would be so challenging? After all, 3D video games, like first-person shooting games, already provide all means to create the correct perspective view for any position in the scene. This is true, but bear in mind that the content is fully described in 3D format, with 3D shapes painted with 2D textures. OpenGL rendering technology will – for each user viewpoint – project any 3D point in space to the right pixel on screen to obtain rigorously correct 2D projections. With two such projections – one for each eye – stereoscopic viewing is enabled. It is then the visual cortex in our brain that does all the work to recombine the slight parallax differences of the stereo images into an imaginary 3D picture we 'see'; actually, we 'imagine'. With synthetic content designed in 3D modelling software environments like Blender or Unity, there is no big deal in following this approach. However, with real scenes we see in daily life, it is much more challenging to capture the third dimension: cameras only capture 'flat' images, and even though there exist 3D scanners, they do not comply to some requirements needed to obtain high-quality 3D content, especially when one wants to capture real people into 3D.

This phenomenon of a 'creepy look' to the person is referred to as the 'uncanny valley' effect of Figure 2.6, which states that we feel more empathetic to content with increasing levels of realism, except when approaching an almost natural feeling, where any tiny detail not corresponding to what we would experience in daily life directly and irremediably destroys any empathy to the person we look at. This is the valley that content creators want to avoid at any cost when capturing people in 3D. It is even more recommended to make one's content look more 'cartoonish' than trying to convince someone to be empathetic with content in the uncanny valley.

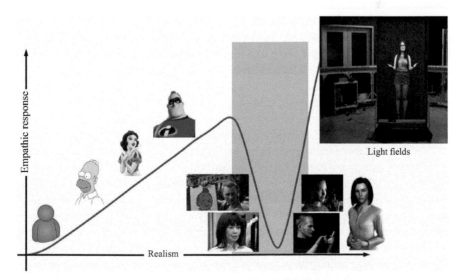

Figure 2.6   The uncanny valley effect with empathy (vertically) versus realism
(horizontally). Courtesy: UHasselt, Belgium

Of course, here we did not go much into the application details and the business opportunities and services that 3DoF or 6DoF virtual reality, augmented reality or mixed reality (VR/AR/XR) offer. This textbook is indeed more oriented toward the underlying technology of VR/AR/XR. Nevertheless, [23] gives an excellent overview of VR/AR/XR applications, as well as their technological strengths and weaknesses. Carefully reading, this study will give the reader insight into all the technological challenges ahead. This textbook addresses some of them, incorporating experience that the authors have gathered in actively following the MPEG-I standardization activities, also contributing to some of the solutions that have been retained for the final standard, published by the end of 2021 [22,24] (including the systems layer aka OMAF [25]). For static images, similar light field technology was developed in the JPEG-PLENO activities, published a bit earlier by mid-2021 [26].

2.3   The challenge of stereoscopic to holographic vision

Everyone knows stereoscopic viewing in cinema theatres, but did you know that experiments have been conducted in the end of the nineteenth century for building autostereoscopic displays, which are stereoscopic without wearing glasses [27]. Lippmann also experimented with such techniques in the early twentieth century, which he called integral photography. Still today, so-called Lippmann holograms give stunning results [28].

Coming back to the stereoscopic viewing, one must aware that – even 6DoF technology becoming eventually mature – there remain other challenges in the visualization pipeline. The most well-known is the 'eye accommodation and vergence' (EAVE) conflict that is a direct consequence of how our visual cortex mentally reproduces a depth impression starting from two flat images our eyes are focusing on. Depth impression comes from a slight, horizontal displacement – so-called disparity – between the left and right images that are presented to each corresponding eye through filters, for example low-cost anaglyph and polaroid glasses used in 3D cinema being the most well-known ones. A large disparity corresponds to foreground objects, while a small disparity to background objects, with zero-disparity mathematically corresponding to the background at infinity (e.g. stars in a sky-dome).

Thanks to the disparity between left- and right-eye images, the visual cortex in our brain reconstructs a 3D representation of the scene with a depth impression, implicitly providing information to the eyes about where to converge to (cf. the above 'eye vergence'), but also where to focus on (cf. the above 'eye accommodation'). It is exactly here that starts the EAVE conflict: while the brain 'sees' the objects at a specific depth, and hence expects that the eyes would also focus at the same depth, physically the eyes always focus on the images they see on the display, that is most often far away from the position where the brain perceives the object in space. In the same way, the eyes are forced to verge in a fixed way to the display in front of them in the VR goggles, while the physical eye vergence depends on the object's position in space. In summary, there exists a conflict between what the brain 'sees/perceives' in 3D in its reconstruction process from the stereoscopic images on one hand, and on the other hand how the eyes optically behave when watching these stereoscopic images. This creates an 'eye accommodation and vergence' (EAVE) conflict, which is an important cause for cybersickness in VR [29]. A similar phenomenon happened in 3D cinema with – in its early days – content with monsters jumping outside the screen toward the spectator, hence creating severe EAVE conflicts. Since then, this has been mitigated by creating 3D content that so to speak 'stays in the screen space' close to where the eyes physically focus, at the expense of drastically reducing the 3D effect and even the 'raison d'être' of 3D cinema.

A good approach to alleviate the EAVE conflict problem is to achieve truly holographic visualization in the VR goggles. True holography creates light points in space, on which the eyes will focus (and verge) at the user's own free will: if he/she wants to focus on a front portion of a nearby object, the eye will do so (through the visual cortex control) and that portion of the object will be sharp, while the rear portion of the object will most probably remain blurred, as we would experience in real life. Real holography, however, is technologically still incredibly challenging, since pixels should be of the size of the wavelength of light, that is around half a micrometre. An alternative is to recreate a so-called light field, that is the field of light or all light rays around us – including their direction – hitting at extremely high density the eye (pupil). We will revisit this approach in Section 10.4, applying view synthesis of the later Chapter 12 to create micro-parallax images. Technology starts to reach this level for small regions to light (the eye pupil), so we may expect such technology coming soon on the market. In the meantime, the solution that is often followed to mitigate the EAVE conflict is to artificially shift and sharpen the image regions that the user is looking at (hence, some eye tracking technology is involved here) and blur all others around, while at the same time adapt the focal length of the lenses in the VR goggles (e.g. electrically controlled varifocal lenses). In this way, the user's eyes react in the opposite way, coming close to the true 'eye accommodation and vergence' the user would experience with a real object he/she would look at. We will revisit this subject in Chapter 10 when talking about the design of VR goggles.

But let us now start with the first topic: 'What is the technology used in 3D games?'. Starting from there, we will gradually move toward MPEG-I's light field technology, throughout the chapters of this textbook.

References

[1] Comments and Observations by John Dennis, StereoWorld, Volume 15, Number 1, March-April 1988.
[2] M. Carnavalet, *Paris in 3D: From Stereoscopy to Virtual Reality 1850-2000*. Hardcover – October 1, 2000, Publisher : Booth-Clibborn; 1st Edition (October 1, 2000).

[3] S. A. Gamble, Wolfson College, 'The Hologram and its Antecedents 1891–1965: The Illusory History of a Three-Dimensional Illusion,' dissertation submitted for the degree of Doctor of Philosophy, University of Cambridge, 2004.

[4] S. F. Johnston, *Holographic Visions: A History of New Science*. Oxford University Press, ISBN 978-0-19-857122-3, 2006.

[5] G. Ogram, 'Magical Images: A Handbook of Stereo Photography,' ASIN : B01JO6XI90, ATBOSH Media Ltd., 2016.

[6] F. Pagot and R. Pookutty, 'Immersive 3-D: The secrets of beautiful stereo cinematography,' ASIN : B08PRXMDW7, The Perfect Edition, 2020.

[7] S. Aukstakalnis, *Practical Augmented Reality: A Guide to the Technologies, Applications, and Human Factors for AR and VR*. ISBN-13: 978-0134094236, Addison Wesley, 2017.

[8] Stereo human factors: Robert Harry Black, 'Human factors in the perception of stereoscopic images,' Thesis submitted in accordance with the requirements of the University of Liverpool for the degree of Doctor in Philosophy, January 2017.

[9] Various slides from previous courses by: D.A. Forsyth (Berkeley/UIUC), I. Kokkinos (Ecole Centrale/UCL). S. Lazebnik (UNC/UIUC), S. Seitz (MSR/Facebook), J. Hays (Brown/Georgia Tech), A. Berg (Stony Brook/UNC), D. Samaras (Stony Brook). J. M. Frahm (UNC), V. Ordonez (UVA), CS4501: Introduction to Computer Vision Camera Calibration and Stereo.

[10] C. Kim, A. Hornung, S. Heinzle, W. Matusik, and M. Gross, 'Multi-perspective stereoscopy from light fields,' *ACM Transactions on Graphics*, vol. 30, no. 6, 2011, 10 pages, cf. https://dspace.mit.edu/handle/1721.1/73503.

[11] Museo della Scienza e della Tecnologia "Leonardo da Vinci", cf. https://en.wikipedia.org/wiki/Stereoscope#/media/File:IGB_006055_Visore_stereoscopico_portatile_Museo_scienza_e_tecnologia_Milano.jpg.

[12] Gift of Weston J. Naef, in memory of Kathleen W. Naef and Weston J. Naef Sr., 1982, cf. https://www.metmuseum.org/art/collection/search/302466.

[13] https://en.99designs.be/blog/trends/virtual-reality-design/.

[14] https://virtualspeech.com/blog/history-of-vr.

[15] https://commons.wikimedia.org/wiki/File:Virtual_Reality_Headset_Prototype.jpg.

[16] P. Collier, 'The development of photogrammetry in World War 1,' *International Journal of Cartography*, vol. 4, no. 3, pp. 285–295, 2018, doi: 10.1080/23729333.2018.1497439.

[17] P. R. Wolf, B. A. Dewitt, and B. E. Wilkinson, *Elements of Photogrammetry with Applications in GIS*. 1st edition in 1974, 4th edition in 2014, ISBN: 978-0-07-176111-6, Mc Graw Hill.

[18] D. Scaramuzza and F. Fraundorfer, 'Visual Odometry, Part I: The First 30 Years and Fundamentals,' *IEEE Robotics & Automation Magazine*, pp. 80–92, 2011.

[19] S. Daniel. 'Very first view synthesis: View synthesis using stereo vision.' Lecture Notes in Computer Science, ISBN 978-3-540-48725-8, 1999.

[20] Intel Sport, F. Yeung, B. Salahieh, K. Loza, S. Jayaram, and J. Boyce, 'Delivering object-based immersive media experiences in sports,' *ITU Journal: ICT Discoveries*, vol. 3, no. 1, 18 May 2020.

[21] T. Rhee, S. Thompson, D. Medeiros, R. D. Anjos, and A. Chalmers, 'Augmented virtual teleportation for high-fidelity telecollaboration.' *IEEE Transactions on Visualization and Computer Graphics*, vol. 26, no. 5, pp. 1923–1933, 2020, doi:10.1109/TVCG.2020.2973065.

[22] Text of ISO/IEC DIS 23090-12(E), Information technology – Coded representation of immersive media – Part 12: Immersive Video, ISO/IEC JTC1/SC29/WG04, 2021.

[23] XR4ALL (Grant Agreement 825545 in European Union's Horizon 2020 Research and Innovation Programme – eXtended Reality for All), 'D4.2: Revised Landscape Report,' Fraunhofer HHI, Nov. 2020.

[24] Text of ISO/IEC DIS 23090-5 Visual Volumetric Video-based Coding and Video-based Point Cloud Compression 2nd Edition, ISO/IEC JTC1/SC29/WG04 MPEG2020/N0065, Online. Jan. 2021.

[25] Text of ISO/IEC FDIS 23090-2(E), Information technology – Coded representation of immersive media – Part 2: Omnidirectional Media Format, ISO/IEC JTC1/SC29/WG03, 2021.

[26] ISO/IEC FDIS 21794-2(E), Information technology – Plenoptic image coding system – Part 2: Light field coding, ISO/IEC JTC1/SC29/WG01, 2021.

[27] W. Funk, 'History of autostereoscopic cinema,' Proceedings Volume 8288, Stereoscopic Displays and Applications XXIII; 82880R, 2012, https://doi.org/10.1117/12.909410.

[28] H. I. Bjelkhagen, 'Super-realistic-looking images based on colour holography and Lippmann photography,' Proceedings Volume 4737, Holography: A Tribute to Yuri Denisyuk and Emmett Leith; (2002), https://doi.org/10.1117/12.474952.

[29] S. K. Rushton and P. M. Riddell, 'Developing visual systems and exposure to virtual reality and stereo displays: some concerns and speculations about the demands on accommodation and vergence.' *Appl. Ergon.*, 1999, doi: 10.1016/S0003-6870(98)00044-1.

Chapter 3

3D gaming and VR

3D gaming and virtual reality (VR) use extremely specific 3D graphics technology to project 3D images onto the user's eyes; they have little to do with playing a 2D video as we know it when looking at a movie on a TV screen. Therefore, this chapter is devoted to explaining the main ingredient of 3D graphics. Along the way, the reader will become aware of the OpenGL's ingredients and their complexity, suggesting that 3D technology is sometimes still challenging, even today 30 years after its conception. Fortunately, there are many opportunities to reduce the rendering complexity, but this often comes with a price to pay with respect to rendering quality. And this, sometimes, can on its turn be compensated by yet another trick. We will give a general overview of all these magic tricks in this chapter.

3.1   OpenGL in VR

OpenGL is one of the most famous 3D technologies. GL stands for Graphics Library, and Open indicates it is open source and completely royalty free: whoever uses OpenGL drivers on a PC does not have to pay a penny to anyone for using it. Historically, OpenGL was developed in the 1990s, then taken over by the Khronos Group, a standardization committee for open standards in 3D, and has since then gradually evolved to a very mature 3D software framework. It has all the necessary APIs and drivers to work smoothly with all graphics processing units (GPUs) that nowadays reach outstanding performances, supporting real-time 3D applications, from video gaming to VR.

As shown in Figure 3.1, a typical VR application will have a 3D model of the scene that has to be rendered to both eyes of the user wearing the VR headset. The position of the headset is continuously tracked with internal accelerometers and/or external tracking devices (a), and with this position in mind, the OpenGL application (b) computes from the 3D model (c) what the user would see (d) for his/her specific head position, when staring at the virtual 3D scene. A pair of stereoscopic images are calculated in a blink of an eye, and projected in the headset, immersing the user into the virtual world.

An important aspect is what kind of content is to be rendered in the headset? Is it synthetic content with a cartoonish-alike look and feel, or is it content that must be rendered at ultra-realistic quality levels, in such a way that it looks very real and natural? In the former case, like in the example of Figure 3.1 with a 3D model of

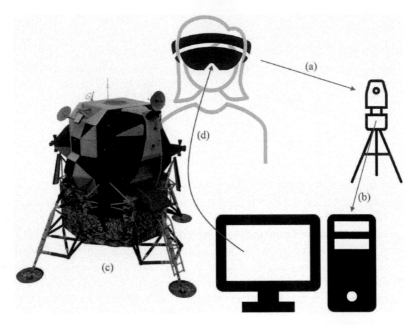

Figure 3.1   VR tracking and rendering system: (a) track the user's head,
(b) calculate the 2D image on a PC (c) starting from a 3D model,
(d) with the final rendering on the headset. Reproduced under a
Creative Commons license from [1]

the lunar landing module, OpenGL provides satisfactory results. In the latter case, one must go far beyond OpenGL, using raytracing techniques that may give results indistinguishable from reality, like in the Apollo 11 example of Figure 3.2. However, because of its complexity, raytracing was far from real-time, even a couple of years ago. Only recently, in 2019, Nvidia has proposed real-time raytracing solutions with powerful GPUs.

3.2   3D data representations

In this section, we will rapidly review the most prevalent 3D data representation formats that are used in the OpenGL pipeline, which itself will be presented in Section 3.3.

3.2.1   Triangular meshes

The easiest way to represent a 3D object is to approximate its shape by interconnected triangles, as exemplified in Figure 3.3 for a simple object like the cube. Note that the triangles are obtained by splitting the quads that automatically appear when subdividing each face of the cube. Many 3D objects are indeed represented by quads, but triangles have the advantage that their surface is a perfect plane: three non-collinear points

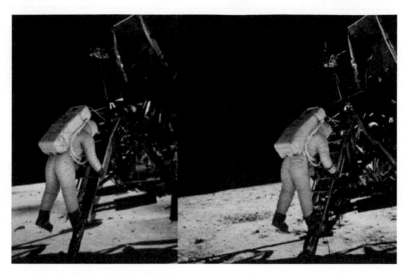

Figure 3.2   3D rendering of the lunar module of Apollo 11 (left) compared with a real photograph (right). Reproduced under a Creative Commons license from [2]

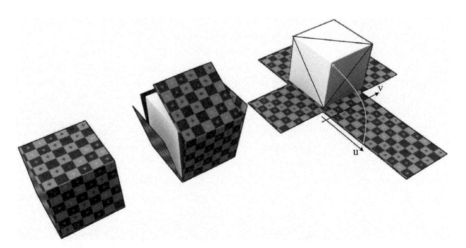

Figure 3.3   A triangulated 3D model of an object (cube) with a 2D texture mapped onto it, using (u,v) coordinates. Reproduced under a Creative Commons license from [3]

always describe a plane, while four points might induce a fold in the plane to be able to connect them all. The planarity of triangles is an important asset when performing OpenGL rendering since a line on a triangle will always be projected as a line on the screen. Further details will be given in the next section about this issue.

To give a more realistic effect, the cube in Figure 3.3 is wrapped around with a 2D texture, using a so-called UV mapping, where U and V are the two coordinates (ranging

*Figure 3.4   3D object (left) and its UV texture mapping (right). Reproduced under
a Creative Commons license from [1]*

from 0 to 1) of the 2D texture. Note that the 2D texture is perfectly rectangular, but conceptually, this is not even needed, since each vertex on the cube is linked to the texture coordinates, explicitly indicating how the texture is mapped onto the cube. As such, the cross-shaped texture might also be used. In general, different regions of the object are mapped side by side in the texture map, creating a mosaic of patches, as exemplified in Figure 3.4. By convenience, big patches are often clustered at one side of the texture, while small patches at the other side, though this is not strictly required.

The triangular meshes on which these textures are mapped should be sufficiently numerous for well describing the shape of the object. For instance, though the lunar module of Figure 3.5 is made of cubical shapes, some parts are cylindrical, or even have an irregular shape (the base structure of the lunar module) and therefore need much more triangles to well describe their shape. One easily ends up in hundreds of thousands and even millions of triangles, as at the bottom-left of Figure 3.5.

Of course, when in the VR animation, the lunar module is far away from the moon, any observer on the moon will hardly see its details. Therefore, 3D objects are often represented at various levels of detail, as exemplified at the bottom of Figure 3.5, where the general shape of the lunar module is preserved despite a reduction of the number of vertices and faces with two orders of magnitude. This comes handy to keep a good quality-speed trade-off. For instance, in a 3D game where we observe the lunar module far away from the moon while it is docking to the command module for travelling back to earth, the visual quality of the rendering will hardly be impaired by this reduced number of triangles, while at the same time speeding up the rendering pipeline to keep fluent animations. Of course, the decision to gradually reduce the number of triangles per object in the 3D game or VR animation will highly depend on the variability of the execution time. Reference [4] shows for a generic OpenGL pipeline how the number of triangles and their number of pixels projected on the screen influence the OpenGL rendering time. This helps in better deciding when to reduce the level of detail for each object, at each point in time. A rich spectrum of

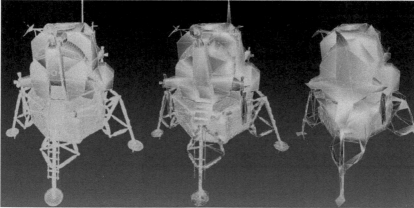

Figure 3.5   *Levels of detail of a 3D model of the lunar module (top) with (left) 230 k vertices and 430 k faces, (middle) 6.5 k vertices and 13.7 k faces and (right) 760 vertices and 1,180 faces. Reproduced from NASA public domain (top); Reproduced under a Creative Commons license from [1] (bottom)*

simplification opportunities exists, all put under the umbrella of level of detail (LoD) [5–8]; we will here focus on the mesh simplification approaches.

To obtain the results of Figure 3.5, we have used the clustering decimation tool of Meshlab – a free and open-source tool providing simple 3D rendering – to get the object at various levels of detail. In fact, many different mesh simplification tools exist, each with their pros and cons. For instance, when the shape is very regular, the mesh simplification rules are simpler. We will return to this topic in the next section. Meanwhile, the interested reader is referred to [5,7] for an overview on available mesh simplification algorithms. To evaluate the quality of the simplification process, the Metro tool was developed in the 1990s [9,10]: it allows to measure the errors introduced by the simplification process, calculating the distance between a vertex and the planar patch that replaces it after simplification.

Also be aware that the visual quality not only depends on the shape deformation of the 3D object after mesh simplification but also on the textures used as materials. Often, rich textures can well hide shape imperfections. In the same line of thoughts, when the object becomes visually ridiculously small, it is recommended to replace it by a rectangle showing a 2D image of the object (outside the object's silhouette, the pixels are transparent to let background colours come through). This is called a sprite or billboard [8], which does not have any UV mapping; it is merely a simple, planar image put there in the scene. It gives sufficient realism for far-away objects, while drastically reducing the workload in the OpenGL pipeline.

3.2.2   Subdivision surfaces and Bézier curves

The mesh simplification tools may sometimes become quite complex because the vertex connectivity can change from vertex to vertex, which introduces special cases that the mesh tool must support. Subdivision surfaces have a constant (or almost constant) vertex connectivity, which reduces the complexity of the mesh simplification process. For instance, in Figure 3.6, a big triangle at level 1 can be subdivided (thus refined) into four triangles to obtain level 2 by connecting (and slightly displacing) its edges' midpoints. Inversely, the four triangles can easily be replaced by one single triangle with little effort, reaching a simple level of detail mechanism. After a relatively small number of subdivision stages – here labelled as levels – a very smooth surface (here a sphere) can be obtained.

Note that the vertex connectivity is mostly equal to six. In general, however, when a graphics designer creates a mesh, the vertex connectivity may vary heavily, and the subdivision rule must adapt to such a situation. This is the case with the Catmull-Clark subdivision [11], for which one can find code on [12,13] that includes Raytracing code we will revisit in Chapter 7.

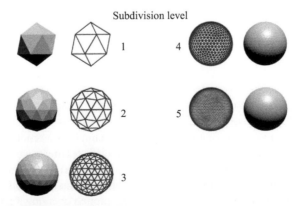

Figure 3.6   3D mesh subdivision at various subdivision levels. Reproduced under a Creative Commons license from [14]

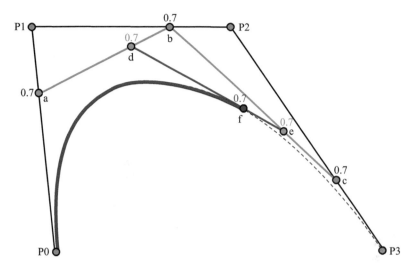

Figure 3.7   Bézier curve with four control points and one point (t = 0.7) created with the Casteljau algorithm

In the 1960s, Mr. Bézier, then working with Renault in designing the body-works of cars, developed a technique to draw a smooth curve at any resolution. These curves are now called Bézier curves. Such curves are defined by four control points, two of which define the start and endpoint of the curve, while the two others describe the convex hull of the curve, as well as the tangents in the start and endpoints, cf. Figure 3.7 [15].

Mathematically, in each coordinate x(t), y(t), or z(t), a Bézier curve is weighted sum (weighting coefficients depend on the control point coordinates) of four Bernstein polynomials with the free parameter t ranging from 0 to 1:

$$B_0(t) = (1 - t)^3$$
$$B_1(t) = 3.t \cdot (1 - t)^2$$
$$B_2(t) = 3.t^2 \cdot (1 - t)$$
$$B_3(t) = t^3$$

(3.1)

We will not further go into the mathematical details. We highly recommend [15] for more details on Bézier curves, as well as another family of 'smooth curves' known as splines.

Interestingly, any point of the Bézier curve can be constructed by three successive iterations as shown in Figure 3.7: take on each segment between the starting and endpoint, the point at position t (=0.7 in the figure) and connect successive points with a line; then repeat the operation three times, on segments [a,b] and [b,c] first, then on segment [d,e]. The last segment at parameter value t gives the Bézier point for that specific value t. In the example of Figure 3.7, point f is so created for $t = 0.7$. Repeating this operation for each t-value builds up the Bézier curve, as

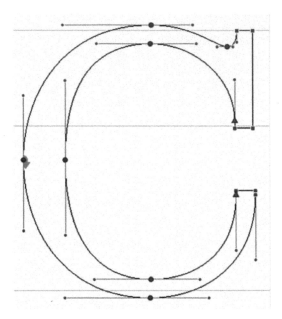

*Figure 3.8   Bézier curves in postscript and PDF characters, here the letter C.
Reproduced under a Creative Commons license from [16]*

shown by the thick solid red curve for *t*-values smaller than 0.7, and the dashed red curve for *t*-values larger than 0.7 (with $t = 1$ being the maximum value). That we need three iterations is related to the power three in (3.1), because we must take three times a linear interpolation of a previously linear interpolated value, yielding a third power in t.

This construction is called the Casteljau algorithm, named after his inventor, who was also working for (another) car manufacturer. Its rigorous mathematical proof can be found in many OpenGL textbooks, including [27]; we will not further dig into its details.

As an anecdote, Bézier curves have been used in many applications since their invention. Most people are probably not even aware of that. One of these applications is postscript and PDF printing, as explained in Box 3.1.

Box 3.1:   Postscript and PDF printing of Bézier characters

A decade after the first laser printers were invented (also in the 1970s), Adobe invented the postscript language for printing characters at any resolution. Instead of using a lookup table for printing a pixel in black or white, the letters were defined with smoothly connected Bézier curves and a handful of control points, as shown here for the letter C, cf. Figure 3.8 [16]. In this way, using the Casteljau algorithm, it is possible to change the character resolution at will: with more pixels to print, more Casteljau iterations over various *t* values were used to keep a perfectly smooth character.

Also, when drawing a smooth curve with Powerpoint, one unconsciously uses a Bézier curve. This is easy to verify by right-clicking on 'edit points' which will bring the two tangent lines of the curve for further editing.

Ever since its invention, the Bézier curve has been widely used in everyday applications. In the early days of OpenGL, enthusiasts looked for an emblematic object to show OpenGL's capabilities, and in 1974, Martin Newell came up with a teapot, all made of Bézier patches – Bézier curves in each of the surface dimensions – as shown in Figure 3.9. Besides simple objects like cylinders and spheres, the OpenGL 'standard object library' hence ended up in one more elaborated object: the teapot. This explains why in OpenGL tutorials one often finds that teapot.

3.2.3   Textures and cubemaps

In previous sections, we have already seen that shapes of the object can be simplified the more objects lie far away, which eventually may end up in sprites that are 2D images fully replacing the object. In general, for far away objects, also in the case of

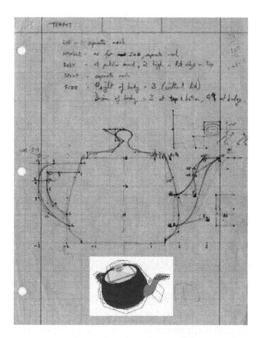

Figure 3.9   Bézier curves and patches for the well-known OpenGL teapot, superimposed on its first sketch in history. Courtesy: Computer History Museum

*Figure 3.10   Cubemap (a) and its cross-shaped texture (b), allowing the rendering
of various viewpoints (c), (d) and (e), with the characteristic that all
lines remain straight. Reproduced under a Creative Commons
license (a) from [3] and (b-e) from [17]*

panoramas, it makes little sense to give elaborated shapes to them; a simple planar
image suffices. The cubemap has been developed for this very purpose: it is a cube with
panoramic textures put on its six faces, like in Figure 3.3, but here the cube represents
the outer world, not an object inside the world. Figure 3.10 shows an example for
various head poses of the user looking to a part of the surrounding cubemap.

Such a cubemap simplifies the 3D rendering process by just taking a part of the
surrounding texture, almost handling it like a sprite, but it has also the advantage
that vertical and horizontal lines remain straight in any viewing direction in the
box, cf. Figure 3.10. Vertical lines might converge when looking up or down, but
they will certainly not become curves. This is different when using a spherical
cubemap – or should we say, 'sphere map' (an alternative name is 'skybox') – as
one would find in a planetarium dome. From the projection from the middle of the
dome towards the dome itself, one can always take care that horizontal and vertical
lines look horizontal and vertical from the central point of view where the projector
is positioned. However, for the spectators outside the centre, a line that is projected
through a plane on the dome will look curved from a point outside that plane.

Figure 3.11 A cubemap, holding inside another cube that is highly reflective. Courtesy: BlenderArtists.org [18]

Spherical skyboxes are therefore not often used in 3D graphics, especially not in 3D gaming where the user moves all around in the scene, hence does not stand in the middle of the spherical skybox. However, in VR, one often assumes that the user is standing in the middle of the surrounding sphere (or cube), hence such curvilinear distortion will not occur ... unless special actions are taken in the rendering to enable 6DoF movements outside the centre, like in real free navigation, which is another story that will be addressed later in Chapter 11.

Finally, cubemaps also allow us to see the surroundings not directly, but indirectly after reflection, like in the example of Figure 3.11. Here, the cubemap is made of the six textures shown at the right, creating the background scenery at the left. An additional very reflective, cubical object is put in the centre of the scene, with its three visible faces reflecting the surrounding cubemap.

3.3 OpenGL pipeline

Figure 3.12 gives a high-level overview of the 3D graphics processing pipeline that calculates a 2D screen projection of a 3D scene. The scene's 3D objects that are described as a collection of triangles are pushed through all the modules, two of which are programmable: the vertex and fragment shaders, which borrow their name of 'shader' from the fact that they are heavily involved into the light and shading calculations, we will see later. To be complete, there exist also geometry and compute shaders for more advanced calculations, but we will not consider them in this textbook.

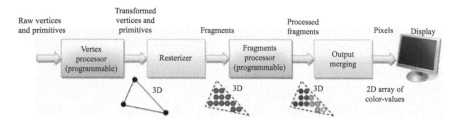

Figure 3.12   OpenGL processing pipeline with vertex and fragment processors, aka shaders. Reproduced under a Creative Commons license from [19]

Historically, the OpenGL pipeline started in versions 1.x and 2.x with fixed functions for the light equations of Section 5.1 of Chapter 5, but gradually, instead of parametrizing them to confer some flexibility, it was chosen to foresee fully programmable functionalities with a dedicated programming language: GLSL, which stands for Graphics Library Shading Language. From OpenGL v3.0 on, the parametrizable functions were deprecated, and today OpenGL (v4.0 and beyond) is fully based on programmable shaders. It has therefore become the programmer's responsibility not only to use but also to program the OpenGL pipeline adequately. It may look like a burden to use shaders, but besides their high flexibility for visual effects, they also provide parallel programming without the programmer even noticing it. For example, when a programmer implements a rotation in a vertex shader instead of using the original OpenGL glrotate function, he/she also pushes this functionality into an ocean of processors that are running in parallel on the graphics card or GPU. It is therefore recommended to program any application functionality as much as possible in GLSL, instead of conventional programming languages like C or C++.

For instance, in Unity, visual effects and interactions are programmed in C#, very much following the GLSL mindset; these functionalities are thus pushed to a parallel processing framework. In Blender, one can program such effects in Python or with a visual interface of interconnecting modules (the node editor), which themselves are transformed into the corresponding GLSL functionalities behind the scenes. It is not the intention of the current textbook to go into the details of how to program in such third-party software; many books exist around the subject, for example [20–25] to name only a few. We would rather like to give a high-level overview of the OpenGL functionalities, so that one is better prepared in using OpenGL (or derivatives thereof, e.g. WebGL) more adequately.

Coming back to Figure 3.12, the 3D objects are processed triangle by triangle to obtain the final 2D rendering. The vertex shader will perform the calculations on the triangle's vertices (e.g. translations, rotations, some parts of the light equations of Section 5.1 of Chapter 5), and then, each triangle passes the rasterizer which will scan the triangle line by line onto the 2D screen. This is done as shown in Figure 3.13, where the 3D triangle vertices and borders are projected onto the 2D screen, followed by filling in each pixel of the screen with a colour that is read from the texture, allocated to that triangle. The rasterizer thus passes overall screen

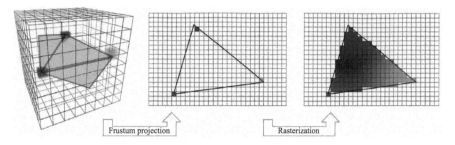

Figure 3.13   Rasterization in the fragment shader. Reproduced under a Creative Commons license from [26]

pixels to know what texel (the equivalent of a pixel on the texture) to allocate to each of these screen pixels, but it is the fragment shader (fragments can be regarded as pixels; after all, what's in a name) that finalizes the colouring of the pixels/fragments. Indeed, the programmable fragment shader modulates the texel colour corresponding to the pixel/fragment with some of the fragment shader's light equations of Section 5.1. It is only after this operation that the pixel colour is complete and ready to be displayed.

Instead of directly 'printing' the pixel colour on screen, all results are held in the Z-buffer; this is a frame buffer that collects all pixels from all triangles before it is transferred to the screen for display. This buffer is called the 'Z'-buffer because it also collects the Z-information (the depth) of the corresponding point in 3D space (the 3D point that gets the texel colour). This is useful, because if two triangles are (partially) projected on the same screen region, for example the two triangles come from two objects lying one behind the other, then the Z-buffer will keep the pixel that is the most in the foreground for display. Note that this approach even allows two triangles to cross each other, where let us say half of the pixels of the first triangle are displayed, as well as the other half of the pixels of the second triangle. The Z-buffer does not even have to calculate the intersection line between the two triangles; it just takes a decision pixel by pixel based on the available Z or depth information.

Applying this full pipeline on each incoming triangle of the 3D scene will eventually create a 2D projection of the scene. Nevertheless, let us put some nuances in this overall scheme.

First, triangles that are at the back of the objects do not have to be rendered. Of course, the Z-buffer mechanism will detect that their pixels are further away than in foreground triangles that will overlap them in the 2D projection, but looking at the triangle's normal, one can directly take a decision whether the triangle is visible or not: backward-facing triangles have a normal pointing backwards, hence detecting this condition can drastically reduce the rendering processing load by discarding them upfront.

Second, some forward-facing triangles might fall fully or partially outside the screen borders. Therefore, a clipping operation is first performed (not shown in Figure 3.12) where one detects whether some of the triangle borders (and hence also the vertices) fall outside the screen region. The interested reader is referred to the method of Cohen-Sutherland of [27] for more details on how this works. Just keep in mind that the method is made to be handled easily with simple hardware because the first graphics cards in history had limited processing power. In fact, a border (and vertex) that fully falls inside the screen region gets a code 0000, while for one falling outside the screen border, at least one of these bits is 1, which can easily be detected with simple logic circuitry. More details can be found in [27].

In the same line of thoughts in simplifying the graphics hardware as much as possible, a method was developed to draw lines on the screen with simple integer arithmetic. Indeed, lines should be decomposed into discrete pixels, and it is not so obvious on deciding which pixel should be coloured and which not. For instance, in Figure 3.13, we observe that the left-most triangle border is approximated by a stair-step shape of coloured pixels, not fully covering the line. Another triangle that would be at its left side needs to have its right border coloured such that no single pixel is left inadvertently black between the two triangles lying side by side. To this end, Bresenham [27] has developed an algorithm that scans the screen from left to right, pixel by pixel, and decides whether the pixel on the same row should be coloured, or the pixel one row upper (in case of a line with a positive slope). Great care was taken at that time to have only integer arithmetic without any division operation, so that simple hardware could handle that properly. In fact, this line drawing mechanism occurs implicitly at every triangle border when colouring a triangle line by line, as in Figure 3.13: for each horizontal row of pixels, one should clearly know what the first pixel is, as well as the last pixel of that row in the triangle. This should perfectly match with the border of the neighbouring triangle at the left and right sides of the current triangle; otherwise, gaps between triangles might occur. Therefore, even though this line drawing mechanism might look innocent, it is a critical operation that should be taken with care. OpenGL developers have probably spent a lot of time debugging it throughout the years, hence we do not recommend enthusiasts in designing a 3D rendering pipeline by themselves; rather take OpenGL source code as a starting point. Furthermore, while still handling all situations properly, OpenGL source code remains sufficiently simple as to be easily ported on a plethora of platforms, including FPGA hardware circuits, for example [28].

Box 3.2:   NASA 3D rendering without OpenGL

NASA has since the early days of the Apollo race to the moon (the 1960s–1970s) developed a lot of 3D based software, for example the stereo matching tool Ames [29], which has its own rasterizer similar to OpenGL, but not using any OpenGL library. It is interesting to have a look at their source code, with only a couple of pages code for their 2D projection; much less than what OpenGL requires. Admittedly, the NASA code only covers orthographic projection; not perspective projection, as we will see in Chapter 4, which probably simplifies the challenge. As a side remark, both projection modes involve additional processing transforming all coordinates towards normalized device coordinates (NDC) ranging from -1 to $+1$, which must be well represented by floating point numbers, no integers anymore. Also, here, the original OpenGL designers took great care in developing code that could easily scale with the compute power over many decades. That surely contributed to OpenGL's success.

Finally, coming back to how texels are projected as pixels in the fragment shader, one should be aware that a horizontal unit step in the pixel domain (on screen) corresponds, in general, to a larger step along the texels. For instance, for a very oblique surface as in Figure 3.14, almost perpendicular to the screen, two adjacent screen pixels will find their origin on the object texture at two very different places therein; all in-between texels may be considered as lost. Two successive raster lines on screen will have this effect completely independently of each other, and this erratic pixel-texel selection may cause very disturbing speckle effects in the final rendering, as shown in Figure 3.14(a). To overcome these artefacts, a so-called mipmapping (Multiple in Place mapping) was developed in OpenGL, which is a kind of level of detail for textures instead as for meshes, as was presented earlier in Section 3.2.2. This creates projections that are much more regular and smoother, as shown in Figure 3.14(b). The main idea is to create multiple resolutions of the same texture, as shown in Figure 3.14(a), and then take the resolution where the texel step would be one, or close to one; in the latter case, two texture resolutions are needed and a linear interpolation between two successive levels is followed to find the texel colour to be displayed. Details are beyond the scope of this textbook, but Figure 3.15(b) gives a glimpse on the trilinear interpolation used in mipmapping [30–32]; we call it trilinear, because it is linear over three dimensions. In the figure, the amplitude of four pixels of one mipmap level are represented by a vertical bar; the pixel amplitude of the upper mipmap level is also represented by a bar. The trilinear interpolation now works over three coordinates: two (here represented by the coordinates s and t) correspond to the image dimensions in each level of the pyramid in the figure, while the third one u is a linear interpolation 'vertically' from one image to the next. A linear interpolation

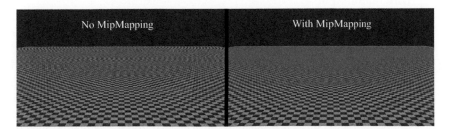

Figure 3.14   3D rendering without (left) and with mipmapping (right).
Reproduced from Public Domain [33]

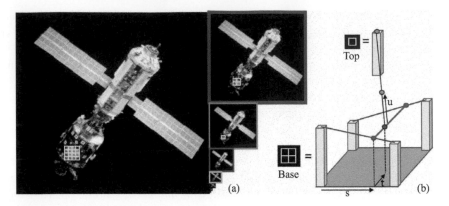

Figure 3.15   Mipmapping (a) with trilinear texture interpolation (b). Reproduced from Public Domain [33]

over each of these dimensions determines which colour will be given to a pixel with texture coordinates (s, t, u), where u is somehow related to the depth of the corresponding point in the 3D scene.

With all the descriptions so far, we got a good picture on how OpenGL works for projecting images on the screen, but in the next chapters, we will take a closer look at what happens under the hood. A very important aspect will be the projection types and how that relates to camera models used in photography. Another aspect will be the light equations that give 'life' to the OpenGL images; without them, one would end up with dull images, far from providing a realistic look.

References

[1]   https://www.solcommand.com/,   cf.   http://artist-3d.com/free_3d_models/ dnm/model_disp.php?uid=3815.
[2]   NVIDIA: Apollo Investigation, Mission Failure, NVIDIA's attempt to justify additional lighting used during creation of the Apollo 11 imagery by Marcus Allen, cf. https://www.aulis.com/nvidia.htm.
[3]   https://commons.wikimedia.org/wiki/File:Cube_Representative_UV_ Unwrapping.png.
[4]   G. Lafruit, L. Nachtergaele, K., Denolf, and J. Bormans. '3D computational graceful degradation'. *IEEE International Symposium on Circuits and Systems*, DOI: 10.1109/ISCAS.2000.856118, 2000.
[5]   F. P. Brooks, Editor(s): D. Luebke, M. Reddy, J. D. Cohen, A. Varshney, B. Watson, R. Huebner. In *The Morgan Kaufmann Series in Computer Graphics, Level of Detail for 3D Graphics*, Morgan Kaufmann, 2003, pp. ix, https://doi.org/10.1016/B978-155860838-2/50000-5.
[6]   E. Puppo and R. Scopigno. Simplification, LOD and Multiresolution Principles and Applications, In *Tutorial Eurographics* '97.

[7]   P. Lindstrom. Model Simplification Using Image and Geometry-based Metrics. Ph.D. Dissertation. Georgia Institute of Technology, USA. Advisor(s) Greg Turk. Order Number: AAI9994428, 2000.

[8]   S. Jeschke, M. Wimmer, and W. Purgathofer. 'Image-based Representations for Accelerated Rendering of Complex Scenes'. *Eurographics 2005 State of the Art Reports*, pp. 1–20, August 2005.

[9]   M. Corsini, M. C. Larabi, G. Lavoué, O. Petřík, L. Váša, and K. Wang, 'Perceptual metrics for static and dynamic triangle meshes'. *Computer Graphics Forum*, vol. 32, no. 6, pp. 251–251, https://doi.org/10.1111/cgf. 12001 First Published online: May 18, 2013.

[10]   P. Cignoniy, C. Rocchiniz and R. Scopigno. 'Metro: measuring error on simplied surfaces'. *Computer Graphics Forum*, vol. 17, no. 2, pp. 167–174, Eurographics (1998), https://doi.org/10.1111/1467-8659.00236.

[11]   E. Catmull and J. Clark. 'Recursively generated B-spline surfaces on arbitrary topological meshes'. *Computer Aided Design*, vol. 10, no. 6, pp. 350–355, 1978.

[12]   Intel Corporation. 'Embree Overview: High Performance Ray Tracing Kernels 3.13.0-alpha.0', https://github.com/embree/embree.

[13]   'Intel® Embree High Performance Ray Tracing Kernels: Subdivision Geometry'. https://embree.org/tutorials.html.

[14]   https://commons.wikimedia.org/wiki/File:Icospheres_at_different_levels_of_subdivision.png.

[15]   H. Prautzsch, W. Boehm, and M. Paluszny. *Bézier- and B-spline techniques*. Springer Berlin Heidelberg, ASIN: B0014CSJ7Y, 2002.

[16]   https://math.stackexchange.com/questions/3520859/are-cursives-and-circle-polygons-or-two-other-different-things/3520919#3520919.

[17]   https://www.humus.name/index.php?page=Cubemap&item=Yokohama.

[18]   https://blenderartists.org/t/hdri-images-to-blender-cube-maps-converter/670079.

[19]   C. He and M. Li. 'Efficient spatial anti-aliasing rendering for line joins on vector maps'. https://arxiv.org/abs/1906.11999.

[20]   K. Halladay. *Practical Shader Development: Vertex and Fragment Shaders for Game Developers*. Apress, ASIN: B07QKWND51, 2019.

[21]   K. A. Lammers. *Unity 4 Shaders and Post-Processing Effects Cookbook*. Packt Publishing, 2013.

[22]   J. Dean. *Mastering Unity Shaders and Effects*. Packt Publishing, 2016.

[23]   C. Conlan. *The Blender Python API: Precision 3D Modeling and Add-on Development*. Apress, 2017.

[24]   J. Brook. *Blender Shader Nodes For Beginners*. ASIN: B01H5P2BL8, 2016.

[25]   E. Valenza. *Blender Cycles: Materials and Textures Cookbook*. Packt Publishing, ASIN: B00U2MI8LY, 2015.

[26]   J. S. Gao, A. G. Huth, M. D. Lescroart, and J. L. Gallant. 'Pycortex: an interactive surface visualizer for fMRI'. *Frontiers in Neuroinformatics*, vol. 9, pp. 23, 2015, https://doi.org/10.3389/fninf.2015.00023.

[27]   S. R. Buss. *3D Computer Graphics: A Mathematical Introduction with OpenGL*. Cambridge University Press, ASIN: B00INYG428, 2003.

[28]   J. Lee, W.-N. Chung, T.-H. Lee, J.-H. Nah, Y. Kim, and W.-C. Park. 'Load Balancing Algorithm for Real-Time Ray Tracing of Dynamic Scenes'. vol. 8, pp. 165003–165009, *IEEE Access*, August 2020, DOI: 10.1109/ACCESS.2020.3019075.

[29]   R. A. Beyer, O. Alexandrov, S. McMichael, *et al.* 'The Ames stereo pipeline: NASA's open source software for deriving and processing terrain data'. *Earth and Space Science,* vol. 5, no. 3, August 2018 (documentation, release 2.7.0, 2020).

[30]   B. Cyganek, and J. Paul Siebert. *An Introduction to 3D Computer Vision Techniques and Algorithms.* Wiley–Blackwell, 2009.

[31]   A. T. Áfra, I. Wald, C. Benthin, and S. Woop. 2016. Embree ray tracing kernels: overview and new features. In *ACM SIGGRAPH 2016 Talks (SIGGRAPH '16).* Association for Computing Machinery, New York, NY, USA, Article 52, 1–2. DOI: https://doi.org/10.1145/2897839.2927450.

[32]   J. de Vries. *Learn OpenGL: Learn modern OpenGL graphics programming in a step-by-step fashion.* Kendall & Welling, 2020.

[33]   https://commons.wikimedia.org/wiki/File:Mipmap_Aliasing_Comparison.png.

Chapter 4

Camera and projection models

In this chapter, we will mathematically describe how a 3D scene is projected to a camera view. This corresponds to the core functionality of OpenGL and should thus be well understood; many derivations are inspired from [1]. The relationship between OpenGL and the pinhole camera model will also be studied, showing that the model is only valid in the hyperfocal regime.

Before we dig into the details, let us first expose some mathematical terminology that will be useful in the remainder of this textbook.

4.1 Mathematical preliminaries

In 3D graphics, there are several mathematical concepts that are often used, going from homogeneous coordinates to scalar products, cross products and quaternions. The latter will be addressed in Section 6.2; it would be too early to speak about that here. However, the other three concepts are sufficiently important now to give a short overview in this section.

First, all points in space will be represented in vectorial notation with a bar on top of each letter, but at the same time, we will also keep the Cartesian notation in mind, represented by a column vector. For instance, a 3D point P will be represented by its vector $\overline{P}$ and the column vector of its Cartesian coordinates, as follows:

$$\overline{P} = \begin{pmatrix} P_x \\ P_y \\ P_z \end{pmatrix} \tag{4.1}$$

where the subscripts indicate whether we take the x, y, or z-coordinate of the vector. This over-bar notation $\overline{P}$ will be used throughout the text to make a clear difference between a vector and a scalar. In a figure, however, a vector is clearly drawn by an arrow and no over-bar notation will be used then.

The scalar product of two such vectors $\overline{P}$ and $\overline{Q}$ can also be represented in various ways. Its vectorial notation is $\overline{P} \cdot \overline{Q}$ (keep in mind though that it represents a scalar value), but we can also express this in Cartesian coordinates:

$$\overline{P} \cdot \overline{Q} = \begin{pmatrix} P_x & P_y & P_z \end{pmatrix} \cdot \begin{pmatrix} Q_x \\ Q_y \\ Q_z \end{pmatrix} = \overline{P}^t \cdot \overline{Q} \tag{4.2}$$

Here we see a peculiar trick that will be used throughout the textbook: we can express the scalar product in two ways that look very similar, but that hide a

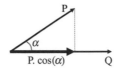

Figure 4.1   The scalar product between two vectors P and Q

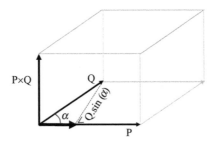

Figure 4.2   Cross product between vector P and Q

different underlying representation. In this equation, we use the left-hand side as a representation for the scalar product, while the right-hand side shows how the things are really calculated in Cartesian coordinates. It might look a bit counter-intuitive to mix these two representations, but it is simple to differentiate them by checking whether the transpose superscript is present or not.

To be complete, a scalar product has yet another interpretation, as shown in Figure 4.1: it is a scalar value that represents the length of the projection through $\cos(\alpha)$ of the vector $\overline{P}$ onto the vector $\overline{Q}$. This will come handy whenever we have a cosine function that we want to hide away by using a scalar product.

Another mathematical concept that is often used is the cross product $\overline{P} \times \overline{Q}$, which hides a $\sin(\alpha)$. As shown in Figure 4.2, the cross product is a vector that is perpendicular to both $\overline{P}$ and $\overline{Q}$, and its length is equal to the surface of the trapezium spanned by $\overline{P}$ and $\overline{Q}$. Undergraduate textbooks give the following formulas for the cross product:

$$\overline{P} \times \overline{Q} = \begin{vmatrix} \overline{1}_x & \overline{1}_y & \overline{1}_z \\ P_x & P_y & P_z \\ Q_x & Q_y & Q_z \end{vmatrix}$$

$$\|\overline{P} \times \overline{Q}\| = \|\overline{P}\| \cdot \|\overline{Q}\| \cdot \sin \alpha \qquad (4.3)$$

where the $\overline{1}_x$, $\overline{1}_y$ and $\overline{1}_z$ vectors correspond to unity vectors in the x, y and z-dimensions.

There is one more equation that is interesting in the context of 3D graphics:

$$\overline{P} \times \overline{Q} = \begin{pmatrix} 0 & -P_z & P_y \\ P_z & 0 & -P_x \\ -P_y & P_x & 0 \end{pmatrix} \cdot \begin{pmatrix} Q_x \\ Q_y \\ Q_z \end{pmatrix} \qquad (4.4)$$

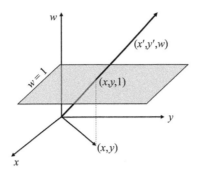

Figure 4.3 Homogeneous coordinates, inserting an additional w-coordinate

Here, the cross product is represented as the multiplication of a matrix with a point (the second point Q), suggesting that the point Q undergoes a transformation based on that matrix (which depends on the first point P), which is anti-symmetric and is called the cross matrix $P_{[\times]}$:

$$P_{[\times]} = \begin{pmatrix} 0 & -P_z & P_y \\ P_z & 0 & -P_x \\ -P_y & P_x & 0 \end{pmatrix} \tag{4.5}$$

The equality of (4.4) can easily be proven by explicitly calculating the matrix product and comparing it with the cross product determinant representation of (4.3). This matrix representation will come very handy when calculating a 3D rotation with the Rodriguez formula, cf. Section 6.1.2.

Now comes a last 'trick' often used in 3D graphics; it is the trick of using homogeneous coordinates, on which all above vector calculus can be applied.

Let us first explain the homogeneous coordinates in 2D space. We start with a point (x,y) in an image, as in Figure 4.3, and we add a third dimension w (not z), which will transform the 2D point P into a 3D line that most often has no direct physical meaning; it is just an imaginary line that helps in doing some calculus, as we will see further. In fact, every 3D point P' with (x',y',w) coordinates on this line represents the unique 2D point P with (x,y) coordinates in the image plane. To go from one to the other, one should use the following equations:

$$\begin{cases} x = \dfrac{x'}{w} \\ y = \dfrac{y'}{w} \end{cases} \tag{4.6}$$

Clearly, taking $w=1$, we draw parallel to the image plane a new plane at height $w=1$, intersecting the 3D line. The (x,y)-coordinates of that intersection point is also directly the physical point P. However, for $w \neq 1$, the physical 2D coordinates must be found back by applying (4.6).

One may wonder why making such difficult detours. The reason is simple: we want to express everything with linear equations, using matrices and vectors;

nothing else. If a physical phenomenon needs to find something by dividing a value by another value (we will see later that the perspective projection is one of them), then we can hide that second value into w and do all linear equations. For instance, a point P undergoing a hypothetical transformation M with division to create point Q, would in 2D be expressed for example as

$$\begin{cases} Q_x = \dfrac{m_{11} \cdot x + m_{12} \cdot y + m_{13}}{m_{31} \cdot x + m_{32} \cdot y + m_{33}} \\ Q_y = \dfrac{m_{21} \cdot x + m_{22} \cdot y + m_{23}}{m_{31} \cdot x + m_{32} \cdot y + m_{33}} \end{cases} \tag{4.7}$$

In homogeneous coordinates, it is much simpler to put the rotation and translation together in a matrix with a third-dimension w, as follows:

$$\begin{pmatrix} Q'_x \\ Q'_y \\ w \end{pmatrix} = \begin{pmatrix} m_{11} & m_{12} & m_{13} \\ m_{21} & m_{22} & m_{23} \\ m_{31} & m_{32} & m_{33} \end{pmatrix} \cdot \begin{pmatrix} x \\ y \\ 1 \end{pmatrix} \tag{4.8}$$

After having performed this multiplication, we can recover the physical coordinates of Q by division through w, yielding exactly what we were looking for in (4.7).

Of course, we can go one step further and represent a 3D point in space by 4D homogeneous coordinates, using exactly the same principles. For instance, a point P undergoing a rotation R and translation t in 3D, creating point Q, can be represented as

$$\begin{pmatrix} Q_x \\ Q_y \\ Q_z \\ Q_w \end{pmatrix} = \begin{pmatrix} r_{11} & r_{12} & r_{13} & t_x \\ r_{21} & r_{22} & r_{23} & t_y \\ r_{31} & r_{32} & r_{33} & t_z \\ 0 & 0 & 0 & 1 \end{pmatrix} \cdot \begin{pmatrix} P_x \\ P_y \\ P_z \\ P_w \end{pmatrix} \tag{4.9}$$

The exact nature of the r_{ij} coefficients is not important in this discussion; we will return on this topic in Section 6.1.1 of Chapter 6. All we want to show here is that homogeneous coordinates also work for 3D points.

Interestingly, combining various rotations and translations one after the other becomes now an easy job: each rotation-translation pair is now a 4×4 matrix, and all we must do is to multiply them all. Without this trick of homogeneous coordinates, we would end up in explicitly separating the successive rotations R_i and translations t_i from each other, ending up in unreadable formulas, like this one after three steps of a rotation-translation pair:

$$Q = R_3 \cdot [R_2 \cdot (R_1 \cdot P + t_1) + t_2] + t_3 \tag{4.10}$$

Observe how P is now embedded in the middle of the equation, hence it will be a difficult job to get it out in obtaining a simple formula like $Q = M \cdot P$, as we had before in (4.4). Homogeneous coordinates do not have that problem and that is the main reason to use them all over in the 3D graphics calculus.

As a final remark, note that when $w = 0$, we end up in a little interpretative problem: the physical coordinates would be infinite by division by zero. However, looking back to (4.9), we see that w only appears thanks to the translation vector.

This means that $w = 0$ corresponds to a transformation that only involves translations, which basically means that the direction of a vector is not changing (no rotation). Therefore, by convention, $w = 0$ is interpreted as representing a direction in space, not a physical point.

With this arsenal of mathematical tools, we can now continue our journey to camera and projection models.

4.2   The pinhole camera model

The pinhole camera model is probably the most important model that represents conventional cameras used throughout VR applications. It is therefore important to well understand what it exactly covers and what it does not cover at all in its mathematical formulas using a linear matrix formalism.

The pinhole camera is a faithful representation of the very first camera that was built in history: the camera obscura. As shown in Figure 4.4, light rays pass through a tiny hole (pinhole) made with a needle in the front panel of a black box (literally) and pinch the rear panel covered with a photographic emulsion, capturing the intensity of the respective light rays. In this way, a 2D projection of the 3D scene is obtained on the rear panel, albeit upside-down since points high (low) in space follow a down (up) travelling light path for reaching the corresponding 2D point at the bottom (top) of the rear photographic panel.

Since the tiny hole does not let much light enter into the black box, several minutes of exposure time are needed to fix a 2D image projection onto the photographic emulsion. To overcome this limitation, one may think of enlarging the tiny hole to let more light rays enter, but this would cause a blurry image since each point in space would be projected onto different 2D points on the rear panel, causing overlapping image effects, as shown in Figure 4.5. This, however, can be easily resolved using a converging lens that will concentrate all light rays from a far-away point in space onto a single point on the photographic emulsion, well-lit in a minimum of time. Not surprisingly, the distance from the lens centre to the rear panel (also called the image plane) is referred to as 'the focal length' of the lens.

An important note is in place here with respect to the 'far-away' aspect of the point in the scene (lying on the so-called object plane). For a point on any distance a from the lens, geometrical optics tells that its image plane projection through a lens is found at a distance b, with both distances being related to each other through the focal length f, according to the equation:

$$\frac{1}{a} + \frac{1}{b} = \frac{1}{f} \tag{4.11}$$

Obviously, for a finite value of a, the distances b and f are not equal, which does not correspond to what we have defined as the focal length f in Figure 4.5. However, when a reaches infinity, (4.14) yields that $b = f$, which is exactly what is provided in Figure 4.5. This regime is known in photography as the 'hyperfocal regime', where points in space are sufficiently far away that they are always in focus on the

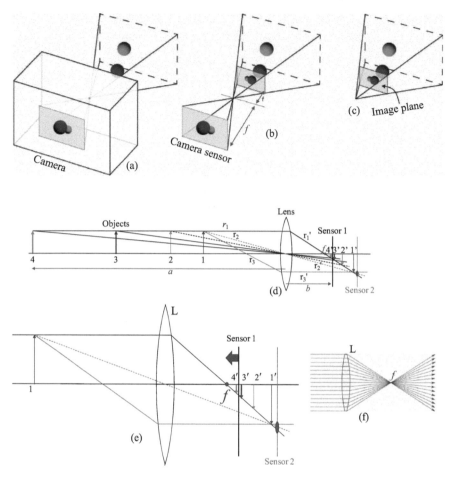

Figure 4.4   Camera obscura (a) following the pinhole model (b), also represented as a pyramid (c). When inserting a lens, some optical laws apply (d, e) reaching only a perfect match with the pinhole camera model in hyperfocal regime (f) with objects imaged from far away. (a–c) Reproduced under a Creative Commons license from [2]; (f) Reproduced from Public Domain [3]

image plane at the focal distance from the lens. This is exactly what the pinhole camera model presumes: all points in space are projected in focus on the image plane, and instead of explicitly drawing the three main light rays of Figure 4.5 to find the projected point, it is sufficient to follow one light ray that passes the pinhole – that is the lens centre – to hit the image plane – that is the rear photographic panel of the camera obscura – exactly in the point we were seeking.

All this brings us to a big simplification of the pinhole camera model: the lens centre is now called the camera optical centre, represented as the single converging point of all light rays in the double pyramid representation. The image plane is the

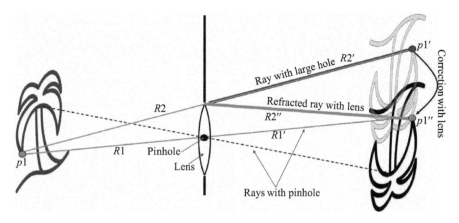

Figure 4.5   A lens inserted in an enlarged hole of the pinhole camera (centre) ensures that the light rays converge again at the right place, avoiding ghosting (right)

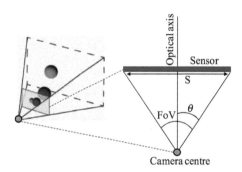

Figure 4.6   Pinhole camera model and field of view. Reproduced under a Creative Commons license from [2] (left)

basis of the pyramid the furthest from the scene, capturing the upside-down projected image through a camera sensor made of pixels. A further simplification can be obtained by discarding this pyramid: after all, the pyramid the closest to the scene holds the same image (not up-side-down) of the scene, while clearly showing the 'field of view' (FoV), that is over which angular sector the scene has been captured. As shown in Figure 4.6, the FoV and focal length f are geometrically related as follows to the sensor size S:

$$S = 2 \cdot f \cdot \tan\theta \tag{4.12}$$

where θ is half the FoV angle, hence

$$\text{FoV} = 2 \cdot \tan^{-1}\left(\frac{S}{2f}\right) \tag{4.13}$$

From now on, we will follow this pyramidal representation of the pinhole camera model, where the top of the pyramid is the camera optical centre, and its orthogonal projection onto the (front) image plane is called the 'principal point'. Theoretically, the principal point is the centre of the image plane, but in practice, this is often not true and special calibration techniques are needed to find the exact position of the principal point. Intuitively, this is particularly important, because any displacement of the principal point corresponds to a displacement of the camera optical centre, resulting itself in a change of orientation of the incoming light rays, and hence a change in position of the points in space that create the 2D points on the image plane. Such mistakes in principal point position estimation can lead to severe errors in the pose estimation problems we will tackle in Chapter 8.

4.3   Intrinsics of the pinhole camera

The relation between the various parameters of the pinhole camera model is expressed in the so-called intrinsic matrix K of the camera [4,5]. To be frank, this matrix K is not used in OpenGL, which rather uses its explicit projection matrices, as we will show in the next section. Nevertheless, we present it here to make a link with the pinhole camera model, which is a good approximation of what one encounters in photography or computer vision, where this matrix K is very often used.

The matrix K expresses how a point (X,Y,Z) in space is projected on the front image plane of the pinhole camera model (and pyramid), expressed in homogeneous coordinates (x',y',w'), following the representation of Figure 4.7:

$$\begin{pmatrix} x' \\ y' \\ w' \end{pmatrix} = \begin{pmatrix} f_x & 0 & p_x \\ 0 & f_y & p_y \\ 0 & 0 & 1 \end{pmatrix} \cdot \begin{pmatrix} X \\ Y \\ Z \end{pmatrix}$$

$$\begin{pmatrix} x' \\ y' \\ w' \end{pmatrix} = \begin{pmatrix} f_x & 0 & p_x \\ 0 & f_y & p_y \\ 0 & 0 & 1 \end{pmatrix} \cdot (R|t) \begin{pmatrix} x \\ y \\ z \\ w \end{pmatrix}$$

(4.14)

where f_x and f_y are the focal lengths in the x and y direction of the image plane, expressed in pixels (not in mm like on commercial cameras) and (p_x, p_y) the coordinates of the principal point, after shifting the origin of the image from its bottom-left corner to this particular point. All are called the intrinsics of the camera under test.

Note that the capital letters X, Y and Z are the 3D camera coordinates (with Z along the optical axis) of a point in space, corresponding to the point's world coordinates (represented in lower case) that are rotated and translated towards the camera coordinates. The rotation R and translation t are concatenated into the 3×4 matrix $(R|t)$. Consequently, any multiplication with a column vector requires four dimensions, hence the point in space is represented by its homogeneous coordinates (x,y,z,w). What we finally see in the camera image is a 2D point without any depth information Z anymore, explaining why it is represented by its 3D homogeneous coordinates; not 4D coordinates. Nevertheless, that hidden Z-coordinate is important since it appears through w' in the denominator of the 2D

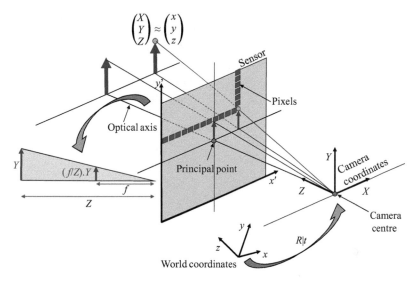

Figure 4.7: *Pinhole camera projection in world and camera coordinates. The concept of the principal point on the real optical axis is of great importance. Reproduced under a Creative Commons license from [6]*

physical coordinates $(x'/w', y'/w')$. Indeed, if the principal point would be zero, that is the x' and y' coordinates start at zero at the optical axis, instead of the bottom-left pixel in the image, then we would obtain:

$$x_{\text{phys}} = \frac{x'}{w'} = f_x \cdot \frac{X}{Z}$$

$$y_{\text{phys}} = \frac{y'}{w'} = f_y \cdot \frac{Y}{Z}$$

(4.15)

clearly showing the scaling with the depth Z that occurs in a perspective camera.

A specific setting is reached when Z is equal to f, yielding no scaling (i.e. scaling factor 1), which corresponds to intuition: a point in space that coincidentally falls on the image plane is seen at exactly the same position in the image.

In all above equations, f_x and f_y can also be expressed as a function of the focal length f expressed in mm: the number of pixels per mm multiplied with the focal length in mm will yield the focal length in number of pixels. For instance, today's high-quality camera sensors have pixels of typically 4 μm size, hence there are 250 pixels per mm, which for typical focal lengths of 12–25 mm used in machine vision leads to f_x and f_y numbers in the range of 3,000 to slightly above 6,000 pixels.

4.4 Projection matrices

Projection matrices are an essential part of the OpenGL pipeline, especially in its practical implementation on a graphics card. They represent the projection of the 3D scene (made in OpenGL of triangles, remember) to the 2D screen, and their

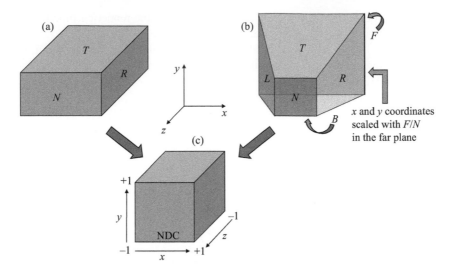

Figure 4.8   Mapping from world coordinates to the normalized device coordinates (c), in orthographic projection (a) and perspective projection (b). Reproduced from [1]

peculiar structure (we will see that in a minute) helps in making relatively simple implementations of OpenGL on various platforms. For this reason, we want to spend some time on how OpenGL projection matrices are defined.

So far, we have assumed that each triangle in 3D space would be projected onto the 2D screen, taking perspective scaling into account, that is a triangle far away in space (large z-values) will be projected onto a smaller surface onto the screen than the same triangle positioned nearby (small z-values). But how does the OpenGL pipeline take care of this? The answer is simple: through projection matrices doing all necessary scaling and translation operations.

In this process, the graphics card will map a volume in space towards so-called normalized device coordinates (NDC) using numbers ranging from -1 to $+1$, hence easily represented by a floating-point data representation to hold as much precision as possible. As shown in Figure 4.8, the original volume is delimited by six faces, creating the so-called view frustum, with the left (L), right (R), top (T), and bottom (B) faces representing the borders of what will eventually become visible on the screen. There is also a near (N) and far (F) face; the near one may be thought of as the screen on which the scene will be projected (though this is not necessarily true, but for simplicity, let us assume this for a moment). For the far face, it may be surprising to have such limiting border in the far end of the scene, since – in reality – whatever object that lies beyond the near face must be visible on the screen, possibly scaled down to a minimum size (remember the story of levels of detail in Chapter 3). The latter is exactly the reason for using a far face: any object – even a complex one made of millions of triangles – will hardly be visible if it is positioned extremely far away in the view frustum. Instead of asking the OpenGL pipeline to spend a lot of processing power on such objects, it is easier to exclude them from the rendering pipeline once further away than a specific threshold, represented by the far face *F*.

Note that – in contrast with most textbooks – we choose to represent all view frustum faces with an upper-case letter, not a lower-case one. This comes handy to make the difference between the focal length *f* and the far face *F*, a confusion that makes one lose a lot of time when studying openGL.

4.4.1   *Mathematical derivation of projection matrices*

Before jumping to the exact mathematical formulation of the projection matrix, let us first introduce a trick that allows the equations to remain linear, though a scaling determined by *z* is involved through a division process. We use the trick of 'homogeneous coordinates', where instead of representing a point in 3D space with three coordinates *x*, *y* and *z*, one rather uses the four-dimensional homogeneous coordinates (x, y, z, w) with the understanding that to recover the physical coordinates $(x_{phys}, y_{phys}, z_{phys})$ one has to divide the homogeneous coordinates by the fourth coordinate *w*.

Also note that all coordinates are represented by column vectors, which will simplify subsequent matrix calculus that involves any transformation *P* (*P* refers to a 'Projection' in this section) that transforms a point *X* in space to another point *X'*. To clearly indicate that $\overline{X}$ and $\overline{X}'$ are column vectors holding the point's coordinates, the over-bar notation is used:

$$\overline{X} = \begin{pmatrix} x \\ y \\ z \\ w \end{pmatrix} \text{ and } \overline{X'} = \begin{pmatrix} x' \\ y' \\ z' \\ w' \end{pmatrix} \tag{4.16}$$

$$\overline{X'} = P \cdot \overline{X}$$

where *P* is obviously a 4×4 matrix, $\overline{X}$ the homogeneous coordinates of a point in space before projective transformation and $\overline{X}'$ the homogeneous coordinates after transformation.

We will now derive the projection matrices for two important projections that are used throughout this textbook: the orthographic and the perspective projection. Both scale their coordinates to stay within the NDC, but the perspective projection matrix also includes some transformations to obtain perspective illusions.

Let us start with the orthographic projection of Figure 4.9, where all coordinates of the view frustum are translated and scaled towards the $(-1, +1)$ range. This can be obtained by first translating the view frustum cube over the average of two opposing

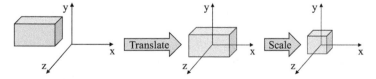

Figure 4.9   Translate and scaling operations to come to the normalized device coordinates in orthographic projection. Reproduced from [1]

sides towards the world coordinates' origin, and then later scale all its sides so that they reach a length two, that is the distance from -1 to $+1$. In matrix notation, we obtain:

$$P_{\text{ortho}} = \begin{pmatrix} \dfrac{2}{R-L} & 0 & 0 & 0 \\ 0 & \dfrac{2}{T-B} & 0 & 0 \\ 0 & 0 & \dfrac{2}{F-N} & 0 \\ 0 & 0 & 0 & 1 \end{pmatrix} \cdot \begin{pmatrix} 1 & 0 & 0 & -\dfrac{L+R}{2} \\ 0 & 1 & 0 & -\dfrac{T+B}{2} \\ 0 & 0 & 1 & -\dfrac{F+N}{2} \\ 0 & 0 & 0 & 1 \end{pmatrix} \quad (4.17)$$

where the first translation operation is the right factor and the subsequent scaling operation is the left factor in the multiplication. This finally results in the orthographic projection matrix:

$$P_{\text{ortho}} = \begin{pmatrix} \dfrac{2}{R-L} & 0 & 0 & -\dfrac{R+L}{R-L} \\ 0 & \dfrac{2}{T-B} & 0 & -\dfrac{T+B}{T-B} \\ 0 & 0 & \dfrac{2}{F-N} & -\dfrac{F+N}{F-N} \\ 0 & 0 & 0 & 1 \end{pmatrix} \quad (4.18)$$

With this projection matrix, any point X in space will be brought back into the NDC cube, where each side is ranging from -1 to $+1$. Nothing else will be done, and we will see later that any set of parallel lines in space remain parallel after transformation with the orthographic projection matrix, yielding strangely looking renderings like the left side in Figure 4.10, which are sometimes used in architectural design because they keep distances between points. In most other applications, however, the perspective projection is used instead. Let us have a closer look at it.

The derivation of the perspective projection is a little bit more involved than of the orthographic projection. In fact, it starts with an orthographic projection for finding the equations in x' and y', further scaled with the focal length, as in (4.15) to obtain the depth-dependent scaling. However, here we use the near plane instead (lying at the focal length). Furthermore, there is a little detail not to overlook, that is that OpenGL uses a right-handed coordinate system, and with the x and y dimensions aligned along an image with left-to-right and bottom-to-top directions, the positive z-direction is oriented towards the camera, while the negative z-direction is oriented into depth. As such, we must use $-N$ instead of N, yielding:

$$x' = \frac{2}{R-L} \cdot \left(-N \cdot \frac{x}{z}\right) - \frac{R+L}{R-L}$$
$$y' = \frac{2}{T-B} \cdot \left(-N \cdot \frac{y}{z}\right) - \frac{T+B}{T-B} \quad (4.19)$$

Equation (4.19) clearly shows in his parentheses the effect of scaling with z, before following the orthographic transformation of (4.18).

For z', however, another transformation is followed to represent the depth in a better way, closer to what we experience in everyday's life, that is stereo vision. Indeed, in Chapter 12, we will see that we experience parallax or disparity between our eyes, and it is up to the brain to transform that back into a depth perception.

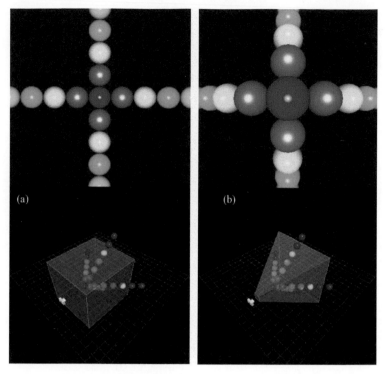

Figure 4.10   Ortho (a) and perspective rendering (b). Courtesy: Song Ho Ahn [7]

Depth and disparity are inverse proportional to each other. Wishing to hold information about disparity rather than depth, the OpenGL designers have chosen to use the following transformation from z (depth) to z′:

$$z' = \frac{A}{z} + B \qquad (4.20)$$

where $1/z$ corresponds to a disparity value, and at the same time introduces a scaling with z, like what we have encountered in (4.16).

We now map the near (N) and far (F) planes to −1 and +1 respectively, for obtaining a valid NDC, but here too, the OpenGL right-handed coordinate system requires to inverse the signs in z and z′, yielding for the constants A and B:

$$A = \frac{2NF}{F - N}$$
$$B = \frac{F + N}{F - N} \qquad (4.21)$$

And for the transformation from z to z′, we obtain

$$z' = \frac{-2NF}{F - N} \cdot \frac{1}{z} + \frac{F + N}{F - N} \qquad (4.22)$$

Equations (4.18) and (4.22) tell us how to transform x, y and z into x', y' and z' to obtain the perspective transformation in NDC notation. To simplify the equations, we left- and right-multiply with z so that we get rid of the $1/z$ factor in the right side of the equations:

$$z \cdot x' = \frac{2}{R-L} \cdot (-N \cdot x) - \frac{R+L}{R-L} \cdot z$$

$$z \cdot y' = \frac{2}{T-B} \cdot (-N \cdot y) - \frac{T+B}{T-B} \cdot z$$

$$z \cdot z' = \frac{-2NF}{F-N} + \frac{F+N}{F-N} \cdot z$$

$$w' = -z$$

(4.23)

where the last equation brings the minus signs at the right hand-side of the equations to the left side, while also taking care that once we have calculated the homogeneous coordinates, we get physical coordinates as expected, for example for the first equation in (4.23):

$$\frac{-z \cdot x'}{w'} = \frac{-z \cdot x'}{-z} = x'$$

(4.24)

Now, we can rearrange all equations of (4.23) into one set of matrix equations, obtaining:

$$\begin{pmatrix} -z \cdot x' \\ -z \cdot y' \\ -z \cdot z' \\ w' \end{pmatrix} = \begin{pmatrix} \frac{2N}{R-L} & 0 & \frac{R+L}{R-L} & 0 \\ 0 & \frac{2N}{T-B} & \frac{T+B}{T-B} & 0 \\ 0 & 0 & -\frac{F+N}{F-N} & \frac{-2NF}{F-N} \\ 0 & 0 & -1 & 0 \end{pmatrix} \cdot \begin{pmatrix} x \\ y \\ z \\ w \end{pmatrix}$$

(4.25)

At the end of the day, we get for the perspective projection matrix:

$$P_{\text{pers}} = \begin{pmatrix} \frac{2N}{R-L} & 0 & \frac{R+L}{R-L} & 0 \\ 0 & \frac{2N}{T-B} & \frac{T+B}{T-B} & 0 \\ 0 & 0 & -\frac{F+N}{F-N} & \frac{-2NF}{F-N} \\ 0 & 0 & -1 & 0 \end{pmatrix}$$

(4.26)

Note the difference between P_{ortho} and P_{pers} in their third and fourth columns, which are roughly speaking switched. Doing so, the w' coordinate that was equal to w in P_{ortho}, becomes in P_{pers} equal to z' (disregarding its sign) due to the identity coefficient in the third column instead of the fourth. This subtle difference makes P_{pers} introduces a scaling through the division by w' – equal to z' – which was absent in P_{ortho}. This makes all the difference in projective appearance between orthographic and perspective projection, as shown in Figure 4.10.

Of course, Figure 4.10 just shows the visual effect of applying orthographic or perspective projections. Nothing suggests where that comes from. This is what we will do in the next section, starting from the projection matrices we have developed above.

Box 4.1: Camera centre equation

It may sometimes be helpful to determine the camera centre. For the perspective projection, we may start from the equation of intrinsics K and extrinsics $(R|t)$, stating that by definition the camera centre C will be projected on the origin of the camera coordinates, represented by the vector $\mathbf{0}$:

$$\begin{aligned} P \cdot C &= K \cdot (R|t) \cdot C = 0 \\ K \cdot R \cdot C + K \cdot t &= 0 \\ C &= -R^{-1} \cdot t = -R^t \cdot t \end{aligned} \tag{4.27}$$

The camera centre coordinates is thus not dependent on the K matrix; it only depends on the extrinsics.

4.4.2 Characteristics of the projection matrices

Orthographic projections keep parallel lines (in 3D) parallel (in 2D on the screen), while the perspective projection will transform parallel lines (in 3D) to convergent lines (in 2D on the screen), with the convergent point also known as the vanishing point.

To prove this, let us define any line in 3D space with a free parameter t:

$$\begin{aligned} x &= x_0 + m_x \cdot t \\ y &= y_0 + m_y \cdot t \\ z &= z_0 + m_z \cdot t \end{aligned} \tag{4.28}$$

With the same m_x, m_y and m_z values, any two lines with different values of x_0, y_0, and/or z_0 will be parallel in 3D, since their relative slopes are identical; we will represent them with the same value m:

$$m = m_x = m_y = m_z$$

Let us also represent the projection matrix with its non-zero coefficients p_{ij}:

$$P = (p_{ij}) \; \forall i,j$$

$$P_{\text{ortho}} = \begin{pmatrix} p_{11} & 0 & 0 & p_{14} \\ 0 & p_{22} & 0 & p_{24} \\ 0 & 0 & p_{33} & p_{34} \\ 0 & 0 & 0 & 1 \end{pmatrix}$$

$$P_{\text{pers}} = \begin{pmatrix} p_{11} & 0 & p_{13} & 0 \\ 0 & p_{22} & p_{23} & 0 \\ 0 & 0 & p_{33} & p_{34} \\ 0 & 0 & -1 & 0 \end{pmatrix} \tag{4.29}$$

where the non-zero coefficients that are always $+1$ or -1, independently of (L,R,T,B,N,F) are put explicitly as ± 1.

We now inject (4.28) into (4.14) and let t grow to high values (and beyond, that is infinity), which will also increase the depth value z. The idea is to see what happens in the limit when we follow a long, long line into the depth dimension; (4.28) makes sure that it is indeed a straight line. In the limit, we find for P_{ortho} the following physical coordinates x'_{phys} and y'_{phys} (z'_{phys} is hardly interesting, since we look to the 2D image of the line on screen space), with a ratio corresponding to the slope of the line in the limit situation:

$$\lim_{t\to\infty} \frac{y'_{phys}}{x'_{phys}} = \lim_{t\to\infty} \frac{p_{22}\cdot y_0 + p_{11}\cdot m\cdot t + p_{24}}{p_{11}\cdot x_0 + p_{11}\cdot m\cdot t + p_{14}} = \frac{p_{22}}{p_{11}} \tag{4.30}$$

Clearly, in P_{ortho}, for any large value of t, the physical camera coordinates change in the same way for all points, keeping the same relative slope, independently of their starting point (x_0, y_0); these parameters have disappeared from the right hand-side result in (4.30). Hence, all these lines represent parallel 2D lines on screen, as expected for P_{ortho}.

For P_{pers}, when letting t going to infinity after injecting (4.28), we get:

$$\lim_{t\to\infty} x'_{phys} = \lim_{t\to\infty} \frac{p_{11}\cdot(x_0+mt)+p_{13}\cdot(z_0+mt)}{-(z_0+mt)} = -(p_{11}+p_{13})$$
$$\lim_{t\to\infty} y'_{phys} = \lim_{t\to\infty} \frac{p_{22}\cdot(x_0+mt)+p_{23}\cdot(z_0+mt)}{-(z_0+mt)} = -(p_{22}+p_{23}) \tag{4.31}$$

In P_{pers}, the physical coordinates for large z values (t tending to infinity) converge to the same constant values over all points, independently of the x_0, y_0 and z_0 values that represent the starting point of the corresponding line in 3D. It is not even the ratio (i.e. the line slope) of the two equations in (4.31) that tends to a constant; it is each physical coordinate itself that reaches a constant value. This means that – wherever 3D parallel lines start in P_{pers} – they always end up in the same point on the 2D screen, called the vanishing point.

References

[1] E. Lengyel. *Mathematics for 3D game programming and computer graphics.* Delmar Cengage Learning; 2011.
[2] https://ksimek.github.io/pinhole_camera_diagram/.
[3] https://commons.wikimedia.org/wiki/File:Convex_lens_-_perfect.svg.
[4] L. W. Kheng. 'Camera models and imaging'. CS4243 Computer Vision and Pattern Recognition, Department of Computer Science School of Computing National University of Singapore. https://comp.nus.edu.sg/~cs4243/lecture/camera.pdf
[5] C. Stamatopoulos. 'Orientation and Calibration of Long Focal Length Cameras in Digital Close-Range Photogrammetry'. PhD thesis. The University of Melbourne, 2011.
[6] https://tex.stackexchange.com/questions/96074/more-elegant-way-to-achieve-this-same-camera-perspective-projection-model.
[7] http://www.songho.ca/opengl/gl_transform.html.

Chapter 5

Light equations

Light equations are really a cornerstone in OpenGL; they give 'life' to the images that are rendered. Without them, one would end in very dark and/or unrealistically looking images. We therefore 'devote a couple of sections to them, exposing their mathematical equations that must be programmed to get things 'alive'. These equations will then run on each vertex and/or fragment of the scene, putting some load on the rendering pipeline. Even worse, in search of photo-realistic rendering results, one may even have to use raytracing techniques (cf. Chapter 7) that will basically iterate multiple times on each pixel to find the colour that best approaches reality, easily overloading the rendering pipeline. We hope the interested reader will then become aware of the level of complexity involved in OpenGL, and how this may impact virtual reality applications. Based on these insights, we will gradually move towards other image-based techniques that enable both photo-realistic quality and reasonable processing cost, cf. Chapter 12.

In the newer versions of OpenGL (v3 and beyond), light equations must be programmed in the shader language by the user him/herself; function calls to predefined light equations are deprecated. Beyond the disadvantage to knowing how to master these light contributions for programming them correctly, there is also a big advantage in having the flexibility to add special light effects by oneself, including shadows, which have a profound impact on how one experiences the visual impression at rendering.

For instance, in mimicking the moon pictures taken by the astronauts of Apollo 11 with the aim to verify the light conditions, Nvidia 3D designers have modelled the lunar landing zone and simulated various light conditions with direct light equations as used in OpenGL and multi-path light transport equations as used in raytracing. Some results are depicted in Figure 5.1, which shows the large impact of including or excluding some light sources (here ambient light, cf. Section 5.1.2) in the rendering. Interestingly, even after applying raytracing with a single light source (the sun), the rendered image still misses something to look sufficiently authentic: compared to Figure 5.2 (right), which is a real picture taken on the moon, the astronaut of Figure 5.1(c) still looks quite dark/grey compared to the bright white colour seen in the real picture.

Figure 5.2 (left) shows a new raytracing taking all effects into account, including the reflection of light on the photographer astronaut (Neil Armstrong) facing the lunar module, which effectively adds a lot of light to the scene to make it look as authentic as Figure 5.2 (right).

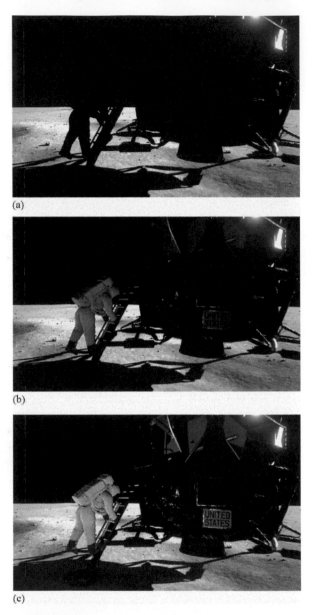

Figure 5.1   3D light effects on a 3D model of the lunar landing module of Apollo 11 with the sun coming from the right: (a) without ambient light, (b) with ambient light, and (c) with multi-path light reflections, that is raytracing with only the sun as light source. Reproduced under a Creative Commons license from [1]

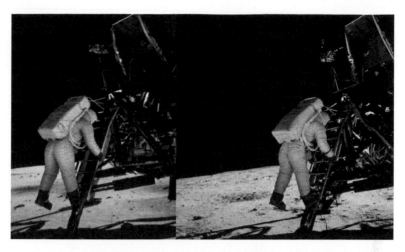

Figure 5.2   Raytracing (left) simulating the original picture (right) taken of the lunar module of Apollo 11, while the astronaut (Buzz Aldrin) goes down the ladder to join his colleague taking the picture (Neil Armstrong). Observe from the shadows on the ground that sunlight is coming from the right. Reproduced under a Creative Commons license from [1]

All this shows that high-quality OpenGL renderings need a good understanding of light equations.

In this chapter, we will briefly explain the main light equations used in 3D rendering. As said before, these equations (or slight modifications thereof) must be programmed in the shaders explicitly. We will not explain how to do that in this textbook; many books exist on this subject, for example, [2–5], just to name a few.

5.1   Light contributions

In this section, we will give the mathematical formulation of the four most important, yet simple light equations, that is emissive, ambient, diffuse and specular light. Many other light models exist like Cook-Torrance and various others explained in detail in [6]. For ultra-realistic renderings (using raytracing, cf. Chapter 7), it is highly recommended to take a look at these more elaborated models.

In all models below, we will take a point on the object surface for which we would like to calculate the light contribution, with a normal $\overline{N}$ perpendicular to the local surface. From the object point of interest, we draw the unit vector $\overline{L}$ to the light source, so that the arrow points to the light source (rather than showing the opposite direction in which the light travels, which would be more intuitive, but most textbooks do not follow this approach; we neither). The angle between $\overline{L}$ and $\overline{N}$ is the angle of incidence α, which will play an important role in most light equations. The intensity of the light source is represented by a scalar value $\overline{I}$, which typically depends on the colour channel red (R), green (G) and blue (B), indicated by the corresponding index. We thus have I_R, I_G and I_B light intensities. Finally, there is also a unit vector $\overline{E}$ in the user's eye direction; it has an angle β with $\overline{N}$. It is in this eye direction $\overline{E}$ that we would like to know which fraction of the incoming light $\overline{L}$ will hit the eye.

Note that the material surface has a reflection coefficient k, which not only depends on the material but will also be different for the three main colour channels R, G and B; hence, for each material, we have three reflection coefficients k_R, k_G and k_B. In reality, each wavelength λ has its own reflection coefficient k_λ, but we will simplify our derivations to be restricted to each one of the three colour channels R, G and B. Whenever the reader sees a light equation with the coefficient k, it is implicitly assumed that a similar equation should be applied three times, once per R, G and B colour channel.

Except in the case of laser light, light spreads out in various directions, hence its intensity decreases with the distance to the source. The light strength per m^2 of the sphere will decrease with the square of its radius r, since the surface of a sphere increases with r^2 and the total amount of light emitted over all directions remains constant.

Physically, we should speak of the power and radiance of light, but we will not go into the details of the terminology; we only want to define a light modulation as a function of distance. In practice, instead of using only a $1/r^2$ function, old versions of OpenGL (v1 and v2, where light equations were still hard-coded with function calls) define a modulation function also including $1/r$, therefore obtaining a light intensity variation I as a function of the point source intensity I_0, as follows:

$$I = \frac{I_0}{1 + k_1 r + k_2 r^2} \tag{5.1}$$

Since anyway, starting from OpenGL v3 on, these light equation functions are deprecated and the programmer must explicitly create shaders for them, he/she has anyway the freedom to deviate from (5.1) and can hence define any modulation function, even a constant one, which is perfectly acceptable (to be empirically checked) for small 3D scenes.

5.1.1 Emissive light source

Emissive light corresponds to light emitted by a light source and is therefore typically constant. A non-constant light source might be a spotlight, emitting a lot of light from its centre, gradually decreasing towards its borders. It would hence include a directional parameter that would modulate the light intensities I_R, I_G and I_B. In view of the programmer's freedom to foresee ad hoc shaders for whatever visual effect, the details of implementing spotlights are kept to the programmer's discretion. Here also, OpenGL and GLSL textbooks are very helpful, for example [3,4,7]. Many derivations in the following sections are reproduced from [2].

5.1.2 Ambient light

Ambient light is a constant light contribution that holds for any point in the scene. It is typically used to mimic fog, where light is so much scattered in all directions that it diffuses uniformly over the scene. To show that ambient light is important, observe that Figure 5.1(a) does not include ambient light, hence all objects in the shadows are black, which does not reflect what a real picture taken on the moon would show. Since the surface of the moon is slightly reflective with 8% of the sunlight being diffused in all directions and hitting each point in the scene in a uniform way, we must add ambient light to the scene to reach the slightly more plausible effect of Figure 5.1(b).

When debugging a shader that adds light to the scene, it is recommended to always add a constant ambient light source into the scene, since it represents a constant value that will always show up the objects in the scene. Other light sources like diffuse and specular light use an equation that involves L, N and E, and if the programmer has wrongly programmed these equations, he/she might end up with no light anywhere, ending up in a fully black-rendered scene. Adding a slight ambient light constant contribution overcomes this issue.

5.1.3   Diffuse light

In the explanation of ambient light in the previous section, we already used the word 'diffusion' of light. To be completely correct, the ambient light added in Figure 5.1(b) should not have been taken as an arbitrary constant value that seems to give a plausible rendering result; it should rather have been calculated using the sunlight direction $\overline{L}$, and the lunar surface reflection coefficient, as we will do in this section. Note that if you have no clue about the material properties and the incident light angles, it is simpler to use an ambient light constant value. Indeed, from the pictures taken in Figure 5.1, we do not know the precise position of the sun. Nevertheless, the shadows seem to be elongated, suggesting that the sun is low at the horizon. In fact, the Apollo 11 flight plan had foreseen to land on a region on the moon with the sun showing 4° to 15° angle with the horizon (cf. Box 5.1), exactly to have long elongated shadows to better estimate the crater's depth for choosing a safe landing zone. This angle is exactly the angle α between $\overline{L}$ and $\overline{N}$, which plays an important role in the diffuse light equation, as we will explain now.

As shown in Figure 5.3, light falling under an angle α onto the surface will spread its intensity I over an elementary cylinder with cross-section S. The same intensity is spread over a larger surface element S′ onto the object surface, with

$$S = S' \cdot \cos \alpha \qquad (5.2)$$

Each point on the object surface will hence capture a light density I of I_0/S':

$$I = \frac{I_0}{S'} = \frac{I_0}{S} \cdot \cos \alpha = \frac{I_0}{S} \cdot (\overline{N}.\overline{L}) \qquad (5.3)$$

where the last equality comes from the properties of the scalar product between the two unity vectors $\overline{N}$ and $\overline{L}$. This is very handy, since by this principle one can replace the cosine (or sin) of angles by a vector notation, which keeps its validity in 3D, even though the equation has been derived in a 2D plane of Figure 5.3.

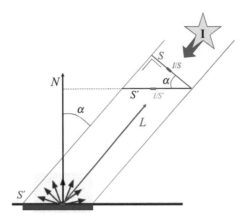

Figure 5.3   The surface S′ captures the light rays from the source I and diffuses them in all directions

Actually, since all incoming and outcoming light rays are always in a 2D plane, somehow oriented in 3D space, it makes a lot of sense to derive everything with 2D vectors that instantaneously become 3D vectors through generalization. Only if light would not stay in the same plane after reflection (like birefringence [8]) would this approach fail. In all equations we show in this textbook, the planar derivation approach remains perfectly correct.

Let us come back to our diffuse light equation. Note that (5.3) can become negative for angles larger than 90°, which has no physical meaning since this would mean that the light source is shining from within the object. Therefore, (5.3) is often extended to (5.4), where the maximum between a zero and negative value provides the zero value and the maximum between a zero and positive value retains the latter:

$$I = I_0 \cdot k_d \cdot \max\left(0, \overline{N} \cdot \overline{L}\right) \tag{5.4}$$

where I_0 is the incoming light intensity, I is the light intensity diffused evenly in all directions and k_d is the material dependent diffuse coefficient. As said before, this equation is valid for the three main colour components R, G and B, hence I, I_0 and k_d have colour dependent values.

It is important to observe that a material subject to diffuse light will actually capture the energy of a light source shining from a specific direction and will evenly distribute this energy in all directions, hence the magnitude of diffuse light is independent of the eye vector $\overline{E}$; we say that diffuse light is Lambertian, that is independent of the view direction. Nevertheless, there is a dependence with the incoming light source direction: a light source shining perpendicularly on the surface creates the highest amount of diffuse light, while light that shines tangential to the surface is not captured by the surface, which hence does not diffuse light in that configuration

Box 5.1:   Lunar landing cos function

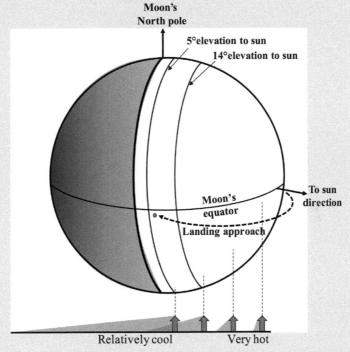

Reproduced from [9]

To ease the landing of the Apollo 11 lunar module on the moon, NASA has chosen a region on the moon where the sun would be low at the horizon, so that shadows would be highly stretched, giving some indirect information of the lunar relief to the landing crew, who were the first to land on the moon. A region where the sun shows 4° to 15° angle with the horizon was eventually chosen. Looking back to (5.3), this angle is not the angle between $\overline{N}$ and $\overline{L}$, but rather its complement. Hence, instead of taking the cosine of this angle, one must take the sine, which for 4° to 15° ends up in only one tenth to one quarter of the sunlight energy effectively captured by the moon surface in that region. Knowing that in full sunlight the moon temperature rises to 120° C or 393 Kelvin, this 0.1 to 0.25 fraction comes very handy to ease the temperature regulation within the astronaut's suite, avoiding its melt-down and/or the astronaut cooking inside his suit. Maybe, the shadow elongation was not the real reason to land in this low-shining region of the moon?

5.1.4   Specular light

5.1.4.1   Specular shininess factor

Specular light is quite different from diffuse light: it is like an imperfect reflection in the mirror, where directions close to the one with a perfect mirror reflection

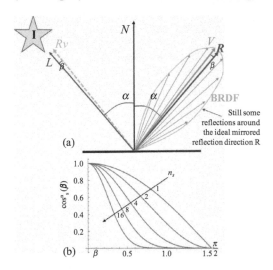

(a)

(b)

Figure 5.4   Specular light reflection with its corresponding BRDF (a), which
follows a cosine-power law that depends on the shininess n_s (b)

$\overline{R}$ also reflect a portion of the incoming light, as in the example of the lunar module of Figure 5.2. This directional reflection is schematically shown in Figure 5.4 with the reflection bubble at its right side. For a view direction or eye direction $\overline{E}$ close to the perfect mirror reflection direction $\overline{R}$, a lot of light will be reflected, that is close to a reflector factor of 1. However, when the eye direction $\overline{E}$ deviates from $\overline{R}$ with increasing angle β (not related to α!), then a smaller portion of light is reflected, eventually decreasing well below a reflection factor of 1 at large β angles. A good approximation to this behaviour is obtained by taking the cosine of β and modulating this function, as in Figure 5.4 (right), with a shininess coefficient n_s:

$$I = I_0 \cdot k_s \cdot (\cos \beta)^{n_s} \tag{5.5}$$

where we also included the specular coefficient k_s telling how specular the material is. After all, a material might be 30% diffusive and 70% specular (for a colour component), in which case $k_s = 0.7$. Such specular surfaces are typically metallic, but the forehead of a person will also be specular when lightened by a spotlight, with the reflection of the spotlight visible over a relatively small range of viewing angles. The viewing zone in which specularity is observed is mainly dependent on n_s, as we will now explain.

In (5.5), $n_s = 1$ yields a cosine function, hence β should then increase up to 90° to make I vanish in the eye direction $\overline{E}$. At for instance 45°, the contribution of the cosine is sqrt(2)/2 = 0.7. For $n_s = 2$, we would then obtain in (5.5) the factor $0.7^2 = 0.49$, which is roughly 1/2. At further increasing n_s to for example 4, we obtain $0.7^4 = 0.5^2 = 0.25$, that is roughly ¼. In general, increasing n_s to high values will push down the cosine function as in Figure 5.4(b), effectively making the bulb of Figure 5.4(a) narrower. If the eye direction remains somewhere in the large part of the bulb – thus at rather low angles β – one sees light that is reflected from the light source onto the surface. For eye directions far from the perfect reflection direction $\overline{R}$, one does not see any (or much) light anymore, which corresponds to what one would experience looking into a metallic object with a slightly rough surface (hence, not perfectly mirroring surface).

One understands that the shininess coefficient must be chosen empirically (typically a value in the order of 10–20) to give a plausible specular reflection. Of course, the inclusion of the cosine function is purely arbitrary, providing an even more empirical model, but in practice, this model approximates sufficiently well simple specular surfaces. Moreover, this model has the advantage that one can again replace the cosine function by a scalar product:

$$\cos \beta = \overline{E} \cdot \overline{R} \tag{5.6}$$

where the perfect reflection direction $\overline{R}$ can be calculated as shown in Figure 5.5. First, take the projection of the vector $\overline{L}$ onto the normal $\overline{N}$, which is a vector of amplitude $(\overline{N} \cdot \overline{L})$ in the direction of $\overline{N}$, hence is the vector $(\overline{N} \cdot \overline{L}) \cdot \overline{N}$ (this is a vector notation, so do not try to simplify to something like $\overline{N}^2 \cdot \overline{L}$; this does not hold). Calculate the difference vector $\overline{D}$ between $\overline{L}$ and its projection on $\overline{N}$:

$$\overline{D} = \overline{L} - \left(\overline{N} \cdot \overline{L} \right) \cdot \overline{N} \tag{5.7}$$

This vector $\overline{D}$ is perpendicular to $\overline{N}$. Finally, $\overline{R}$ being the symmetrical vector of $\overline{L}$ along $\overline{N}$, it is easy to see that $\overline{R}$ can be obtained from $\overline{L}$ by subtracting twice the vector $\overline{D}$ from $\overline{L}$:

$$\overline{R} = \overline{L} - 2 \cdot \overline{D} = 2 \cdot \left(\overline{N} \cdot \overline{L} \right) \cdot \overline{L} - \overline{L} \tag{5.8}$$

Combining (5.5)–(5.8), one obtains an expression for the light intensity in the eye direction $\overline{E}$ for specular objects only involving the incoming light direction $\overline{L}$. Though this equation is not super-complex, the equation of $\overline{R}$ (5.8) is somewhat cumbersome, and therefore an alternative has been proposed using a so-called halfway vector, introduced in next section.

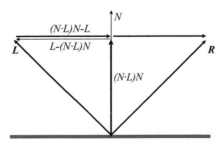

Figure 5.5   Calculating the perfect reflection direction R from the light direction L and the surface normal N

5.1.4.1.1   Specular light with the halfway vector

The halfway vector $\overline{H}$ is by definition the vector midway between the light vector $\overline{L}$ and the eye vector $\overline{E}$:

$$\overline{H} = \frac{\overline{L} + \overline{E}}{2} \tag{5.9}$$

When $\overline{E}$ falls on the perfect reflection direction $\overline{R}$, then $\overline{H}$ coincides with the normal $\overline{N}$. The more the eye direction $\overline{E}$ deviates from $\overline{R}$ at increasing angle β, as in Figure 5.6, the more the halfway vector $\overline{H}$ deviates from $\overline{N}$ at increasing angle γ, therefore the angle γ and β follow the same trend (though they are not the same angle). Therefore, instead of using $\cos(\beta)$ as in (5.5), let us replace it with $\cos(\gamma)$, somehow compensating for the difference in β and γ by defining another shininess coefficient n_{sH}:

$$I = I_0 \cdot k_s \cdot (\cos \gamma)^{n_{sH}} \tag{5.10}$$

All this may look very arbitrary, but let us not forget that anyway (5.5) is a very empirical model, so after all, the choice of using (5.10) instead is not that unjustified. γ being the angle between $\overline{N}$ and $\overline{H}$, we can easily express its cosine:

$$\cos \gamma = \overline{N} \cdot \overline{H} \tag{5.11}$$

Following the same reasoning as for (5.4) in introducing a max function to address angles larger than 90° for which there is no reflection possible (the light would then travel beyond a tangential direction to the surface), we can now combine (5.10) and (5.11) into the final specular light reflection equation:

$$I = I_0 \cdot k_s \cdot \left[\max \left(0, \overline{N} \cdot \overline{H} \right) \right]^{n_{sH}} \tag{5.12}$$

where $\overline{H}$ is the halfway vector defined in (5.9). This equation is much more manageable than the one which would include the perfect reflection direction $\overline{R}$ (5.8) and is therefore also most often used for specular light.

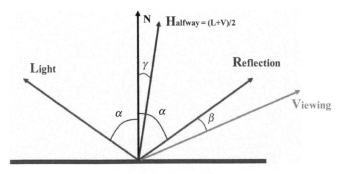

Figure 5.6   Halfway vector for specular light calculations

5.2   Physically correct light models

More accurate – and complex – light models exist in the literature, with the Cook-Torrance light model being probably one of the best known. These models fall beyond the scope of this textbook; nevertheless, the interested reader is referred to [6] for a very detailed overview of existing models.

Also note that some materials show a very anisotropic behaviour, for example, the Ward model of Figure 5.7 that nevertheless can be quite simply programmed in a shader, using bitangent Fresnet coordinates [3,5,7]. This is a coordinate system with one normal and two tangent vectors that follow the local curvature of any surface, as exemplified in Figure 5.8. Simply changing the coefficients of the light equations along one or the other tangent gives the authentic impression of Figure 5.7.

For practical shader programming providing many nice visual effects on a large range of materials and objects, the interested reader is referred to some of the following books [7,11–15], with the latter even explaining how to proceed for an ultra-realistic rendering of diamonds.

Be aware, however, that getting very realistic renderings (preferably with raytracing, as will be explained in Chapter 7) with good light equations – directly programmed into the image synthesis software or made up with a so-called node editor like in the 3D editing software Blender using interconnected modules that are transformed into shaders behind-the-scene – is a painstaking process that requires a lot of experience and finetuning. It is therefore sometimes easier to avoid any equations and just measure the light reflection for any incoming light and viewing angle, which is captured in a bi-directional reflection distribution function (BRDF) that may be highly asymmetrical when switching incoming light and viewing angles (hence the name 'bidirectional'). Measuring BRDF functions is not an easy

Figure 5.7   Ward light model. Reproduced under a Creative Commons license from [10]

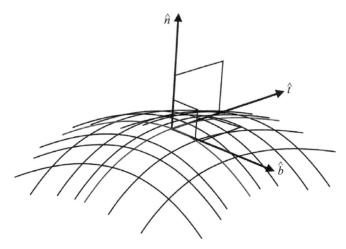

Figure 5.8   Bitangent Fresnet coordinates with two tangent vectors $\hat{t}$ and $\hat{b}$, orthogonal to $\hat{n}$. Reproduced from Public Domain [16]

task either, but once done, all light effects are put in a lookup table instead of using parametric equations that are always an approximation of reality.

Also be aware that, though advanced specular light equations and/or asymmetric BRDF functions call for a lot of effort in designing an authentic-looking 3D scene, they remain unavoidable if one really wants to create an ultra-realistic scene: the Lambertian assumption that each point in the scene emits light in the same way along any viewing direction does not hold in practice. Nevertheless, for reaching realistic 3D renderings of real scenes from a couple of photographs (cf. Chapter 12), the Lambertian assumption – even though wrong – is often followed to make the problem tractable. Consequently, many studies follow the Lambertian assumption, anyway.

5.3   Light models for transparent materials

Light also traverses transparent materials like glass, also impacting the final rendering, though often this is only used in more advanced rendering methods, like the raytracing which will be explained in Chapter 7. We therefore also develop the corresponding equations here, to prepare for it following the derivations of [2]. It is also a good exercise for practicing a bit of vector calculus in the context of 3D rendering.

In transparent media, there is not only a mirror-alike reflection of light but there is also a refraction of light where a light ray $\bar{L}$ will bend towards the normal direction when passing through a denser material, as suggested by Snell's law:

$$\eta_L \cdot \sin \alpha = \eta_T \cdot \sin \theta \tag{5.13}$$

where α is the incident angle and θ is the refracted or transmitted light ray angle.

Referring to Figure 5.9, the unit vectors $\bar{L}$ and $\bar{N}$ are known, as well as the incident angle α, and we are looking for a formula expressing the transmitted light

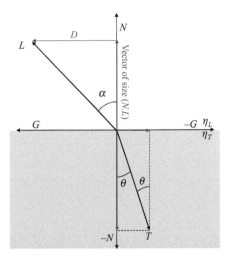

Figure 5.9 Transmitted light through a transparent object

ray $\overline{T}$ that is also a unit vector. Decomposing $\overline{T}$ into its horizontal and vertical components, we find respectively the horizontal vector with amplitude $\sin(\theta)$ pointing to the right, and the vertical vector with amplitude $\cos(\theta)$ pointing downwards. Their respective directions are expressed by the horizontal unit vector $\overline{G}$ (a sign change brings it to the right) and the vertical unit vector $\overline{N}$ (a sign change brings it downward). Note that $\overline{G}$ is perpendicular to $\overline{N}$, hence parallel to what we have called the difference vector $\overline{D}$. $\overline{G}$ can thus be derived from $\overline{D}$ on the condition that we know the amplitude of the vector $\overline{D}$, which by visual inspection of Figure 5.9 is equal to $\sin(\alpha)$ × amplitude of $\overline{L}$, the latter being 1 since by definition $\overline{L}$ is a unit vector. Therefore, we obtain for vector $\overline{G}$:

$$\overline{G} = \frac{\overline{D}}{\sin \alpha} \tag{5.14}$$

Let us now further develop $\overline{T}$, using (5.14) and Snell's law of (5.13) to replace any occurrence of the unknown angle θ by the known incidence angle α. We obtain:

$$\overline{T} = -\overline{N} \cdot \cos \theta - \overline{G} \cdot \sin \theta$$

$$\overline{T} = -\overline{N} \cdot \cos \theta - \frac{\overline{D}}{\sin \alpha} \cdot \sin \theta \tag{5.15}$$

$$\overline{T} = -\overline{N} \cdot \cos \theta - \overline{D} \cdot \frac{\eta_L}{\eta_T}$$

In (5.15), we still have θ in the first term, which will be replaced again by α with (5.13):

$$\cos \theta = \sqrt{1 - \sin^2 \theta} = \sqrt{1 - \left(\frac{\eta_L}{\eta_T}\right)^2 \cdot \sin^2 \alpha} = \sqrt{1 - \left(\frac{\eta_L}{\eta_T}\right)^2 \cdot [1 - \cos^2 \alpha]} \tag{5.16}$$

Injecting (5.16) into (5.15), we obtain

$$\overline{T} = -\overline{N} \cdot \sqrt{1 - \left(\frac{\eta_L}{\eta_T}\right)^2 \cdot [1 - \cos^2\alpha]} - \overline{D} \cdot \frac{\eta_L}{\eta_T} \tag{5.17}$$

By (5.7), we have already derived in a previous section an expression for $\overline{D}$. We also know that α is the angle between $\overline{L}$ and $\overline{N}$, hence its cosine is the angle between these two vectors. Injecting these expressions into (5.17), we obtain

$$\overline{D} = \overline{L} - (\overline{N} \cdot \overline{L}) \cdot \overline{N}$$

$$\overline{T} = -\overline{N} \cdot \sqrt{1 - \left(\frac{\eta_L}{\eta_T}\right)^2 \cdot [1 - \cos^2\alpha]} - [\overline{L} - (\overline{N} \cdot \overline{L}) \cdot \overline{N}] \cdot \frac{\eta_L}{\eta_T} \tag{5.18}$$

$$\overline{T} = \left\{\frac{\eta_L}{\eta_T} \cdot (\overline{N} \cdot \overline{L}) - \sqrt{1 - \left(\frac{\eta_L}{\eta_T}\right)^2 \cdot \left[1 - (\overline{N} \cdot \overline{L})^2\right]}\right\} \cdot \overline{N} - \frac{\eta_L}{\eta_T} \cdot \overline{L}$$

This equation expresses the transmitted ray $\overline{T}$ only as a function of the incoming ray $\overline{L}$, the normal $\overline{N}$ on the transmissive surface and the material properties; no single outcoming angle occurs in the formula. This is the equation that is used for instance in raytracing programs.

5.4 Shadows rendering

Shadows give an important clue on the position of the objects in space and should therefore also be considered as an integral part of the final rendering. For instance, a soccer player running around on the playground in a virtual 3D game without shadows gives the impression that he/she is floating in the air. With shadows, however, it is visually clear that his/her feet are standing on the ground, where the shadows start, which gives a more realistic rendering of the game.

As shown in Figure 5.10, the shadowed region only contains ambient light; no direct light can reach any point in the shadow. The renderer should hence know in each point of the scene whether its light effects only contain ambient light, or on the contrary involve all light contributions, including diffuse and specular light emanating from a light source the region under interest directly sees. To test for this, we first render the scene from the light source viewpoint, putting a virtual camera over there ①. The Z-buffer will contain depth information from the part of the scene directly facing the light source. Any point beyond will have a depth that is larger than what is captured in the Z-buffer depth map from position ①. Hence, when rendering the scene from the user's viewpoint ②, we can for each point in the scene determine whether it is lying beyond the frontier between the region that is directly lit or not, hence knowing whether it is lying in the shadow and which light contribution should be considered. In practice, the OpenGL code that creates shadows is a bit more complex than what we just described; details can be found in [3,8].

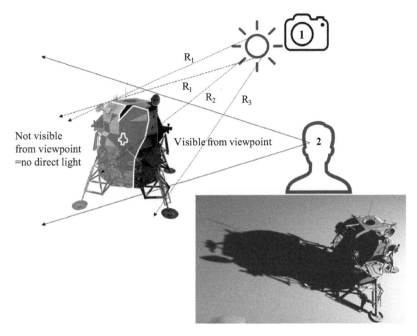

Figure 5.10   Visible and invisible regions in shadow mapping. Reproduced under a Creative Commons license from [17]

Note that in Figure 5.10 the shadow behind the lunar module is smooth because the light source is not a single point, but rather a collection of light points, each emitting a light ray R_i. For instance, a point on top of the lunar module will see two different light rays R_1 and R_1' that each create a shadow. The final shadow will be the overlap of all shadows from each individual light point in the light source. More details can be found in [18] on how to construct these shadows.

5.5   Mesh-based 3D rendering with light equations

In Chapter 3, we have seen the main processing steps in an OpenGL rendering pipeline, but we did not yet include any light effects. Now that we have seen how various light effects can be grasped in relatively simple equations, it is time to add them somewhere in the pipeline using the GLSL (Graphics Library Shader Language) shader programming language. As already warned many times before, this is the game programmer's responsibility: starting from OpenGL 3.0, any light equation functions originally present in OpenGL 1.x to 2.x are now deprecated. So, whatever we do, we must program these light equations into shaders. The question is which shaders: vertex or fragment shaders?

The answer to this question is somewhat related to the number of triangles and their size used in the objects, cf. the level of detail discussion in Section 3.2.2. This is also related to the way the normals that are heavily used in most light equations

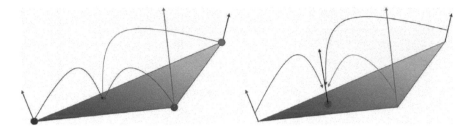

Figure 5.11   Gouraud shading (left) versus Phong shading (right)

are calculated. In fact, there are two ways to handle this, referred to as Gouraud and Phong shading.

5.5.1   Gouraud shading

Gouraud shading was developed in the early days of 3D rendering, aiming at reducing the complexity of the calculations involved in light equations. As shown in Figure 5.11, the idea is to calculate the light equation in each vertex of the triangle to be rendered, each vertex having a normal averaged over all adjacent triangles. These calculations can hence be done in the vertex shader with at most three calculations per triangle. Later, any pixel within the triangle gets a colour interpolated from the three vertices, which is a relatively simple operation that is done in the fragment shader. Gouraud shading hence pushes the heavy processing towards the vertex shaders instead of the fragment shaders. The price to pay, however, is that the cosine of the angle between the light vector $\overline{L}$ and the normal $\overline{N}$ that should have been calculated (through $\overline{N}{\cdot}\overline{L}$) is not guaranteed to be correct, especially when the light source is close to a large triangle with a potentially large variation in the direction of the vector $\overline{L}$.

5.5.2   Phong shading

Undoubtedly, the normal is an important parameter in the light equations. In contrast to Gouraud shading, where each pixel does not explicitly hold a normal, Phong shading will explicitly calculate a normal in each pixel of the triangle by interpolating the normals from the vertices, prior to any light calculation. The light equations are hence evaluated within each pixel, with the right normal $\overline{N}$, but also the correct light direction $\overline{L}$, guaranteeing that all light effects are correctly calculated. This comes at the price of a high computational load within the fragment shaders that now take up the full processing load, fully freeing the vertex shaders.

Nowadays graphics cards on desktop computers are sufficiently powerful to handle Phong shading without overload and/or lag, hence Phong shading is now the preferred way to handle light calculations. Note also that whatever the size of the triangles, Phong shading performs correct calculations, while Gouraud shading might introduce severe approximations, especially with large triangles and nearby point sources.

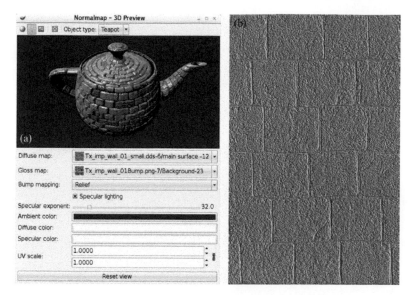

Figure 5.12   Bump map texture (b) modulates the normal, and hence the lighting effects on the object surface (a). Reproduced under a Creative Commons license from [19]

5.5.3   Bump mapping

In the interpolation process to get normals from the vertices (in Phong shading) in each pixel of a specific triangle, the normal direction will change smoothly from one pixel to the next one. There might be situations, however, where one would like to abruptly change the normal direction between adjacent pixels, for example, to mimic the cement seams between bricks or create a rough looking surface like an orange skin. Figure 5.12 shows an example of the emblematic OpenGL teapot that is covered with a brick wall, while not explicitly giving their geometry.

This can be achieved by giving indications on how the normals are oriented using a texture image – the bump map – where each tri-coloured pixel corresponds to the three Fresnel coordinates of the normal in the pixel under consideration. Figure 5.12 shows an example with reddish colours at one side of the objects and green/blueish colours at the other side, showing the large difference in local normal orientation. These abrupt directional changes will drastically modify the contribution of the $(\overline{N}\cdot\overline{L})$ term in the light equations, pixel by pixel, creating local shadow spots on the material's surface, hence giving an authentic look to the scene. The big advantage of this approach is that we do not require a multitude of tiny triangles to describe the surface and its local normal orientation; only a texture and a small number of triangles to describe the general shape of the object are required.

5.5.4   3D file formats

Many different 3D file formats exist, probably more than 30. It is hence impossible to discuss them all here. Nevertheless, there are – for simple scenes – three file

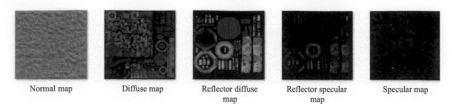

Normal map   Diffuse map   Reflector diffuse   Reflector specular   Specular map
                                          map   map

Figure 5.13   Texture mapping on the lunar module of Figure 3.4: various maps in
the OBJ file format contributing to the lighting calculations

Figure 5.14   ToysTable test scene captured from the camera positions (a) to create
a point cloud (b) with photogrammetry. The 2D texture (c) put on the
mesh of the reconstructed 3D scene (a) is clearly made from multiple
patches originating from the objects

formats which are sufficiently simple to be handled by beginners: the PLY, STL
and OBJ file formats, which are also supported in readable ASCII (always handy
when one wants to debug a 3D program source code).

So far, we have seen that 3D scenes can be modelled with a collection of
triangles, made of triples of vertices. Also the normal on these triangles (or in the
vertices) are indispensable to handle light equations in the rendering correctly. The
PLY and STL file formats do support these items well. The interested reader is
referred to Wikipedia to find detailed information on these file formats.

To make the scene look more appealing, we saw in Chapter 3 that textures are
wrapped onto the triangles with UV mapping. As shown in the example of
Figure 3.4 for the Apollo lunar module, the UV mapping is rather straightforward
with a clear link between a texture region and the 3D object. For complex scenes,
however, it may happen that the sub-textures are so much packed together in a very
weird way that results like the one of Figure 5.14(c) are obtained. Here we see that
a single texture packs all the information of the full scene.

Finally, we have seen in the previous section how additional textures help in giving information for the light equations. The OBJ file format is probably the simplest one to support multiple textures, cf. Figure 5.13, each having a light equation contribution. The first one in the figure is the bump map for the Apollo 11 lunar module, and all others are all kinds of diffuse and specular coefficients that are defined pixel by pixel, as in a bump map. Indeed, though the k_d and k_s coefficients in (5.4), (5.5) and (5.12) are often considered to be constant for a specific material, the OBJ file format allows one to define these coefficients (and others) per pixel providing even more realism in the scene at little cost: the cost of also storing or transmitting a JPEG file, most often of around 100 kB only.

References

[1] NVIDIA: Apollo Investigation, Mission Failure, NVIDIA's attempt to justify additional lighting used during creation of the Apollo 11 imagery by Marcus Allen, cf. https://www.aulis.com/nvidia.htm.

[2] E. Lengyel. *Mathematics for 3D game programming and computer graphics.* Delmar Cengage Learning; 2011.

[3] P. Nerzic. *Synthèse d'images avec OpenGL.* D-BOOKER éditions; 2017.

[4] S. R. Buss. *3D computer graphics: A mathematical introduction with OpenGL.* Cambridge University Press, ASIN; 2003.

[5] J. de Vries. *Learn OpenGL: Learn modern OpenGL graphics programming in a step-by-step fashion.* Kendall & Welling; 2020.

[6] V. Pegoraro. *Handbook of digital image synthesis: Scientific foundations of rendering.* CRC Press; 2020.

[7] K. Halladay. *Practical shader development: Vertex and fragment shaders for game Developers.* Apress, ASIN; 2019.

[8] See https://en.wikipedia.org/wiki/Birefringence.

[9] D. Baker. *Haynes NASA Moon Missions 1969-1972 (Apollo 12, 14, 15, 16 and 17) operations manual: An insight into the engineering, technology and operation of NASA's advanced lunar flights.* J H Haynes & Co Ltd; 2019.

[10] https://commons.wikimedia.org/wiki/File:Brushed_aluminium.jpg.

[11] K. A. Lammers. *Unity 4 shaders and post-processing effects cookbook.* Packt Publishing; 2013.

[12] J. Dean. *Mastering unity shaders and effects.* Packt Publishing; 2016.

[13] C. Conlan. *The Blender Python API: Precision 3D modeling and add-on development.* Apress; 2017.

[14] E. Valenza. *Blender cycles: Materials and textures cookbook.* Packt Publishing, ASIN; 2015.

[15] J. Brook. *Blender shader nodes for beginners.* ASIN; 2016.

[16] https://commons.wikimedia.org/wiki/File:Tangent_normal_binormal_unit_vectors.svg.

[17] https://computergraphics.stackexchange.com/questions/4146/better-shadow-mapping-techniques.

[18]   J.-M. Hasenfratz, M. Lapierre, N. Holzschuch, and F. X. Sillion. 'A survey of real-time Soft Shadows Algorithms'. *Computer Graphics Forum*, vol. 22, no. 4, pp. 753–774, 2003. doi: 10.1111/j.1467-8659.2003.00722.x. https://hal.archives-ouvertes.fr/inria-00281388.
[19]   https://gamebanana.com/tools/948.

Chapter 6

Kinematics

This chapter is related to all aspects of kinematics in 3D, including rigid body animations (rotations and translations), as well as deformable object simulations and collision detection. Simple animations can be programmed within the vertex shaders, but more complex animations with deformable objects will need dedicated calculations into the physics engine, which may use compute shaders. In case of geometry simplifications, cf. the levels of detail in Chapter 3, dedicated geometry shaders can handle the vertex connectivity constraints.

This chapter only provides the core elements involved in kinematics, since this is a vast domain, impossible to cover in one single chapter. We therefore restrict ourselves to a general overview with links to seminal work that the interested reader can consult by him/herself.

6.1 Rigid body animations

An object is animated by moving its vertices in space, which can be done in the vertex shader. If all vertices undergo the same transformation rule, we have rigid body animation; otherwise, the object will undergo deformations.

Rigid body animations are obtained with rotations and translations, which in homogeneous coordinates can be represented as follows:

$$
\begin{pmatrix} x' \\ y' \\ z' \\ w' \end{pmatrix} = \begin{pmatrix} R_{11} & R_{12} & R_{13} & T_x \\ R_{21} & R_{22} & R_{23} & T_y \\ R_{31} & R_{32} & R_{33} & T_z \\ 0 & 0 & 0 & 1 \end{pmatrix} \cdot \begin{pmatrix} x \\ y \\ z \\ w \end{pmatrix}
\tag{6.1}
$$

where the upper-left 3x3 submatrix of R_{ij} coefficients corresponds to the rotation in 3D space, and the T_x, T_y and T_z values represent the translation T in x, y and z, respectively.

For a rotation in 2D, we obtain the well-known expression of R made of $\cos \alpha$ and $\sin \alpha$, with α the rotation angle around the axis perpendicular to the plane of rotation. For instance, a 3D point rotated in the plane (x,y) results in a constant z-value and rotation equations:

$$
R = \begin{pmatrix} \cos \alpha & -\sin \alpha & 0 \\ \sin \alpha & \cos \alpha & 0 \\ 0 & 0 & 1 \end{pmatrix}
\tag{6.2}
$$

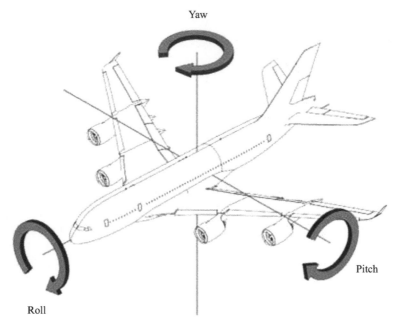

Figure 6.1   Roll, pitch and yaw in the 3D animation of an object. Reproduced under a Creative Commons license from [1]

6.1.1   Rotations with Euler angles

Rotations in the planes perpendicular to one of the world axes are called Euler rotations with Euler angles α, β and γ around respectively the x, y and z-axes. When the object is flying around, the rotation around the flight direction is called the roll, while the other two perpendicular rotation angles correspond to the pitch and yaw, as represented in Figure 6.1.

In an aircraft, the roll creates a turning action, the pitch an ascending or descending angle (the throttle must be adjusted accordingly to keep the same air speed) while the yaw following the position of the rudder pedals is rather used to bring the airplane in a perfect tangential position compared to the circular flight path induced by the roll. These three rotation actions together create a single, composed rotation with a rotation matrix obtained through multiplication of the individual rotation matrices, in reversed order. For instance, if the airplane is first taking off (pitch) and then takes a turn (roll + yaw) to leave the airfield, then the rotation matrix becomes:

$$R(\text{pitch}, \text{roll}, \text{yaw}) = R_z(\text{yaw} = \gamma) \cdot R_y(\text{roll} = \beta) \cdot R_x(\text{pitch} = \alpha) \qquad (6.3)$$

with

$$R_x(\alpha) = \begin{pmatrix} 1 & 0 & 0 \\ 0 & \cos\alpha & -\sin\alpha \\ 0 & \sin\alpha & \cos\alpha \end{pmatrix}$$

$$R_y(\beta) = \begin{pmatrix} \cos\beta & 0 & -\sin\beta \\ 0 & 1 & 0 \\ \sin\beta & 0 & \cos\beta \end{pmatrix}$$

$$R_z(\gamma) = \begin{pmatrix} \cos\gamma & \sin\gamma & 0 \\ -\sin\gamma & \cos\gamma & 0 \\ 0 & 0 & 1 \end{pmatrix}$$

(6.4)

Clearly, in an airplane, the yaw is a corrective action, also when a lot of crosswind occurs, as explained in Box 6.1.

The interested reader may verify that the matrix multiplication of (6.4) will become a relatively complicated expression, difficult to intuitively apprehend. If instead of using a pitch, roll and yaw, one would prefer to perform a rotation around an arbitrary axis in space, it would clearly become difficult to decompose this rotation into its three Euler rotations. The next section will alleviate this problem by finding a generic expression for any rotation in space.

Box 6.1: Airplane crosswind

At landing, an airplane has no roll or yaw, only a pitch. However, at severe crosswind, the airplane is turning against the wind with the rudder, causing a yaw (not a roll that would bring one wing lower than the other, which would be extremely dangerous at landing). The airplane holds this 'crab position' until touch-down, where suddenly the rudder pedals are brought back in their default position, instantaneously turning the airplane back in the direction of the runway for a safe landing.

Box 6.2: Apollo 11 roll

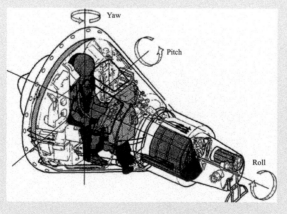

Reproduced under a Creative Commons license from [2]

In its flight from earth to the moon (and vice versa), the Apollo 11 capsule was constantly rolling at a speed of three turns an hour to ensure thermal equilibrium over the full capsule. Indeed, in space sunlight warms up the lit side of an object rapidly, while the back side in the shadow is subject to low temperatures. To mix up these warm and cold temperatures, the capsule was constantly rolling, reaching an acceptable average temperature. It is also this rolling that causes the impression that the earth turns around the capsule at the return flights, as one can see in Apollo 11 documentaries. Without rolling, the astronauts would constantly have the same picture of the earth that would only increase in size, without any other apparent movement.

Also note that if the radius of the spacecraft and/or the turning speed would be large, then a centrifugal force is created, sufficiently large to mimic a gravitational field, like in the 2001 Odyssey movie. The rolling of Apollo 11, however, was not meant for that.

6.1.2   Rotations around an arbitrary axis

As (6.4) suggests, once we know the three Euler angles, one can find the composed rotation matrix. However, the opposite is not obvious. Moreover, one is often confronted with the situation of taking a rotation around an arbitrary axis in space, rather than referring to the x, y, z-axes in world coordinates. Rodrigues' rotation formula addresses this challenge: knowing the rotation axis and rotation angle, what is the equation leading to the rotation matrix? In the early OpenGL version, this equation was present in the gl_rotate function, but in current OpenGL versions, it is the programmer who must implement this equation by himself/herself in vertex shaders. Since it is an important formula, it is a good exercise to do all the maths here instead of deferring (hiding) them away in an annex, so let us briefly give the different steps.

The situation is depicted in Figure 6.2, summarizing the derivations of [3]: the vector $\overline{P}$ turns over an angle alpha around the axis $\overline{N}$ (here represented as a vertical axis for simplicity: everything is done with vector calculus, independent of the x,y, z-axes) to obtain the vector $\overline{Q}$.

Decomposing vector $\overline{P}$ in its orthogonal components $\overline{P}_r$ and $\overline{P}_p$, with $\overline{P}_p$ being the projection on the $\overline{N}$ axis of rotation, we observe that $\overline{P}_p$ does not move during the

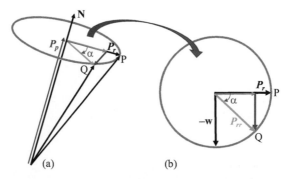

Figure 6.2   Rodrigues rotation around the axis $\overline{N}$ (a) with a top view (b)

rotation, while $\overline{P}_r$ turns over the top plane of the cone, spanned over $\overline{P}_r$ and $\overline{w}$, the vector perpendicular to the plane spanning $\overline{P}$ and $\overline{N}$. After rotation in the plane perpendicular to the $\overline{N}$ axis, $\overline{P}_r$ ends up in $\overline{P}_{rr}$ and the final vector $\overline{Q}$ is the sum of $\overline{P}_{rr}$ and $\overline{P}_p$.

Let us put all these steps in mathematical equations.

$\overline{P}$ projected towards $\overline{P}_p$ has the direction $\overline{N}$ with the scalar product between $\overline{N}$ and $\overline{P}$ being its magnitude. We hence get

$$\overline{P}_p = \left(\overline{N} \cdot \overline{P} \right) \cdot \overline{N} \tag{6.5}$$

$\overline{P}_r$ can be calculated as the difference between $\overline{P}$ and $\overline{P}_p$:

$$\overline{P}_r = \overline{P} - \overline{P}_p \tag{6.6}$$

Since w is perpendicular to the plane spanning $\overline{P}$ and $\overline{N}$, we get

$$\overline{w} = -\overline{N} \times \overline{P} \tag{6.7}$$

where the minus sign makes the correspondence between the right-handed coordinate system and the vector $\overline{w}$ shown in Figure 6.2.

By turning the vector $\overline{P}_r$ in the plane perpendicular to the axis $\overline{N}$, we get the vector $\overline{P}_{rr}$, which decomposed along $\overline{P}_r$ and $\overline{w}$ yields:

$$\begin{aligned} \overline{P}_{rr} &= \overline{P}_r \cdot \cos \alpha - \overline{w} \cdot \sin |\alpha| \\ \overline{P}_{rr} &= \overline{P}_r \cdot \cos \alpha + \overline{w} \cdot \sin \alpha \end{aligned} \tag{6.8}$$

where the change in sign for α comes from the fact that this angle is negative in the direction of the arrow shown in Figure 6.2, since in the right-handed coordinate system a turning screwdriver moves along vector $\overline{N}$ with a positive angle, which is in the opposite direction from angle α.

Finally, since $\overline{Q}$ is the sum of $\overline{P}_{rr}$ and $\overline{P}_p$, we get

$$\overline{Q} = \overline{P}_{rr} + \overline{P}_p \tag{6.9}$$

Putting (6.6), (6.7) and (6.8) together, we obtain

$$\overline{Q} = \left(\overline{P} - \overline{P}_p \right) \cdot \cos \alpha + \left(\overline{N} \times P \right) \cdot \sin \alpha + \overline{P}_p \tag{6.10}$$

The remaining $\overline{P}_p$ can be replaced by (6.5), yielding:

$$\begin{aligned} \overline{Q} &= \left(\overline{P} - \left(\overline{N} \cdot \overline{P} \right) \cdot \overline{N} \right) \cdot \cos \alpha + \left(\overline{N} \times \overline{P} \right) \cdot \sin \alpha + \left(\overline{N} \cdot \overline{P} \right) \cdot \overline{N} \\ \overline{Q} &= \overline{P} \cdot \cos \alpha + (1 - \cos \alpha) \cdot \left(\overline{N} \cdot \overline{P} \right) \cdot \overline{N} + \left(\overline{N} \times \overline{P} \right) \cdot \sin \alpha \end{aligned} \tag{6.11}$$

Since we would like to express $\overline{Q}$ as a function of $\overline{P}$, in the form $\overline{Q} = R \cdot \overline{P}$, we must find a way to extract $\overline{P}$ from the terms with $\overline{N} \cdot \overline{P}$ and $\overline{N} \times \overline{P}$, as follows.

Recall that $\overline{N} \cdot \overline{P}$ is a scalar product; hence its result is a scalar, as indicated by the parentheses in the equation below. The multiplication of a scalar with a vector is also a vector times the scalar, hence it is commutative, and the scalar product and $\overline{N}$ can be switched:

$$\left(\overline{N} \cdot \overline{P} \right) \cdot \overline{N} = \overline{N} \cdot \left(\overline{N} \cdot \overline{P} \right) = \left(\overline{N}^t \cdot \overline{N} \right) \cdot \overline{P} \tag{6.12}$$

The last part of the equation holds a transpose, when reinterpreting the product of $\overline{N}$ with itself. In fact, the transpose makes that $\overline{N}$ as a column vector gets multiplied with a row vector (transpose of a column vector), yielding a 3×3 matrix, which after multiplication with the column vector $\overline{P}$ produces a new vector.

A cross product can be written as a cross matrix times a vector, as already exposed in (4.4) and (4.5) of Chapter 4:

$$\overline{N} \times \overline{P} = N_{[\times]} \cdot \overline{P} \tag{6.13}$$

From (6.11)–(6.13), we thus get:

$$\overline{Q} = \cos\alpha \cdot \overline{P} + (1 - \cos\alpha) \cdot \left(\overline{N}^t \cdot \overline{N}\right) \cdot \overline{P} + \sin\alpha \cdot \left[\overline{N}\right] \times \overline{P}$$

$$\overline{Q} = \left\{\cos\alpha \cdot I + (1 - \cos\alpha) \cdot \left(\overline{N}^t \cdot \overline{N}\right) + \sin\alpha \cdot N_{[\times]}\right\} \cdot \overline{P} \tag{6.14}$$

with I the identity matrix.

Equation (6.14) is known as the Rodrigues equation with rotation matrix R:

$$\overline{Q} = R \cdot \overline{P}$$

$$R = \cos\alpha \cdot I + (1 - \cos\alpha) \cdot \left(\overline{N}^t \cdot \overline{N}\right) + \sin\alpha \cdot N_{[\times]} \tag{6.15}$$

The Rodrigues equation is often used in 3D graphics because it expresses in a relatively simple vectorial formula the rotation with angle α around any axis $\overline{N}$ in space.

6.1.3   *ModelView transformation*

In Chapter 4, we have seen that the projection matrix scales all the scenes within a normalized device coordinates (NDC) cube, with a near plane $\overline{N}$ in front of which the OpenGL viewing camera will be positioned (the camera focal plane is often put at the near plane, but this is not mandatory). This requires that the camera be moved (rotation and translation) towards that near plane, with a so-called view transformation.

At the same time, the objects in the scene are described in their local coordinates that should be placed somewhere (rotation and translation) in the scene's world coordinates. This is the model transformation.

The combined transformation that positions the objects in the NDC cube, as well as positioning the camera in front of the cube is called the ModelView transformation. This is an important transformation that should always be present in one of the code lines in a vertex shader, something like the code in Listing 6.1.

Listing 6.1 Shader code with the 4×4 ModelView matrix and its inverse and transpose

```
1.  Uniform mat4 mat4ModelView;
2.  Uniform mat4 mat4Projection;
3.  Uniform vec3 Normal;
4.  Void main ()
5.  {
6.        PointPosition = mat4ModelView * vec4(glVertex, 1.0);
7.        gl_Position = mat4Projection * PointPosition;
8.        gl_Normal = Vec3(mat4ModelViewInverseTranspose *Vec4(Normal,0.0));
9.  }
```

Note that this code embeds vector and matrix calculus with the vec3, vec4 and mat4 types; this makes shaders very readable. We observe that the normal in line 8 undergoes an 'inverse and transpose' of the ModelView transformation. To better understand why, let us represent the ModelView transformation by a matrix M. This M transformation is applied on the vertices, hence by linearity also the difference between vertices – that is, triangle edges or vertex tangents $\overline{T}$ – undergo the same transformation M. The question is now how each normal $\overline{N}$, perpendicular to $\overline{T}$, is transformed? Let's call this transformation Q and seek for its expression.

By definition, $\overline{N}$ and $\overline{T}$ are orthogonal, so

$$\overline{N}^t \cdot \overline{T} = 0 \tag{6.16}$$

where the transposed notation is used to have a product between a row and column vector to mimic the scalar product that is zero, cf. Section 4.1 of Chapter 4.

The transformed normals and tangents in a rigid transformation are also orthogonal, hence:

$$\begin{aligned}
(Q \cdot \overline{N})^t \cdot (M \cdot \overline{T}) &= 0 \\
\left(\overline{N}^t \cdot Q^t\right) \cdot (M \cdot \overline{T}) &= 0 \\
\overline{N}^t \cdot (Q^t \cdot M) \cdot \overline{T} &= 0
\end{aligned} \tag{6.17}$$

Since by (6.16), the outer factors $\overline{N}^t$ and $\overline{T}$ yield a value 0 by themselves, the inner factor should be the identity matrix:

$$\begin{aligned}
(Q^t \cdot M) &= I \\
Q^t &= M^{-1} \\
Q &= (M^{-1})^t
\end{aligned} \tag{6.18}$$

The last equation explains why we have an inverse and transposed in the shader's code when handling normals. Note that for an orthonormal transformation, inverse and transpose are identical operations, hence if there are no scaling operations and only rotation and/or translation operations, Q and M are equal. Therefore, most often we can also use the ModelView transformation directly on the normal, though in general it is the transposed of the inverse that needs to be taken, as given in the code of Listing 6.1.

6.2 Quaternions

In the context of 3D rotations, another mathematical concept has been introduced to be able to use analytical equations that are simpler than (6.6): the quaternions. The mathematical theories behind quaternions are vast, hence we will restrict ourselves to its basic ingredients. The interested reader should consult specialized literature in the field, as well as open-source libraries to use quaternions properly.

A quaternion q is like a complex number with a scalar and imaginary part, but instead of having only the i-component for the imaginary part, three components i, j

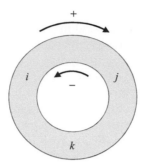

Figure 6.3   Sign rules used in the multiplication of imaginary parts in quaternions

and k are used with

$$i^2 = j^2 = k^2 = -1 \qquad (6.19)$$

For instance, $q_1 = s_1 + x_1 \cdot i + y_1 \cdot j + z_1 \cdot k$ and $q_2 = s_2 + x_2 \cdot i + y_2 \cdot j + z_2 \cdot k$ are two quaternions with scalar parts s_i and imaginary parts (x_i, y_i and z_i).

We can multiply any two (or more) quaternions by using the distributive multiplication laws. Doing so, we obtain some coefficients that are combination pairs of i, j and k, for example $x_1 \cdot y_2 \cdot i \cdot j$. Each pair of imaginary coefficients can be replaced by the third component, following the principles of Figure 6.3: when going clockwise the multiplication of two imaginary coefficients gets a + sign, counter-clockwise one must use a − sign. For example, i times j is $+k$, while j times i is $-k$. This indicates that the order of the imaginary coefficients is important, hence quaternions are non-commutative.

To return to the subject of rotations around an axis n, with rotation angle α, the quaternion rotation identity of [3] tells that if we define a quaternion q, as follows:

$$q = \cos \frac{\alpha}{2} + \overline{N} \cdot \sin \frac{\alpha}{2} \qquad (6.20)$$

Then any vector $\overline{U}$ undergoing the Rodriguez rotation of (6.10)–(6.11) to become vector $\overline{V}$ follows the quaternion equation:

$$\overline{V} = q \cdot \overline{U} \cdot q^{-1} \qquad (6.21)$$

where q^{-1} is the inverse of q, obtained by inverting all the signs in its imaginary part, divided by its norm, that is:

$$\begin{aligned} q_1 &= q_r + q_i \cdot i + q_j \cdot j + q_k \cdot k \\ q_1^{-1} &= \frac{q_r - q_i \cdot i - q_j \cdot j - q_k \cdot k}{\sqrt{q_r^2 + q_i^2 + q_j^2 + q_k^2}} \end{aligned} \qquad (6.22)$$

For rotations, unit quaternions are often used, with the denominator being equal to 1.

Equation (6.22) is analytically clearly much simpler than (6.20), bringing the 3D community to favour the quaternions over the original Rodriguez matrix equations. Of course, behind the scenes, quaternions are 4-dimensional entities that somehow replace the 4×4 homogeneous matrix calculations (or the 3×3 matrix calculations with their imaginary part only), so somehow quaternions have judiciously hidden away their complexity. Nevertheless, their complexity is still there, since the rotation corresponding to the quaternion q is given by (without proof):

$$R = \begin{pmatrix} 1 - 2s\left(q_j^2 + q_k^2\right) & 2s\left(q_i q_j - q_k q_r\right) & 2s\left(q_i q_k + q_j q_r\right) \\ 2s\left(q_i q_j + q_k q_r\right) & 1 - 2s\left(q_i^2 + q_k^2\right) & 2s\left(q_j q_k - q_i q_r\right) \\ 2s\left(q_i q_k - q_j q_r\right) & 2s(q_i q_k + q_i q_r) & 1 - 2s\left(q_i^2 + q_j^2\right) \end{pmatrix} \tag{6.23}$$

with

$$s = \frac{1}{\sqrt{q_r^2 + q_i^2 + q_j^2 + q_k^2}} \tag{6.24}$$

which becomes one for a unit quaternion.

Back and forth transformations from rotation matrix to quaternions can introduce rounding errors one should be careful about (or at least aware of).

6.2.1 Spherical linear interpolation

There is one domain where quaternions are often used with respect to rotations, that is their linear interpolation. To better understand the concept, let us take the example of an OpenGL camera view made of a pinhole camera looking at a scene. At time stamp t_1, this camera has a specific orientation given by an up vector and a rotation around it; its position can hence be represented by a quaternion q_1. During the animation, the camera is moving (and rotating), and we would like that at time stamp t_2 it has a position represented by quaternion q_2. Suppose now that t_1 and t_2 are very distant time stamps, for example $t_1 = 0$ s and $t_2 = 30$ s, and we would like to find 'the smoothest' camera positions for timestamps t in between t_1 and t_2. The best approach is to find the equivalent quaternions q by spherical linear interpolation, aka slerp.

The idea is that the linear interpolation of q_1 and q_2 on the four-dimensional sphere yields (after normalization) q, which still lies on the sphere along the shortest interpolation path. The so-obtained quaternion q being equivalent to an axis and rotation angle, we can find the corresponding camera position: its up vector is the axis of q, while the rotation angle will give its orientation towards the scene. Note that this slerp process is linear in four dimensions, though the sphere would suggest differently. Here, clearly, having used quaternions, we stay with a linear operation, which would otherwise be difficult to obtain on the original 3×3 matrices, suggesting the superiority of using quaternions in this use case.

6.3 Deformable body animations

6.3.1 Keyframes and inverse kinematics

Animations can also be obtained by indicating at several key points in time how the object is looking, providing the rotation and translation each individual segment or vertex has undergone to go from the previous keyframe to the actual one. Without putting any constraints, each vertex can move independently of the others; hence, the object might undergo a deformation.

For animating a person or animal, it is obviously better to foresee a fixed link between the vertices that follow a skeleton, and then make the skeleton move with keyframes. This approach gives the highest flexibility in defining an animation of the object vertices. It has first been used in the quake II MD2 file format, as exemplified in [4] providing also some OpenGL example code to show how to make everything work properly, even with texture coordinates that may also need to be regularly updated.

Of course, the vertices of the skeleton cannot move completely freely; they must follow constraints imposed by the joints and fixed-length segments, and these constraints may result in rather complex calculations. For instance, a robot arm is made of several segments that rotate one around another (and not necessarily in any direction), but most often without the possibility to reduce the segment length. In that case, we would like to know which rotation angles should be imposed to each segment for reaching with the top of the last segment a predefined point in space. This is called inverse kinematics [5].

A method often used for this purpose is Cyclic Coordinate Descent, where one coordinate after the other is cyclically chosen (hence the name of the method) to descent to the optimal solution, iterating until the required point in space is reached by the arm of linked segments [5,6]. It may sometimes fail to find a stable solution; hence it remains an active field of research to find improvements. The interested reader is referred to studies like [5] for more details.

6.3.2   Clothes animation

When the characters wear clothes, vertex shaders can also be used to calculate their deformations as a function of their weight, as well as the tissue elasticity and damping characteristics. The main idea is that the tissue is subdivided into a grid, where each element is allocated a vertex, on which all acting forces are calculated. This includes the gravity force:

$$\overline{F}_{\text{gravity}} = m \cdot \overline{g} \tag{6.25}$$

As well as a spring (elasticity) and damping forces, acting between two adjacent vertices (or even beyond). The spring force is a vector aligned between the vertex $\overline{Q}$ and $\overline{P}$, with an amplitude determined by the distance between $\overline{Q}$ and $\overline{P}$, keeping in mind that for a default distance d, no force occurs, hence:

$$\overline{F}_{\text{spring}} = k_{\text{spring}} \cdot (\|\overline{Q} - \overline{P}\| - d) \cdot \frac{\overline{Q} - \overline{P}}{\|\overline{Q} - \overline{P}\|} \tag{6.26}$$

The damping force depends mainly on the speed of change imposed on the vertex, like when the wheels of a car are suddenly pushed up by a bump on the road, hence:

$$\overline{F}_{\text{damper}} = k_{\text{damper}} \cdot \left(\frac{d\overline{Q}}{dt} - \frac{d\overline{P}}{dt} \right) \tag{6.27}$$

Figure 6.4   Deformations of a tissue falling onto a sphere

Listing 6.2 gives an example of source code using these equations, taking two adjacent nodes on which forces, acceleration, velocity and positions are calculated following normal physics equations (lines 5 to 23). A simple collision detection of the tissue against a sphere (height $<=$ upper circle of the sphere) and the ground (height $<=$ 0) is added in lines 24 to 28. We will see a more advanced collision detection mechanism in Section 6.4. The movement of the tissue is shown at some key moments in Figure 6.4, which corresponds to a plausible movement; perhaps not physically perfectly correct, but at least sufficiently plausible to be accepted as a physical movement.

Listing 6.2 C++ code for the example of Figure 6.4. Reproduced from [7]

```
1.   Uniform vec3 force=gravity;
2.   for (int j=0; j<numberOfSprings; j++)
3.   {
4.
5.     // take two adjacent nodes to calculate forces on
6.     If (springs[j].node1==i) {
7.       vec3 tensionDirection = currentNode[spring[j].node2].position-currentNode[i].position;
8.       tensionDirection.Normalize();
9.       force +=springs[j].tension* tensionDirection;
10.  }
11.    If (springs[j].node2==i) {
12.      vec3 tensionDirection = currentNode[spring[j].node1].position-currentNode[i].position;
13.      tensionDirection.Normalize();
14.      force +=springs[j].tension* tensionDirection;
15.  }
16.
17.    // calculate acceleration, velocity, and new position
18.    vec3 acceleration = force/currentNode[i].mass ;
19.    nextNode[i].velocity=currentNode[i].velocity+ acceleration*(float)timePassed;
20.    nextNode[i].velocity*=dampFactor;
21.    nextNode[i].position= currentNode[i].position+
22.      (nextNode[i].velocity+ currentNode[i].velocity)/2*(float)timePassed;
23.
24.    // check for a collision with the sphere or floor
25.    If (nextNode[i].position.GetSquaredLength()<sphereRadius*sphereRadius)
26.      nextNode[i].position= nextNode[i].position.GetNormalized()*sphereRadius;
27.    If (nextNode[i].position.y<floorPos)
28.      nextNode[i].position.y=floorPos;
29. }
```

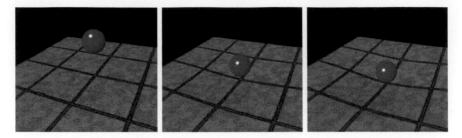

Figure 6.5   Bouncing ball animation

Simple kinematics animations can also be obtained with vertex and fragment shaders, like in Listing 6.3 and Listing 6.4 for the example of Figure 6.5 from [8,9],
which is a very good starting point for whoever wants to learn GLSL quickly. The
vertex shader changes the ball position (*y* coordinate), as well as some of the floor's
x- and *z*-coordinates to create a bending when the ball bounces on the floor.
Completely unrelated to the vertex shader animation, the fragment shader does
nothing else than calculating some light equations, which clearly hold in just a
couple of statements. This example shows the strength of vector notations in GLSL
for simple animations and lighting.

Listing 6.3 vertex shader of the bouncing ball

```
1.  void main(void)
2.  {
3.      // Normalize and scale
4.      vec3 pos = 5.0 * normalize(vec3(gl_Vertex));
5.
6.      // Basic Bounce with changing y position
7.      float t = fract( time_0_X * bounceSpeed ) ;
8.      float center = bounceHeight * t * (1.0 - t);
9.      pos.y += center + BounceMin;
10.
11.     // Bend
12.     if (pos.y < GroundHeight)
13.     {
14.         // Bend in Z direction
15.         float squeeze = (1.0 - exp2(1.0 * (pos.y - GroundHeight)));
16.         pos.y = GroundHeight - squeeze * squeezeHeight;
17.         // Flatten in XZ direcion
18.         vec2 xyNorm = vec2(normalize(vec3(gl_Normal.xy,1.0)));
19.         pos.xz += squeeze * xyNorm * squeezeHeight;
20.     }
21.
22.     gl_Position = gl_ModelViewProjectionMatrix * vec4(pos, 1.0);
23.     // gl_NormalMatrix the inverse of the upper 3x3 of the view matrix
24.     vNormal  = gl_NormalMatrix * gl_Normal;
25.     vViewVec = -vec3((gl_ModelViewMatrix * vec4(pos, 1.0)));
26. }
```

Listing 6.4 fragment shader of the bouncing ball

```
1.  void main(void)
2.  {
3.    vec3 nLightVec = normalize(vec3(lightDir.x, lightDir.y, -lightDir.z));
4.    // Simple diffuse and specular lighting
5.    vec3 nNormal = normalize(vNormal);
6.    float diffuse = clamp( (dot(vNormal, nLightVec)) , 0.0 , 1.0 );
7.    vec3 reflectVec = reflect(-normalize(vViewVec), nNormal);
8.    float specular = pow(clamp( dot(reflectVec, vec3(nLightVec)) , 0.0 , 1.0 ), 32.0);
9.    gl_FragColor = ballColor * diffuse + 0.8 * specular;
10. }
```

6.3.3   Particle systems

When one wants to mimic the movement of a flame, fireworks, or smoke, a particle system is often used. As the name suggests, it is a collection of particles (tiny triangles or quads) that move, according to some plausible movement. For instance, for welding sparks, as in Figure 6.6 [10], the particles emerge upward from a point and then follow a parabolic movement downward, here even colliding with a horizontal plate (just detect whether their height is larger or smaller than the table height). Instead of keeping each particle to be a point, one can give a lifetime to the particle, highlighting successive positions over time, like in Figure 6.6(b). Also, their color and size might change in time, creating the effect of Figure 6.6(b). By empirically finetuning the various parameters, genuinely nice visual effects can be obtained for sparks, flames, etc. Listing 6.5 gives the source code for the fragment shader creating a wobbling effect that eventually creates the flames of Figure 6.6.

Listing 6.5 Main function of the fragment shader for a flame effect

```
1.  void main(void)
2.  {
3.    // Wobble for the noise to get a more realistic appearance
4.    float wobbX = 2.0 * cos(6.0 * vTexCoord.x + time_0_X);
5.    float wobbY = 7.0 * (1.0 - vTexCoord.y) * (1.0 - vTexCoord.y);
6.    float wobble = sin(time_0_X + wobbX + wobbY);
7.
8.    vec3 coord;
9.
10.   // Wobble more in the flames than at the base
11.   coord.x = xScale * vTexCoord.x + wobbleScale * (vTexCoord.y + 1.0) * wobble;
12.   // Create an upwards movement
13.   coord.y = yScale * vTexCoord.y - burnSpeed * time_0_X;
14.   // Move in Z to get some randomness
15.   coord.z = randomnessRate * time_0_X;
16.   float noisy = texture3D(Noise, coord).x;
17.
18.   // Define the shape of the fire
19.   float t = sideFadeSharpness * (1.0 - sideFade * vTexCoord.x * vTexCoord.x);
20.   // Get the color out of it all
21.   float heat = saturate(t + noisy - yFade * vTexCoord.y);
22.   vec4 flame = texture2D(Flame, vec2(heat,0.0));
23.   gl_FragColor = flame;
24. }
```

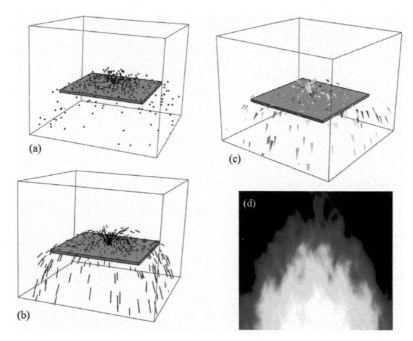

Figure 6.6   Particle system (a) which mimicks sparkles (b,c) and fireworks (d) depending on the lifetime of each particle's position. Reproduced under a Creative Commons license from [11]

To be complete, particles can also be used for defining fur or hair: all the positions taken by the particle during its lifetime are kept alive, creating a continuous line, corresponding to one hair brand. Here too, a lot of finetuning should be applied. More details can be found in [12].

6.4   Collisions in the physics engine

While objects are moving around in the scene, collisions may appear. Detecting and handling collisions is a tedious task; we will here only give a glimpse on the subject. We recommend the interested reader to use existing software libraries to handle all possible collision cases, for example, bullet [13] or SOFA [14]. A mathematical background to collision detection can be found in [15], including hierarchical trees.

Bullet can be used standalone as a library for a user-programmed OpenGL application, but it is also an integral part of the Blender 3D editing software. Using this physics engine in Blender is not an easy task; the interested reader is referred to a good tutorial book for more details [13]. SOFA is also a bullet-based physics engine, developed for interactive physical simulations targeting biomedical applications, where also the elasticity of tissue is considered. The reader is referred to [14] for a good tutorial in the field. For more information w.r.t. the physical laws that can be put in such systems, we highly recommend the books [16,17].

Box 6.3: Proto-earth moon

The collision of a meteor with the earth in formation (proto-earth made of not yet solidified magma) four billion years ago is believed to be at the origin of our moon formation. Since then, the moon turns around the earth, always facing the same half-spherical surface to the earth. It is on this face that all Apollo missions have landed. The moon's backside has been subject to many meteor impacts (much more than its frontside) which can also be handled by collision detection. Though the physics engines of gaming platforms can handle such scenarios, specialized software has been developed in the course of history, for example [18] to take all physical effects into account; gaming software is often restricted to create plausible physics, not necessarily scientifically, perfectly correct ones.

The remainder of the chapter is focused on the basic principles that can be used in collision detection. It is in no way complete; it only gives a flavor of some interesting tricks to keep in the back of one's mind when using physics engines.

6.4.1 Collision of a triangle with a plane

Let us start with the simple example of a point $\overline{P}$ moving on a straight line in the vector direction $\overline{V}$, expressed with the equation:

$$\overline{P}(t) = \overline{S}_0 + t \cdot \overline{V} \tag{6.28}$$

where $\overline{S}_0$ is the starting point, reached at $t = 0$.

We would like to know when this point $\overline{P}$ will collide with an infinitely large plane π passing through point $\overline{P}_0$, and having normal $\overline{N}$. The vector $\overline{P}-\overline{P}_0$ is orthogonal to the normal $\overline{N}$, for any point $\overline{P}$ in the plane, hence

$$\left(\overline{P} - \overline{P}_0\right) \cdot \overline{N} = 0 \tag{6.29}$$

A collision will occur in the intersection point where (6.28) and (6.29) are valid at the same time, hence

$$\left(\overline{S}_0 + t \cdot \overline{V} - \overline{P}_0\right) \cdot \overline{N} = 0$$
$$\left(\overline{V} \cdot \overline{N}\right) \cdot t + \left(\overline{S}_0 - \overline{P}_0\right) \cdot \overline{N} = 0 \tag{6.30}$$
$$t = \frac{\left(\overline{P}_0 - \overline{S}_0\right) \cdot \overline{N}}{\overline{V} \cdot \overline{N}}$$

which will provide the exact point $\overline{P}$, injecting this t-value into (6.28).

If instead of having an infinitely large plane π, we would have only a triangular region on the plane that is physically present, then of course, we would have to check whether the candidate collision point of (6.30) is really lying within the triangle; if not, there is still no collision. A simple check consists in using barycentric coordinates. For point $\overline{P}$ lying in the triangle, its projection on each side of the triangle should be positive and smaller than the length of the corresponding triangle edge. If so, then the intersection point $\overline{P}$ is indeed a collision point, otherwise not.

This leads to the simple test expressed in Listing 6.6 [19].

Listing 6.6 Barycentric coordinates to evaluate whether the intersection point of a ray with a triangle lies within the triangle or not

```
1.   Bool triangleIntersect(ray, tv1, tv2, tv3)
2.   {
3.      // e1 and e2 are two triangle edges; s1 is perpendicular to ray direction and e2.
4.      vec3 e1 = tv2-tv1;
5.      vec3 e2 = tv3-tv1;
6.      vec3 s1 = cross(ray.d, e2);
7.
8.      float divisor = dot(s1, e1);
9.      if (divisor ==0)
10.        return false;
11.     float invDivisor = 1.f/divisor;
12.
13.     // the actual test on barycentric coordinates starts here
14.     vec3 d = ray.o – tv1;
15.     float b1 = dot(d, s1)*invDivisor;
16.     if (b1 < 0 || b1 > 1)
17.        return false;
18.
19.     vec3 s2 = cross(d, e1);
20.     float b2 = dot(ray.d, s2)*invDivisor;
21.     if (b2<0 || b1+b2 > 1)
22.        return false;
23.
24.     float t = dot(e2, s2)*invDivisor;
25.     if (t<ray.min_t || t>ray.max_t)
26.        return false ;
27. }
```

Determining the collision of a triangle against another triangle might work in the same way, if we consider each vertex of the first triangle as being point $\overline{P}$. We so-obtain three t values, one for each vertex of the first triangle, and it is at the minimum value of this triplet of t-values that we get a collision. In practice, however, the situation is a bit more complex. Indeed, as in the example of Figure 6.7, it might well be that two vertices of the first triangle collide within the second triangle at time stamps t_1 and t_2, but that the third vertex of the first triangle does not intersect the second triangle, in which case this vertex is not colliding with the second triangle. This does not mean that the first triangle is not colliding at all with the second one; it just means that one edge is colliding as in Figure 6.7(b), and physically, this means that the triangle gets a rotational momentum, probably bouncing back with a spin into space. At that point in time, it becomes increasingly difficult to track the chain of events analytically with a simple equation like the ones we saw before. Therefore, in practice, even simple collision detections are evaluated numerically, subdividing the object's path into short

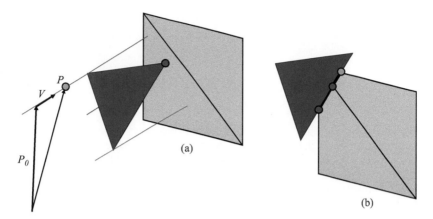

Figure 6.7   Collision between two triangles, one being part of an object (a) and degenerate scenario where an edge of the triangle collides with the object (b)

linear segments, corresponding to small t-steps. In each iteration, one may calculate linear intersections as we did before, but each of these must be updated, according to the outcome of the physical movement that is induced by the collision.

In the example above, where a first triangle punches one edge onto a second triangle, if the t-step has been taken larger than the minimum of t_1 and t_2 that would have been evaluated analytically with (6.30), then the t-step was taken too large, since the collision takes place at a lower t-value than the one following the cumulation of t-steps. In that case, we should numerically backtrack, that is discard the last t-step calculations, reduce the t-step for example by half and redo the calculations, hoping that this time we are not yet (or just reaching) the first intersection point. This example shows clearly how difficult it is to evaluate collisions, calling for all kinds of numerical recipes to handle them correctly. It is probably for this reason that one can sometimes observe mistakes in collision detections, even in high-end products, like the animation movie 'Frozen' where the character's/Elsa's hair braid passes through her shoulder at one point in time, cf. Figure 6.8. Since the movement is very rapid in the animation movie, one hardly notices this problem. What is, however, rather surprising is that the collision detection between her ponytail and body does not work, while between her hand and her hair braid, it works perfectly; otherwise, the latter could not have been pushed forward.

6.4.2   Collision between two spheres, only one moving

When the geometric primitive is represented by multiple points, like the vertices of a triangle, the previous section suggests that the collision detection might become more complicated than expected. Let us therefore take a simpler example of two colliding spheres, where only one is moving. The equations and principles that we develop here will be very useful in many other contexts, as we will see later.

Figure 6.8   Incorrect collision detection with Elsa's ponytail passing through her shoulder in the animation movie Frozen. Reproduced from [20]

Let us take a sphere S_1 that has radius r_1 and a centre point $\overline{P}$ that moves along a line, passing through $\overline{C}_1$ at $t = 0$, as shown in Figure 6.9. For the line along which the sphere is moving, we may write

$$\overline{P}(t) = \overline{C}_1 + t \cdot \overline{V} \tag{6.31}$$

where $\overline{C}_1$ is any starting position, for example the centre point $\overline{C}_1$ of the sphere at $t = 0$, and $\overline{V}$ is the directional vector (one may think of the velocity vector) in which the sphere is moving.

Another sphere S_2 with centre point $\overline{C}_2$ and radius r_2 is static. Its equation for any point $\overline{P}$ is given by

$$\|\overline{P} - \overline{C}_2\|^2 = r_2^2 \tag{6.32}$$

One would be tempted to inject (6.31) into (6.32) to find a solution for t, as we did in the previous section. Be aware, however, that (6.31) is just telling how the centre of the first sphere S_1 is moving in space; it does not hold the equation of the sphere S_1 itself. We can nevertheless use these two equations if we add an interesting interpretation that is often followed in collision detection.

In fact, sphere S_1 collides with sphere S_2 at the very moment that the centre point $\overline{C}_1$ of S_1 is at a distance r_1 away from the surface of S_2, as shown in Figure 6.9. Said differently, if we enlarge sphere S_2 uniformly over an additional radius r_1, beyond its radius r_2, the dashed sphere S_2' in Figure 6.9 will have the centre point $\overline{C}_1$ at its surface at the very moment t that sphere S_1 collides with sphere S_2. Consequently, finding the intersection point of (6.1) – the movement of

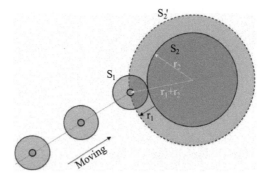

Figure 6.9   A moving sphere colliding with a static sphere

the sphere S_1 centre point – with the enlarged sphere S_2' with radius r_1+r_2 will yield the parameter t where sphere S_1 touches sphere S_2.

Defining r to be the radius of the enlarged sphere S_2':

$$r = r_1 + r_2 \tag{6.33}$$

And injecting (6.31) into (6.32) with this new radius r of (6.33), yields:

$$\left(\overline{C}_1 + t \cdot \overline{V} - \overline{C}_2\right) \cdot \left(\overline{C}_1 + t \cdot \overline{V} - \overline{C}_2\right) = r^2$$
$$\left(\overline{V} \cdot \overline{V}\right) \cdot t^2 + 2\left[\overline{V} \cdot \left(\overline{C}_1 - \overline{C}_2\right)\right] \cdot t + \left(\overline{C}_1 - \overline{C}_2\right) \cdot \left(\overline{C}_1 - \overline{C}_2\right) - r^2 = 0 \tag{6.34}$$

which is a quadratic equation in t, which can be solved with its discriminant, yielding two solutions:

$$t_{1,2} = \frac{-b \pm \sqrt{b^2 - 4ac}}{2a} \tag{6.35}$$

where the a, b and c scalars are obtained by identification with (6.34):

$$\begin{cases} a = \overline{V} \cdot \overline{V} \\ b = 2\left[\overline{V} \cdot \left(\overline{C}_1 - \overline{C}_2\right)\right] \\ c = \left(\overline{C}_1 - \overline{C}_2\right) \cdot \left(\overline{C}_1 - \overline{C}_2\right) - r^2 \end{cases} \tag{6.36}$$

Note that (6.36) holds scalar products (of vectors) that yield scalar values to a, b and c. Moreover, (6.35) suggests two values of t, but in fact only the smallest one corresponds to the sphere S_1 touching or entering the sphere S_2. The other t-value corresponds to the sphere S_1 getting out of S_2 after having fully traversed it.

Equations (6.34)–(6.36) representing the intersection of a line with a sphere is not only used in the context of collision detection, but also for raytracing, as we will see in Chapter 7. It is hence an important set of equations to keep in mind.

6.4.3   Collision of two moving spheres

When two spheres are moving, the equations of the previous section must be transformed in yet another way. We will not derive all formulas here; the interested reader is referred to [21]. The main idea is that each sphere will have its couple of equations, like (6.31) and (6.32) of the previous section for providing the movement of their centre, as well as describing their surface. Then we express that the two spheres collide when the distance between their centres reaches r_1+r_2, but we do that by finding t that minimizes the centre distance and checking that this minimum is smaller or equal to r_1+r_2. It might indeed happen that the distance between the two spheres is always larger than r_1+r_2, in which case we may state that the spheres are not colliding. If they are colliding, however, we end up in a quadratic equation like (6.34), again yielding two solutions for t, the smallest one being the solution to consider. More details can be found in [22]. The take-away message here is that relatively simple quadratic equations with scalar products can provide solutions to whether spheres collide or not. This will be very helpful in collision detection using spherical bounding boxes, we will encounter in a while.

6.4.4   Collision of a sphere with a plane

Let us take one step further with the collision of a sphere against a plane, as shown in Figures 6.10 and 6.11.

As in previous sections, the centre of the sphere is a point $\overline{P}$ that follows a line with parameter t, cf. (6.31). According to Figure 6.10, when the sphere touches the

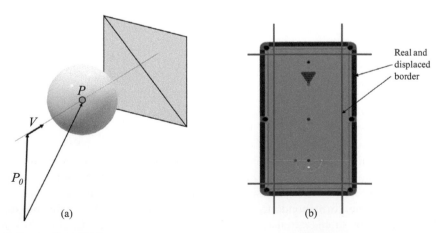

Figure 6.10   Collision of a sphere with a plane (a) applied to a snooker table scenario (b)

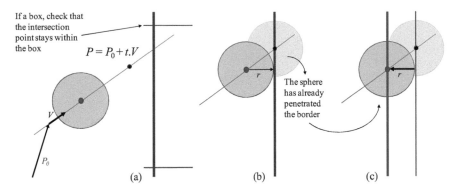

Figure 6.11 *Collision of a sphere with a plane: side-views before the collision (a) and beyond the collision (b) with the sphere already penetrating the object, requiring a correction in positioning the object plane (c)*

plane P_i, its centre point $\overline{P}$ is lying at exactly a distance r from the plane, with r being the radius of the sphere. If we now move the plane to the left in Figure 6.11, exactly over the distance r, yielding plane P_{i-r}, then we find the perfect conditions to evaluate the parameter t at which point $\overline{P}$ intersects plane P_{i-r}, which is the same time at which the sphere touches the plane P_i. The solution is like the equations of Section 6.4.1 where one finds a time t where the point travelling line intersects the displaced plane.

If instead of an infinitely large plane P_i or P_{i-r}, we now have a rectangle on the plane, we still must check whether the intersection point I at value t is really lying within the rectangle. This also can be done as described in Section 6.4.1.

6.4.5   Collision of a sphere with a cube

For checking whether a sphere hits a cube or not, it is obvious that we should apply the recipe of the previous section to each face of the cube. However, is this enough? Not really, since we might think of the sphere touching one edge of the cube, instead of a face, as shown in Figure 6.12. To check the condition that the sphere touches the edge, one should use the same trick as before by moving the surface of collision over a distance r, but this time it is not a plane that is moved, but an edge that we turn into a cylinder with radius r.

There is still one more condition to be checked, it is the scenario where the sphere might touch one corner of the cube, hence to deal with this condition, spheres of radius r are added in each cube's corner. For this situation, we end up in verifying the collision of two spheres, explained before in Section 6.4.2.

We clearly see in this example that collision detection can become rapidly complex, even for simple geometric primitives such as cubes, triangles, cylinders and spheres. Therefore, there is a need to find some ways to simplify collision detection, or at least its first stages. This is the subject of the next section.

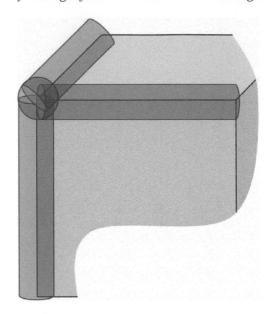

Figure 6.12   Collision of a sphere with a cube

6.4.6   Separating axes theorem and bounding boxes

Without proof, the separating axes theorem (SAT) claims that two objects of whatever shape (hence, they can be a collection of triangles as one would often do in 3D) are separated (not colliding or penetrating each other) if and only if one can find at least one projection direction, where their respective projections are separated, as shown in Figure 6.13.

It is important to understand that one single separated projection is sufficient to claim the two objects are separated. On the contrary, if one tries out any possible projection plane when he/she turns around the objects, and none of these projection planes are separated, then the two objects themselves are not separated either. More details on the actual mathematical calculations involved can be found in [15,21].

For instance, for the two objects A and B of Figure 6.13, we might check on the interconnection line between their centres whether they overlap or not, with in the latter case the separating line being perpendicular to the interconnection line. This is a simpler operation than all the calculations we have seen in all previous sections.

Suppose now we have two triangular objects A and B that are lying somewhere in space, with A being a bit larger than what we had before, for example we extend A with a shape that resembles a rabbit ear. A simple method would be to use bounding boxes A12 and B2 that best fit the objects (they are somewhat oriented along the principal axes) and check whether they overlap or not, also using the SAT. In fact, the bounding boxes are there to ease the verification process w.r.t. to object separation by collecting its triangles into one entity and avoiding that we check each possible triangle of one object with each possible triangle of the other object from the very start.

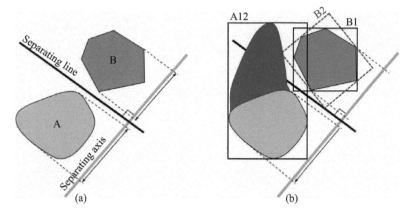

Figure 6.13   Separating axis theorem in collision detection: a clear separation line exists between the objects in (a), but not in (b) with calculations based on the bounding boxes

The simplest bounding boxes to use are the so-called axes aligned bounding boxes (AABB) which edges follow the *x, y* and *z*-directions, simplifying the SAT test calculations. Unfortunately, we see in Figure 6.13(b) that these bounding boxes overlap, so we might be tempted to conclude that the two objects collide. However, visually, this is clearly not the case, and changing the bounding box orientation does not help here. This is because too much space has been lost between the object and the cubical bounding boxes.

Perhaps, we should choose another strategy, and rather use (1) spherical bounding boxes (all directions behave in the same way, so that will ease the calculations without the need for AABB), and (2) use a collection of spheres to delimit as tight as possible the objects, as in the example of Figure 6.14(a) [23]. Here, the object A (the rabbit ear, let us say) is fully embedded in the A1 to A8 spheres, and this collective bounding box is visually separated from the spherical bounding box of object B. It is visually, however, not possible to find a separating line. So, instead of considering all these spheres altogether, let us check for the separability of each bounding sphere Ai with the one of object B. We will find out that separation is achieved for each Ai-B combination to test, hence the objects are separated.

In Figure 6.14(a), we did not have to do an SAT for each triangle of object A with each triangle of object B, so we have clearly gained in processing time. But, perhaps, we can do better? For instance, we might make sub-collections Ci of the bounding spheres Aj of (a), where these Ci are themselves bounding spheres at a higher level, yielding the hierarchical tree of Figure 6.14(b). A 3D representation is given in Figure 6.14(d), where each colour corresponds to another hierarchical level. We observe that bounding spheres C1 and C3 are colliding with the one of object B, but bounding sphere C2 does not collide with the one of object B. Therefore, all its children bounding spheres A3, A4, A5 and A6 will for sure not

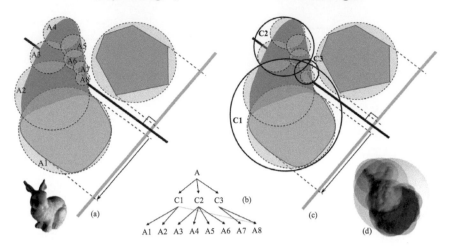

Figure 6.14   Separating axes theorem applied on two objects (a), with an hierarchical subdivision (b) helping in taking decisions in (c,d)

collide with object B neither. Instead of doing the SAT test on each of these A3 to A6 bounding spheres, we could limit the SAT test (for that region) to one single test. Of course, we still must check the SAT for the remaining bounding spheres, but overall, we have gained a lot of processing time.

This approach of successively splitting the bounding volume into smaller bounding boxes that gradually better surround the object is called a Bounding Volumes Hierarchy (BVH) [23,24]. It really saves a lot of processing time, by first traversing large volumes and checking for a possible collision, before proceeding to sub-volumes, only when the outcome is uncertain from the SAT tests in the higher levels of the hierarchy. The attentive reader understands that this hierarchical object SAT approach does not need to check triangle by triangle whether two objects are separated or not; it might already give a positive answer to this question at a higher level in the hierarchy with clusters of triangles, that is sub-boxes at a certain level in the graph.

How to create such BVH is another challenge, though. Spheres are nice with their isotropic behaviour (everything is the same in all directions), but the AABB boxes method encountered before gives even simpler calculations. This comes at the expense of possibly losing more space between the object and the surrounding bounding box, which will probably lead to a higher probability of inconclusive SAT tests at higher levels of the hierarchy. An overview of how to handle BVH can be found in [24], for example octrees that gradually subdivide the bounding volume into eight (oct) smaller boxes by splitting each dimension in two [25], Kd-trees where the split in each dimension is not strictly in the middle [26], etc. For a real-time application where many collision detections are involved, it is worth putting some effort in a well-constructed BVH that will drastically reduce the SAT testing over the various levels. Various collision detection libraries exist, also for WebGL [27].

As a final remark, the bullet library that handles collisions does not impose – in its simplest form [13] – to use such octrees or Kd-trees, but nevertheless allows the programmer to subdivide the object into multiple portions, each having its own bounding box, be it cubical or spherical, or even cylindrical. Think for instance of a pin in a bowling game: its head is spherical; its neck and body are cylindrical with different radii. Such aggregated bounding boxes can better fit the object, which will highly simplify the separating axes testing procedure, without complex tree structures. For simple game applications, this approach provides probably the best compromise.

References

[1]   https://en.m.wikipedia.org/wiki/File:Flight_dynamics_with_text_ortho.svg.

[2]   https://en.wikipedia.org/wiki/File:Mercury-spacecraft-control.png.

[3]   J. Vince. *Quaternions for computer graphics*. Springer London Ltd; 2011.

[4]   D. Henry. MD2 file format (Quake 2's models). 2004. http://tfc.duke.free.fr/coding/md2-specs-en.html#:~:text=The%20MD2%20model%20file%20format, Model's%20geometric%20data%20(triangles)%3B.

[5]   Y. Chen, X. Luo, B. Han, Y. Jia, G. Liang and X. Wang. 'A general approach based on Newton's method and cyclic coordinate descent method for solving the inverse kinematics.' *Applied Sciences*. 2019; 9(24): 5461. https://doi.org/10.3390/app9245461.

[6]   B. Kenwright. 'Inverse kinematics – cyclic coordinate descent (CCD).' *The Journal of Graphics Tools*. 2012; 16(4): 177–217.

[7]   http://www.paulsprojects.net/opengl/cloth/cloth.html.

[8]   N. Tatarchuk. 'Beginner shader programming with RenderMonkey'. ATI Research. https://developer.amd.com/wordpress/media/2012/10/Tatarchuk-GDC03-Beginner_Shader_Programming_with_RenderMonkey.pdf.

[9]   AMD GPUOpen. https://gpuopen.com/archived/rendermonkey-toolsuite-ide-features/.

[10] Wolfram demonstration projects. Particle system: Fountain. https://demonstrations.wolfram.com/author.html?author=Yuzhu+Lu.

[11] Y. Lu. 'Wolfram Demonstrations Project'. cf. https://demonstrations.wolfram.com/author.html?author=Yuzhu+Lu.

[12] L. Quan, and T. Kanade. *Image-based modeling*. Springer-Verlag New York Inc.; 2010.

[13] C. Dickinson. *Learning game physics with bullet physics and OpenGL*. Packt Publishing, 2013.

[14] F. Faure, C. Duriez, H. Delingett, *et al.* SOFA: A multi-model framework for interactive physical simulation. In: Payan Y. (eds). *Soft Tissue Biomechanical Modeling for Computer Assisted Surgery*. Studies in Mechanobiology, Tissue Engineering and Biomaterials, vol 11. Springer, Berlin, Heidelberg; 2012. https://doi.org/10.1007/8415_2012_125.

[15] C. Ericson. In The Morgan Kaufmann Series in Interactive 3D Technology, Real-Time Collision Detection. Morgan Kaufmann; 2005, page iv. https://

doi.org/10.1016/B978-1-55860-732-3.50021-8. (https://www.sciencedirect. com/science/article/pii/B9781558607323500218).

[16]   G. Palmer. *Physics For Games Programmers*. APress; 2005.

[17]   T. Mullen and E. Coumans. *Bounce, Tumble, and Splash!: Simulating the Physical World with Blender 3D*. Sybex; Pap/Cdr edition; 2008.

[18]   R. W. K. Potter. Numerical modelling of basin-scale impact crater formation. PhD thesis, Imperial College London, 2012. http://hdl.handle.net/10044/1/9322.

[19]   M. Pharr, W. Jakob, and G. Humphreys. *Physically based rendering: From theory to implementation*. Morgan Kaufmann Publishers, 2016.

[20]   https://preview.redd.it/uwbuubpl3paz.gif?format=mp4&s=76c9cedb8a8511 94c4f1e225f9fef0c9ed4d7dba.

[21]   Kenwright. Game collision detection: A practical introduction. CreateSpace Independent Publishing Platform; 2015.

[22]   E. Lengyel. *Mathematics for 3D game programming and computer graphics*. Delmar Cengage Learning, 2011.

[23]   M. Kaluschke, R. Weller and G. Zachmann. 'A volumetric penetration measure for 6-DOF haptic rendering of streaming point clouds.' *2017 IEEE World Haptics Conference (WHC)*. 2017. pp. 511–516. doi: 10.1109/ WHC.2017.7989954.

[24]   S. Dinas, and J. M. Banon. 'A literature review of bounding volumes hierarchy focused on collision detection'. *Ing. Compet.* [online]. 2015;17(1):49–62.

[25]   D. Ströter, J. S. Mueller-Roemer, A. Stork *et al.* OLBVH: Octree linear bounding volume hierarchy for volumetric meshes. *Vis. Comput.* 36, 2327– 2340 (2020). https://doi.org/10.1007/s00371-020-01886-6.

[26]   H. Wang, X. Zhang, L. Zhou, X. Lu and C. Wang. 'Intersection detection algorithm based on hybrid bounding box for geological modeling with faults.' *IEEE Access*. 2020; 29538–29546. doi: 10.1109/ACCESS.2020.2972317.

[27]   R. Yogya, and R. Kosala. 'Comparison of physics frameworks for WebGL-based game engine, ICASCE 2013'. *International Conference on Advances Science and Contemporary Engineering*, Jakarta, Indonesia. Edited by Ford Lumban Gaol; EPJ Web of Conferences, Volume 68, ID.00035. March 2014. DOI:10.1051/epjconf/20146800035.

Chapter 7

Raytracing

So far, we have seen the main aspects of the OpenGL pipeline, from the rendering with light equations to the animation and collision detection, the latter not being strictu sensu a default library of OpenGL, but nevertheless being used by many 3D editing software tools, like Blender. In the example of Box 5.1 of Chapter 5, we have seen how subtle light effects can be, and one of the main drawbacks of OpenGL is exactly that all lighting is done with a single-bounce light equation approach, that is the photons coming from a light source bounce only one time onto the surfaces before hitting the viewer's eyes. In scenes with mirror-alike reflections, this can be a serious limitation. For example, two metallic spheres put side by side will reflect each other's texture, as exemplified in Figure 7.1, and there is no way to handle this in OpenGL (though clever shader programming can come close to it, cf. [1]).

Raytracing therefore proposes a multi-bouncing lighting approach where conceptually the photons of a light source bounce multiple times over the objects' surfaces before reaching the eyes. At each bounce, the photons get the colour of the object's surface, creating a mixture of colours after multiple bounces. For instance, white light bouncing on a red object will become reddish, but after a second bounce on a green object, the mixture of red and green gives a yellow/orange colour, reaching a richer colour palette and colour gradations in the rendered image than OpenGL. Recall the example of Figure 5.2 with the astronaut coming down the ladder the raytraced solution (left) comes pretty close to the real picture taken on the moon (right), though there are still tiny differences that probably come from 3D modelling imperfections (like the moon surface, which is really too smooth in the raytraced result).

Raytracing as we just explained has, however, has the big drawback that only a fraction of all ejected photons will eventually reach the screen in the simulation process, giving the rendering a rather dark impression, often degraded by speckle noise. To overcome this issue, in practice raytracing is performed the other way around, in the inverse light direction, as shown in Figure 7.2. Light rays are 'emitted' from the screen pixels towards the scene, and at each bounce, the local colour contribution with conventional OpenGL light equations is evaluated and stored. Since this process goes in the inverse direction of light, we rather speak about path tracing than raytracing, nevertheless the two concepts are equivalent. Note that if the light from the light source is cut by any object, no light will reach the object under consideration. This can be evaluated with a shadow feeler ray that

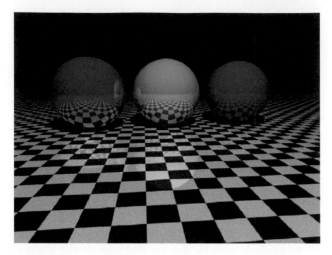

Figure 7.1   Two spheres reflecting in one another. Reproduced from Public Domain [2]

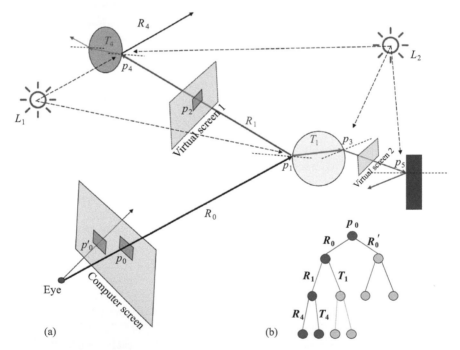

Figure 7.2   The raytracing process (a) with its hierarchical structure of reflected R_i and transmitted T_i rays (b)

goes from the first bouncing point p_1 to the light source L_1. If the shadow feeler ray gets cut, no local light contribution should be considered at this stage of the process in point p_1 or pixel p_0.

At the same time, the perfect reflection direction R_1 from the Eye's vector point of view is evaluated; this light ray will bounce once again onto another object, here the top-left ellipsoid, where it gathers its local light contribution in point p_4. In fact, it is as if we would place the screen along this reflection light ray R_1 and again evaluate the light that comes into the virtual screen pixel p_2. In the second bouncing point p_4, there will be again a reflection ray R_4 that can be handled in the same way.

Besides the reflective ray R_1 in p_1, we also have a ray T_1 that is transmitted through the spherical object, hitting point p_3 where it will get refracted, hitting in p_5 a rectangular object at the very right of the picture. Both in p_3 and p_5, there are light contributions (the feeler rays to L_2 are not cut by other objects). For instance, for capturing the light contribution of p_5 that will influence p_3, we might think of a virtual screen (2) put on their interconnecting ray and repeat the recursive process as we explained before. In the end, all these intersection points p_i contribute to the colour pixel p_0 by following the rays in the reverse direction—as photons would do—from p_5 to p_3, then p_1 (which itself gets a contribution from p_2), and finally p_0, which gets the agglomerated colour of all these light contributions. The tree structure of Figure 7.2(b) summarizes the recursive process: starting from pixel p_0, one gets an arborescence of reflected and transmitted rays that all capture some light as represented by the nodes. In practice, it is not one single ray that is sent from each pixel, but rather a multitude (here R_0 and R_0', cf. next section), which colours are averaged to produce the colour of the pixel on the computer screen, here p_0.

This approach clearly handles the example of the two spheres in Figure 7.1: somewhere in the middle of the screen, an intersection point will bounce from the right sphere to the left one, where there will be a bounce back to the right sphere. In this way, with the successive reflection rays R_i, one obtains multiple back-and-forth reflections in each sphere of Figure 7.1.

The question now pops up: 'How many iterations do we need to follow to obtain good visual results?'. In fact, the back-and-forth reflections process can only be stopped when the light contribution gets too small. At each bounce, there is a reflection coefficient k_r smaller than 1, which gradually reduces the light contribution over the many iterations. With $k_r = 0.9$, two steps yields a reduction to $0.9^2 = 0.81 \approx 0.8$, and four steps yields $0.9^4 = (0.9^2)^2 = 0.8^2 = 0.64$. In practice, four to maximum ten iterations are sufficient to claim that the light contributions become negligible, as shown in the example of Figure 7.3.

Figure 7.4 shows the raytracing of the Blender Classroom scene in its Cycles rendering engine with seven recursive levels. Light is coming from the ceiling (the four lamps) and the right-most windows; all other light contributions are indirect light. Figure 7.4 shows zoom-ins with (a) the results obtained without the indirect light contribution of glossy material, while (b, c) include all indirect light contributions, and (c) gives the final rendering with many rays per pixel, making the image less noisy than (a) and (b). We clearly notice the differences in the metal frame of the chairs; especially the metal tubes behind the chair back have large portions that do not get direct light, neither from the ceiling, nor from the windows. Without a recursive multi-bounce rendering approach, one would get very unrealistic renderings like in Figure 7.3(a). In general, there is thus a lot of indirect light involved in rendering images realistically.

Figure 7.3   An ultra-realistic rendering of the classroom Blender scene (d) at various processing levels (b,c) applied on the 3D model (a). Reproduced from [3]

As a final remark, the realistic look comes more from the indirect light contributions than from innovative light equations; the light equations used in OpenGL can do already a nice job in providing quite realistic renderings, on the condition that multiple light bounces are followed. Of course, more advanced lighting equations provide even better results, and in this Classroom example, the light equation parameters have been well-tuned to provide quasi photorealistic results. The interested reader is encouraged to study [4] for an in-depth overview of advanced light equations (and more, e.g., OpenGL projection equations, octrees, sampling functions in raytracing, etc.).

As we suggested before, raytracing is not part of the OpenGL framework, which is not foreseen to handle recursive calls. Nevertheless, simple raytracing that for example only uses reflections is sufficiently simple to be able to convert its recursive nature into an iterative call of the raytracing function [1]. At each call, an

Figure 7.4   Raytracing in preview mode excluding indirect light from glossy materials (a), and with indirect light (b). (c) Gives the final rendering with many more rays per pixel than in preview mode, overcoming the noisy rendering (b)

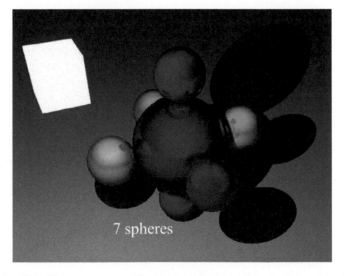

7 spheres

Figure 7.5   WebGL raytracing with simple reflective objects. Reproduced from [1]

intermediate result is kept into a frame buffer, and after all iterations, the final ray-tracing result is obtained by combining (multiplying) these intermediate buffer images. Figure 7.5 shows a visual WebGL example of a simple raytracing with reflections on spheres. Simple shaders in Unity can also mimic retracing quite well [5].

Another interesting situation hardly covered by OpenGL is given in Figure 7.6. Here, the rendering will contain the results of light rays passing through the sphere. In fact, instead of limiting ourselves to the reflection rays in each intersecting or bouncing point q, we may add the refracted or transmitted ray, following (5.18)

Figure 7.6   Raytracing with transparent spheres. Reproduced from [6]

from Chapter 5. A transmitted light ray will itself reach an exit point (equivalent to a bouncing point, but at the other side of the object) which will also contribute to the colour in pixel p by any light it gathers from the raytracing beyond the exit point. The transmitted light rays are mandatory if one wants to well-simulate transparent objects with raytracing.

Let us now summarize the process in the pseudo-code of Listing 7.1. Since each colour evaluation step in a bouncing point p calls for two additional light evaluations along directions $d_{ReflectedRay}$ and $d_{TransmittedRay}$, which themselves require the same equations as in the first step, we clearly end up in a recursive process. Each recursion phase is associated to a level parameter in decreasing order, so that once we have reached level 0, where the recursion stops, all remaining evaluations go the other way around up to the highest level for providing the final colour to the pixel p.

Listing 7.1 Pseudo-code for raytracing, reproduced from [7]

```
1.    void startRayTracer()
2.    {
3.       positionEye = eye position in world coordinates;
4.       for (each pixel p of the virtual screen)
5.       {
6.          d = unit vector from positionEye toward the center of p;
7.          colorP = rayTracer(positionEye, d, numberOfLevels);
8.       }
9.
10.   // The recursive raytracer function
11.   Color rayTracer(p, d, level)
12.   {
```

```
13.    if (ray from point p in the direction d does not intersect any object)
14.      Return backgroundColor;
15.    else
16.    {
17.      // intersection point put on black first
18.      q = first intersection point;
19.      computedColor = black;
20.
21.      // compute local light contribution in intersection point
22.      for (each light source L)
23.      {
24.        if (feeler ray from q to L does not intersect an object)
25.          // object is illuminated by light source L
26.          computedColor += color computed at q with Phong lighting model
27.        else
28.          // shadow region
29.          computedColor += color ambient light at q with Phong lighting model
30.      }
31.      // if not yet at the last recursion level
32.      If (level > 0)
33.      {
34.        // call rayTracer again for relflected and transmitted ray
35.        dReflectedRay = unit vector from q in direction of perfect reflection
36.        dTransmittedRay = unit vector from q in direction of transmission
37.        computedColor += kReflection * rayTracer(q, dReflectedRay, level-1);
38.        computedColor += kTransmission * rayTracer(q, dTransmittedRay, level-1);
39.      }
40.      return computedColor;
41.    }
42. }
```

7.1   Raytracing complexity

Clearly, each pixel p_i will call a recursion tree of N levels, each level requiring a local light calculation and two additional recursive light calculations R_i and T_i, as shown in Figure 7.2(b). For five levels, we require 2^5 calculations, which may involve several processor instructions, let us say 100 to make our point. This would represent 3,200 clock cycles. With a UHD image of $1,920 \times 1,080$ pixels, corresponding to approximately 2 Mpixels, we would end up with 2 million times 3,200 clock cycles, that is 6.4 billion clock cycles. With today's processors running at 4 GHz, this would represent less than 2 seconds, which is rather small in view of the well-known claim that raytracing is execution time hungry.

In practice, to avoid speckle noise, each pixel p_i is subdivided into $n \times n$ subpixels (typically $n = 4$), each running the full raytracing process. Subdividing each pixel randomly in $n \times n$ positions out of which the path tracing is started avoids aliasing, which typically occurs with a regular sampling. With 16 subpixels per pixel, the execution time would increase with a factor 16, reaching not more than half a minute overall. This is still much lower than the several tens of minutes to half an hour or hours that non-optimized raytracing needs for fully rendering the image. So, where is the famous raytracing complexity hiding, then?

To answer this question, we should have a closer look at what happens in all stages of the raytracing. So far, we may claim that the actual calculation of the light equations, as well as the recursive function calls are not the cause for extremely long execution times. There must be something else we overlook. In fact, we said that there are bouncing points b_i, but we did not tell what needs to be calculated to get these points. Perhaps there lies the hidden complexity?

Indeed, finding for each ray a bouncing point p_i is less innocent than we would think. After all, the objects are made of millions of triangles, and to find each bouncing point, we must evaluate the intersection of the ray with triangles, as done for the collision detection in Section 6.4.4 of Chapter 6. For a single triangle, this might not be so difficult, but since we do not know where the triangles are lying in space compared to the ray, we should actually check each triangle for an intersection, which calls for millions of operations per ray to consider. Moreover, if we find multiple triangles being intersected, we must find the very first one in the list, the closest to the screen (or virtual screen), which calls for a ranking operation. All this represents a huge task, even if we find some optimization technique ... and do not forget that this should be done for each light ray to consider in each pixel. Our previous calculation of half a minute for a UHD image should now be multiplied by the number of triangles, which may be millions, drastically increasing the complexity. That is the real reason for the raytracing complexity!

Is there a way to overcome this execution time explosion? Yes, by finding an organizational structure of the triangles so that we know beforehand which trian-gles can directly be excluded from the intersection checks.

Using the octree structure, already encountered in Section 6.4.6 for collision detection, or more generally, the Bounding Volumes Hierarchies of that section, we can indeed drastically reduce the number of intersection calculations drastically. Indeed, for a light ray in a certain direction traversing this spatial structure, we can find which sub-blocks are traversed by the ray; only the triangles from these sub-blocks might potentially be intersected by the ray. This represents a fraction of all available triangles, hence we can drastically reduce the number of checks to per-haps 10 or 100 instead of millions (of course, it highly depends on the scene structure, so these numbers are only indicative). For 100 intersection tests per ray, the total execution time would be 100 times the half a minute figure for an UHD image, which is 3,000 seconds, a bit less than an hour. This is a very realistic execution time figure for raytracing.

In 2019, Nvidia has come up with its new RTX architecture that holds a dedicated geometry shader for subdivision surfaces and memory optimizations, as well as a couple of thousands of compute cores. Thanks to that, real-time raytracing has come into reach, which was inconceivable, only a couple of years ago. Nvidia's OptiX backend for Cycles rendering in Blender can only work on Nvidia's RTX graphics cards, and also gives huge performance gains [8]. Furthermore, Foveat rendering in a VR headset can also provide big performance gains by rendering high-resolution sub-images in front of the pupil and lower resolution sub-images in the peripheral viewing zone [9]. The era of real-time VR raytracing has thus begun!

Following references are recommended to the reader interested in learning raytracing by example, digging into readable source code: Intel's Embree [10], Google's PBRT [11], Cycles in Blender [12], and a relatively short, self-contained tutorial [6]. You may even program raytracing in Unity's shader language [7]. Recently, Eevee was developed for Blender [13,14], but this is not a raytracer; it is rather a single-bounce rasterizer like OpenGL, yielding results close to Cycles, if one knows how to give indications to the rendering engine about multiple light bounces. Embree has evolved the last couple of years to a high-end raytracing tool with many scientific papers with an advanced BVH [15,16]. PBRT is a bit older, but is very well documented [11] and even enables sub-scattering that causes the glowing effect with marble objects, like in Figure 7.7, or in the skin of a human being [17–19]. They use a slightly different terminology, speaking for instance of a BSDF function (instead of BRDF) with S referring to 'scattering' and BSSSDF

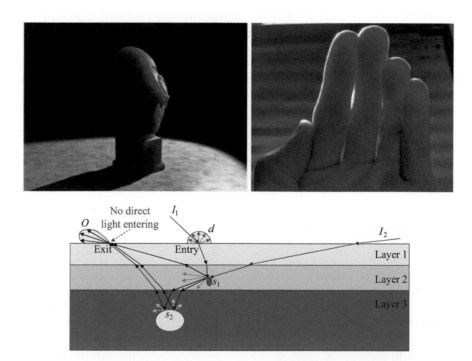

Figure 7.7   Raytracing glowing effects (top) with subsurface scattering modelled with a multi-layer stack (bottom). Reproduced under a Creative Commons license from [20] (top-left) and [21] (top-right)

with SSS being the abbreviation of sub-surface scattering. Anyway, a great tool to explore if one wants to understand raytracing in detail.

The sub-surface scattering results of Figure 7.7 (top) are obtained by representing the object's surface as multiple layers, applying the lighting equations on each of them, including on small scattering objects s_i that are present in these layers, for example, skin impurities. Note how the incoming light I_1 is scattered over the various layers, creating an exit point BRDF with a peculiar shape, very different from the simple diffusive scattering d in the entry point. This is what gives the glowing effect in the fingers of Figure 7.7 (top-right); it does not only come from the light I_2 behind the fingers that traverses them (light sources I_1 and I_2 have two different incoming light directions).

Whatever the raytracing tool you choose, be aware that many differences may occur from one raytracing tool to another; after all, the raytracing's main principles are known since a couple of decades, leading to many improvements over time. One of them is related to the question whether taking only the reflective and transmitted ray paths is sufficient for high-quality rendering? Indeed, when bouncing on a diffusive material, it would be more logical to have many different 'reflective directions' (in theory, all directions) rather than only one (and another transmitted ray direction). Though more advanced raytracing tools indeed do such things, with a denser sampling along important directions of the BRDF, this principle must be used with care, since it gives in the recursive arborescence of Figure 7.2(b), not with two but rather B branches, yielding a total complexity of B^N rather than 2^N. For B equal to a modest value of 8, $B^N = 8^N = (2^N)^3$ represents already the cubic power of 2^N, which in the above examples having $2^5 = 32$ branches in the binary tree, yields $32^3 = 32{,}768$ branches in the N-array tree, that is more than a thousand times more complex. Furthermore, for simple scenes, the binary tree approach (reflection, transmission) gives good results thanks to the subpixels approach. Indeed, neighbouring sub-pixels will also cause neighbouring reflection rays to appear, where each reflection ray samples another nearby portion of the BRDF. It is true, however, that this will not sample all directions evenly; it will rather be a direction bundle that is favoured. Nevertheless, the visual results are very satisfactory.

7.2   Raytracing with analytical objects

Bounding volume hierarchies (BVH) are important tools to test for ray intersection (like collision detection) providing large speed-up gains. Reference [22] uses this concept to do real-time raytracing on FPGA. Nvidia has also included a dedicated mesh subdivision shader that is extremely helpful in speeding up the processing by testing ray intersection first on low-resolution versions of the mesh.

Another approach to speed up the processing is to use analytical objects in the scene, like spheres, cylinders, boxes, etc. Ray intersections can be calculated analytically with a few steps, instead of representing the object with many triangles that would have to be tested on intersections one by one. Of course, one would claim that doing raytracing on such 'very smooth objects only' will result in

*Figure 7.8   3D object described with intersections and unions of analytical
objects. Reproduced under a Creative Commons license from [23]*

completely artificial scenes, but that is not completely true. For instance, Figure 7.8 shows a camera fully described with analytical surfaces, and clearly its rendering looks quite realistic, while the creation of the objects is also relatively simple. Indeed, if one would start with two spheres, one can describe the lens by intersecting two transparent spheres, and there is a way to combine the maths for each sphere into a final solution in an elegant way.

To explain this, let us use two spheres that we either intersect to create a lens, as in Figure 7.9, or that we unite with some degree of penetration to create a snowman. As before, rays are shot from the screen pixels towards the scene, and each ray intersects objects in the scene. The intersection of a line with a sphere was already presented in Section 6.4.2 and can here be reused in the raytracing context. Indeed, the intersection point will be the origin of any local light equation as summarized in Listing 7.1. Other geometric primitives can be handled in the same way; the interested reader is referred to [5,24] for finding the solution for all scenarios up to the torus, which yields a polynomial in t of the fourth degree, with an analytical solution for its four roots (Box 7.1).

Box 7.1:   Galois theory fourth-degree equation

The intersection of a ray with a sphere that can be represented by a polynomial of the second degree provides up to two intersection points having the parameter values t_1 and t_2 that are given by an analytical formula obtained as the solution from the corresponding second-order polynomial equation. Likewise, a torus that is a surface that can be represented by a fourth-degree polynomial will have up to four intersection points, and these too can be given by an analytical formula (which is quite complex). If we would have a surface that is described by a fifth-degree polynomial, one would expect to obtain five intersection points, each described by a complex analytical formula. In fact, this is not true: Galois theory tells us that an analytical formula for the solution of a N-degree polynomial equation can only be found up to $N = 4$, because all values of N below 4, that is 1, 2 and 3 are primes. Starting from $N = 5$, $N - 1 = 4$, which is not prime and this does not allow (for a mysterious reason far beyond the scope of this book) to find an analytical equation for the roots of any generic fifth-degree polynomial. This is the reason why in many raytracing programs, all surfaces up to the fourth degree (a torus) are considered for analytical evaluation; not any others.

To be precise, however, there are some special cases where the coefficients of a fifth-degree polynomial (or beyond: sixth-, seventh-degree, etc.) are such that it is still possible to find an equation for the roots, but for any fifth-degree polynomial where the coefficients a, b, c, d and e are arbitrary, no analytical solution can be found involving the basic arithmetic operations (mathematicians call these 'radicals'): additions, subtractions, multiplications, divisions and nth-power roots. Of course, one can always find a numerical solution using Newton's gradient descent method that iteratively approximates the roots with their numerical values.

In our example of two spheres, either for the lens, or for the snowman, the roots of the quadratic equation for spheres will yield two t-values for each sphere, so four values in total: $[t_1, t_2]$ for the first sphere and $[t_3, t_4]$ for the second sphere, as shown in Figure 7.9. Each tuple represents the incoming and exit points of the ray intersections with the corresponding sphere.

Figure 7.9 shows how these two tuples can be combined to find the relevant t-values for the lens object or the snowman. Since the lens is the intersection of the two spheres, also the intersection of the two tuple intervals must be taken, retaining

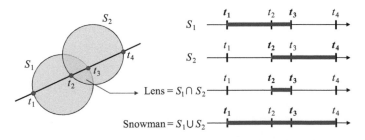

Figure 7.9   Describing an object as the intersection of two spheres, creating a lens or snowman, for which the intersection rules at the right apply

only t_3 and t_2 (in that order). t_3 is the incoming intersection point to the lens, t_2 the exit point. For the snowman, knowing that it is the union of the two spheres, we also take the union of the tuple intervals, yielding entrance point t_1 and exit point t_4.

In this way, raytracing with analytical objects becomes relatively simple, but of course, it still has its limitations. For instance, a natural scene with trees with thousands of leaves will be hard to model with simple geometric primitives like spheres, cylinders, cones, etc.

7.3 VR challenges

So far, we have learned how OpenGL works, as well as extensions thereof, like collision detection and raytracing. We have seen how the OpenGL 3D-to-2D projection works, how this relates to the pinhole camera model and animations (rotation, translations, etc.), and finally, how light equations are used in every point of the scene to create visually appealing results. Though the principles are easy to grasp, one clearly feels that to reach a high level of photo-realism in the visual rendering, heavy raytracing computations are required, jeopardizing the animation speed. For VR applications running for instance on smartphones or embedded VR headsets, it is hard to believe that this is the way to go for an enjoyable free navigation experience. The next chapters will therefore gradually introduce computer vision techniques that reconcile quality with speed at a reasonable compute cost.

References

[1] M. Broeker. 'WebGL raytracer'. http://mbroecker.com/project_webgltracer. html.

[2] https://commons.wikimedia.org/wiki/File:Raytracing_reflection.png.

[3] https://download.blender.org/demo/test/classroom.zip.

[4] V. Pegoraro. *Handbook of Digital Image Synthesis: Scientific Foundations of Rendering*. CRC Press; 2020.

[5] V. G Subramaniyan. 'Raytracing using unity: A quick start'. ASIN: B07N5HTYB4 (kindle edition only).

[6] D. Cross. Fundamentals of ray tracing. 2013. http://cosinekitty.com/ raytrace/.

[7] E. Lengyel. *Mathematics for 3D Game Programming and Computer Graphics*. Delmar Cengage Learning; 2011.

[8] M. Larabel. 'Blender 2.81 Benchmarks On 19 NVIDIA Graphics Cards - RTX OptiX Rendering Performance Is Incredible'. November 2019. https://phoronix.com/scan.php?page=article&item=blender-281-optix&num=1.

[9] https://developer.nvidia.com/gtc/2020/video/s22029.

[10] A. T. Áfra, I. Wald, C. Benthin, and S. Woop. 'Embree ray tracing kernels: Overview and new features'. in *ACM SIGGRAPH 2016 Talks (SIGGRAPH' 16)*. Association for Computing Machinery, New York, NY, USA. 2016. Article 52, 1–2. doi: https://doi.org/10.1145/2897839.2927450.

[11]   M. Pharr, W. Jakob, and G. Humphreys. *Physically based Rendering: From Theory to Implementation*. Morgan Kaufmann Publishers. 2016.

[12]   F. Steinmetz and G. Hofmann. *The Cycles Encyclopedia*. Blender Foundation.

[13]   H. San. Blender Eevee Rendering Engine: Fundamentals. Kindle edition; 2019.

[14]   J. Lampel. Cycles vs. Eevee – 15 Limitations of Real Time Rendering in Blender 2.8. https://cgcookie.com/articles/blender-cycles-vs-eevee-15-limitations-of-real-time-rendering.

[15]   K. Vaidyanathan, S. Woop, and C. Benthin. Wide BVH traversal with a short stack: The Eurographics Association. 2019. https://doi.org/10.2312/hpg.20191190.

[16]   R. Wiche, and D. Kuri. Performance evaluation of acceleration structures for cone-tracing traversal. *Journal of Computer Graphics Techniques*. 2020; 9(1).

[17]   See http://npsg.uwaterloo.ca/models/biospec.php.

[18]   B. Querleux. *Computational Biophysics of the Skin*. Jenny Stanford Publishing; 2014.

[19]   G. Borshukov and J. P. Lewis. 'Realistic human face rendering for "The Matrix Reloaded"'. SIGGRAPH '05: ACM SIGGRAPH 2005 Courses, Pages 13–es, 2005. https://doi.org/10.1145/1198555.1198593.

[20]   https://commons.wikimedia.org/wiki/File:Subsurface_scattering.jpg.

[21]   https://en.wikipedia.org/wiki/Subsurface_scattering#/media/File:Skin_Subsurface_Scattering.jpg.

[22]   J. Lee, W.-N. Chung, T.-H. Lee, J.-H. Nah, Y. Kim, and W.-C. Park. 'Load balancing algorithm for real-time ray tracing of dynamic scenes'. *IEEE Access*. 2020; 8: 165003–165009. doi: 10.1109/ACCESS.2020.3019075.

[23]   M. Scharrer. 'Strange crystal'. cf. https://mscharrer.net/povray/strange_crystal/4/.

[24]   S. R. Buss. *3D computer graphics: A mathematical introduction with OpenGL*. Cambridge University Press, ISBN: 978-0521821032, 2003.

Chapter 8

2D transforms for VR with natural content

In the study of OpenGL, we have considered the projection of 3D points (and objects) towards the 2D screen. When objects are explicitly modelled in 3D, like synthetic content created in Blender, all 3D information is available to perform a 2D projection that will display the corresponding image. It often happens, however, that only 2D projections of the real world are available, while requiring image transformations that mimic a 3D effect. For this purpose, we first review the so-called homography, a 2D transformation that gives useful 3D perspective illusions. We will take a shortcut to explain intuitively the most important aspects without rigorously developing all mathematical derivations; we will only stress the most important ones that will be used in the remainder of the textbook. Let us therefore start with the affine transform.

8.1 The affine transform

The affine transform is the 2D companion of the orthographic projection, expressed in (4.18). Since we are only interested in what is visualized on the screen (with z equal to the Near plane), we will rapidly restrict the equations to 2D physical screen coordinates, expressed in 3D homogeneous coordinates (x, y, w).

Inspecting (4.18), we observe that the 4D homogeneous coordinates (thus, the ones also including z) have a w remaining unchanged: in contrast to the perspective projection, it will not include a combination of x, y or z, that will end up in the denominator of the physical coordinates (by the division with w). We have also seen in Section 4.4.2 that the orthographic projection keeps parallel lines in 3D also parallel in 2D, which corresponds to the affine transform in 2D.

To better explain what all this implies in 2D, let us write down the generic transformation of a point (x, y, w) into (x', y', w') in 3D homogeneous coordinates, representing 2D physical coordinates $(x/w, y/w)$:

$$\begin{pmatrix} x' \\ y' \\ w' \end{pmatrix} = \begin{pmatrix} h_1 & h_2 & h_3 \\ h_4 & h_5 & h_6 \\ h_7 & h_8 & h_9 \end{pmatrix} \cdot \begin{pmatrix} x \\ y \\ w \end{pmatrix} \tag{8.1a}$$

Note that if we scale all matrix coefficients with a scaling factor λ, x', y' and w' will scale accordingly, but the physical coordinates obtained as x'/w' and y'/w' will not change. Therefore, we can set one coefficient to an arbitrary value (e.g. $h_9 = 1$) and evaluate all others, without any change in the results:

$$\begin{pmatrix} x' \\ y' \\ w' \end{pmatrix} = \begin{pmatrix} h_1 & h_2 & h_3 \\ h_4 & h_5 & h_6 \\ h_7 & h_8 & 1 \end{pmatrix} \cdot \begin{pmatrix} x \\ y \\ w \end{pmatrix} \tag{8.1b}$$

As we will see later, this generic (8.1b) corresponds to the homography, not the affine transform. Indeed, knowing that the affine transformation keeps w unchanged (i.e., it does not include the influence of x and y), the first two coefficients of the last row must be set to zero. The exact equation of an affine transform then becomes:

$$\begin{pmatrix} x' \\ y' \\ w' \end{pmatrix} = \begin{pmatrix} h_1 & h_2 & h_3 \\ h_4 & h_5 & h_6 \\ 0 & 0 & 1 \end{pmatrix} \cdot \begin{pmatrix} x \\ y \\ w \end{pmatrix} \tag{8.2}$$

where the last row indeed keeps w unchanged.

This equation reminds us of the 'raison d'être' of the homogeneous coordinates: the inclusion of a rotation and translation into a single matrix, as follows (in 2D):

$$\begin{pmatrix} x' \\ y' \\ w' \end{pmatrix} = \begin{pmatrix} r_1 & r_2 & t_x \\ r_3 & r_4 & t_y \\ 0 & 0 & 1 \end{pmatrix} \cdot \begin{pmatrix} x \\ y \\ w \end{pmatrix} \tag{8.3}$$

where the upper-left 2×2 sub-matrix is orthogonal, holding sine and cosine functions with

$$r_1 = r_4 = \cos \theta$$
$$r_2 = -r_3 = \sin \theta$$

An affine transform is slightly more generic, in the sense that this upper-left 2×2 sub-matrix will not necessarily be a rotation; it can be a combination of a rotation and a shear transform, as follows:

$$\begin{pmatrix} x' \\ y' \\ w' \end{pmatrix} = \begin{pmatrix} 1 & s & 0 \\ 0 & 1 & 0 \\ 0 & 0 & 1 \end{pmatrix} \cdot \begin{pmatrix} r_1 & r_2 & t_x \\ r_3 & r_4 & t_y \\ 0 & 0 & 1 \end{pmatrix} \cdot \begin{pmatrix} x \\ y \\ w \end{pmatrix} \tag{8.4}$$

The fist matrix in (8.4) will increase the x-value with $s \cdot y$ compared to the identity. If s is positive, this means that the larger y (let us also assume a positive y value), the larger the transformed x becomes. This results in gradually pushing the pixels of a vertical line towards the right with increasing y, hence it indeed creates a shear effect.

Note that (8.4) complies with the generic expression for the affine transformation given in (8.2).

Since orthographic projections are not often used in VR, the affine transform is not the most interesting one to consider. This is different for the homography, which we will tackle now.

8.2   The homography

The homography is the 2D companion of the perspective projection, expressed in (4.26). To see how a 3D object, for example a flat rectangle in space, is transformed, let us also consider the rotation and translation that occurs in the ModelView transform of Section 6.1.3; we will not include a shear transform here to simplify our discussion. For instance, we may induce a rotation around the y-axis only, which is the vertical axis (recall that the z-axis lies in the opposite depth direction in OpenGL). Such rotation provides a perspective illusion to the rectangle, as exemplified in Figure 8.1. The question is now how we can obtain such an effect with a 2D transform, generically described by (8.1)? Do we need all the matrix values, or – as before with the affine transform – can some of them be set to zero?

Box 8.1:   Extrinsics calibration

The calibration of extrinsics is the process of finding the pose (position and orientation) of one camera compared to another. A simple way to obtain this is by putting a checkerboard pattern as in Figure 8.1 in the scene and observe the perspective distortions that occur over the various camera views. It is intuitively clear that the way the checkerboard square changes shape in the 2D projective image gives somehow information about its position to the camera. Correlating this information over all cameras yields their respective poses.

We will see in Sections 8.3–8.6 that this is closely related to detecting homographies. In the 1980s and 1990s, many people have been searching for good calibration approaches, the most influential ones being Bouguet [1], Tsai [2] and Zhang [3,4]. More recently, an excellent mathematical overview was given in [5]. In the meantime, many of these methods have been implemented in OpenCV [6], which is probably the best starting point for any beginner, but other methods have since then been investigated for specific applications, for example [7–10]. All methods need to find correspondences of corner points (or lines) over the various cameras, and this is somewhat a weak point (at least in the past) because it relies on good feature detectors (that now exist). The method of [11,12] overcomes this problem by using a single moving led light point that one can reliably track in all views.

Other aspects of calibration are the removal of lens distortions, which we will review in Section 10.1, as well as the colour correction so that all camera views have the same colour tone. This is also a never-ending field of research, which we will not dig further into in this textbook. The interested reader is referred to some simple, yet effective tutorials (not an exhaustive list) [13–17].

Figure 8.2 already gives hint to answer this question. Starting from the Mona Lisa image, the transform given at the bottom of Figure 8.2 creates the transformed

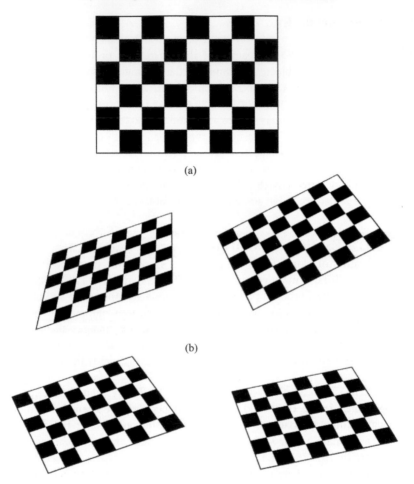

Figure 8.1   Perspective transformations obtained with the homography (b) on the
checkerboard image (a)

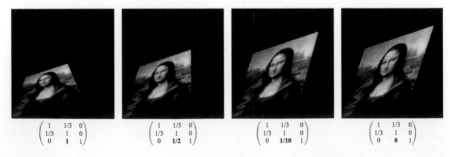

Figure 8.2   Various Mathematica ImagePerspectiveTransformation calls on the
Mona Lisa image (top) and their parameter settings (bottom)

Mona Lisa images at the top, using the ImagePerspectiveTransformation function from Mathematica [18]. The parameter h_8 is gradually decreased over the four images, reaching zero in the last one. We clearly see that this parameter plays an important role in the trapezoidal shape of the image: with relatively high values (larger than the other parameters), a trapezoid is created, while for small values (1/10 and 0), the Mona Lisa image borders get two by two parallel to each other. This already suggests that the trapezoidal shape is related to non-zero values in the last row of (8.1) and (8.1b).

To better apprehend what is really happening behind the scenes, let us suppose we have a flat textured rectangle that is captured by a perspective pinhole camera from a direction perpendicular to the rectangle. Under this reference camera pose, we see a 2D perspective view perfectly corresponding to a rectangle, as shown in Figure 8.1(a). Now, we change the camera pose so that it is not perpendicular anymore to the rectangle and observe that the closest vertical border appears much larger after perspective 2D rendering than the farthest vertical border, as exemplified in Figure 8.1(b). Also observe that the two horizontal borders in reference camera pose are now converging towards each other in the new camera pose. This is quite different from the affine transform where parallel lines in 3D space remain parallel in the rendered 2D space, as discussed in the previous section. While the affine transform could be represented with the simplified matrix of (8.2), that is, with two zero coefficients in the last row, we feel here that the homography will most probably need more. Inspection of the perspective projection matrix of (8.26) of Section 4.4 indeed reveals that its w' coefficient is not constant and equal to w, but rather changes with x, and y (and z if we take the 3D equivalent). Keeping the same behaviour in its 2D counterpart – and hence also in (8.1b) by letting h_7 and/or h_8 being non-zero – explains why parallel lines in the reference camera pose can become convergent in an arbitrary camera pose of Figure 8.1(b). Let us explain that with the example of rectangle R_{ref} in Figure 8.3.

We start with a rectangle R_{ref} of Figure 8.3 that undergoes an affine transform as before. For simplifying the visual inspection (yet without loss of generality), we will only take the rotation (here around 45°, and shear zero) and translation, yielding the rectangle R_a (the subscript a refers to *affine*). Now, instead of heaving zero values in the last row of (8.2) to (8.4), the homography adds non-zero coefficients h_7 and/or h_8, which means that w' changes with x, and y. Without loss of generality, let us assume that the last row coefficients h_7 and h_8 are positive. This means that with increasing positive values of x, y, and w' also increases. The points a, and b that are closer to the origin than points c, d will hence have a smaller corresponding w' value (which will be anyway larger than 1, since $h_9 = 1$). Consequently, when dividing the homogeneous coordinates x' and y' by w', the physical points a and b will move inward towards a' and b' over a much smaller distance than the points c and d jumping over a large distance towards c' and d'. The rectangle R_a has thus become a trapezium R_h (the subscript h refers to *homography*) with corners a', b', c' and d', suggesting a perspective rendering effect, like in Figure 8.1.

All this clearly suggests that having non-zero coefficients h_7 and/or h_8 in (8.1b) makes all the difference with the affine transform: a perspective illusion is obtained

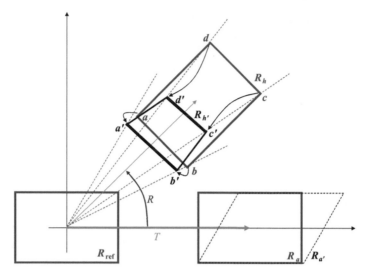

Figure 8.3   A 2D rectangle transformed under a 3D rotation and translation can give a perspective impression when applying a scaling in homogeneous coordinates

with a so-called homography. More information about the comparison between an affine transform and the homography can be found in [19]. In summary, the concept of homography is essential when trying to mimic 3D by 2D-only, and we will extensively use this feature in the remainder of the textbook.

8.3   Homography estimation

To estimate the homography, one should find corresponding points between the image before transformation (with coordinates x, y, w) and the image after transformation (with coordinates x', y', w'). Here, we will present the most well-known method, the direct linear transform (DLT), though there exist many variants with varying robustness against noise, for example [20–22]. Interestingly, [22] even presents an approach by training a deep neural network for homography estimation.

Starting from (8.1b), the DLT method states in column vector notation:

$$\overline{X'} = H.\overline{X} \tag{8.5}$$

Left and right cross-multiplying (taking the cross-product) and considering that the cross product of a vector with its own is zero, we obtain

$$\overline{X'}.H\overline{X} = 0 \tag{8.6}$$

Which in matrix cross notation gives:

$$X'_{[\times]}H\overline{X} = 0 \tag{8.7}$$

Explicitly writing the equations in (x, y, w)-coordinates yields:

$$\begin{pmatrix} 0 & -w' & y' \\ w' & 0 & -x' \\ y' & x' & 0 \end{pmatrix} \cdot \begin{pmatrix} h_1 x + h_2 y + h_3 w \\ h_4 x + h_5 y + h_6 w \\ h_7 x + h_8 y + w \end{pmatrix} = 0 \qquad (8.8)$$

Since the homography imposes that two triangles from a quad must be lying in the same plane, the matrix H is of rank 2 (this is just an intuitive explanation for a mathematical aspect that goes beyond the scope of the textbook), so that only two of the three equations are really independent. Let us choose the first two rows:

$$\begin{cases} -w'(h_4 x + h_5 y + h_6 w) + y'(h_7 x + h_8 y + w) = 0 \\ w'(h_1 x + h_2 y + h_3 w) - x'(h_7 x + h_8 y + w) = 0 \end{cases} \qquad (8.9)$$

Rearranging the terms as to split off the unknowns into a column vector yields:

$$\begin{pmatrix} 0 & 0 & 0 & -w'x & -w'y & -w'w & xy' & yy' & y'w \\ xw' & yw' & ww' & 0 & 0 & 0 & -xx' & -x'y & -x'w \end{pmatrix} \begin{pmatrix} h_1 \\ h_2 \\ h_3 \\ h_4 \\ h_5 \\ h_6 \\ h_7 \\ h_8 \\ 1 \end{pmatrix} = \mathbf{0}$$

$$(8.10)$$

We see that each point pair (x, y, w) and (x', y', w') yields two independent equations, hence a minimum of four-point pairs are required to solve for the eight unknowns h_1 to h_8. Note that (8.10) can also be extended with many more point pairs, obtaining an over-determined system of equations that might be solved with a least-squares approach and singular value decompositions (SVD) [20,23]. This may be, however, a dangerous approach in view of some points being outliers, possibly impeding the correctness of the homography evaluation. In these circumstances, the approach in the following section is recommended. Also, other more robust approaches exist for estimating an homography; the interested reader is referred to [21,23–28] for more details.

8.4   Feature points and RANSAC outliers for panoramic stitching

One of the many applications in homography estimation is the stitching of two images to create a panoramic image, as in the example of Figure 8.4. Even though the images might well have been taken by laterally moving in front of the scene between the two snapshots, in practice, at least one of the pictures must be stretched to make them fit the two pictures correctly together. In this example, the algorithm will even detect that

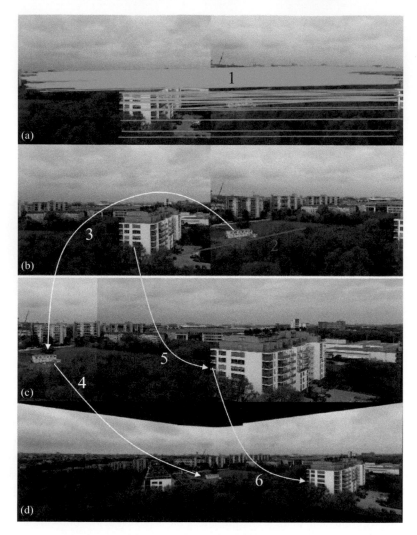

Figure 8.4   Creating panoramic images, finding corresponding points (a), calculating transformation parameters like the translation and scaling (b), stitching successive pairs of images (c) until the full panoramic stitching (d) is obtained over all captured images

the two images must be switched to find a contiguous link between them, cf. the transition from Figure 8.4 (b) to (c).

To be able to calculate the homography, a feature point detector should find the corresponding points in the two images. This is represented by the almost horizontal blue lines (a bundle of them is labelled by '1') connecting corresponding feature points.

Many feature point detectors exist; a good tutorial overview can be found in [29,30]. Figure 8.5 shows the basic principles for the family of SIFT alike feature detection. Around the pixel of interest, several directions (here eight) are identified,

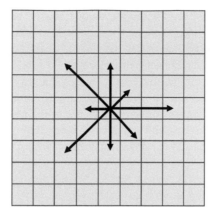

Figure 8.5   Feature point detection looking at the histogram in various directions of a central point of interest

along which the feature detector builds up statistics of the underlying pixels, for example the directional distribution of the pixel colour. Often a gradient operator is also used in the process to identify sudden colour changes indicating the underlying pixel might belong to an edge or a corner, which are useful distinctive features. If a pixel in a first image shows similar statistics (i.e., similar surrounding distributions, gradients, etc.) to another pixel in the second image, then the feature detector has found a matching point pair in the images. Most often, the feature point detector does a good job and correctly identifies corresponding feature points. Nevertheless, sometimes, it may get it wrong, as exemplified in the diagonal red line of Figure 8.4(b), which wrongly matches the top of a tree in one image to another tree in the other image. This situation may sometimes occur, and clearly represents outliers compared to the general trend of horizontal lines in the figure. If we would use a least-squares approach in estimating the homography, these outliers might (and will) seriously impact the outcome. Indeed, the relative position of the outliers is so different from the general trend of the horizontal connecting lines that taking up the outliers in the estimation might change the overall horizontal direction into a diagonal one, which intuitively is very different from what one would expect.

RANSAC (RANdom SAmple Consensus) [31], a method developed in the 1980s, is exactly taking care of detecting outliers so that they are not taken up in the estimation process. RANSAC is a very generic approach that can be used for outlier detection in any situation where one knows the expected behaviour of the system. It can be used to find outliers in a line detection, but it can also be used in finding outliers in the homography estimation. Whenever one knows the underlying model, RANSAC can be applied.

In our specific example of matching panoramic pictures, instead of applying a least squares estimation on all observation points at once, one may rather take randomly small subsets of points (at least two for a line and four point pairs for a homography), typically by dropping one point of a previously taken subset and randomly selecting a new point, replacing it. For each subset, an estimation or model fit is done and compared with all previous ones. If one estimation provides a quite different result from all others, the subset of points (or the newly selected point) is considered an outlier. After a while, outliers are all excluded (at least probabilistically) and the remaining inliers can then safely be used for estimating the parameters that will provide the best fit with the a priori model. For the case of homography estimation, least squares or SVD are all valid methods to use at this stage of the process. Of course, since in each step of the processing, an eight points DLT estimation has been done and statistically integrated into the parameter model estimation, there is no need to really add an additional step of least squares or SVD.

As a side remark, though RANSAC is used in literature since its very beginning, some studies [21] suggest that RANSAC does not always deal well with outliers, while a modified version of least squares – the least median of squares (LMS) – would be more appropriate.

Finally, to come back to Figure 8.4, we now understand the full stitching process [32,33] as indicated by the numbers. First, features between pictures are matched (1) with a feature detector. RANSAC takes care that outliers like the diagonal line (2) are discarded in the homography parameter estimation process. The system detects that the two images should be switched (negative translation) in (b), yielding the images in (c) that are transformed with the homography and seamlessly overlap (except for some sudden colour changes along the seam, close to (4)). This process is repeated with more images to create the full panoramic view of (d), where we clearly see the homographic/perspective distortions. Note also that the beige, small building is repeated over steps (3) and (4), while the large white building in the foreground is repeated over (5) and (6). More details about the stitching process can be found in [32].

8.5   Homography and affine transform revisited

A rapid inspection on (8.1b) reveals that for a homography there are eight unknowns to be found when estimating it from the images corresponding to two camera poses, like in Figure 8.1. By intuition, since image pixels have two coordinates x and y, finding four corresponding points in the two images will suffice to solve for the eight unknowns. For the time being, let us recall that the homography can transform a perfectly rectangular 2D image into a 2D trapezoidal image, giving the illusion of a plane in 3D space having a wanted perspective distortion.

Let us now compare this with the situation of an affine transform, as shown at the bottom of Figure 8.6. Having only six unknowns in (8.2) suggests that only three point pairs should be found to compute all unknowns. Said differently, if a piece of an image is represented by a triangle (always made of three points), and we know how the triangle is transformed to create a new image, then we can find the corresponding affine transform. This might be interesting to create a special effect, as at the top of Figure 8.6 reproduced with some modifications from [34], where one wants to give the illusion of a 2D sunset image that is mapped onto a 3D object, the tower, while having no information whatsoever about the depth for neither of them; the tower is also just a 2D image. For doing so, one can put a triangular grid onto the tower image

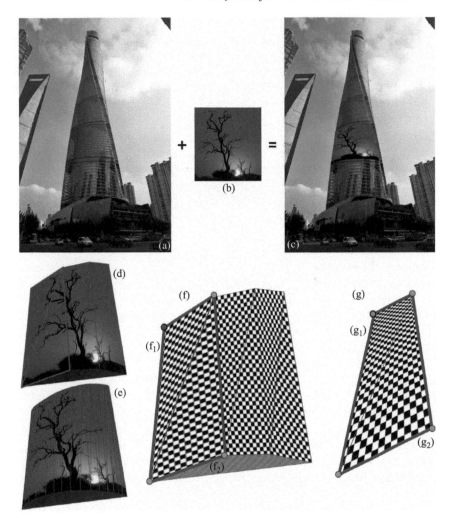

Figure 8.6   *Special effect with the affine transform, fitting a rectangular image (b)
onto an object shape (a) triangle by triangle (as in (d) for large
triangles or (e) for more refined triangles) without knowing the actual
3D shape of the object (tower, c). An affine transform allows each
triangle in (d, e) to be processed separately as shown in (f_1, f_2), while a
perspective transformation will apply additional constraints to keep
both triangles (g_1, g_2) into the same apparent plane (g) in 3D.
Reproduced under a Creative Commons license from [35,36]*

and let that correspond with a triangular grid of the sunset image, like with texture
coordinates in 3D graphics; thus we create the transition of Figure 8.6 (a)–(c), yielding
the wallpaper effect with (b). Each triangle in the sunset image is then mapped with its
own affine transform onto the corresponding triangle of the tower.

The same approach using triangles could have been used in any homography example: split any rectangle (*f*) in the scene, in two triangles (*f₁*) and (*f₂*), and apply an affine transform instead of the homography to cover the image. This, however, is not always recommended (and often, not recommended at all). Indeed, the homography imposes that the two triangles it transforms in one step are really lying in the same plane (*g*) = (*g₁*, *g₂*) (the plane in 3D space that is projected as a trapezium onto the screen). If one uses an affine transform instead (actually two: one for each triangle, represented by (*f₁*) and (*f₂*) in Figure 8.6), this constraint is lost and each triangle is transformed in its own way, most probably creating a 'fold' along their common borders in the displayed image. Such a fold is acceptable in the example of Figure 8.6, where each triangle in (*c*) should give the illusion that it best follows the façade of the twisted tower (*a*). However, with a perfect flat façade, the transform should keep the triangles coherent over a single perspective viewing experience, that would be best obtained with a homography, giving a slight perspective stretch on the triangles (*e₁*) and (*e₂*) or (*g₁*) and (*g₂*), seen as one single entity.

Though we have so far (in the OpenGL context) always worked with triangles as the basic ingredient to operate on, the homography example shows that this can be counterproductive for visual effects. Therefore, once again, when working with images to give 3D illusions, one should first consider working with homographies rather than with affine transforms.

8.6   Pose estimation for AR

In the panoramic stitching example of Figure 8.4, we observe that the partial images undergo a trapezoidal distortion mimicking a perspective transform corresponding to divergent camera poses.

In general, pose estimation is an important tool in VR, but even more in augmented reality (AR), where virtual objects must be positioned in space, in perfect correspondence with the real objects that a camera on the user's head-mounted device detects in the scene. Typically, a rectangular marker is put in the scene and tracked over time with the camera [37–39]. Its image will show perspective deformations (a homography) that correspond to the relative translation and rotation of the camera compared to the rectangular marker positioned in 3D space. It is with this information that a virtual object can be well positioned in the rendering process, as shown in Figure 8.7, with the virtual cat standing on a pile of real books. The rectangular marker corresponds to the purple book on top of the pile.

There exist excellent methods to find the pose, like the one implemented in OpenCV based on [23]. Their mathematical developments being quite extensive, we will not fully develop them here. We will rather take a simple case first, and later extend it.

Reference [11] gives a simple process to extract the rotation and translation from one camera pose to another, by taking for granted that the first pose is the reference, with the optical axis of the camera perfectly perpendicular to the planar marker under interest. The normal to the plane corresponds to this optical axis (in the opposite direction), yielding the world coordinate axes (*R₁*, *R₂*, *R₃*) in

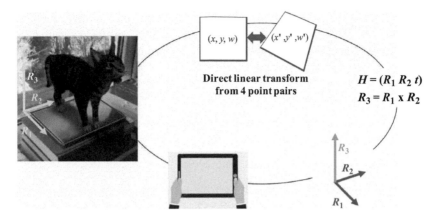

*Figure 8.7   Augmented reality with pose estimation of scene objects to render the
virtual object (cat) with the correct pose over the real world*

Figure 8.7, with the planar marker positioned at $z = 0$. For simplicity, we assume
the origin of the image is set at the camera's optical centre (i.e., the offset for the
principal point is zero; after all, we may choose our offset wherever we want) and
we also consider that the intrinsic matrix K is further normalized (i.e. f_x and f_y are
virtually put to 1), that is, we may assume K is equivalent to the identity matrix. If
not, the inverse of K can be put in the equations for more genericity, introducing
explicitly some scaling or normalization, as we will see at the end of this section.

The marker rectangle seen from the real camera position (with unknown pose)
looks typically perspectively distorted. The corresponding homography H (which
we can estimate with any image-based method from previous sections) now tells
how a point $p = (x, y)$ is transformed into a point $p' = (x', y')$ in the plane of the
marker. At the same time, in terms of the projection matrix, we know that p is
projected to p' according to

$$\overline{p'} = K \cdot (R|t) \cdot \overline{p} \tag{8.11}$$

where p holds a zero value for its z-coordinate.

In the first step, as we said before, let us simplify this expression by taking K equal
to the identity matrix. We will correct this situation later to come to a generic K matrix.
To further simplify the mathematical derivations, instead of representing R with all its
scalar coefficients, we will represent its columns by R_1, R_2 and R_3 column vectors.
Likewise, we represent the homography matrix H by its column vectors H_1, H_2 and H_3.

The decomposition of $(R|t)$ of (8.11) into this representation provides a good
way to compare it to the homography:

$$\begin{pmatrix} \overline{R_1} & \overline{R_2} & \overline{R_3} & \overline{t} \end{pmatrix} \cdot \begin{pmatrix} x \\ y \\ z = 0 \\ w \end{pmatrix} \equiv \begin{pmatrix} \overline{H_1} & \overline{H_2} & \overline{H_3} \end{pmatrix} \cdot \begin{pmatrix} x \\ y \\ w \end{pmatrix} \tag{8.12}$$

Because the z coordinate in this equation is zero, it does not expose any information. Therefore, we must disregard the third row and third column from (8.12), telling that the first two columns of H correspond to the first two columns of the rotation, while the last column of H corresponds to the translation:

$$\left(\overline{R_1} \quad \overline{R_2} \quad \bar{t} \right).\begin{pmatrix} x \\ y \\ w \end{pmatrix} = \left(\overline{H_1} \quad \overline{H_2} \quad \overline{H_3} \right).\begin{pmatrix} x \\ y \\ w \end{pmatrix} \tag{8.13}$$

which is valid for any x, y and w, hence we get

$$\left(\overline{R_1} \quad \overline{R_2} \quad \bar{t} \right) = \left(\overline{H_1} \quad \overline{H_2} \quad \overline{H_3} \right) \tag{8.14}$$

Since we can estimate the homography (cf. previous sections), we have almost fully found R and t. The only information we are now missing is the last column $\overline{R_3}$ of the rotation R to find the camera pose. However, knowing that a rotation is an orthogonal transform, by definition its first two columns correspond to the unit vectors of the first two axes of the transformed coordinate system, while the third column corresponds to the third axis, orthogonal to the first two. Consequently, the third axis must be the cross-product of the first two, that is:

$$\overline{R_3} = \overline{R_1} \times \overline{R_2} \tag{8.15}$$

Figure 8.7 shows how the vectors relate to the reference rectangle in the scene.

The calculation is a bit more involved when K is not equal to the identity matrix. A good overview of the process can be found in [40] and will briefly be repeated here with our own notations.

Instead of (8.14), we now have K also appearing in the equation, hence

$$K.\left(\overline{R_1} \quad \overline{R_2} \quad \bar{t} \right) = \left(\overline{H_1} \quad \overline{H_2} \quad \overline{H_3} \right) \tag{8.16}$$

Thus:

$$\begin{aligned} \overline{R_1} &= K^{-1}\overline{H_1} \\ \overline{R_2} &= K^{-1}\overline{H_2} \end{aligned} \tag{8.17}$$

Since R_1 and R_2 are orthogonal, their scalar product is zero. Expressing this directly in vector notation with a transpose expression for the scalar product, we get

$$\begin{aligned} \left(K^{-1}\overline{H_1}\right)^t \left(K^{-1}\overline{H_2}\right) &= 0 \\ \overline{H_1}^t (K^{-t}K^{-1})\overline{H_2} &= 0 \end{aligned} \tag{8.18}$$

Moreover, R_1 and R_2 have both norm one, and are thus equal, yielding

$$\begin{aligned} \overline{H_1}^t (K^{-t}K^{-1})\overline{H_1} &= \overline{H_2}^t (K^{-t}K^{-1})\overline{H_2} \\ \overline{H_1}^t (K^{-t}K^{-1})\overline{H_1} - \overline{H_2}^t (K^{-t}K^{-1})\overline{H_2} &= 0 \end{aligned} \tag{8.19}$$

Note that the factor $K = K^{-t}K^{-1}$ appears multiple times in (8.18) and (8.19), and this is an unknown that made it difficult to find R_1 and R_2 in (8.17).

Fortunately, one can show that this factor is a symmetric and positive definite matrix, hence can be represented with only six unknowns:

$$K = K^{-t}K^{-1} = \begin{pmatrix} k_1 & k_2 & k_3 \\ k_2 & k_4 & k_5 \\ k_3 & k_5 & k_6 \end{pmatrix} \tag{8.20}$$

Reordering (8.18) and (8.19) now allows us to solve for the unknown k_i of (8.20). We can even find the K matrix itself, instead of the product $K = K^{-t}K^{-1}$ by using the Cholesky factorization, applicable to such symmetric, positive definite matrices. The vectors R_1 and R_2 are then found through (8.17). The reader is further referred to [23] for all mathematical details and robust, generic solutions, going beyond the general principles exposed above.

We can now summarize the full pose estimation process given in Figure 8.7. The perspective deformations of the reference rectangle (marker) seen through the camera allow to find the rotation R and translation t required to go from this marker to the camera view. With calculations performed in real-time, it is hence possible to know exactly the position of the camera anytime, compared to the marker (here the book) on the table. Using a tablet with a camera, pointing to the scene, the camera view can be displayed on the screen, and at the same time, the virtual object we want to place in the scene (here the cat) is rotated and translated accordingly, before 3D rendering on the screen. In this way, the cat comes exactly to the right place in the image, seamlessly integrated into the scene to support augmented reality applications. These basic principles are implemented in augmented reality software tools, like OpenVG [41] and Vuforia [42], with additional temporal filtering to obtain larger robustness in the pose estimation.

Note that the markers can be as simple as the checkerboard patterns of Figure 8.1. These are often used in multi-camera applications where the camera poses are required, for example in fusing images from various cameras into one another for a specific use, like synthesizing any virtual viewpoint to the scene without prior 3D scanning of the scene. More on this topic in Chapter 12.

Finally, the marker can also be any flat picture out of which enough feature points are extracted and tracked to enable the calculations presented above.

References

[1] Camera Calibration Toolbox for MATLAB®. http://vision.caltech.edu/bouguetj/calib_doc/.

[2] R. Tsai. 'A versatile camera calibration technique for high-accuracy 3D machine vision metrology using off-the-shelf TV cameras and lenses'. *IEEE Journal on Robotics and Automation*. 1987; 3(4): 323–344. doi:10.1109/JRA.1987.1087109.

[3] Z. Zhang. 'Flexible camera calibration by viewing a plane from unknown orientations'. *Proceedings of the Seventh IEEE International Conference on Computer Vision*. 1999, vol. 1, pp. 666–673. doi: 10.1109/ICCV.1999.791289.

[4]   Z. Zhang. 'A flexible new technique for camera calibration'. *IEEE Transactions on Pattern Analysis and Machine Intelligence*. 2000; 22(11): 1330–1334. doi:10.1109/34.888718.

[5]   W. Burger. 'Zhang's Camera Calibration Algorithm: In-Depth Tutorial and Implementation'. Technical Report HGB16-05, May 2016.

[6]   Camera Calibration and 3D Reconstruction. https://docs.opencv.org/master/d9/d0c/group__calib3d.html.

[7]   A. Schmidt, A. Kasiński, M. Kraft, M. Fularz, and Z. Domagała. 'Calibration of the multi-camera registration system for visual navigation benchmarking'. *International Journal of Advanced Robotic Systems*. 2014; 11(6). https://doi.org/10.5772/58471.

[8]   J. Rehder, J. Nikolic, T. Schneider, T. Hinzmann and R. Siegwart. 'Extending kalibr: Calibrating the extrinsics of multiple IMUs and of individual axes'. *2016 IEEE International Conference on Robotics and Automation (ICRA)*. 2016, pp. 4304–4311. doi: 10.1109/ICRA.2016.7487628.

[9]   T. Ewbank. Efficient and precise stereoscopic vision for humanoid robots. Master's thesis. University of Liège, 2016–2017.

[10] _Kalibr toolbox. https://github.com/ethz-asl/kalibr

[11] T. Svoboda, D. Martinec and T. Pajdla. 'A convenient multicamera self-calibration for virtual environments'. *Presence*. 2005; 14(4): 407–422. doi: 10.1162/105474605774785325.

[12] Solving your calibration problems. https://vrtracker.xyz/solving-calibration-problems/.

[13] O. V. Thanh, T. Canham, J. Vazquez-Corral, R. G. Rodríguez and M. Bertalmío. 'Color stabilization for multi-camera light-field imaging'. *ICASSP 2020–2020 IEEE International Conference on Acoustics, Speech and Signal Processing (ICASSP)*. 2020, pp. 2148–2152, doi: 10.1109/ICASSP40776.2020.9053088.

[14] J. Stankowski, K. Klimaszewski, O. Stankiewicz, K. Wegner, and M. Domański. 'Preprocessing methods used for Poznan 3D/FTV test sequences'. ISO/IEC JTC1/SC29/WG11 MPEG 2010/M17174, m17174, Kyoto, Japan, January 2010.

[15] S. Gurbuz, M. Kawakita and H. Ando. 'Color calibration for multi-camera imaging systems'. *2010 4th International Universal Communication Symposium*. 2010, pp. 201–206. doi: 10.1109/IUCS.2010.5666228.

[16] Color Correction Matrix (CCM). https://imatest.com/docs/colormatrix/.

[17] T. Senoh, N. Tetsutani, and H. Yasuda. Proposal of trimming and color matching of multi-view sequences. ISO/IEC JTC1/SC29/WG11 MPEG2018/M47170, Geneva, Switzerland. March 2019.

[18] https://reference.wolfram.com/language/ref/ImagePerspectiveTransformation.html

[19] D. Barath and L. Hajder. 'Novel Ways to Estimate Homography from Local Affine Transformations'. In *Proceedings of the 11th Joint Conference on Computer Vision, Imaging and Computer Graphics Theory and Applications - Volume 3: VISAPP, (VISIGRAPP* 2016), pp. 432–443.

[20] D. Kriegman. Homography estimation. *Computer Vision I CSE 252A*. Winter 2007.

[21] E. Dubrofsky. Homography estimation. Master's thesis. The University of British Columbia, 2007.

[22] D. DeTone, T. Malisiewicz, and A. Rabinovich. Deep image homography estimation. 2016. arXiv:1606.03798 [cs.CV].

[23] D. DeTone, T. Malisiewicz, and A. Rabinovich. Deeper understanding of the homography decomposition for vision-based control. arXiv:1606.03798.

[24] M. Wadenbäck. Homography-based positioning and planar motion recovery. Lund University. 2017.

[25] Basic concepts of the homography explained with code. https://docs.opencv.org/master/d9/dab/tutorial_homography.html.

[26] A. Agarwal, C. Jawahar and P. Narayanan 'A survey of planar homography estimation techniques'. Centre for Visual Information Technology International Institute of Information Technology, Hyderabad, India. 2008.

[27] E. Dubrofsky. Homography estimation. Master's thesis. The University of British Columbia, 2009.

[28] L. McMillan, Jr. 'An image-based approach to three-dimensional computer graphics'. PhD thesis. University of North Carolina, 1997.

[29] S. A. K. Tareen and Z. Saleem. 'A comparative analysis of SIFT, SURF, KAZE, AKAZE, ORB, and BRISK'. *2018 International Conference on Computing, Mathematics and Engineering Technologies (iCoMET)*. 2018, pp. 1–10. doi: 10.1109/ICOMET.2018.8346440.

[30] D. G. Lowe. Distinctive Image Features from Scale-Invariant Keypoints. *International Journal of Computer Vision* 60, 91–110 (2004). https://doi.org/10.1023/B:VISI.0000029664.99615.94.

[31] M. A. Fischler and R. C. Bolles. Random sample consensus: a paradigm for model fitting with applications to image analysis and automated cartography. *Commun. ACM*. 1981; 24(6): 381–395. doi: https://doi.org/10.1145/358669.358692.

[32] R. Szeliski. 'Image alignment and stitching: A tutorial'. *Foundations and Trends® in Computer Graphics and Vision*. 2007; 2(1): 1–104. http://dx.doi.org/10.1561/0600000009.

[33] R. Szeliski and H.-Y. Shum. 'Creating full view panoramic image mosaics and environment maps'. In *Proceedings of the 24th Annual Conference on Computer Graphics and Interactive Techniques (SIGGRAPH '97)*. ACM Press/Addison-Wesley Publishing Co., USA, pp. 251–258.

[34] J. E. Solem. Programming computer vision with Python, 2012.

[35] https://en.wikipedia.org/wiki/Shanghai_Tower#/media/File:Shanghai_Tower_2015.jpg

[36] https://commons.wikimedia.org/wiki/File:African_Sunset,_North_West_Province_(6253199070).jpg

[37] H. Kato and M. Billinghurst. 'Marker tracking and HMD calibration for a video-based augmented reality conferencing system'. *Proceedings 2nd IEEE and ACM International Workshop on Augmented Reality (IWAR'99)*, 1999, pp. 85-94, doi: 10.1109/IWAR.1999.803809.

[38] H. Kato, M. Billinghurst, I. Poupyrev, K. Imamoto and K. Tachibana. 'Virtual object manipulation on a table-top AR environment'. *Proceedings*

IEEE and ACM International Symposium on Augmented Reality (ISAR 2000), 2000, pp. 111–119. doi: 10.1109/ISAR.2000.880934.

[39] P. Joshi. *OpenCV with Python by example: Build real-world computer vision applications and develop cool demos using OpenCV for Python.* 'Chapter 11: Stereo vision and 3D reconstruction'. Packt Publishing; 2015.

[40] B. Frank, C. Stachniss,G. Grisetti, K. Arras, and W. Burgard, Robotics 2 Camera Calibration, University of Freiburg.

[41] L. Kneip and P. Furgale. 'OpenGV: A unified and generalized approach to real-time calibrated geometric vision'. *2014 IEEE International Conference on Robotics and Automation (ICRA)*, 2014, pp. 1–8. doi: 10.1109/ICRA.2014. 6906582.

[42] https://library.vuforia.com/.

Chapter 9

3DoF VR with natural content

In previous chapter, we have made the first step towards 3DoF VR with natural images, introducing the concept of panoramic stitching from the image processing point of view. In the present chapter we will rather focus on what this implies from the camera positioning point of view.

9.1 Stereoscopic viewing

Having a 3D model of the scene and an OpenGL rendering pipeline, it is relatively simple to render the scene stereoscopically by rendering the scene twice, one rendering for the left eye and one for the right eye, taking each eye's position into account. The interested reader is referred to [1,2] for a tutorial on how to program stereoscopic viewing in OpenGL. Here, we give only the recommended high-level settings.

Stereoscopic viewing will take partially overlapping viewports of the projection plane to obtain the left and right eye images that are rendered through red and blue colour filters, resulting in a so-called anaglyph rendering (old-fashioned, yet still effective). The virtual cameras that correspond to the left and right eyes have here parallel optical axes, suggesting the eyes are focusing on infinity. This setting is fine in a cinema theatre, where the audience is sitting far away from the projection screen, but for a VR headset, it is better to create a slight vergence between the eyes, so that their optical axes cross on the display (the projection plane), where the eyes will focus on. This creates a picture like in Figure 9.1 where the eyes will focus on the middle front cactus (no anaglyph shift). All objects behind this point have an anaglyph shift that is opposite (i.e. blue and red colours are inverted) to one of the foreground objects.

Observe, especially at the right wall of Figure 9.2, just below the ceiling that this anaglyph picture is somewhat weird: the circular windows in the left and right image are vertically shifted. This is also very well visible at the top of the background wall, and for the guideposts in front of the picture. Though this image can very well be visualized with anaglyph glasses by well-positioning the picture in front of the viewer's eyes in a relatively severe cross-eyed viewing mode, it will nevertheless cause a lot of headaches to someone viewing it at a large distance on a large screen in a cinema theatre. Indeed, the spectators sitting far away from the projection screen, their eyes are focusing far away with parallel optical axes, therefore any feature in the picture (an object, a corner, a pattern, etc.) should be at the same height in both eyes, similar to Figure 9.3, as exemplified by the yellow

Figure 9.1   Anaglyph rendering with a focus point around the middle cactus. Reproduced from Public Domain [3]

Figure 9.2   Anaglyph rendering of the Ambras castle. Reproduced under a Creative Commons license from [4]

horizontal lines. Do not be fooled by the apparently different number of windows in the left and right images: there is always a difference between the left and right images, including that some features are visible in one image and not in the other, mostly at the image borders.

Figure 9.3   Rectified left and right eye rendering, corresponding to the stereoscopic image pair in a cinema theatre (parallel viewing axes). Reproduced under a Creative Commons license from [4]

The transformation of Figure 9.2 into Figure 9.3 is called 'rectification', suggesting that something has been rectified or corrected in the image: it is a 'perspective correction' that counteracts the cross-eyed viewing by taking care in having the two eyes looking perfectly straight with parallel optical axes, seeing the objects in both eyes at the same horizontal line. This rectification process is achieved by applying the homography that we have seen in Section 8.2. More details on the rectification process will be given in Chapter 12. At this point of our discussion, let us just keep in mind that rectification is an unavoidable step in good stereoscopic viewing (including anaglyph [5–7]), as well as for any stereoscopic post-processing, like stereo matching that will be explained in Chapter 12.

Finally, stereoscopic rendering is also used in 3D movies where the scene is captured in 2D with two cameras. The rectified left and right images, for example, of Figure 9.3, are then projected on the screen with different polarization (left and right circular) or with slightly different colours [8]. The latter might look like anaglyph, but in fact what happens is that the two images are fully coloured with red, green and blue lasers that have a slightly different colour between left and right for the same colour channel. For instance, the red colour R1 for the left eye is slightly different from the red colour R2 for the right eye, and that slight difference is imperceptible for the human, but sufficiently large to be filtered by two different colour filters (narrow band filters with thin film technology), one for each eye. Likewise, the green and blue colour channels for left and right eye can also be well filtered and sorted out, so that the eye captures the correct fully coloured image for proper stereoscopic visualization.

9.2   360 panoramas

9.2.1   360 panoramas with planar reprojections

VR typically uses stereoscopic viewing but goes one step further by at least being able to view the scene all around us, which is referred to as 360° viewing, as shown in Figure 9.4 of the same Ambras castle of Figure 9.2 and Figure 9.3.

Figure 9.4   360° viewing of the Ambras castle. Courtesy: Andrew Bodrov [9]

Before digging into the details on how to create such 360 panoramas, let us first look at a few pitfalls which should not be overlooked.

Firstly, each eye should have a similar yet different 360 panorama; it is not sufficient to take two overlapping viewports of the same picture to have correct stereoscopic viewing (unless all objects are far away, which is not the case for the foreground parts of the left and right wall in Figure 9.4).

Secondly, 360 viewing implies that the person viewing the scene does not move forward/backward or left/right: he/she must remain in a central point and only allow the three head rotations (roll, pitch and yaw), corresponding to three degrees of freedom (3DoF). We will see in Chapter 12 how this constraint can be overcome to reach six degrees of freedom (6DoF) with three additional translations (frontal, lateral and vertical), allowing full free navigation. For now, just remember that this will only be possible by adding depth information to 'magically' recreate the parallax in any viewing position and viewing direction.

Thirdly, continuing the previous line of thoughts, creating 360 panoramas involves much more processing than one would expect. Indeed, a 360 panorama can be created with a cubemap having six images taken in perpendicular directions. In practice, however, pictures are not taken in perpendicular directions, and then – inevitably – one must project the images onto a sphere before a reprojection onto a cube like a skybox can take place. The spherical image might also be captured directly through a ball lens, but this causes severe distortions that must be carefully compensated (aside from the relatively small image resolution of such single shot 360° panorama). Let us therefore have a closer look at how such 360 panoramas can be captured with conventional pinhole cameras. Free software can be found all over the Internet.

Figure 9.5 shows the example of Microsoft IDE with pictures taken from the central roadway on our university campus. The principles of panoramic stitching have already been explained in Chapter 8; we here rather focus on the origins of the trapezoidal shape of each viewport.

Note, before we start the discussion, that the pictures have been taken one after the other, so that some pedestrians have moved from one image to the next,

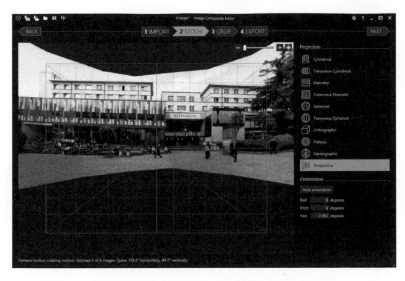

Figure 9.5   Panoramic stitching (on a cylinder) with Microsoft IDE

dislocating them when performing the stitching. This problem can be overcome by first filtering the pictures to remove moving objects, as explained in [10].

The example of Figure 9.5 clearly shows that the best way to have the largest possible resolution (number of pixels) in the 360 image with a conventional pinhole camera is to capture multiple views of the scene from different viewing directions and somehow stitch these images together in a projection plane, as shown in Figure 9.6(a) and (b). Before stitching, the image captured in the image plane of the pinhole camera is projected onto another plane that is not necessarily parallel with it. For instance, in the configuration of Figure 9.6(b), the left-most camera (cam1) has an optical axis that is not orthogonal to the projection plane. The reprojection of the image plane to the projection plane will inevitably stretch the image. In fact, an easy way to see that is just to let the projection plane intersect the view frustum and that intersection shape will be a scaled version of the real reprojection operation.

The cross-section of the projection plane with the view frustum of all cameras corresponds to the size and shape of the stitched image. In the example of Figure 9.6(a), the rectangular view frustum of cameras 2 and 3 create in the stitched image a rectangular and trapezoidal domain, here delimited by the white border in the figure. Clearly, the rectangular view frustum of camera 3 has been transformed into a trapezium in the planar projection process. This corresponds to a homography that we already encountered in Section 8.2. A front view of the stitched area shape over the three cameras is shown in Figure 9.6(b), explaining the image border shape of Figure 9.5.

When stitching the pictures of a long facade of a building, it is probably wiser to use the camera configuration of Figure 9.6(c), perfectly aligned in height and with perfect parallel optical axes looking straight to the building. Here clearly, the reprojection of the pictures from the image plane of each camera's view frustum to

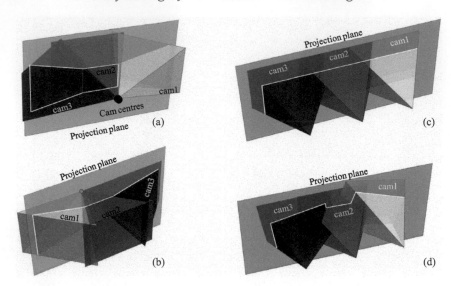

*Figure 9.6   Planar projections with rotated cameras (a,b) in rear (a) and front
view (b), parallel cameras (c) and almost parallel cameras (d)*

the projection plane creates a perfectly rectangular image, represented by the white
border in the figure. This image can be used without any cropping to make a poster
or even as wallpaper. Unfortunately, in practice, one would take his/her favourite
photography devices, and take three pictures side by side, each one a couple of
meters apart, which is inevitably sloppy and ends up in the whimsical shape configuration of Figure 9.6(d). Indeed, one can never have sufficient control over the
successive camera positions to ensure that they are perfectly aligned to reach
Figure 9.6(c). Nevertheless, so-called registration and rectification software tools
can correct the situation of Figure 9.6(d), or at least take care that the stitching
between the three images provides satisfactory results.

The principle of these tools is to recover the camera position (extrinsics) and
all intrinsic camera parameters so that the reprojection on the projection plane of
Figure 9.6 can be done correctly. Figure 9.7 shows an example with two pictures
taken from the same scene from a similar viewpoint, but at two totally different time
instances; one in winter and one in summer, represented by the images 1 and 2,
respectively, in Figure 9.7(a) and(b). The idea is to see a time-lapse of the construction from one specific viewpoint, though we cannot guarantee that the camera
positions perfectly coincide. We therefore estimate their positions as being the
camera centres C_1 and C_2 in Figure 9.7(c), and then reproject the image from
camera 1 onto the image plane P of camera 2, yielding the slightly trapezoidal
shape of image 1 in Figure 9.7(c,d). To clearly show the time-lapse effect, the two
images are blended, superimposing the information of both images.

A closer look to Figure 9.7(d) reveals at the left and bottom borders of image 1
that the lighting conditions in taking these two pictures were different (winter vs.
summertime). Therefore, colour correction between the two pictures is required.

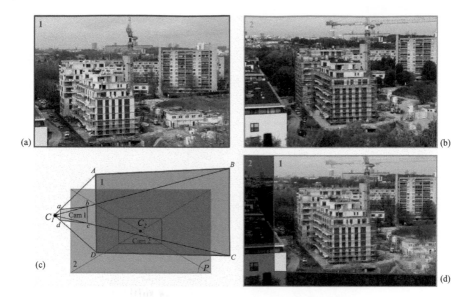

*Figure 9.7   Stitching two images (a,b) to create a planar panorama (d) taking the
estimated camera poses(c) into account*

Various solutions exist [11,12], but the simplest yet effective way is to adapt the
colours such that the colour histogram of one picture matches as closely as possible the
other picture's histogram. For instance, the front white building at the left side of the
image of Figure 9.7(d) is sharp white in image 1 and slightly gray in image 2, which
after cross-histogram equalization would bring us back to the same white colour over
the full building's facade. The same applies for all other colours. Of course, one must
be cautious; in this example, the green leaves of the trees are present in image 2 during
summertime, but not in image 1 corresponding to wintertime, creating an unbalance in
the green colour component of their respective histograms. Colour equalization is a
research topic on its own, going far beyond the current textbook.

9.2.2   Cylindrical and spherical 360 panoramas

With the planar reprojections we have just seen, the panoramic image gets extremely
stretched at the left and right extremes, therefore it is highly recommended to rather
project the images onto a cylinder or sphere, as shown in Figure 9.8. The reprojections
are now intersections of the camera's view frustum with the cylinder or sphere.

In the cylindrical reprojection of Figure 9.8(a), any vertical line in the image
will remain vertical on the cylinder. However, horizontal lines, for instance, the
horizontal borders of the image, will be projected onto a curve bending up or
down for the top and bottom portions of the image. The white curved line in cam2
of the figure shows this effect for a horizontal line at the bottom of the image.
The more the bottom plane of the camera's view frustum is moving downward
(e.g. with smaller camera focal lengths), the larger the horizontal lines will bend
to their corresponding curves on the cylinder. This may cause severe image

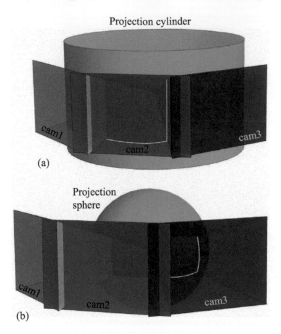

Figure 9.8   Reprojection of the pinhole camera images onto a cylinder (a) and sphere (b)

distortions, but at least, adjacent pinhole cameras – whatever their direction – will perfectly fit/overlap their cylindrical projections in creating one smooth panoramic image (after blending and possible colour correction). Figure 9.9 clearly shows this cylindrical bending phenomenon in the stitched images. The corresponding site [13] gives an overview of various reprojection approaches, accompanied by some examples and an interactive formula sheet giving an indication of what happens when changing camera parameters.

This cylindrical projection approach has been followed in creating lunar panoramas from the Apollo missions, as exemplified in Figure 9.10, with a zoom-in of its right portion given in Figure 9.11. As an anecdote, there exist conspiracy theories that no one has ever landed on the moon, suggesting that these pictures were taken in a studio on earth. One argument that supporters of this theory see as a proof is that something is wrong with the shadows in Figure 9.11: they converge, while the sun may be regarded as being infinitely far, hence its light rays – and hence the shadows – must be parallel. Figure 9.11 shows that the non-parallelism of the shadows is just a perspective effect, fully explainable with the perspective projection matrices, already encountered in Chapter 4.

At first sight there might even be something else that looks weird in the picture of Figure 9.11: the sun is shining towards the photographer (the astronaut) and his shadow goes towards the sun, not away from the sun. Of course, this is perfectly normal, since the right side of Figure 9.10 is what one sees at the other side (than the sun) of the cylindrical 360 panorama, where the sun shines in the back of the astronaut.

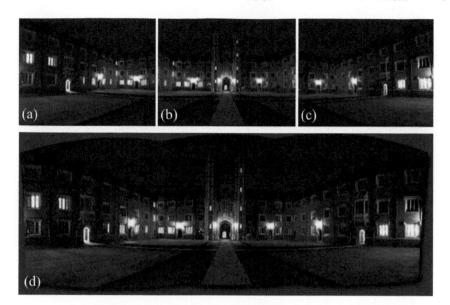

Figure 9.9   *Cylindrical reprojection and stitching of pinhole camera views (a, b, c) to a cylinder (d), clearly showing distorted horizontal lines. Courtesy: Cambridge in Colour [14]*

Figure 9.10   *Lunar cylindrical 360 panorama. Reproduced from NASA public domain [15]*

Figure 9.11   *Zoom-in on the right viewport of Figure 9.10. Reproduced from NASA public domain [15]*

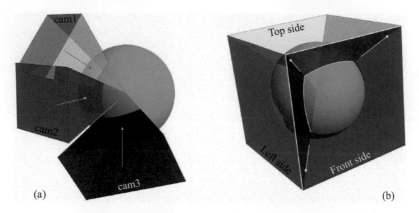

*Figure 9.12   (a) Projection of pinhole camera views onto a sphere, and
(b) reprojection from the sphere towards an ideal cube*

Note that the upper and bottom faces of the cylinder remain unfilled, but as long as the viewer does not rotate his/her head too much up or down, this does not cause any problem in the VR experience.

If viewing the scene in VR upward and downward is required, then one must consider a spherical projection. As before, one will first capture 2D images all around a central point, as shown in Figure 9.12(a), stitch these images together onto a surrounding sphere, and then finally project the result back onto a simple, ideal structure, for example the cubical skybox or cubemap of Figure 9.12(b), which can easily be handled in OpenGL. Such a process creates the cubemap of Figure 9.4.

Any distortion like the curved white line on the sphere in Figure 9.12(b) will get undistorted and become a straight line back on the cubemap, if and only if the viewing is done from the centre of the cubemap (this is assumed since we are in a 3DoF viewing scenario). Therefore, except for the perspective projection effects (e.g. parallel lines in space converge in the 2D image), a cubemap does not present any distortion in 3DoF viewing. An extension to stereoscopic viewing with ana-glyph is straightforward by having virtually two cubemaps, one for each eye [16].

9.2.3   360 panoramas with equirectangular projection images

In Figure 9.12, we have seen how an image on a sphere can be reprojected to the six sides of a cube. There exists another representation that is often used: the equir-ectangular projection images that are the unfolded version of a spherical map (represented by the earth map in Figure 9.14) towards a rectangular image.

The easiest way to explain such image formation is to start with the acquisition process using an omnidirectional capturing device like the Ricoh theta of Figure 9.13: two wide-angle lenses capture each 180° of the surrounding scenes, through a clever optical setup made of prisms. As such, we do not have the irre-gularly spaced camera setup of Figure 9.12(a) anymore, nor the six sides of the cube in Figure 9.12(b); we can now restrict the device to two capturing sides, represented by the front and rear side pinhole camera of Figure 9.14(a). Be aware that the wide-angle lenses have peculiar distortions that ask for some precautions

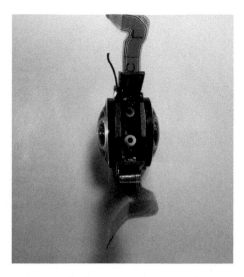

Figure 9.13   Ricoh theta omnidirectional optical sensor

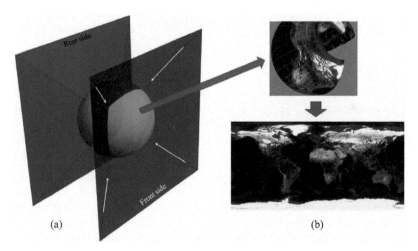

(a)   (b)

Figure 9.14   Reprojection of a dual wide angle lens image (a) onto an earth map image (b)

when stitching the two images into one panoramic view [17], but for now we make an abstraction of these issues; more will be explained in Chapter 10.

If we would look at the image on the sphere of Figure 9.14(a), we would see an image that faithfully represents reality as the earth sphere at the top of Figure 9.14(b). It makes, however, more sense to represent the spherical surface in a rectangular image, that is the equirectangular projection (ERP) image. This image is created by doing the exact opposite of the capturing action of Figure 9.14(a): we project the image of the sphere through the pinhole camera view frustum (the pyramid corresponding to the front side) back onto a plane. Figure 9.15 shows for three different heights on the sphere what exactly happens. Each height – that is a latitude on the sphere – is

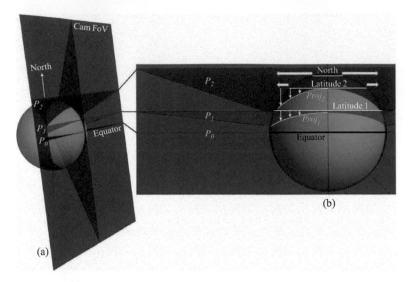

Figure 9.15   Origin of the distortions caused by 2D projections (a) in an equirectangular image (b)

associated with a plane P_i that indicates how a point on the sphere is projected on the front plane of the pinhole camera. To simplify our discussion, we will follow the other direction, that is starting from a point on the front plane, how is it projected to the sphere. Clearly, any point on the horizontal border of plane P_0 is projected onto the sphere along its equator. A horizontal line, here, does not get distorted. However, if we take the horizontal border of plane P_1 that is projected towards the centre of the sphere, we clearly see in Figure 9.15(b) that the midpoint will be projected on the corresponding latitude (Latitude 1, which is actually an orthographic projection of the plane border), but that all other points of that horizontal line will be projected downward (in the northern hemisphere) to a curved line, that is the intersection line $Proj_i$ of plane P_1 with the sphere. This means that this line stays below the latitude of its midpoint. In essence, any horizontal line in 3D space will be projected onto a curved line in Figure 9.15(b). Moreover, the higher the plane P_i in the northern hemisphere, the more the corresponding curved line $Proj_i$ bends more severely downward, compared to its corresponding latitude.

Finally, also be aware that the latitude circles on the sphere are smaller when moving upward to the north pole; hence when creating the ERP image, those circles will have to be stretched even more horizontally, as represented by the horizontal arrows in Figure 9.15(b).

All these observations put together, we now better understand why ERP images have these peculiar distortions as exemplified in Figure 9.16, where the front side of Figure 9.14(a) and Figure 9.15(a) correspond to the sharp left side of Figure 9.16 (the middle and border regions correspond to the empty spaces in Figure 9.14(a), while the bordered region in the right side of Figure 9.16 corresponds to the rear side of Figure 9.14(a)). At half-height, we are at the equator where no distortion occurs, while at roughly one-fourth height we have two clear features that are horizontal lines in space, but that gets completely bent in the ERP image: the upper part of each window

Figure 9.16 Equirectangular projection with an omnidirectional capture.
Courtesy: InterDigital

follows the $Proj_i$ curve, while the start of the ceiling follows the $Proj_2$ curve. Furthermore, at the top border of the image, we are close to the north (but not yet at the north pole) where features (here a golden template) are stretched horizontally.

We want to emphasize again that this image is not as such represented in the VR goggles: a projection from the ERP image to the sphere is performed, automatically inversing the former projection operation (from sphere to plane) and hence eliminating all these distortions.

As a final remark, many other approaches different from the spherical mapping exist, and the interested reader is referred to [18] for the pros and cons. The websites [13] and [19] give a number of examples and provide a calculator for the number of snapshots to be taken to create a panoramic or 360° image under various photographic conditions and overlaps between the successive snapshots. Some shareware is also provided to ease the stitching process with high levels of control, that is [20].

Finally, [21] gives a nice overview of stitching tools for the Pannini wide-angle projection, named after an 18th Century Roman painter, who made remarkable paintings with spectacular views and relatively little distortions in this way. In the same line of thoughts of avoiding as much distortions as possible, [22] presents an interesting method that adapts the projection to the actual content for preserving as much as possible straight lines and salient objects in the scene. Of course, such projection cannot be captured in a simple mathematical formulation and might hence be of limited benefit in immersive VR with the user wearing goggles. Nevertheless, one might imagine applications of 360 navigation on the rectangular desktop PC screen, for example real estate virtual visits, where the user wants to see as little distortions as possible.

References

[1]   R. C. H. Lo, and W. C. Y. Lo. 'OpenGL data visualization cookbook'. 2015.
[2]   J.-M. Réveillac. 'Créez vos photos en 3D – Matériel, prise de vue, développement: Matériel, prise de vue, développement'. Dunod, 2011.

[3]   See https://commons.wikimedia.org/wiki/File:3D_dusk_on_Desert.jpg.

[4]   https://commons.wikimedia.org/wiki/File:Stereo_agl_Ambras_Castle._Spanish_Hall_-_008.jpg.

[5]   R. Bhardwaj, and K. Jain. 'Development of a system for photogrammetric rectification of tilted images'. *International Journal of Advanced Research Science and Engineering*. 2017; 6(9).

[6]   I. Ideses, and L. Yaroslavsky. 'Three methods that improve the visual quality of colour anaglyphs'. *Journal of Optics A: Pure and Applied Optics*. 2005; 7(12)

[7]   C. Kim. '3D reconstruction and rendering from high resolution light fields'. PhD thesis. ETH Zurich, Switzerland, Diss. ETH No. 22933, 2015.

[8]   H. Jorke, and M. Fritz. 'Stereo projection using interference filters'. *Proceedings of the Stereoscopic Displays and Virtual Reality Systems XIII*. Volume 6055, 60550G. 2006. https://doi.org/10.1117/12.650348.

[9]   www.360pano.eu.

[10] Z. Zhang. Panoramic image reconstruction with the removal of moving foreground, Master's thesis. ULB, 2019–2020.

[11] O. Vu Thanh, T. Canham, J Vazquez-Corral, R. G. Rodríguez, and M. Bertalmío'. 'Color correction: Color stabilization for multi-camera light-field imaging'. *IEEE International Conference on Acoustics, Speech and Signal Processing (ICASSP)*. May 2020. doi: 10.1109/ICASSP40776.2020.9053088.

[12] T. Senoh, N. Tetsutani, and H. Yasuda. 'Color correction: Proposal of trimming and color matching of multi-view sequences'. ISO/IEC JTC1/SC29/WG11 MPEG2018/m47170, March 2019.

[13] See https://cambridgeincolour.com/tutorials/image-projections.htm.

[14] https://www.cambridgeincolour.com/tutorials/image-projections.htm.

[15] Apollo Surface Panoramas, AS12-47-6982 – AS12-47-7006. https://www.lpi.usra.edu/resources/apollopanoramas/pans/?pan=JSC2007e045376&zoom=True.

[16] R. Wiche and D. Kuri. 'Performance evaluation of acceleration structures for cone-tracing traversal'. *Journal of Computer Graphics Techniques*. 2020; 9(1) 1–16.

[17] T. Ho and M. Budagavi. Dual-fisheye lens stitching for 360-degree imaging. arXiv:1708.08988.

[18] Cambridge in Colour, Panoramic Image Projections. https://cambridgeincolour.com/tutorials/image-projections.htm.

[19] See https://panocatcher.com/panoplanner/.

[20] PTAssembler. Panoramic and high resolution image mosaic creation software. www.tawbaware.com/ptasmblr.htm.

[21] See http://tksharpless.net/vedutismo/Pannini/.

[22] R. Carroll, M. Agrawal, and A. Agarwala. Optimizing content-preserving projections for wide-angle images. *ACM Transactions on Graphics*. 2009; 28(3), Article 43, 9 pages. DOI: https://doi.org/10.1145/1531326.1531349.

Chapter 10

VR goggles

In previous chapters, we have surveyed various methods to model or capture 3D content, be it synthetic or 360 panoramas of real/natural scenery. We have also explained how to make stereoscopic images that will be interpreted by the visual cortex as a 3D scene. The final step is the rendering process itself in the VR goggles, where optics play an important role, especially with respect to wide angle lens distortion. For a more complete overview of generations of HMD designs, the interested reader is referred to [1].

10.1   Wide angle lens distortion

Wide angle lens distortion is not only an important aspect when rendering the content in VR goggles, it is also important at the acquisition stage. The descriptions of this chapter are hence applicable both at the acquisition, as well as at the rendering stages in the end-to-end pipeline.

10.1.1   Wide angle lens model

Obviously, it is important to capture images with a wide field of view (FoV) to create a good immersive experience in 360 panoramic VR. In this domain, lenses with 120° FoV is not an exception, but obtaining such large FoV with a pinhole camera would require an extremely small focal length (cf. Eq. (4.12) with the focal length transformed back into mm), which is very difficult to reliably manufacture for a large aperture, capturing sufficient light.

Fisheye lenses are therefore another kind of lenses very often used in VR: they allow 'compacting' a large FoV into a relatively small image, albeit at the cost of image distortions. With two of such lenses at both sides of a device, one can capture 360° images and videos [2,3].

The best way to understand fisheye lenses is to compare them with the pinhole camera model, as shown in Figure 10.1. The pinhole camera corresponds to the double pyramid with the CMOS camera sensor at the bottom, but as we saw in Section 4.2, the upper pyramid is sufficient to understand the visualization process of the pinhole camera: a light ray from a point in space intersects the upper image plane in its 2D projection point $P1$. The corresponding fisheye lens would not have projection point $P1$, but rather projection point $P1'$, which is the orthogonal/

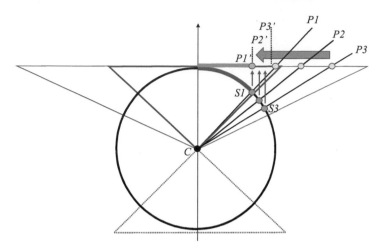

Figure 10.1   Fisheye lens circular reprojection model compared to the pinhole camera model

orthographical projection onto the image plane of point *S1* (*S* stands for sphere), which itself is the intersection of the light ray from point *P1* to the camera centre *C*. This kind of fisheye camera model is therefore also referred to as the 'orthographic fisheye camera', which is actually the camera that moves point *P1* the most inward to Point *P1'*, compared to other types of fisheye lens cameras (because there exist many others, cf. [4]).

Note that for equidistant points *P2*, *P3*, ... *Pn*, the corresponding fisheye lens points *P2'*, *P3'*, ... *Pn'* are getting closer and closer to each other when the intersection points *S2*, *S3*, ... *Sn* move more to the bottom of the first circle quadrant. This is exactly what causes the 'compacting effect' mentioned earlier: scene points at the border of the image get squeezed to each other, while central points undergo hardly any distortion. Since the vertical central axis is an axis of rotational symmetry, the same effect occurs for all points on the same concentric circle in the image plane.

This explains the rather unique artistic effect one obtains in Figure 10.2 when capturing scene from a drone with a fisheye lens camera looking straight downward: the centre of the image remains relatively undistorted, but all the scene surroundings are all compacted together into a narrow ring at the outer part of the image. When the drone moves forward, all the border circles holding textures of objects all around will turn the left part counter-clockwise, the right part clockwise, with a 'singular point' at the top or bottom where everything pops up or vanishes, causing a kind of slipstream moving object effect.

When, however, the camera is oriented with its optical axis pointing horizontally to a subject, the fisheye lens distortion gives high distortion on the ground and in the sky.

Figure 10.2   Fisheye lens camera image. Reproduced under a Creative Commons license from [5]

10.1.2   Radial distortion model

As shown in Figure 10.3(a), VR goggles are made of a display with each half covering the left and right eye, respectively. Lenses in between the user's eyes and the display provide visual comfort with the eyes' accommodation constantly in rest, that is the eyes virtually focusing on objects at infinity. These lenses have another important function, as shown in Figure 10.3(c): they spread out the relatively small FoV spanned by the display with height h to a larger FoV corresponding to the eyes' peripheral viewing zone of approximately 120° (here represented by H). Indeed, each light ray emitted from the display to the lens with incident angle θ will be refracted under incident angle θ' to the eye. Consequently, the light rays originating from the display are bent when traversing the lenses, such that the extension (towards the screen) of the portions of light rays closest to the eyes spans a much larger virtual display of height H, larger than h, ending at point W. This trick gives a real sense of immersion with a relatively small display size, hence also a small form factor of the VR goggles.

The downside of these lenses, however, is that they create a large distortion, known as the pincushion distortion (we will explain its details later). To counteract this effect, a pre-distortion is applied – on purpose – to the image on the display in the opposite way, aka barrel distortion, cf. Figure 10.3(b), so that the final image captured by the eye through the VR goggle lens with its pincushion distortion gets at the end its expected appearance. For instance, lines that should be observed as straight lines to the user in (a) are typically bent on the display panel.

Let us explain how all this works in more details: first by following the example of Figure 10.4, where the object is taken at increasing focal distances from (a) to (d), using two different cameras between (a,d) and (b,c), clearly identifiable

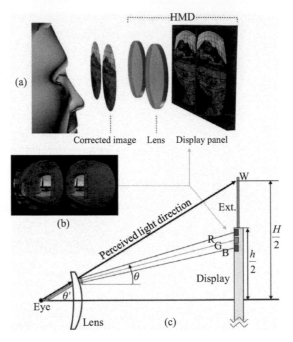

Figure 10.3   *VR goggles lens distortions impose the image to be pre-distorted (a),
obtaining (b). Chromatic lens distortions require the decomposition
of pixel colours (c). Reproduced under a Creative Commons license
from [6]*

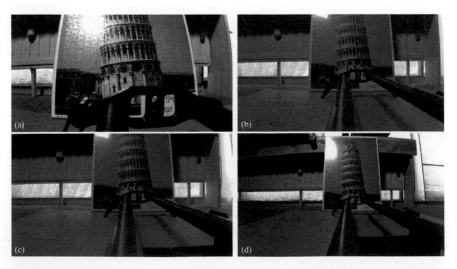

Figure 10.4   *Radial distortion with increasing focal lengths from (a) to (d). Note
that (b) and (c) exhibit much less distortion than (a) and (d)*

by the difference in colour tones. Note that the camera in (b,c) yields images with little radial distortion, while (a) clearly exhibits large radial distortions. Visual inspection of (d) compared to (a) would make one believe when looking at the central Pisa tower poster that (d) has less distortion than (a), but this is an illusion. In fact, we will see later that the distortion increases with the distance from the principal point (in first approximation, the centre of the image) and since the Pisa tower poster spreads over a larger width in (a) than in (d), its distortion looks also more pronounced. Nevertheless, when looking at the wooden tablet above the radiator that extends over almost the full width of the image (d), we clearly observe a large radial distortion too in the image (d).

At each focal length, the radial distortion can be modelled with a simple mathematical relation between the coordinates (x_d, y_d) of the distorted image and the coordinates (x, y) of its undistorted/ideal counterpart:

$$\begin{cases} x = x_d \cdot (1 + k_1 r^2 + k_2 r^4 + \ldots) \\ y = y_d \cdot (1 + k_1 r^2 + k_2 r^4 + \ldots) \end{cases} \tag{10.1}$$

where r represents the radial distance from the centre (rigorously, the principal point), here represented by the origin $(0, 0)$, while k_1 and k_2 are constants that determine the scaling effect for the lens under test. Note that many more powers of r^2 may be added through more constants k_3, k_4, etc.

This simple distortion model tells that the circle's new radius r made of distorted points (x_d, y_d) has been scaled with a factor including even powers of the ideal image's radius of the circle spanning the original pixels (x, y).

In this model, the coordinate system has its origin in the principal point (p_x, p_y), hence some coordinates (x, y) and (x_d, y_d) can be negative, while – by symmetry – the scale factor is not dependent on the sign of each coordinate; this explains why only even powers are retained in (10.1). Shifting the origin of the image to its non-zero principal point, an offset must be included in the former equation, yielding:

$$\begin{cases} x = x_d + (x_d - p_x) \cdot (k_1 r^2 + k_2 r^4 + \ldots) \\ y = y_d + (y_d - p_y) \cdot (k_1 r^2 + k_2 r^4 + \ldots) \end{cases} \tag{10.2}$$

The reader is referred to the seminal papers of Brown, back in the 1960s and even one as old as 1919 [7–9] for other distortions that may appear in lenses, for example the tangential distortions, cf. the addition terms in (10.2) below compared to (10.1), but these distortions are not dominant and can be safely discarded in a first approximation, especially in high-quality lenses that one may find on the market nowadays. We will therefore safely continue with the radial distortion model only.

One little side note is in place here. Recently [10], another radial distortion model has been proposed to approximate radial distortion; it is called the Division Model, which actually switches the coordinates (x, y) and (x_d, y_d) in (10.1), effectively moving the k_1 and k_2 terms to the denominator (hence its name Division Model) as follows:

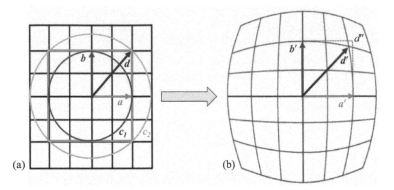

Figure 10.5   (a) Lens distortion modelled with concentric circles, yielding barrel distortion (b)

$$\begin{cases} x = p_x + \dfrac{x_d - p_x}{1 + k_1 r^2 + k_2 r^4 + \cdots} \\ y = p_y + \dfrac{y_d - p_y}{1 + k_1 r^2 + k_2 r^4 + \cdots} \end{cases} \qquad (10.3)$$

Remarkably, with this arrangement, most often the parameter k_2 is totally negligible, which eases the calibration process. That is a good reason to envisage that Division Model, but the reader should well understand that in no way there is a mathematical relation between the radial distortion model of (10.3) and the Division Model: one is not obtained from the other; they are both merely approximations of what happens in reality with the concentric circles around the principal point.

Coming back to our radial distortion model of (10.2), and following the graphical representation of Figure 10.5 with vectorial point positions, circles and squares, we observe that the circles C_1 and C_2 of Figure 10.5(a) represent the ideal, undistorted image (x, y) that will get scaled evenly in all directions. It is then sufficient to follow this scaling process to know what happens with all vectors having an endpoint on these circles, here a and b on circle C_1, and d on circle C_2.

With circle C_1 being scaled, the perpendicular vectors a and b that follow the square grid will end up on a new square grid in Figure 10.5(b). Interestingly, vector d in Figure 10.5(a) is a diagonal vector with its endpoint falling on the square grid, but also on circle C_2. If circle C_2 is scaled with the same scaling factor as for C_1, the transformed vector d' in Figure 10.5(b) will stay on the same square spanned by a' and b', hence would yield point d'. In contrast, if C_2 is less scaled up than C_1, then the transformed vector d' ends inside the square spanned by a' and b'. Consequently, the horizontal and vertical grid lines ending in d' are bent inwards within the square spanned by a' and b', creating the so-called barrel distortion of Figure 10.5(b).

We notice that the sign of k_1 and k_2 in (10.4) will determine whether the scaling factor in the distortion is larger or smaller than one. With positive valued k_1

and k_2, the scaling factor gets larger than 1, and even more than the radius increases. In this case, diagonal vectors like d and d' will get much more enlarged than horizontal and vertical vectors, hence the corners of the square grid are stretched outward, creating a pincushion shape. Likewise, the barrel distortion of Figure 10.5(b) has k_1 and k_2 values that are negative.

Box 10.1:   Intrinsics calibration process

Camera calibration is the process of finding the parameters from the lens distortion model. As it was the case for the extrinsics calibration Box 8.1, a checkerboard is presented in front of the camera and its distortions through the camera lens are captured by the sensor. Many software tools exist in fitting the detected features over the various checkerboard positions, which allows afterwards to estimate the camera parameters. OpenCV has some standard functions [11–15], but other approaches might give better results in some application contexts, for example detecting other features than corners (lines and ellipses) with the Hough Transform [16–19], using singular value decomposition or sparse bundle adjustment [20,21], following the inverse radial distortion model [21–24], high-order polynomial models [25–27], or even models more appropriate for fisheye and ball lenses [28–30].

Note that the magnitude of any radial distortion depends on the focal length of the lens, hence changing the setting of a camera objective will require that k_1 and k_2 are re-calibrated. For instance, consumer cameras have a built-in look-up table for (f, k_1, k_2)-settings (with f the focal length), obtained from factory calibration. One easily understands that such calibration can vary in time, or even on the application settings. For instance, using a camera underwater, within a hermetic box, will cause focal length changes that the user is unaware of, because of the difference in densities between air and water. If the camera parameters are not adapted accordingly, the pincushion distortion will not be taken away [31].

10.1.3   VR goggles pre-distortion

We have just seen how we can get a large field of view with special lenses, and at the same time get rid of their pincushion distortion by pre-distorting on purpose the images to be sent to the VR goggles with barrel distortion. These are the images one can see on a PC display that shows what the person wearing the VR goggles sees, but in fact, this person does not see any barrel distortion anymore, thanks to the subsequent pincushion distortion of the goggle lenses. Nevertheless, the barrel distortion must be calculated, and this is best done in the vertex and/or fragment shaders of the OpenGL pipeline that is anyway present in a system for 3D synthetic content rendering. If the lens grid density of Figure 10.5 is sufficiently high, the non-linear transformation of the radial distortion can be taken care of by the vertex shader.

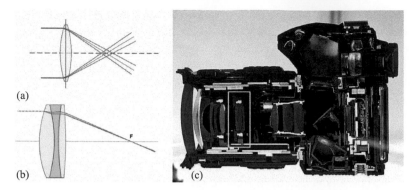

Figure 10.6   Chromatic aberrations in lenses (a) and methods to counteract with doublet or triplet lenses (b) as used in photography (c). Reproduced under a Creative Commons license (a) from [32], (b) from [33] and (c) from [34]

Besides this barrel pre-distortion, there is yet another interesting trick that is used in VR goggles; it is the chromatic aberration compensation, obtained also by some modifications of the image, prior to its rendering in the VR goggles. To make a comparison, in photography for instance, such chromatic aberrations also occur, but they are compensated optically by ingenious combinations of lenses, as shown in Figure 10.6(c).

Let us have a look at Figure 10.6 to better understand the phenomenon. When light passes a lens, it is bent, or what is called scientifically 'refracted', so that it propagates in another direction. This refraction is, however, colour dependent, hence white light that enters the lens will be decomposed into the primary colours, like in a prism. The three primary colours – red, green and blue – of a light ray that enters the lens will hence be refracted slightly differently, not reaching the same focal point, therefore causing chromatic aberration onto the image plane.

To counteract this effect in photography, a second lens in Figure 10.6, which is concave instead of convex, will create the opposite effect of bending/refraction, making it possible to make a second colour (here green) exit the lens doublet in the same way as a first coloured light ray (here red). We have hence reduced the aberration, but still the third colour (here blue) does not exist in the same way as green and red. Therefore, a third lens (convex again) is introduced to refract the blue-coloured light ray such that it follows exactly the same path as the previous green and red-light rays. In summary, in photography, a triplet of lenses is required to compensate for the chromatic aberrations. This is the reason for the high cost of objectives for photography: they are made up of a couple of triplets (most often three for tele-objectives) that must move very pre-cociously when changing the focal length of the objective. All this mechanical system is undoubtedly expensive, but also heavy, hence not the ideal solution for VR.

In VR goggles, however, we do not capture light; we rather send light in the direction we want by design. Looking back to Figure 10.3(c), the coloured pixels of the display in the VR goggles emit light towards the lens, and each colour component (R, G, B) has a slightly different incidence angle θ to the lens. Somehow, we

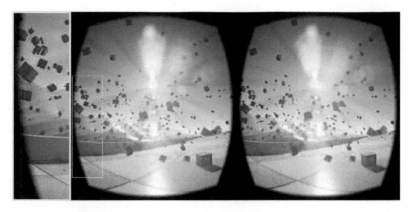

Figure 10.7   Pre-distorting the image chromatically so that the optical system in the VR goggles will recover the image correctly. Reproduced under a Creative Commons license from [35]

might take care that the refraction in the lens brings these three colour components back under the same outgoing angle θ', as shown close to the eye position in Figure 10.3(c). In this way, our eye captures the true light impression, represented by the black 'perceived light direction' in the figure (remember that the lens is there for achieving a large field of view).

For instance, let us suppose for a while that we want the person who wears the VR goggles, and that we want to address the chromatic aberration problem, which is severe at the image borders, and almost non-existent in the centre of the image. We first decompose each full-coloured pixel into its three colour components, then pre-calculate the displacement each colour component will undergo when passing through the lens, and finally apply this displacement in the opposite direction onto the raw image in the VR goggles display. This is exactly what is shown in Figure 10.7: the image is first decomposed into its colour channels, which are slightly distorted to account for the chromatic aberration, and this is then automatically reversed optically in the lens, bringing the three colour components back together for obtaining the wanted colours all over the screen.

Here too, the chromatic aberrations and their required pre-distortions can be handled properly in the vertex and/or fragment shaders of the OpenGL pipeline.

10.2   Asynchronous high frame rate rendering

Since the user's position – and especially his/her head position – can change very rapidly, these sudden changes in viewing direction might cause a delayed, saccadic rendering of the stereoscopic image pair in the VR goggles. This might cause delay cyber sickness because of so-called sensory-conflict movements, where head movements and the HMD visual feedback are not coherent with each other [36,37]. Psychovisual tests even seem to suggest that higher resolution images and higher levels of realism in the rendered images increase the motion cyber sickness [38].

To overcome (or reduce) this problem, the images are calculated at high frame rates, typically 90 or 120 frames per second (fps), which is three to four times more rapid than the image flow in a regular video on TV, limited to 25 or 30 fps. At such high framerates of 120 fps, the GPU must be powerful enough to calculate a stereoscopic pair of images at high resolution (HD = 1,920×1,080 pixels, around 2 Mpixels or UHD = 3,820×2,160 pixels, around 8 Mpixels) every 8.3 ms. Each image has thus to be calculated in around 4 ms. Today, this has become possible with the powerful GPUs available on the market, but a decade ago this was still a challenge.

Let us now imagine that we want to visualize 360° videos that by nature are based on captured content using moving picture cameras. Most cameras capture content typically at 30 fps (33 ms frame period), while for VR, it is recommended to refresh the HMD images at 120 fps (a bit larger than 8 ms frame period), consequently the acquisition and rendering pipelines are not running at the same pace. It is therefore good practice to foresee different threads for their respective processing activities and possibly sync them by a semaphore mechanism with data double buffering.

In the example of Figure 10.8, the camera images are captured every 33 ms and transferred to the GPU for some pre-processing (e.g. radial distortion removal). Some operations might also be done on the CPU already (e.g. colour correction), at the side of the cameras, which one can try to fit in the subsequent 33 ms. At the end of this time period, the texture images are ready for further processing on the GPU in the next 8 ms (if this time period is really occurring 'after' the 33 ms) corresponding to the 120 fps rendering. Since there is no certainty that a 'freely running' (or not perfectly synced) rendering pipeline will start its processing exactly after the 33 ms, it may happen that the start of such 8 ms period occurs somewhere before the end of the 33 ms. Hence, it is recommended to foresee a slack period of 8 ms at the end of the 33 ms, allowing only a 'guaranteed' processing time of 25 ms (the equivalent of 40 fps) at the capturing side, cf. the red text in the centre of Figure 10.8.

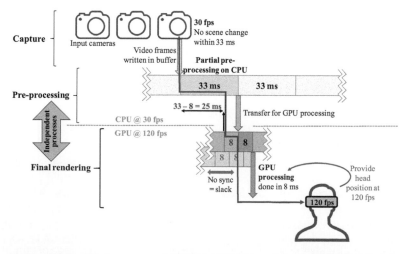

Figure 10.8   Multi-camera captures at 30 fps with rendering at 120 fps

We hence end up in three successive processing actions, as shown in Figure 10.8:

1. Acquisition of images,
2. Pre-processing of these images at the CPU side during the next 25 ms, storing the data in a double buffer, and
3. GPU processing and rendering during 8 ms by capturing the last valid data from the double buffer of (2).

With pre-processing and rendering running independently from each other, the 8 ms time periods have slack and might shift somewhat, resulting in a total processing time ranging from (25 ms + 8 ms = 33 ms) along the red path to (33 ms + 8 ms = 41 ms) along the grey vertical arrows.

10.3   Stereoscopic time warping

Some years ago, user PCs did not necessarily have the required GPU performance for rendering all stereoscopic images in real-time, with up to 120 Hz of refresh rates to accommodate for the possible high acceleration rates (sometimes up to 2g according to [39]). To address the challenge of guaranteeing proper operation on a wide range of PCs, Oculus Rift were the first to propose so-called 'time warping' in case insufficient processing time was available to render both images of a stereoscopic pair [39]. These images might be a viewport to 360° videos as in the previous section, but it might also be an OpenGL rendering of synthetic 3D content; it does not make much difference in how to handle the situation.

To fix our thoughts, let us take the example of a 100 Hz refresh rate in the VR goggles, which means that to render a stereoscopic pair of images, only 10 ms are available. If each image of the stereoscopic pair can be rendered within 5 ms, no problem occurs. However, if the left image takes already 7 ms processing time before its rendering for the user's head position at hand (hence for the corresponding rotation and translation matrices of the left eye's camera view), only 3 ms would be left over for the right image, which is less than half the processing time that was required for the left image. Left and right images being similar, it is hard to believe that the rendering of the right image will be finalized in time. Instead of ending up with only half of the image being processed in time, the headset driver approximates the right image rendering by using the previously rendered right image that is slightly shifted to follow the user's head position; this is the image warp approach (which to be completely correct should rather be a homography, but this may already involve a too high computation cost and is therefore not followed). Of course, this is only an approximation of the rotation and translation matrices related to the right eye, but nevertheless, the rotation matrix corresponding to the right eye's image is partially already taken into account in the left image, hence the approximation is not necessarily crude, as one would expect.

10.4   Advanced HMD rendering

10.4.1   *Optical systems*

Let us also mention that prosumer VR goggles also add some means to obtain high-resolution images for projection on the fovea of the eye, cf. Figure 10.9. Indeed, the

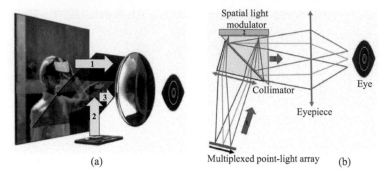

Spatial light
modulator

Collimator

Eye

Eyepiece

Multiplexed point-light array

(a)   (b)

Figure 10.9   (a) Varjo high-resolution fovea rendering and lower resolution
rendering in the periphery and (b) light field rendering in an HMD.
(a) Courtesy: Varjo and (b) Reproduced from [40]

retina of the human eye has a central region that is densely covered with photo-sensitive cells, while the peripheral area has a much lower density of cells. Moreover, the stereoscopic effect of interpreting depth is also mostly covered in the central region of the eye. It is therefore important that – for the same overall budget of pixels over the image – a large part of the pixels is concentrated in the central part of the VR lenses, while the peripheral pixel regions are less populated. Varjo – a VR goggles manufacturer – has recently proposed the use of half-reflective mirrors to achieve this goal, cf. Figure 10.9(a): a high-resolution OLED display is mirrored towards the centre of the eye through path (2,3) in the figure, while a peripheral image is directly projected through the mirror from a lower-resolution display behind through path 1. In this solution, each image serves its purpose dedicated to its specific region of the eye's retina. Of course, an eye-tracking system is required to track the eye and redirect with micro-actuators the high-resolution image straight into the pupil. This is nevertheless more ingenious than foreseeing a single, uniform, high-resolution display for each single eye: with an eye acuity of up to 60 pixels per degree (in the fovea), an FoV of 120° would require – at this pixel density – as much as 7,200 pixels horizontally, thus close to an 8k display for a single eye. This is technologically probably close to be into one's reach today, but remains an overkill, ending up in VR goggles with a large form factor that is not comfortable, and in view of the first VR headsets (e.g. NASA, cf. Figure 2.2) looks a bit like 'being back to the future'.

A better approach to reach high-resolution displays is to time-multiplex the images at a very high rate so that compositions of images can be obtained with clever optical systems. Figure 10.9(b) shows such an approach to create a light field HMD, which can come very handy for the eye accommodation problem addressed in the next section.

The system consists in sending a light bundle from a single point at a time emanating from the point-light array at the bottom of Figure 10.9(b). By refraction through two prisms, the light reaches the spatial light modulator (SLM) at the top of the figure, where it is modulated before reaching the eye after having bounced through the prisms system. The image formation hence follows the (1,2,3) processing path with each time another point source that is illuminated.

Note that for a different light point in the point-light array, a different light output position in front of the eye is obtained, as well as a slightly different incidence angle to the eye. In this way, we obtain both spatial and angular visual information, which is precisely what is called a light field that – if well designed – may confer proper eye accommodation.

10.4.2   Eye accommodation

Historically, since the very beginning of 3D cinema and virtual reality (VR) with stereoscopic HMDs the question rose whether stereoscopic 3D visualization devices would (or not) have a negative impact on the human visual system (HVS), for example Rushton and Riddell's overview study [41] of 20 years ago, as well as more recent publications clearly pinpointing possible irreversible symptoms of cyber-sickness and degraded sight under prolonged stereoscopic use scenarios [42–47]. An even older paper from 1957 [48] already studied the Eye Accommodation and VErgence (EAVE) relations.

Polarized stereoscopic glasses used in 3D cinema allow to perceive the scene's objects floating in the air, far outside the screen, but unfortunately at the same time the spectator's eyes are constantly optically focused and directed to the point of interest on the screen, cf. the blue and red-light rays in Figure 10.10. This creates an EAVE conflict between the brain's virtual perception and the opto-physical realm that the HVS experiences. To mitigate this conflict, cinema theatres gradually moved in the early days from scenes with virtual monsters jumping on one's lap to 3D projections with very limited perceived depth of field, thereby seriously questioning the raison-d'être of 3D cinema. For VR headsets, some recommendations can be made [49], but they do not solve all problems at all.

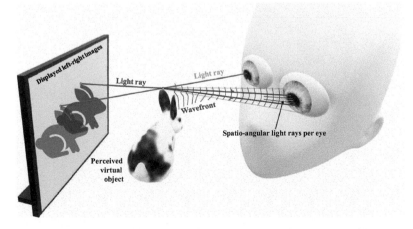

Figure 10.10   Eye accommodation and VErgence (EAVE) requires that each eye captures micro-parallax light field images, mimicking the wavefront that emanates from physical objects

In recent years, however, eye tracking and varifocal lens technology in VR headsets made it possible to artificially mimic natural vision. Eye-tracking in the VR headset detects what the user looks at, determines the depth of that region in the 3D virtual scene (by reading the Z-buffer in the 3D rendering pipeline, cf. Section 3.3 of Chapter 3) and then varies the focal length of the lenses (hence the name 'varifocal') in the headset accordingly. In this way, the user's eye lenses are 'optically forced' to react, taking the 'opposite/inverse contraction/focal length' of the varifocal lens, which artificially gives the user the illusion that his/her eyes react in a natural way, as if physical objects were present in the scene. This technique, however, can hardly differentiate depth differences at object silhouettes (the 'regions with a single focal length' are quite large) and it calls for a closed-loop approach (i.e. detect eyes position and modify the varifocal lens instantaneously) with zero-delay (otherwise the user is already looking to another region of the virtual scene when setting the varifocal lens), which results in a very delicate system [50–52]. Moreover, this can only work in a per-user setting, hence for individual headsets only; not for a large shared 3D display in a cinema theatre.

With the advent of glasses-free 3D light field displays [20,53], a passive multi-user approach was made possible, projecting various images in adjacent directions, so that any spectator – irrespective of his/her position – captures the correct image pair, for a glasses-free stereoscopic experience. Nevertheless, EAVE is still missing since most often only the large parallax aspects which are responsible for the main stereoscopic impression are covered in today's light field display technology, cf. the two main eye directions of Figure 10.10.

To obtain correct EAVE, the density of light rays should be extremely high to recover micro-parallax, that is the slight variations between adjacent light rays hitting the pupil, cf. the right side of Figure 10.10. Indeed, in the real world with

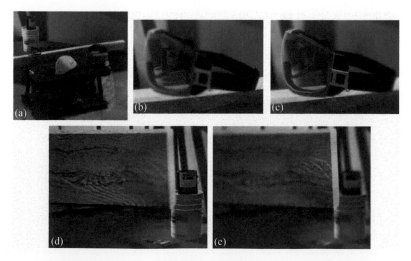

Figure 10.11   Unity scene (a) with eye accommodation on background (b,d) and foreground objects (c,e). Courtesy: Creal

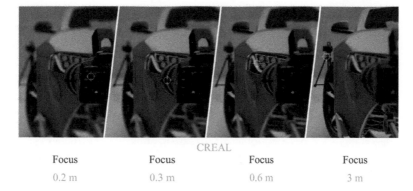

CREAL

Focus	Focus	Focus	Focus
0.2 m	0.3 m	0.6 m	3 m

Figure 10.12   View through a light field VR headset looking to objects at 3 m (left) and 0.3 m (right). Courtesy: Creal

physical objects in space, each eye receives many minimally different views at the same time; this corresponds to the wavefronts in Figure 10.10. Pinlight displays [54] with the working principles of Figure 10.9(b) are currently one of the most promising candidates to achieve this goal for virtual and augmented reality applications. An example is provided in Figure 10.11 where the objective lens of a camera can focus on foreground or background objects of a light field image, without changing any parameters of the light field image and display. In fact, it is the user's eyes that focus on the object of interest by the user's own will. Figure 10.12 shows the visual effect when the user's sight focuses at 3 m distance (left) versus 0.3 m distance (right).

Chapter 12 will present a similar solution for static imagery (to achieve very high light ray densities), which are called holographic stereograms.

References

[1]   O. Cakmakci, and J. Rolland, 'Head-worn displays: A review'. *J. Display Technol.*, vol. 2, pp. 199–216, 2006.

[2]   C. Premachandra and M. Tamaki, 'A hybrid camera system for high-reso-lutionization of target objects in omnidirectional images'. *IEEE Sens. J.*, vol. 21, no. 9, pp. 10752–10760, 2021, doi: 10.1109/JSEN.2021.3059102.

[3]   M. Wohl, *The 360° Video Handbook: A Step-By-step Guide to Creating Video for Virtual Reality (VR)*. Michael Wohl; 2019.

[4]   C. Hughes, P. Denny, E. Jones, and M. Glavin, 'Accuracy of fish-eye lens models'. *Applied Optics*, vol. 49, no. 17, pp. 3338–47, 2010, doi: 10.1364/AO.49.003338.

[5]   M. Meraji, 'Fisheye lenses-HDR Technique-bagh delgosha-Shiraz'. https://commons.wikimedia.org/wiki/File:Fisheye_lenses-HDR_Technique-bagh_delgosha-Shiraz_%D8%A8%D8%A7%D8%BA_%D8%AF%D9%84%DA%AF%D8%B4%D8%A7%DB%8C_%D8%B4%DB%8C%D8%B1%D8%A7%D8%B2.jpg.

[6]   http://blog.qwrt.de/.

[7]   A. E. Conrady, 'Decentred lens systems'. *Mon. Not. R. Astron. Soc.*, vol. 79, no. 5, pp. 384–390, 1919. https://doi.org/10.1093/mnras/79.5.384.

[8]   D. Brown, 'Decentering distortion of lenses'. *Photogramm. Eng.*, vol. 32, no. 3, pp. 444–462, 1966.

[9]   D. Brown, 'Advanced Methods for the Calibration of Metric Cameras'. DBA Systems, Inc.; 1968.

[10]   P. Drap and J. Lefèvre, 'An exact formula for calculating inverse radial lens distortions'. *Sensors*, vol. 16, no. 6, 807, 2016. https://doi.org/10.3390/s16060807.

[11]   Camera calibration with OpenCV. https://docs.opencv.org/2.4/doc/tutorials/calib3d/camera_calibration/camera_calibration.html.

[12]   V. Devecseri1, L. Raj, and R. T. Fekete, 'Comparison of different multiple camera calibration methods'. XV International PhD Workshop, OWD2013, 19–22 October 2013.

[13]   Camera calibration: Explaining camera distortions. https://ori.codes/artificial-intelligence/camera-calibration/camera-distortions/.

[14]   K. Szczęsny, 'Analysis of algorithms for geometric distortion correction of camera lens'. PhD thesis, Akademia Górniczo-Hutnicza, 2015.

[15]   L. Ma, Y. Chen, and K. Moore. 'Camera calibration: A USU implementation'. ArXiv cs.CV/0307072, 2003.

[16]   Lens distortion correction by analysing the shape of patterns in Hough transform space. https://mro.massey.ac.nz/handle/10179/14984.

[17]   G. Xu, A., Zheng, X. Li *et al.* 'A method to calibrate a camera using perpendicularity of 2D lines in the target observations'. *Sci. Rep.*, vol. 6, p. 34951, 2016, doi: 10.1038/srep34951.

[18]   G. Jiang, and L. Quan, 'Detection of concentric circles for camera calibration'. *Tenth IEEE International Conference on Computer Vision (ICCV'05)*, vol. 1, pp. 333–340, 2005, doi: 10.1109/ICCV.2005.73.

[19]   R. Cucchiara, C. Grana, A. Prati, and R. Vezzani, 'A Hough transform-based method for radial lens distortion correction'. *12th International Conference on Image Analysis and Processing, 2003 Proceedings*, 2003, pp. 182–187, doi: 10.1109/ICIAP.2003.1234047.

[20]   V. V. Lehtola, M. Kurkela, and P. Rönnholm, 'Radial distortion from epipolar constraint for rectilinear cameras'. *J. Imaging*, vol. 3, p. 8, 2017, doi: 10.3390/jimaging3010008.

[21]   C. Stamatopoulos, 'Orientation and calibration of long focal length cameras in digital close-range photogrammetry'. PhD thesis, The University of Melbourne, 2011.

[22]   A. Wang, T. Qiu, and L. Shao, 'A simple method of radial distortion correction with centre of distortion estimation'. *J. Math. Imaging Vis.*, vol. 35, pp. 165–172, 2009, doi: 10.1007/s10851-009-0162-1.

[23]   A. S. R. M. Ahouandjinou, E. C. Ezin, C. Motamed, and P. Gouton, 'An approach to correcting image distortion by self calibration stereoscopic scene from multiple views'. *2012 Eighth International Conference on Signal Image Technology and Internet Based Systems*, 2012, pp. 389–394, doi: 10.1109/SITIS.2012.63.

[24]   A. W. Fitzgibbon, 'Simultaneous linear estimation of multiple view geometry and lens distortion'. *Proceedings of the 2001 IEEE Computer Society Conference on Computer Vision and Pattern Recognition. CVPR 2001*, 2001, doi: 10.1109/CVPR.2001.990465.

[25]   R. Tang, Mathematical Methods for Camera Self-Calibration in Photogrammetry and Computer Vision, PhD Thesis, Institute of Photogrammetry, University of Stuttgart, 2013.

[26]   J. Wang, F. Shi, J. Zhang, and Y. Liu, 'A new calibration model of camera lens distortion'. *Pattern Recognition*, vol. 41, no. 2, pp. 607–615, 2008, https://doi.org/10.1016/j.patcog.2007.06.012.

[27]   J. Weng, P. Cohen, and M. Herniou, 'Camera calibration with distortion models and accuracy evaluation'. In *IEEE Transactions on Pattern Analysis and Machine Intelligence*, vol. 14, no. 10, pp. 965–980, 1992, doi: 10.1109/34.159901.

[28]   G. Krishnan, and S. K. Nayar, 'Towards a true spherical camera'. *Proc. SPIE 7240, Human Vision and Electronic Imaging XIV*, 724002, 2009, doi: 10.1117/12.817149.

[29]   D .C. Brown, 'Decentering Distortion of Lenses'. Corpus ID: 117271607, 1966.

[30]   B. Paul 'Converting a fisheye image into a panoramic, spherical or perspective projection'. 2016, paulbourke.net/dome/fish2/.

[31]   F. Menna, E. Nocerino, F. Fassi and F. Remondino, 'Geometric and optic characterization of a hemispherical dome port for underwater photogrammetry', *MDPI Sensors*, vol. 16, no. 1, 2016, doi: 10.3390/s16010048.

[32]   https://commons.wikimedia.org/wiki/File:Chromatic_aberration_lens_diagram.svg.

[33]   https://thereaderwiki.com/en/Digital_camera.

[34]   https://nl.wikipedia.org/wiki/Apochromaat#/media/Bestand:Apochromat3.svg.

[35]   https://commons.wikimedia.org/wiki/File:Sample_screen_capture_of_Oculus_rift_development_kit_2_screen_buffer.jpg.

[36]   K. Raaen and I. Kjellmo, Measuring latency in virtual reality systems. In: Chorianopoulos K., Divitini M., Baalsrud Hauge J., Jaccheri L., Malaka R. (eds) *Entertainment Computing – ICEC 2015. ICEC 2015. Lecture Notes in Computer Science*, vol. 9353, 2015. Springer, Cham, doi: 10.1007/978-3-319-24589-8_40.

[37]   D. Lu, 'Virtual reality sickness during immersion: An investigation of potential obstacles towards general accessibility of VR technology', Dissertation, 2016.

[38]   M. Pouke, A. Tiiro, S. M. LaValle, and T. Ojala, 'Effects of visual realism and moving detail on cybersickness'. *2018 IEEE Conference on Virtual Reality and 3D User Interfaces (VR)*, 2018, pp. 665–666, doi: 10.1109/VR.2018.8446078.

[39]   B. A. Davis, K. Bryla, and P. A. Benton, Foreword by Philip Rosedale, *Oculus Rift in Action*, Manning Publications, August 2015, ISBN 9781617292194, 440 pages.

[40]   Lightfield-forum, http://lightfield-forum.com/2019/01/patent-how-creal3d-light-field-display-works-without-a-microlens-array/.

[41]   S. K. Rushton, and P. M. Riddell, 'Developing visual systems and exposure to virtual reality and stereo displays: some concerns and speculations about the demands on accommodation and vergence'. *Appl. Ergon.*, 1999, doi: 10.1016/S0003-6870(98)00044-1.

[42]   J.-H. Park, 'Recent progress in computer-generated holography for three-dimensional scenes'. *J. Inf. Disp.*, vol. 18, no. 1, pp. 1–12, 2017, doi: 10.1080/15980316.2016.1255672.

[43]   A. Bulanovs, 'Principles of recording image-matrix holographic stereo-gram'. In *Proceedings of the 53rd International Scientific Conference of Daugavpils University*, Daugavpils Universitates Akademiskais apgads, pp. 1–6, 2012.

[44]   Z.-P. Zhuo, H. Bi, X.-P. Yu, J. Jiang, A.-Q. Xu, and Y.-W. Wang, 'Effects of persistent viewing of 3D TV on human visual function'. *Int. Eye Sci.*, vol. 17, no. 4, pp. 610–614, 2014.

[45]   T. Shibata, J. Kim, D. M. Hoffman, and M. S. Banks, 'The zone of comfort: Predicting visual discomfort with stereo displays'. *J. Vis.*, vol. 11, no. 8, 1–29, 2011, doi: 10.1167/11.8.11.

[46]   L. Ryan, 'Vergence-accommodation conflicts and visual performance in stereoscopic 3-D imagery'. *PhD School of Psychology*, Bangor University, 2015.

[47]   C. Vienne, 'Understanding and improving the quality of experience in 3D media perception: Accommodation/vergence conflict in stereopsis'. Corpus ID: 127385839, 2013.

[48]   E. F. Fincham, and J. Walton. 'The reciprocal actions of accommodation and convergence.' *J. Physiol.* vol. 137, no. 3, pp. 488–508, 1957, doi:10.1113/jphysiol.1957.sp005829. PMID: 13463783; PMCID: PMC1363021.

[49]   G. Kramida, 'Resolving the vergence-accommodation conflict in head-mounted displays'. In *IEEE Transactions on Visualization and Computer Graphics*, vol. 22, no. 7, pp. 1912–1931, 2016, doi:10.1109/TVCG.2015.2473855.

[50]   C. Hughes, P. Denny, E. Jones, and M. Glavin, 'Accuracy of fish-eye lens models'. *Appl. Opt.*, vol. 49, pp. 3338–3347, 2010.

[51]   T. El-Ganainy, and M. Hefeeda, Streaming Virtual Reality Content, arXiv:1612.08350.

[52]   H. Houshiar, J. Elseberg, D. Borrmann, and A. Nüchter 'A study of projec-tions for key point based registration of panoramic terrestrial 3D laser scan'. *Geo-spatial Information Science*, vol. 18, no. 1, pp. 11–31, 2015, doi: 10.1080/10095020.2015.1017913.

[53]   P. Bourke, Computer Generated Angular Fisheye Projections, 2001 http://paulbourke.net/dome/fisheye/.

[54]   A. Maimone, D. Lanman, K. Rathinavel, K. Keller, D. Luebke, and H. Fuchs, 'Pinlight displays: Wide field of view augmented reality eyeglasses using defocused point light sources'. *ACM Trans. Graph.*, vol. 33, no. 4, Article 89 (July 2014), 11 pages, 2014, doi: 10.1145/2601097.2601141.

Chapter 11

6DoF navigation

We have seen in Chapter 9 how a 360 panoramic view created by stitching various camera views together provides a 3 degrees of freedom (3DoF) experience, that is one can look in all directions, for example, in watching live concerts on one's TV screen from home. However, the price to pay is that the viewer is always standing exactly in the centre of the panoramic view. This lack of navigation freedom through the scene represents a serious impediment on an immersive VR experience because it gives the user the impression that all his/her surroundings – even static objects – are moving with him/her, whenever there is a translation from the skybox or cubemap centre. The only way to overcome the resulting cyber sickness is to create positional awareness with the content rendered in the VR goggles moving in the opposite direction of the user's translational movements. These 6 degrees of freedom (6DoF) capabilities require that the content be not only described by textures projected onto a surrounding sphere or cube, but that also the object shapes (geometry) and positions are well-captured. This represents a serious challenge for real content.

There are two main solutions to this real content challenge: the point clouds and depth image-based rendering (DIBR), which show many commonalities, yet also different challenges that will be explained step by step in this chapter.

11.1 6DoF with point clouds

A straightforward approach in capturing point clouds is to use active depth sensing devices, like the well-known Kinect and Intel's Realsense devices, but bear in mind that this will provide a relatively sparse set of coloured points in space. Obtaining high-quality point clouds for VR applications involves a lot of processing steps, some of which will be presented in this chapter. We fill only a fly over the various subjects; the interested reader will be redirected to particularly good papers and books along the way for getting more detailed descriptions.

11.2 Active depth sensing

Active depth sensing is a technique that actively (hence its name) sends light towards the scene of interest, and the reflected light will be captured by the device to infer the depth of the scene. As a rule of thumb, such devices give relatively good results, though not of top-quality because of light dispersion phenomena, unless they are of prosumer or professional quality, with the accompanying price of several thousands of euros. Active depth sensing devices also have a relatively low depth map resolution: while today capturing HD colour images (1,920×1,080 pixels) or even UHD (3,840×2,160 pixels) has become mainstream, a captured depth map is often limited to VGA resolution (600×800 pixels) or worse. This inevitable reduces the quality of the point cloud rendering, which is obtained by pushing each colour pixel in the z-direction over a distance given by the depth map.

Let us now briefly explain the main techniques of active depth sensing, which yield such point clouds.

11.3   Time of flight

As the name suggests, time of flight is a technique that calculates the time of flight of a light pulse that is bouncing back from the surface. It is a technique that has already been used in the Apollo moon exploration program from the late 1960s, and an improved version in 2009 called Lola, cf. Box 11.1. has made a precise cartography of the moon surface with high accuracy, while flying a couple of kilometres over the moon's surface. Similar technology is used in cartography on earth also with so-called Lidar which stands for Light Detection and Ranging. Note that since a ridiculously small amount of light is reflected back to the source, a relatively strong laser source and/or large capturing lens is required, cf. Box 11.1.

Box 11.1:   Moon LOLA

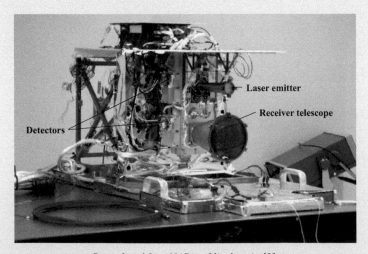

Reproduced from NASA public domain [1]

In 2009, NASA designed a new orbiter, called LOLA which stands for Lunar Orbiter Laser Altimeter (not to be confused with the Apollo simulator Lunar Orbit and Landing Approach from the 1960s), to measure the height map of the moon with time-of-flight technology. It consists of sending a light pulse to the moon's surface and estimating the time it takes to bounce back to LOLA. Since the orbiter is flying 50 km above the moon surface, the travelling time of light over that distance is measurable with an analogue processing module, prior to further digital processing, cf. the functional diagram in [2]. Also, precise optics is needed to capture the tiny amount of light reflected from the moon's surface [3]. The experience that the LOLA team has gathered in its design and measurement performance helped in designing MOLA, the Mars Orbiter Laser Altimeter, that gives valuable data to the Mars Exploration Rover (MER) for augmenting its visual navigation system, cf. Box 11.5.

More importantly, at distances of several km, the time delay between sending and receiving light back is sufficiently large for enabling precise measurements. After all, light is travelling at 300.000 km/s, which over a distance of 3 km represents a round-tip delay of 10 ms, which is measurable with a circuitry having a clock frequency in the order of MHz (1 MHz yields 1 ms sampling rate), which was already available in the 1960s. However, for short distances, let us say 3 m, we would have to sample 1,000 times faster, which is not impossible with today's technology (clock frequencies of GHz), but will be either imprecise or costly. For even shorter distances, like 30 cm, things get 10 times more difficult. Therefore, today's time of flight technology often uses a modulated light source, as explained hereunder.

11.3.1   Phase from a modulated light source

If instead of using a pulsed light source, we now use a continuous light source that is amplitude modulated at let us say a frequency of a couple of kHz up to 1 MHz maximum, the reflected light source will be captured with a phase difference $\Delta\varphi$, as shown in Figure 11.1 [4].

Let us take a cosine modulated signal to explain the process of depth sensing. Suppose that halfway through one period of that periodic signal, there is an object that reflects the signal back towards the source. We may then say that at $\varphi = \pi$, the cosine signal is folded and mirrored to the left in Figure 11.1(a). The signal then arrives at the receiver at $\varphi = 2\pi$, hence in phase with the signal of phase zero that is about to be emitted at that same time instance. The round trip for the total phase traversal of 2π has a length equal to the wavelength λ of the modulated signal.

Let us now move the object under test a bit closer to the source, so that the folding of the signal appears earlier, let us say $\pi/2$ earlier in phase, as shown in Figure 11.1(b). The signal bounced back to the receiver with a phase that is twice the former $\pi/2$, hence reaches the source in anti-phase ($\Delta\varphi = \pi$) compared to the signal it is about to emit. In general, for a phase shift $\Delta\varphi$ at the bouncing front or fold, a total phase shift $\Delta\phi$ twice as large is measured at the receiver and source, as shown in Figure 11.1:

$$\Delta\phi = 2.\Delta\varphi \tag{11.1}$$

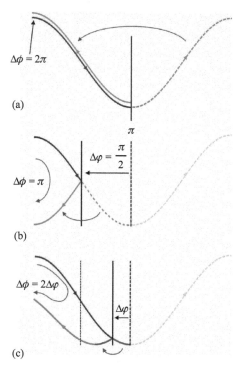

Figure 11.1   Phase shift in time-of-flight due to reflections on objects at various depths (a, b, c)

The fraction of the phase shift $\Delta\phi$ over 2π corresponds to the fraction of the wavelength λ that the total travel distance (back and forth) has been reduced with. An object that is Δx closer to the source than half the wavelength will therefore yield:

$$\Delta x = \frac{\lambda}{2} \cdot \frac{\Delta\phi}{2\pi} = \frac{\lambda}{2} \cdot \frac{\Delta\varphi}{\pi} \tag{11.2}$$

where λ is calculated from the modulation frequency in the order of kHz-MHz; not from the light frequency which is around 400 THz. Consequently, all values in (11.2) are within easily measurable ranges, highly simplifying the implementation of time-of-flight devices.

The distance d between source/receiver and the object under test is half the wavelength, reduced with Δx, which gives

$$d = \frac{\lambda}{2} - \Delta x = \frac{\lambda}{2} \cdot \left(1 - \frac{\Delta\varphi}{\pi}\right) \tag{11.3}$$

Clearly, phase shift $\Delta\varphi$ and distance (depth) d are linearly related. Measuring the phase shift will directly provide the depth of the object.

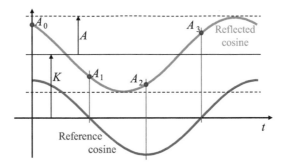

Figure 11.2   Measuring the phase shift by measuring the reflected signal (top) and comparing it with the reference signal (bottom)

This phase shift $\Delta\varphi$ can be measured by sampling the periodic carrier four times a period, each time with an additional phase of $\pi/2$, as shown in Figure 11.2. Since negative values of a cosine function cannot be physically measured, the function is shifted up over a DC component K, larger than its amplitude A, yielding four measured amplitudes A_1, A_2, A_3 and A_4:

$$
\begin{aligned}
A_0 &= K + A \cdot \cos\left(\Delta\varphi\right) \\
A_1 &= K + A \cdot \cos\left(\Delta\varphi + \frac{\pi}{2}\right) \\
A_2 &= K + A \cdot \cos\left(\Delta\varphi + \pi\right) \\
A_3 &= K + A \cdot \cos\left(\Delta\varphi + \frac{3.\pi}{2}\right)
\end{aligned}
\tag{11.4}
$$

Taking the difference between the first and third equation on one hand, and the second and fourth equation on the other hand, allows to eliminate the unknown K value:

$$
\begin{aligned}
A_0 - A_2 &= 2A \cdot \cos\left(\Delta\varphi\right) \\
A_3 - A_1 &= 2A \cdot \sin\left(\Delta\varphi\right)
\end{aligned}
\tag{11.5}
$$

Dividing these two equations finally yields:

$$
\tan(\Delta\varphi) = \frac{A_3 - A_1}{A_0 - A_2}
\tag{11.6}
$$

where the tangent can vary from $-$infinity to $+$infinity, recovering a phase shift $\Delta\varphi$ in the $[-\pi/2, +\pi/2]$ range, hence the measured phase shift $\Delta\phi$ at the source/receiver varies over $[-\pi, +\pi]$ according to (11.1).

In practice, the sampling is done by time-integrating charges (using on/off reading signals) that the back-reflected photons induce in the receiving sensor, without fundamentally changing the equations above. There are, however, some imperfections in the sensor device that might degrade the system's performance. More details can be found in [5,6].

This modulated time-of-flight approach has one drawback, that is that the phase shift varies gradually from $-\pi$ to $+\pi$, therefore it has a cyclic behaviour.

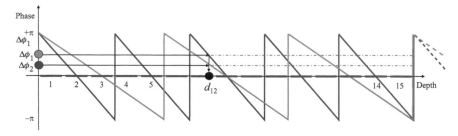

Figure 11.3   The use of multiple carrier frequencies to unambiguously recover depth from different phase shift measurements

Indeed, gradually moving the object away from the light source, the phase difference will gradually decrease, cf. (11.3), and then will suddenly jump back to $+\pi$. There is hence a modulo effect, giving some ambiguity in the distance related to the measured phase difference since many different distances yield the same phase difference.

A way to overcome this limitation is to use multiple carrier frequencies (and wavelengths) that are not a multiple of each other. In this way, the measured phase differences will coincide with only one single distance, as exemplified in Figure 11.3, where one phase signal (green) has a period of three unities, while the other (red) has a period of five unities. Each carrier frequency will provide a measurement of the phase shift, $\Delta\phi_1$ and $\Delta\phi_2$, and only one depth measurement d_{12} is coherent with these two phase shifts simultaneously. This corresponds to the physical depth. After a period of 15 unities ($15 = 3 \times 5$), the pattern repeats itself (the dashed lines at the far-right side), causing possible ambiguities with the two solid lines region. Consequently, any depth measurement without ambiguity must stay within the 15 unities region. Many consumer depth-sensing devices use this approach to measure the distance to objects up to a dozen of meters.

Another approach, often used in higher resolution image depth-sensing devices, is to unwrap the phase jumps by detecting the concentric regions of the phase wrap, adding appropriate jumps of 2π at each border, cf. Figure 11.4(a), yielding very good unwrapped depth images, as shown in Figure 11.4(b). Observe the shadows behind the objects, where no light is captured, nor reflected. These shadow regions play an important role in the view synthesis process of Chapter 12.

The general principles exposed above are heavily used in the well-known Kinect, but much fine tuning and calibration is required to make this work robustly [7–10].

11.3.2   Structured light

Structured light is also an approach that is often used, but rather to measure the shape of an object than to precisely measure its distance to the light source. The basic principle shown in Figure 11.5 reveals that a straight line that is projected in a plane to the object will get curved along the object's shape when observed from another angle, outside the projection plane. Clearly, the line curvature reveals the

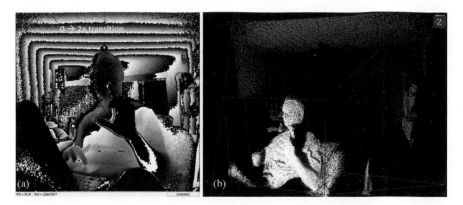

Figure 11.4   *Depth sensing devices have phase wraps (a) that after being undone*
               lead to the depth or point cloud image (b)

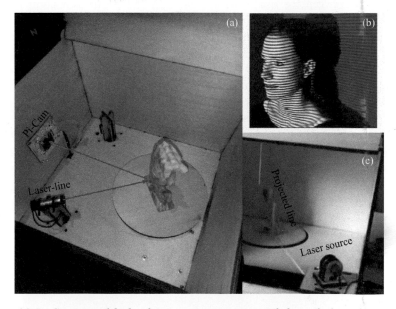

Figure 11.5   *Structured light shape measurements with laser light, camera and*
               turning table (a,c). Typical line deformations on a curved surface (b).
               Courtesy: ESAT-KULeuven, Belgium (b)

object's local shape. By rotating the object on a platform (or moving the projector
in a circle around the object, if it is too bulky) and scanning it line by line, one can
glue all stripes of local shapes together to get the full object's shape.

For a DIY implementation, the interested reader is referred to the description
given in [11,12]. Similar kits are also available from [13] and a couple of excellent
overview studies from [14].

In this approach, one line is projected at a time and time-multiplexing over all possible lines will allow one to measure the shape of the object precisely. Of course, such a process might be time-consuming, hence an approach projecting multiple lines at once will allow measuring shapes almost in real-time, also for video purposes. Though it might look sufficient to project a periodic line pattern on the object, looking at its deformations, complex objects might cause ambiguities in associating the projected line with the observed one [15], in which case an irregular line pattern, like a scan code, is more appropriate [16]. Coding the inter-line distance and the lines' width helps in finding the exact spatial relationship between the lines and their deformations, helping in recovering the object's 3D shape.

Combinations with the time-of-flight approach of the previous section give quite interesting results [17], as well as combining structured light with stereo approaches (cf. Section 12.3 of Chapter 12).

11.3.3   Phase from interferometry

A system in-between the use of structured light and phase estimation is called interferometry. A complete description can be found in [19], but let us explain the main ideas that enabled us to measure at high accuracy, yet low cost (less than thousand euros) of the dragon shape of Figure 11.6(a), to be compared with a time-of-flight laser scan using a device of several ten thousand of euros in Figure 11.6(b). Because of lighting differences, the texture looks different, but the details in the dragon's shape (e.g. the shells) are as precise in both pictures.

Here too, various light stripes are projected with time-multiplexing onto the surface under test, but instead of having to narrow them down to an extremely small width to obtain a high-resolution depth map, it is sufficient to have only three such cosine-modulated patterns projected (more than three for achieving higher

Figure 11.6   Dragon shape with interferometry (a) and professional laser scanner (b)

accuracy) with a phase difference of 120° ($\frac{2\pi}{3}$). This means that the patterns are displaced over one-third of their width, to obtain three images to analyse:

$$I_1(x,y) = K + A \cdot \cos\left(\Delta\varphi(x,y) - \frac{2\pi}{3}\right) \tag{11.6}$$

$$I_2(x,y) = K + A \cdot \cos\left(\Delta\varphi(x,y)\right) \tag{11.7}$$

$$I_3(x,y) = K + A \cdot \cos\left(\Delta\varphi(x,y) + \frac{2\pi}{3}\right) \tag{11.8}$$

where $\Delta\varphi(x,y)$ is the local phase difference at each point (x, y) in the image, as a consequence of the object's shape.

Like in the time-of-flight devices, the phase difference $\Delta\varphi$ can be obtained, independently of the amplitude A and bias K of the light source:

$$\tan(\Delta\varphi(x,y)) = \frac{\sqrt{3}(I_1(x,y) - I_3(x,y))}{2I_2(x,y) - I_1(x,y) - I_3(x,y)} \tag{11.9}$$

which reflects the same information as for the phase shift method, but this time in each pixel of the image (and hence object), making it possible to reach real-time operation in motion picture applications with only three images to project per measurement over the full image. All details can be found in [19]. A description for applying similar methods in reconstructing the shape of a car's windshield can be found in [20].

Finally, [21] compares a similar setup with structured light using grey codes. With photometric non-linearities, sine/cosine waves might cause some artefacts, but when everything is well-calibrated avoiding any non-linearities, the sine/cosine wave approach works very well, with more real-time opportunities.

11.4   Point cloud registration and densification

Pushing the colour pixels from a camera sensor into space, using an associated depth map from a depth-sensing device, will typically create a point cloud as in Figure 11.7(a) with a relatively low resolution because of the limited depth map resolution coming from low-cost, active depth sensing devices.

Typical to depth-sensing devices is that the light they emit diverges over a cone, so that when it hits an object silhouette, a portion of the light is reflected by the object, while another portion travels further to a background object before getting also reflected, as shown in Figure 11.8(c,d). This multipath reflection will inevitably create different depth values for the same point (or should we say, disk) in the scene, and since the final depth value is determined by averaging multiple measurements for the same point, the measurement variability will create so-called flying points along object silhouettes, as shown in Figures 11.8(b) and 11.9. One even observes multiple directions of the flying points because multiple measurement devices were positioned around the scene.

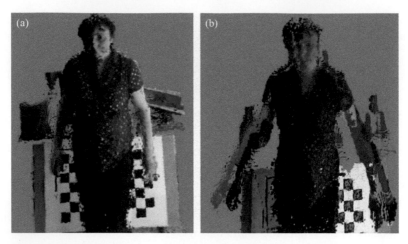

*Figure 11.7   Merging point clouds measured from different devices (a).
Registration errors lead to badly reconstructed point clouds (b)*

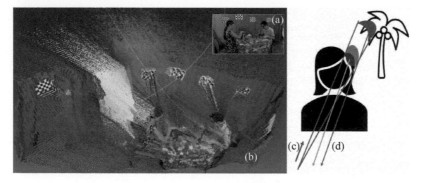

*Figure 11.8   Flying points (b) in the captured scene (a), due to multiple reflection
paths (d) from one emitting source (c)*

One may increase the density of the point cloud by capturing various viewpoints
to the scene, merging them together into a single point cloud, as in Figure 11.7. To
obtain a good merge, the depth sensing device position should be well known, otherwise the constituent points clouds will not coincide in space, dislocating the object or
person, as exemplified in Figure 11.7(b). If everything goes fine, then already quite
good raw point clouds can be obtained, for example Figure 11.10 [23].

The operation of finding the relative position between the various depth-sensing
devices that will create a correct overall point cloud during the merging is called point
cloud registration. It leads to the densification of the point cloud, which can be further
improved by some temporal filtering techniques, like in 4DFusion [24] or [22,25,26].

Even then, the apparent object resolution remains limited, and it is therefore
recommended to continuously scan the objects while moving the active depth
sensing device, so creating successive local point clouds that can be merged into a
much higher density point cloud of acceptable quality.

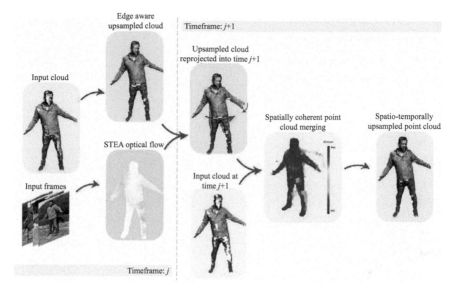

Figure 11.9   Merging various point clouds to create a point cloud of higher density. Reproduced from [22]

Figure 11.10   Good-quality raw point clouds using well-calibrated depth sensing devices. Reproduced from [23]

In some depth-sensing devices, care is taken to have the points organized in a regular grid, so that it remains relatively easy to register them. After all, if the successively acquired point clouds p_i and q_i ($i = 1$ to N) are similar, the technique of singular value decomposition (SVD) finds the principal orientations of the point clouds, yielding a good alignment. The seminal papers in this field are from the 1980s–1990s [27,28], revisited in 2017 [29], where the vectors X and Y with respective components x_i and y_i are created from their centroids $\bar{p}$ and $\bar{q}$:

$$
\begin{aligned}
x_i &= p_i - \bar{p} \\
y_i &= q_i - \bar{q}
\end{aligned}
\tag{11.10}
$$

Finally, the covariance matrix S yields with SVD (Box 11.2) the rotation R and translation t, as follows in Box 11.2:

$$S = X \cdot Y^t = U \cdot \Sigma \cdot V^t$$
$$R = V \begin{pmatrix} 1 & 0 & \cdots & 0 \\ 0 & 1 & & 0 \\ \vdots & & \ddots & \vdots \\ 0 & 0 & \cdots & \pm 1 \end{pmatrix} U^t \qquad (11.11)$$
$$t = \overline{q} - R\overline{p}$$

Box 11.2:   Understanding SVD. Reproduced from [30]

According to [30], an SVD can be interpreted as a succession of a rotation, scaling and another rotation, each corresponding to one factor in the SVD decomposition $S = U \cdot \Sigma \cdot V^t$ as shown in the figure below.

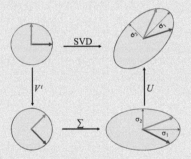

It is therefore not surprising that aligning two-point clouds involves an SVD with the central matrix being made up of unity values since no scaling is needed to rotate one point cloud towards the other. This rotation should be done around the centroids, which explains the introduction of (11.10).

If, however, the point clouds are only very partially overlapping, like in Figure 11.7(b), where we clearly see that the left and the right sides of the lady are captured with two different depth-sensing devices, then the overlap in the point clouds might be insufficient to let the SVD approach work properly. Another method known as the iterative closest point (ICP) method [28] will then probably work better. Its main principles are shown in Figure 11.11, where a rabbit object has two-point clouds to be registered. Here the point clouds are complete, hence the SVD method would work well, but ICP is more robust for more partially acquired point clouds. The final registration in Figure 11.11(c) is obtained by successive iterations, hence the first keyword 'Iterated' in the ICP method: a first guess of the rotation R and translation t was given to go from one camera centre to the other, or equivalently rotate one point cloud to the other. The matching error in the over-lapping point clouds gives indications to modify R and t for obtaining a better

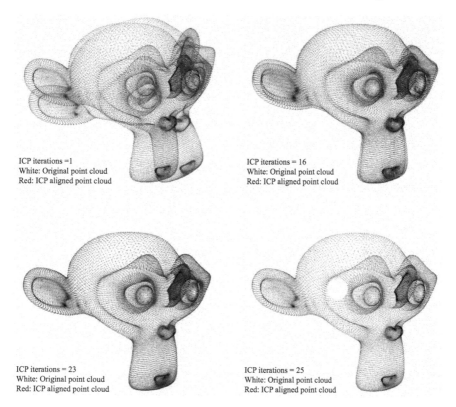

ICP iterations =1
White: Original point cloud
Red: ICP aligned point cloud

ICP iterations = 16
White: Original point cloud
Red: ICP aligned point cloud

ICP iterations = 23
White: Original point cloud
Red: ICP aligned point cloud

ICP iterations = 25
White: Original point cloud
Red: ICP aligned point cloud

Figure 11.11   Iterative closest point (ICP) to densify the point cloud from measurements of various directions. Courtesy: Yassir Ramdani [31]

match. Clearly, the starting point for the iteration process can come from the SVD process mentioned earlier. Some ICP techniques add geometric feature extraction to improve the ICP results, for example, see [32].

Observe in Figure 11.11 how ICP can increase the density of the point cloud because each point cloud has slightly different point positions (it might also be due to noise, so filtering techniques like in [33,34] might help too). Even then, the density of such registered and densified point clouds remains typically low (or insufficient for the target application), and gaps between neighbouring pixels must be filled, either by creating a textured mesh that is spanned onto the point cloud or by increasing the size of each point by oriented circles, also known as splatting, cf. Figure 11.12(b). Reference [25] gives an extensive overview of splatting techniques, and some recommended summaries are given in [35,36]. The most important thing to remember is that, as shown in Figure 11.12, splatting puts disks on the points in space, orienting them with their normal and then projecting them onto the 2D display. In this way, each splat becomes an ellipse that covers its neighbours with a pleasant visual effect that would otherwise not be achieved if we would only enlarge each point in space to become small overlapping spheres.

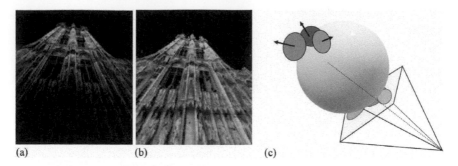

(a)   (b)   (c)

Figure 11.12   Brussels town hall point cloud (a) with splats (b) following the splatting technique (c)

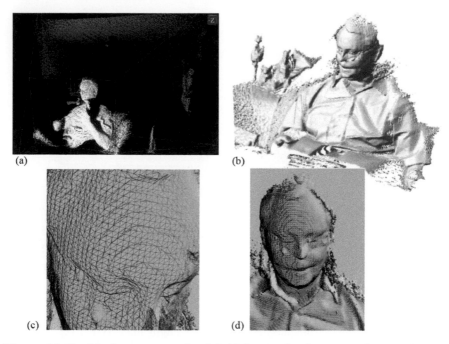

(a)   (b)

(c)   (d)

Figure 11.13   Meshing a point cloud (a,b) from a depth-sensing device, obtaining a regular mesh (c,d)

Another technique for filling the holes between the points in space is to connect them with a mesh. Some depth-sensing devices create point clouds lying on a regular grid, by allocating voxels in a cubical volume, tagging the voxels that correspond to the measured depth, so creating a slice in space corresponding to the frontal surface of the scene, using a so-called truncated signed distance function (TSDF) [37–39]. This also simplifies the task of mesh creation by connecting each new point in space to its neighbours, which are uniquely identified, yielding typical results like in Figure 11.13. For obtained high-quality results, there is also a need to add advanced registration techniques and temporal filtering [40], as in KinectFusion [41] and Fusion4D [24], with remeshing explained in [26]. Also, deep learning methods can help doing all kinds of filtering approaches; an overview is provided in [42]. Without such regular volume, point cloud, and filtering techniques, mesh extraction techniques like Poisson reconstruction [43–45] are required, adding an additional level of complexity. Generic mesh creation and simplification is, however, out of the scope of this textbook. More details can be found in [46].

Finally, relatively cheap Lidar-based depth-sensing devices [46] can also yield good results, densifying the point cloud with semantic information, yielding a kind of inpainting and/or point cloud upsampling [22,47–49].

11.4.1 Photogrammetry

Photogrammetry is the process of reconstructing or measuring a 3D scene using photographic 2D pictures only, without sensing any depth explicitly. It finds its roots during the world wars, with flying reconnaissance squadrons taking hundreds of pictures behind enemy lines, with the aim to reconstruct a geographical map of their territory [50,51]. In these early days, the main purpose was to well align the various pictures to stitch them into a coherent 2D picture, but since then, also with the advent of impressive compute power, the method has evolved, finding also the elevation of each region on the map; the first step towards full 3D reconstruction. Today, the photogrammetric application that is most well-known to a large public is google street [52]. PhotoTourism [53] is another example, more known by experts than the larger public, where photogrammetry is used to find the camera poses, making it possible to rapidly morph one camera view to another. Multi-camera domes that capture objects for 3D cultural heritage preservation [54] also work this way. High level of details can even be reached, even for the reconstruction of trees [55]. Today, various open-source frameworks for photogrammetry exist; the interested reader is referred to [56] for a comparison for cultural heritage applications. Repositories of photogrammetrically reconstructed 3D models can be found in [57].

The beauty of photogrammetry as it exists today is that – starting only from 2D images without prior calibration and depth information (so no depth-sensing devices needed) – it is possible to fully reconstruct the 3D scene but also remove the camera distortions (cf. Chapter 10) and recover the camera poses, all-in-one. This is made possible thanks to the huge number of observations yielding an over-determined system of equations with more observations than unknowns so that it can cope with any additional unknowns like camera pose, radial distortion, etc. without the need of estimating the latter in advance. However, not surprisingly, the method solves a global least squares minimization problem, hence tiny local details like fur are not recovered well, as exemplified in Figure 11.14, where the object was reconstructed individually with a uniform distribution of the camera poses, known to obtain the best results [58].

We will not further dig into the details of this camera placement issue as shown in Figure 11.15, it is intuitively clear that looking to a point in space from very different view directions, the uncertainty on the light ray positions and their intersection – that is the point we want to recover/estimate – is clearly smaller than in a

Figure 11.14   3D reconstruction (left) of objects with a lot of fur (or fine details) from pictures of the original object (right)

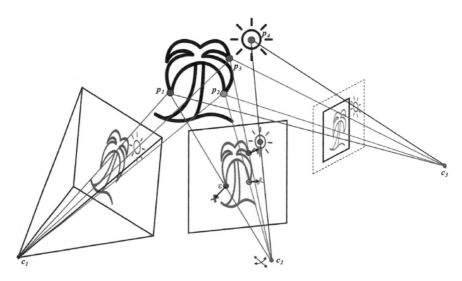

Figure 11.15   Photogrammetry tracks feature points in the captured images to adjust the camera positions c_i and the point positions p_j

scenario with two cameras nearby each other. An exhaustive study of the camera placement can be found in [58], but this goes far beyond the scope of this textbook and will hence not be tackled here.

In what follows, we will spend some time explaining the mathematical aspects of the so-called sparse bundle adjustment (SBA) method, which borrows its name from simple observation of the 3D reconstruction process of Figure 11.15, where each camera centre collects a bundle of light rays emanating from some points in space, and the thought experiment consist in 'adjusting' all the camera poses such that the light rays intersect each other in the corresponding points in space, we want to recover. Note that in practice, because of observation errors, no real intersection points are obtained; the light rays rather come close to each other in virtual intersection points. The method is called 'sparse' because the matrices that are involved in the process are sparse, largely simplifying the mathematical derivations, as well as the complexity of the processing. In literature, some claim that the method is called sparse because in many navigational applications (but not always, for example not in 3D dense reconstructions), only a small number of feature points are tracked with an efficient optical flow and/or feature detector method, for example SIFT (but derivatives exist, like ORB, ASAKA, etc.), as explained in Chapter 9. This feature points sparsity also helps in lowering the complexity of the process, implemented on an embedded device, for example in a drone.

11.4.1.1 SBA

Let us here provide the main steps of SBA, following the tutorial and mathematical derivations of [59] (except for some minor notational differences), which are a very good summary of the seminal paper of [60] on SBA, providing an open source implementation, now also used in many other libraries, like OpenCV [61] and Meshroom.

The main idea of SBA is to minimize the positional error between features found in the captured images of the scene and the projection of the estimated corresponding points in space, as shown in Figure 11.15. These points, as well as the camera positions (their centre) and poses (their orientation), are iteratively slightly displaced to reduce the global error over all feature points. These parametric modifications follow a steepest gradient descent method, aka Levenberg–Marquardt, named after its inventors [62] in the early 1940s. Only its high-level interpretations will be exposed in this section [63].

For SBA to work well, it is important to have an initial guess of the point cloud and camera poses, since SBA is a linearization of a close-to-target non-linear optimization. Any method of Section 11.2 for extracting depth and fusing partial point clouds can be used for this purpose.

Once we have an initial guess of the unknown parameters, we can move on with the mathematical derivations of SBA, based on Figure 11.15. We seek to minimize the squared distance between the observed feature points q_{ij} and the 2D projections $\widehat{q}_{ij}$ of the points p_i:

$$E^2 = \sum_{i,j} \left(q_{ij} - P(C_j, p_i)\right)^2 = \sum_{i,j} \left(q_{ij} - \widehat{q}_{ij}\right)^2 \tag{11.12}$$

Here P represents the 2D projection operator of point p_i through the camera with centre C_j, leading to point $\widehat{q}_{ij}$ in the camera's image plane, while q_{ij} is the corresponding feature (theoretically, at the same place, when all parameters are well estimated) that is detected in the image with conventional image feature detectors. Consequently, q_{ij} does not change with changing camera positions, while $\widehat{q}_{ij}$ does. This fact will also appear in the calculation of the Jacobian J, further on, holding only the values $\widehat{q}_{ij}$.

The idea now is to minimize the overall error E^2 by iteratively changing the camera centres C_j and the estimated point positions p_i in space, until convergence is reached. For instance, when slightly moving a camera centre in Figure 11.15, the projections $\widehat{q}_{ij}$ of the points p_i will change, resulting in a change of E^2, which might be reduced. All the trick is to find an appropriate movement of each camera that will really reduce the global error E^2. Likewise, if we move the estimated points p_i, with or without moving the camera positions, the global error E^2 can also vary and possibly be reduced. In this way, playing on small movements of both the cameras and the points in space, we may hope to find a proper combination of all unknown parameters (camera positions and points in space) that minimizes the global error E^2. Of course, doing this blindly would not yield a satisfactory result. Therefore, we need a mathematically rigorous approach to do so; this is the Levenberg–Marquardt algorithm. Its main steps are given in the remainder of this section.

The minimum of E^2 in (11.12) is reached where its derivative equals zero, which leads to a gradient descent method, yielding:

$$J^T J \cdot \delta x = -J^T \cdot e \tag{11.13}$$

where e is a vector holding each term in (11.12), that is all displacements between q_{ij} and $\widehat{q}_{ij}$ as shown in Figure 11.15, and J is the Jacobian:

$$J = \frac{\partial \widehat{q}}{\partial x} \tag{11.14}$$

with x being the vector of parameters, including the camera parameters represented by c and the points in space by p:

$$x = [c, p] \tag{11.15}$$

Likewise, each error contribution in (11.12) may come from changing camera parameters, or point positions in space, hence, we can also categorize the individual error components of (11.12) as

$$e = [e_c, e_p] \tag{11.16}$$

Before proceeding, let us first make some useful interpretations. Equation (11.13) tells how the parameter vector x must be changed, after observing an error e: x must be changed in the opposite direction of e (the minus sign at the right side of the equation) through the Jacobian, which is the collection of partial derivatives of x to c and p, hence contains the gradients. This equation tells us that once we observe an error e, we know how to adapt the candidate parameters c (cameras) and p (points) to reduce the error e. Visually, referring to Figure 11.15, once we know the small error vectors represented as arrows in the image planes, we know how to move the cameras (c parameters) and the points (p parameters) in order to reduce the global error (the total size of all error vectors in the image planes). This means essentially that the points p_i are pushed towards for example the left and the cameras c_j towards the right for reaching a lower error value. In fact, this is only a single iteration of (11.13) that must be repeated many times for eventually reaching a global minimum.

However, some important modifications must be added to (11.13) to guarantee robustness and convergence. First, it may happen that a feature point corresponding to a point p_i in space has not been detected in the camera's image planes, for instance, p_4 falls outside the window of c_3's camera plane of Figure 11.15. Its contribution has hence to be excluded from (11.13), therefore adding a binary value in the matrix σ_x to include or exclude the contribution of that point:

$$\left(J^T \sigma_x J\right) \cdot \delta x = -J^T \cdot \sigma_x e \tag{11.17}$$

In practice, one may even go further in this interpretation noting that some observations might be reliable and others less. Therefore, σ_x becomes the precision matrix, which can be demonstrated to be the covariance matrix [60]; it is hence a continuous-valued matrix.

Furthermore, the left side of (11.17) might become a matrix with many tiny values that makes the inverse operation numerically unstable. A regularization term with parameter λ is therefore included:

$$\left(J^T \sigma_x J + \lambda \cdot I\right) \cdot \delta x = -J^T \cdot \sigma_x e \tag{11.18}$$

This is the well-known Levenberg–Marquardt 'augmented normal equation' that must be solved to obtain δx at each iteration, until convergence [62]. Different strategies exist for determining appropriate λ values at each iteration, but this is beyond the scope of this textbook.

To better apprehend what all this means, let us calculate the Jacobian following the example of [59] with three cameras (actually, only the camera centres as parameters; in general, intrinsic may also be involved) and four points.

Defining

$$\begin{cases} a_{ij} = \dfrac{\partial \widehat{q}_{ij}}{\partial c_j} \\[2mm] b_{ij} = \dfrac{\partial \widehat{q}_{ij}}{\partial p_i} \end{cases} \tag{11.19}$$

we obtain the configuration of Figure 11.16 with Jacobian J, as well as its product $J^T J$ expressed in (11.13) and (11.18) when $\sigma_x = 0$.

The left side of J corresponds to the impact of changing camera centres C_j for $j = 1$ to 3, while its right side corresponds to the impact of changing point positions p_i for $i = 1$ to 4. For instance, when changing the camera centre C_2 (the second column in J), the projections $\widehat{q}_{ij}$ of each point p_i ($i = 1$ to 4) in camera j also change position, resulting in a change of the a_{i2} values in the centre of all 3×3 diagonal submatrices at the left side of J. Likewise, if point p_3 changes position in space, its

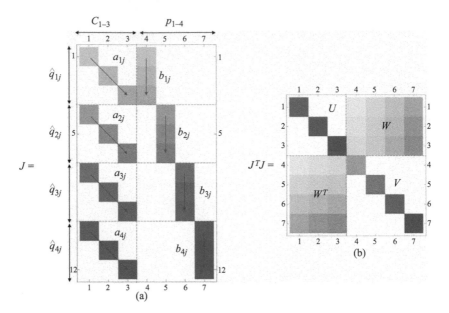

Figure 11.16   (a) The diagonal and column submatrices of the Jacobian J with
$N_a = 3$ and $N_b = 4$, and (b) the product with its transpose

projections $\hat{q}_{3j}$ in the three cameras $j = 1$ to 3 will also change, modifying all three values b_{3j} in the sixth (last but one) column of J.

Visual inspection of Figure 11.16 reveals a sparse structure with only diagonal submatrices at its left side and column matrices at its right side; all other values being zero (white cells in J). Also note that the horizontal dimension of J is equal to the sum (here 7) of the number N_a of camera centres (here 3) and the number N_b of points in space (here 4), while the vertical dimension of J is equal to the product $N_a \cdot N_b$ of these two numbers (here 12). Clearly, the Jacobian can easily become a high (much higher than wide) matrix if the number of cameras and/or points is large. In practice, it is the number of points that is often large, as exemplified in Figure 11.17 for $N_a = 5$ cameras and $N_b = 13$ points, yielding a horizontal dimension $N_a + N_b = 18$ of J, with a vertical dimension of $N_a \cdot N_b = 65$, which starts to be quite large indeed. Interestingly, $J^T J$ in (11.13) is a square matrix with dimensions equal to the lower number, that is 18 in Figure 11.17(c) and 7 in Figure 11.16(b). Note already that $J^T J$ apparently has a particular structure made of two diagonal matrices U and V, and a dense matrix W and its transpose. This will come very handy in subsequent mathematical derivations.

As a side note, many authors follow another organization of the matrix J, where its rows are clustered per camera, collecting the impact of all projected points $\hat{q}_{ij}$ (here with $i = 1$–4) over successive rows, as shown in Figure 11.18(b). The reason for this organization of J' is that since we see all points projected in one camera as one cluster, we get literally a full picture of the image plane of that camera, while moving from one camera to the next corresponds to going down in

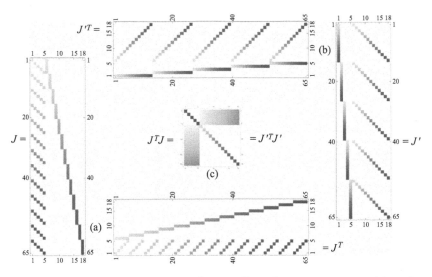

Figure 11.17 *The Jacobians J and J', as well as their transposes in (a) and*
(b) respectively. The product (c) of the Jacobian and its transpose

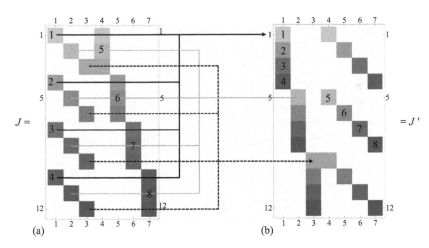

Figure 11.18 *Reorganization of the Jacobian J in (a) towards the Jacobian*
J' in (b)

the matrix J'. This has a more intuitive relationship with applications with robots or
drones moving in the scene and taking each time one image corresponding to one
specific position of the robot or drone over time. This so-called simultaneous
localization and mapping (SLAM) has intuitively a close link to Structure from
Motion (SfM) that is exactly what photogrammetry and SBA do: find the structure
of the (static) 3D scene by moving around, triangulating all captured pictures.
We feel here that the concepts of photogrammetry, SfM, SBA and SLAM are

somewhat interchangeable, with [64] clearly making the link between the pose estimation using SVD as in Box 11.2 and SBA, and [65] discussing the impact of the camera calibration uncertainty on VisualSLAM.

Nevertheless, the structure of J' is merely a simple reorganization of J, shuffling its rows row_J around towards row_J' in J' over all $N_a \cdot N_b$ rows, as follows:

$$\begin{cases} n = \text{Floor}[(row\_J - 1)/b] \\ row\_J' = (n+1) + ((row\_J - 1) - n \cdot N_b) \cdot N_a \end{cases} \tag{11.20}$$

For instance, the values 1 to 4 in the left column of J in Figure 11.18(a) are collected, following the black solid arrows, forming successive rows in the reorganized Jacobian J' in Figure 11.18(b). Similarly, the centre column values 5 to 8 in the right side of J are reordered as a diagonal submatrix in J'. In fact, this reorganization does not change anything in the equivalent structure of $J'^T J'$ in (11.8), as exemplified in Figure 11.17(c), obtained either from (a), that is $J^T J$, or (b), that is $J'^T J'$.

More generally, (11.11) – a refinement of (11.8) – requires a multiplication of one of these Jacobians (J or J') with its transpose and an interleaved covariance matrix σ_x; hence, it is not surprising that following auxiliary values simplify further mathematical derivations:

$$\begin{cases} u_j = \sum_{i=1}^{N_a} a_{ji} \cdot \sigma_{ij} \cdot a_{ij} \\ v_i = \sum_{j=1}^{N_b} b_{ji} \cdot \sigma_{ij} \cdot b_{ij} \\ w_{ji} = a_{ji} \cdot \sigma_{ij} \cdot b_{ij} \end{cases} \tag{11.21}$$

We follow the same conventions as in [59], except that we use lower cases for values, and that the subscripts for transposition are indicated with switched indices i and j, instead of the superscript T. Index i iterates over all points, while index j goes over all cameras.

These values are then rearranged in matrices, which for our example of three cameras and four points yields a 3×3 matrix U, a 4×4 matrix V and a 3×4 matrix W:

$$U = \begin{pmatrix} u_1 & 0 & 0 \\ 0 & u_2 & 0 \\ 0 & 0 & u_3 \end{pmatrix} \tag{11.22}$$

$$V = \begin{pmatrix} v_1 & 0 & 0 & 0 \\ 0 & v_2 & 0 & 0 \\ 0 & 0 & v_3 & 0 \\ 0 & 0 & 0 & v_4 \end{pmatrix} \tag{11.23}$$

$$W = \begin{pmatrix} w_{11} & w_{12} & w_{13} & w_{14} \\ w_{21} & w_{22} & w_{23} & w_{24} \\ w_{31} & w_{32} & w_{33} & w_{34} \end{pmatrix} \tag{11.24}$$

Here, U includes only partial derivatives to the parameters c, and V has only derivatives to the parameters p. W contains a mix of derivatives involving all parameters c and p.

Solving (11.18), one obtains δx, hence also δc and δp, which means that at each iteration the camera and point positions are updated. Reference [59] further transforms this into:

$$
\begin{pmatrix} U & W \\ W^T & V \end{pmatrix} \cdot \begin{pmatrix} \delta c \\ \delta p \end{pmatrix} = \begin{pmatrix} e_c \\ e_p \end{pmatrix}
\tag{11.25}
$$

where the diagonal nature of U and V submatrices will simplify the calculations, as will become clear in a minute.

The reader can verify (also given in [59]) that starting from (11.25), one obtains

$$
\left(U - WV^{-1}W^T \right) \cdot \delta c = e_c - WV^{-1} \cdot e_p
\tag{11.26}
$$

where the factor $\left(U - WV^{-1}W^T \right)$ is called the Schur complement of V, which is a symmetric positive definite matrix that can efficiently be inverted by Cholesky decomposition [66]. Equation (11.26) allows then to calculate δc rather easily, out of which δp can be further derived with

$$
\delta p = V^{-1} \cdot \left(e_p - W^T \cdot \delta c \right)
\tag{11.27}
$$

Since V is a diagonal matrix, its inverse is just the inverse of each value, hence (11.26) can easily be calculated. In fact, only the matrix W is a rather dense matrix with dimensions corresponding to the number of cameras and number of points, respectively. Consequently, the Schur complement of V in (11.26) remains a relatively small matrix with dimensions equal to the number of cameras. This is an important observation since it radically simplifies the calculations in many practical use cases. Indeed, often, the number of points p to evaluate is much higher than the number of camera positions c, typically in the order of millions of points for a dense 3D reconstruction, requiring only around hundreds of camera positions. Clearly, the dimensionality of the vector c being several orders of magnitude lower than the dimensionality of the vector p, it is more advantageous to first calculate δc with (11.26), followed by a simple implementation of the diagonal matrix inverse (inverse of its values) of (11.27) for δp. Nevertheless, with such high number of points, the complexity and especially the memory footprint may become prohibitive large, therefore calling for alternatives to Levenberg–Marquardt, for example the Dog Leg algorithm of [67] and/or distributive approaches [68,69], where a large SBA problem can be decomposed into independent SBA sub-problems which results are only fused at the very end of the process.

The reader is referred to [70,71] for an open-source implementation of the original SBA, [72,73] for its sparse matrix representation format and [74] for a GPU implementation. SBA having proved to be very useful in a wide range of applications, it is widely adopted by many software frameworks such as OpenCV [75,76] with its dedicated wrapper CVSBA [57], OpenVSLAM [77], and open-source 3D reconstruction software pipelines such as Regard3D, Meshroom and Colmap (comparative

Figure 11.19   Meshroom 3D reconstruction results. Reproduced under a Creative Commons license from [80]

studies can be found in [56,78]), just to name a few of the open-source frameworks available on the Internet. Even though Meshroom and Colmap are at the time of writing quite new software packages, they have been developed over the past 10 years under the radar and came out recently. They have interfaces to Blender, as well as a nice GUI; highly recommended for beginners and experts, yielding extremely competitive results, as exemplified in Figure 11.19 [79].

An important remark is that SBA minimizes the global error, not a local one. When using SBA on objects with a lot of fur, like the goat in Figure 11.14(b), there is no guarantee that the local features like each strand of hair will be maintained. For instance, even with several hundreds of camera positions around the goat of Figure 11.14(b) for obtaining a dense point cloud, the SBA approach yields (after remeshing, cf. Section 11.4.1) the peaks of fur bundles as in Figure 11.14(a), rather than natural-looking fur, though the rest of the scene made of smooth objects creates an excellent point cloud and mesh. It is to overcome such problems that the DIBR techniques that will be explained in Chapter 12 are proposed.

Box 11.3:   Laparoscopic photogrammetry

Typically, photogrammetry is used in rigid structure from motion application scenarios, but extensions with elastic structures have also been studied. For instance, in laparoscopy, surgeons put an endoscopic camera into to the patient's body during surgery. This provides only a very small viewport to the inside body, which is probably all right for very precise surgical actions on specific regions of the organ, but it is very difficult to get an overall picture of the 'full scene under surgery'. Stitching various images when the endoscope moves, or even better, creating full 3D reconstructions would greatly help the surgeon. References [81,82] provide examples with real-time, incremental 3D reconstruction during the surgery.

Figure 11.20   A real scene reconstructed with photogrammetry, yielding a point cloud (top) and meshed scene (bottom)

11.4.1.2   SBA for camera calibration

In Section 4.3, we introduced the concept of intrinsics camera calibration, further extended with radial distortion removal in Section 10.1.2, where we encountered a non-linear, quadratic error minimization problem that could already be solved with Levenberg–Marquardt. In fact, not only the camera poses can be solved with SBA, also all intrinsics, for example [83–87], even with large panoramic images that often use fisheye lenses with a lot of distortion, for example [88,89]. Nevertheless, some authors, for example instance [90], recommend to first find intrinsics in an independent calibration process prior to applying SBA for finding the extrinsics.

One can easily include intrinsics in the SBA framework of the previous section by extending the parameter vector c with the focal length, the principal point and/or the radial distortion parameters. The explicit derivation of the corresponding J matrix may be somewhat cumbersome (e.g. p. 19 in [91]), but this does not change the mathematical approach; (11.9) in the previous section might just be a bit larger. Nevertheless, keep in mind that Levenberg–Marquardt is a linearization around the target solution; hence, adding heavily non-linear influences like radial distortion in fisheye lenses might still represent a challenge for convergence. For slight radial distortions, however, SBA is recommended, providing finetuned intrinsic with a reprojection error smaller than one pixel, that is sub-pixel accuracy [92].

PhotoTourism [53] is a good example where SBA is used for recovering camera poses, or said differently, for recovering the rotations and translations for going from one camera position to the next. Annex A of the PhotoTourism paper [53] explicitly exposes an interesting observation, worth mentioning, with respect to the rotation matrix estimation. One would be tempted to use a 3×3 matrix and seek the nine unknowns, but this is not a good idea, since this does not impose any relation between these nine parameters. Indeed, a rotation is an orthogonal transform where all rows (or columns) are orthogonal to each other, and each row (column) has norm one. If this is not baked explicitly within the parameter optimization framework, the numerical values that one might obtain for the nine rotational unknowns might not represent a rotation at all. The easiest approach to circumvent this challenge is to use the Rodriguez formula we have seen in Section 6.1.2 of Chapter 6 with respect to OpenGL, where the rotation is expressed by giving a rotation axis and a rotation angle, which are the only free parameters. Once the SBA optimization finds numerical values for them, the Rodriguez equation will guarantee that the corresponding transform is indeed a rotation, without the need for any additional orthogonalization trick.

Box 11.4:   Special effects

Sparse bundle adjustment is often used in cinema for estimating the camera pose from the captured video, without the need for prior calibration with checkerboards. In this way, the film producer can track the relative position of the camera compared to the scene. During the special effects editing, the editor indicates on one frame of the movie where the object of interest is lying, for example, a building as in Figure 11.21, and then any 3D special effect like adding a circular title turning on top of the building can be added by a simple 3D editing software. The title position is then rendered in 2D (a 2D perspective projection) in perfect sync with the camera pose, and the rendered image is superimposed on top of the already captured 2D video, providing the result shown in Figure 11.21.

All this looks simple, but in practice, pretty advanced editing tools are required, like in [93].

*Figure 11.21   Special effect of adding a 3D title to the scene. Courtesy: Ugo
Cassanello [94]*

11.4.2   SLAM navigational applications

Simultaneous localization and mapping is a family of techniques used in robotics to
localize a robot or drone (i.e. find its pose), while simultaneously constructing the
map or 3D environment in which it moves. A large set of approaches exist; hence we
will restrict ourselves to a couple of them that are related to the mathematical principles developed in the previous section, most often also relying on visual inspection
of the robot's surroundings, which leads to the naming of Visual SLAM or VSLAM.

For instance, the open-source library OpenVSLAM [77] uses aspects of bundle
adjustment, but also other graph-based approaches are implemented using
Levenberg–Marquardt optimization. In [95], special precautions are taken to
additionally obtain good loop-closure when the robot or drone has a closed-loop
navigation path. We therefore spend a minute explaining these concepts hereafter.

11.4.2.1   SBA-based SLAM

Instead of finding millions of points in the scene for reconstructing it as accurately
as possible, as in Figure 11.20, one may choose to drastically reduce this number to
tens or hundreds of points, which will certainly not reconstruct the scene densely.
This is, however, not the target when navigating a robot or drone through a scene; it
is rather its localization that matters. For such navigational applications, one can
still use SBA with a relatively small parameter vector p. The parameter vector c, on
the contrary, will get a high importance and might be extended with the camera
intrinsics estimation. The lunar rover navigation system of Box 11.5 or a satellite
docking system, as for the Rosetta mission are just a few examples where SBA and/
or Levenberg–Marquardt optimizations are used to reach high positional accuracy,
just by using a few feature points. For instance, for guiding the Rosetta satellite
towards its comet, the system could not rely on back-and-forth communication with
earth that would not have allowed direct action for a safe landing. A robust SBA/
Levenberg–Marquardt approach with embedded, low-power processing on the

satellite is a much better solution, as explained in Box 11.5. Obviously, SBA has proven its robustness in critical missions.

Box 11.5:   Lunar rover, Mars lovers and Rosetta Levenberg

Autonomous land rovers and flying drones are typically using SBA-based SLAM to safely navigate through the scene [96]. For instance, Lunar and Mars Exploration Rovers [97,98] use a stereo camera, calibrated with SBA [89], cf. Section 12.2.5 of Chapter 12, to have an initial idea of the depth of some keypoints, which are used for further SLAM improvement. Based on the target destination given by an operator on earth, the vehicle determines a safe path, avoiding big rocks. Also, for the landing of Perseverance on Mars, a camera was used to track feature points during the descent and to estimate the horizontal displacement of the module before touch-down [99]. A similar approach was used for the autonomous navigation of the Rosetta satellite [100,101], comparing multiple images taken at successive time stamps for estimating its position and pose with respect to the comet. Finally, Chang'E-2 lunar orbiter used in the Chinese Lunar Exploration Program [102] also uses a sparse bundle adjustment to find the intrinsics and extrinsics (they call them interior and exterior camera parameters) of the on-board vision cameras. Because of some of their specificities, additional parameters were used than the ones given in this textbook.

Drones are also often guided following this approach, often with complementary measurements (accelerometer, differential GPS, etc.) to obtain extreme navigational accuracy [96]. Also here, the number of tracked feature points is restricted to avoid overloading the embedded device. For drones flying around for photogrammetric applications, the 3D scene reconstruction will never be done on the drone itself: the pictures taken by the drone will be transmitted to the base station and later processed on a powerful PC. Only then it will become possible to increase the number of feature points on the captured images and estimate 3D points up to a level that allows dense 3D reconstructions, that is, several millions of points. In a sense, the SBA is performed twice: once on the drone for navigation only, and a second time with much more feature points on a powerful PC for 3D reconstruction mainly.

11.4.2.2   Probabilistic and graph-based SLAM

There exists also a family of SLAM approaches that rather use so-called odometry, that is measuring the speed of the drone, as well as its approximated pose, integrating the signals from accelerometers [103]. These are probabilistic approaches where for each position, let us say each half a meter, the positional probability is estimated based on all previous measurements. Adding the measurement of the current position (still unknown at a high accuracy level), the maximum a posteriori probability is estimated and used as the best current position estimate of the drone.

The evolution of the positional estimates over the various states that are recorded in a so-called essential graph, keeping track of all measurements and estimated positions over time. At start, we know exactly the position of the drone, but when time passes by, the probability distribution of all its potential positions enlarges. The position that is recorded as the best estimates one may, for simplicity, be considered as the centre of gravity of a positional bubble (this is related to Markov Random Fields and Gaussian processes, but this goes beyond the scope of the current textbook). Note that the positional uncertainty increases, unless there is a clear landmark that is detected by the drone, allowing it to reset its current position to a known one. A sudden decrease of uncertainty will occur, followed by a gradual increase afterwards.

This probabilistic framework is related to Kalman filtering [104,105], which we will not further explain in this textbook, since it is not directly causally related to visual aspects of SBA. In contrast, the essential graph representation of [106] shows many similarities with SBA and Levenberg–Marquardt. Indeed, each position x_i in such a graph is associated with a measurement $\bar{x}_j$, and the difference between these two is equivalent to one term in the error cost function of (11.12). The minimization of the quadratic error over all states is then handled in the same way as for SBA, with an A matrix related to the position x_i and a B matrix to $\bar{x}_j$. The interested reader might verify the mathematical similarity with the Levenberg–Marquardt optimization in SBA, cf. [56].

In summary, though there exist a lot of SLAM techniques, each with their pros and cons (cf. comparative table in [107]), we may nevertheless safely state that there exists somehow a common denominator in a large group of them, that is the Levenberg–Marquardt optimization approach. For visual SLAM, the resemblance with SBA is even more striking, making SBA an outstanding tool, both for navigational applications, as well as for 3D reconstruction use cases.

The enthusiastic reader may now better understand the various steps followed in advanced 3D reconstruction studies such as [108]: it is an intelligent mixture between depth estimation, ICP and probabilistic SLAM techniques, recovering a 3D representation of the scene at high accuracy. There is, however, one subject that is addressed in the study, but that we overlooked so far: the mesh reconstruction from a point cloud. This will be rapidly summarized in next section without in-depth details that would go far beyond the scope of this textbook.

11.5 3D rendering of point clouds

11.5.1 Poisson reconstruction

Once the point cloud has been recovered, following the recipes from previous sections, one would like to visualize it as a fully watertight closed object in the 3D OpenGL rendering pipeline. This requires converting the point cloud into a 3D mesh made of triangles that interconnect the points, possibly even adding more points that are inserted to better follow the local curvatures of the surface to construct. A numerically efficient method is described in [43,45].

The process starts by calculating the normals from the discrete point set, and then estimates an indicator function that tells for any point in space (also other points than the ones given in the point cloud) whether it lies within the object, or outside the object. One feels that this indicator function is somehow related to a gradient that detects 'virtual borders.' This is confirmed in [43,45] proving that the gradient of the indicator function is equal to the vector field obtained after smoothing/filtering the normals, which avoids erratic normal directions and numerical instabilities. The gradient operator is inverted by taking a divergence operator, yielding a Laplacian (divergence of gradient), leading to a classical Poisson equation for which numerical solvers for which open source implementations exist, for example in the Computational Geometric Algebra Library (CGAL) [44]. All details can be found in [44] that reconstructs the surface with an octree representation, embedding various levels of details. From there on, the 3D OpenGL rendering pipeline can do its rendering job.

11.5.2   *Splatting*

Obviously, constructing a 3D mesh from an unordered set of points in space is not an easy task; it calls for heavy numerical methods. One may ask why getting through so much trouble? Recall that the mesh is useful for the OpenGL rendering: each triangle corresponds to a plane structure that can easily be rasterized in the fragment shader. Even when a surface is represented with smooth curves, like a Bezier surface, there is a need to find planar patches that will traverse the fragment shader. From this point of view, it seems inevitable to proceed to meshing for 3D rendering.

However, a good alternative exists with 'splatting', cf. Section 11.4.2. If the points are too small to create a dense image at rendering, a simple solution may be to enlarge these points, which will eventually overlap and fill in the empty gaps between them. This is a simple form of splatting. A more elaborated approach, which yields more pleasant rendering results, consists in creating a flat disk spinning on each point from the point cloud with an orientation given by the local normal, which may be calculated with methods like in [25]. With sufficiently large disks or splats, the rendering looks very similar to what would be obtained with a textured 3D mesh passing through the OpenGL pipeline.

References

[1]   https://www.nasa.gov/sites/default/files/thumbnails/image/lrolola_20080417_hi.jpg.
[2]   D. E. Smith, M. T. Zuber, G. B. Jackson, *et al.,* 'The Lunar Orbiter Laser Altimeter investigation on the Lunar Reconnaissance Orbiter mission,' *Space. Sci. Rev.* vol. 150, pp. 209–241, 2010, doi: 10.1007/s11214-009-9512-y.
[3]   L. Ramos-Izquierdo, V. Stanley Scott III, J. Connelly, *et al.,* 'Optical system design and integration of the Lunar Orbiter Laser Altimeter,' *Appl. Opt.* vol. 48, pp. 3035–3049, 2009.

[4]   M. Hansard, S. Lee, O. Choi, and R. P. Horaud, 'Time of Flight Cameras: Principles, Methods, and Applications,' SpringerBriefs in Computer Science, ISBN 978-1-4471-4658-2, 10.1007/978-1-4471-4658-2, 2013.

[5]   J. Illade-Quinteiro, V. M. Brea, P. López, D. Cabello, and G. Doménech-Asensi, Distance Measurement Error in Time-of-Flight Sensors Due to Shot Noise, *Sensors*, vol. 15, no. 3, pp. 4624–4642, 2015, doi:10.3390/s150304624.

[6]   R. Lange and P. Seitz, 'Solid-state time-of-flight range camera,' *IEEE Journal of Quantum Electronics*, vol. 37, no. 3, pp. 390–397, 2001, doi: 10.1109/3.910448.

[7]   J. Smisek, M. Jancosek and T. Pajdla, '3D with Kinect,' *2011 IEEE International Conference on Computer Vision Workshops (ICCV Workshops)*, 2011, pp. 1154–1160, doi: 10.1109/ICCVW.2011.6130380.

[8]   E. Lachat, H. Macher, T. Landes, and P. Grussenmeyer, Assessment and calibration of a RGB-D camera (Kinect v2 Sensor) towards a potential use for close-range 3D modeling, *Remote Sens.*, vol. 7, pp. 13070–13097, 2015, doi:10.3390/rs71013070.

[9]   Y. Liao, G. Li, Z. Ju, H. Liu, and D. Jiang, 'Joint kinect and multiple external cameras simultaneous calibration,' *2017 2nd International Conference on Advanced Robotics and Mechatronics (ICARM)*, 2017, pp. 305–310, doi: 10.1109/ICARM.2017.8273179.

[10] B. Karan,. Calibration of Kinect-type RGB-D sensors for robotic applications, *FME Transactions,* vol. 43, pp. 47–54, 2015, doi: 10.5937/fmet1501047K.

[11] P. Azad, T. Gockel, R. Dillmann, *Computer Vision: Principles and Practice*. Elektor Electronics, 2008.

[12] J. E. Solem, *Programming Computer Vision with Python: Tools and Algorithms for Analyzing Images*. ISBN-13: 978-1449316549, O'Reilly, 2012.

[13] J. E. Solem, 'FabScan Open source 3D Scanner System,' https://fabscan.org/.

[14] https://www.esat.kuleuven.be/psi/research/structured-light.

[15] T. Moons, L. Van Gool, and M. Vergauwen, *3D reconstruction from multiple images: Part 1: Principles*, Now Foundations and Trends, 2010.

[16] C. Je, S. W. Lee, and R.-H. Park, Colour-stripe permutation pattern for rapid structured-light range imaging, *Optics Communications*, vol. 285, no. 9, pp. 2320–2331, 2012, ISSN 0030-4018, doi: 10.1016/j.optcom.2012.01.025.

[17] G. Agresti, and P. Zanuttigh, Combination of spatially-modulated ToF and structured light for MPI-free depth estimation. In: Leal-Taixé L., Roth S. (eds) *Computer Vision – ECCV 2018 Workshops. ECCV 2018. Lecture Notes in Computer Science*, vol. 11129, 2019. Springer, Cham. doi: 10.1007/978-3-030-11009-3_21.

[18] G. Kramida, Resolving the vergence-accommodation conflict in head-mounted displays, *IEEE Transactions on Visualization and Computer Graphics*, vol. 22, no. 7, pp. 1912–1931, 2016, doi:10.1109/TVCG.2015.2473855.

[19] S. Zhang, *High-Speed 3D Imaging with Digital Fringe Projection Techniques,* ISBN-13: 978-0367869724, Routledge, 2019.

[20] T. Meesen, 'Stereo based Phase Measuring Deflectometry of free-form specular surfaces for industrial inspections applications,' Master thesis, Polytechnical school, Université Libre de Bruxelles, 2021.

[21]   D. Scharstein and R. Szeliski, 'High-accuracy stereo depth maps using structured light,' *2003 IEEE Computer Society Conference on Computer Vision and Pattern Recognition, 2003. Proceedings*, 2003, pp. I-I, doi: 10.1109/CVPR.2003.1211354.

[22]   M. Moynihan, R. Pagés, and A. Smolic, 'Spatio-temporal upsampling for free viewpoint video point clouds,' In *Proceedings of the 14th International Joint Conference on Computer Vision, Imaging and Computer Graphics Theory and Applications (VISAPP)*, vol. 5, SciTePress, 2019, pp. 684–692, ISBN: 978-989-758-354-4.

[23]   R. Diniz, 'Volumetric video capture, object reconstruction and tele-communication methods for Mixed Reality experiences:,' http://www.tele-midia.puc-rio.br/~rafaeldiniz/public_files/monografia.pdf.

[24]   M. Dou, S. Khamis, Y. Degtyarev, *et al.,* 'Fusion4D: real-time performance capture of challenging scenes.' *ACM Trans. Graph.,* July 2016, vol. 35, no. 4, 2016, Article 114, 13 pages, doi: 10.1145/2897824.2925969.

[25]   M. Gross, and H. Pfister, *Point-based Graphics,* ISBN-13: 978-0123706041, Morgan Kaufmann Publishers, 2007.

[26]   A. Collet, M. Chuang, P. Sweeney, *et al.,* 'High-quality streamable free-viewpoint video,' *ACM Trans. Graph.,* vol. 34, no. 4, Article 69 (August 2015), 13 pages, doi: 10.1145/2766945.

[27]   Z. C. Lin, T. S. Huang, S. D. Blostein, H. Lee, and E. A. Margerum, 'Motion estimation from 3-D point sets with and without correspondences,' *Unknown Host Publication Title.* Proceedings of IEEE, 1986, pp. 194–201.

[28]   P. J. Besl and N. D. McKay, 'A method for registration of 3-D shapes,' *IEEE Transactions on Pattern Analysis and Machine Intelligence*, vol. 14, no. 2, pp. 239–256, 1992, doi: 10.1109/34.121791.

[29]   O. Sorkine-Hornung and M. Rabinovich, 'Least-Squares Rigid Motion Using SVD,' Department of Computer Science, ETH Zurich, January 16, 2017.

[30]   'Singular value decomposition,' Wikipedia, https://en.wikipedia.org/wiki/Singular_value_decomposition.

[31]   https://github.com/yassram/iterative-closest-point.

[32]   Y. He, B. Liang, J. Yang, S. Li, and J. He, 'An iterative closest points algorithm for registration of 3D laser scanner point clouds with geometric features,' *Sensors (Basel)*, vol. 17, no. 8, p. 1862, 2017, doi: 10.3390/s17081862. PMID: 28800096; PMCID: PMC5580094.

[33]   G.-J. Anders, and T. Dave, 'Depth Post-Processing for Intel® RealSense™ D400 Depth Cameras,' Revision 1.0.2, https://dev.intelrealsense.com/docs/depth-post-processing.

[34]   L. Keselman, J. I. Woodfill, A. Grunnet-Jepsen, and A. Bhowmik, 'Intel(R) RealSense(TM) Stereoscopic Depth Cameras,' *2017 IEEE Conference on Computer Vision and Pattern Recognition Workshops (CVPRW)*, 2017, pp. 1267–1276, doi: 10.1109/CVPRW.2017.167.

[35]   H. Pfister, M. Zwicker, J. van Baar, and M. Gross. 2000. Surfels: surface elements as rendering primitives. In *Proceedings of the 27th Annual Conference on Computer Graphics and Interactive Techniques (SIGGRAPH'00).*

ACM Press/Addison-Wesley Publishing Co., USA, 335–342, doi: 10.1145/344779.344936.

[36] M. Zwicker, M. Gross, and H. Pfister, 'A Survey and Classification of Real Time Rendering Methods,' Mitsubishi Electric Research Laboratories, Technical Report TR2000-09, 2000.

[37] D. R. Canelhas, T. Stoyanov, and A. J. Lilienthal, 'SDF Tracker: A parallel algorithm for on-line pose estimation and scene reconstruction from depth images,' *2013 IEEE/RSJ International Conference on Intelligent Robots and Systems*, 2013, pp. 3671–3676, doi: 10.1109/IROS.2013.6696880.

[38] R. A. Newcombe, S. Izadi, O. Hilliges, *et al.*, 'KinectFusion: Real-time dense surface mapping and tracking,' *2011 10th IEEE International Symposium on Mixed and Augmented Reality*, 2011, pp. 127–136, doi: 10.1109/ISMAR.2011.6092378.

[39] E. Palazzolo, J. Behley, P. Lottes, P. Giguère, and C. Stachniss, 'ReFusion: 3D Reconstruction in Dynamic Environments for RGB-D Cameras Exploiting Residuals,' arXiv:1905.02082.

[40] W. Martin, *Reconstruction and Analysis of 3D Scenes*, ISBN 978-3-319-29246-5, Springer International Publishing, 2016.

[41] S. Izadi, D. Kim, O. Hilliges, *et al.*, 'KinectFusion: real-time 3D reconstruction and interaction using a moving depth camera.' In *Proceedings of the 24th Annual ACM Symposium on User Interface Software and Technology (UIST'11)*. Association for Computing Machinery, New York, NY, USA, pp. 559–568, 2011, doi: 10.1145/2047196.2047270.

[42] W. Liu, J. Sun, W. Li, T. Hu, and P. Wang, 'Deep learning on point clouds and its application: a survey,' *Sensors,* vol. 19, no. 19, p. 4188, 2019, doi: 10.3390/s19194188.

[43] M. Kazhdan and H. Hoppe, 'Screened poisson surface reconstruction,' *ACM Trans. Graph.,* vol. 32, p. 3, Article 29 (June 2013), 2013, 13 pp. doi: 10.1145/2487228.2487237.

[44] A. Pierre, S. Laurent, and G. Gaël, 'CGAL 5.0.2 – Poisson Surface Reconstruction: User Manual,' https://doc.cgal.org/latest/Poisson_surface_reconstruction_3/index.html.

[45] M. Kazhdan, M. Bolitho, and H. Hoppe, 'Poisson Surface Reconstruction,' *Eurographics Symposium on Geometry Processing*, 2006, Konrad Polthier, Alla Sheffer (Editors).

[46] M. Botsch, L. Kobbelt, M. Pauly, P. Alliez, and B. Levy, *Polygon Mesh Processing,* ISBN-13: 978-1568814261, A K Peters/CRC Press, 2011.

[47] M. Hödlmoser, B. Micusik, and M. Kampel, 'Sparse Point Cloud Densification by Using Redundant Semantic Information,' *Proceedings – 2013 International Conference on 3D Vision*, 3DV 2013, doi: 10.1109/3DV.2013.64.

[48] Z. Li, P. C. Gogia, and M. Kaess, 'Dense Surface Reconstruction from Monocular Vision and LiDAR,' *2019 International Conference on Robotics and Automation (ICRA)*, 2019, pp. 6905–6911, doi: 10.1109/ICRA.2019.8793729.

[49]   J. Bula, G. Mariethoz, and M-H. Derron, 'Dense point cloud acquisition with a low-cost Velodyne VLP-16,' *Geoscientific Instrumentation Methods and Data Systems*, vol. 9, pp. 385–396, 2020, doi: 10.5194/gi-9-385-2020.

[50]   T. Schenk, 'Introduction to photogrammetry.' The Ohio State University, Columbus, 2005, 106.

[51]   B. A. DeWitt and P. R. Wolf, *Elements of Photogrammetry (with Applications in GIS)* (3rd. ed.). McGraw-Hill Higher Education, 2000.

[52]   B. Klingner, D. Martin, and J. Roseborough, 'Street View Motion-from-Structure-from-Motion,' *2013 IEEE International Conference on Computer Vision*, 2013, pp. 953–960, doi: 10.1109/ICCV.2013.122.

[53]   N. Snavely, S. M. Seitz, and R. Szeliski, 'Photo tourism: exploring photo collections in 3D,' *ACM Trans. Graph.*, vol. 25, no. 3, pp. 835–846, 2006, doi: 10.1145/1141911.1141964.

[54]   M. Mudge, 'VAST 2005: The 6th International Symposium on Virtual Reality, Archaeology and Intelligent Cultural Heritage,' *Incorporating 3rd EUROGRAPHICS Workshop on Graphics and Cultural Heritage*, Pisa Italy, November 8–11, 2005, Eurographics Association, 2005.

[55]   OpenGL Transformation, http://songho.ca/opengl/gl_transform.html.

[56]   E.-K. Stathopoulou, M. Welponer, and F. Remondino, 'Open-source image-based 3D reconstruction pipelines: review, comparison and evaluation,' *ISPRS – International Archives of the Photogrammetry, Remote Sensing and Spatial Information Sciences,* Bd. XLII-2/W17, pp. 331–338, 2019.

[57]   A. Maggiordomo, F. Ponchio, P. Cignoni, and M. Tarini, 'Real-World Textured Things: A repository of textured models generated with modern photo-reconstruction tools,' *Computer Aided Geometric Design*, vol. 83, p. 101943, 2020, ISSN 0167-8396, doi: 10.1016/j.cagd.2020.101943.

[58]   W. Förstner, and B. P. Wrobel, *Photogrammetric Computer Vision: Statistics, Geometry, Orientation and Reconstruction,* ISBN-13: 978-3319115498, Springer International Publishing AG, 2016.

[59]   Y. Chen, Y. Chen, and G. Wang,'Bundle Adjustment Revisited,' *Computer Vision and Pattern Recognition*, 2019, https://arxiv.org/pdf/1912.03858v1.pdf.

[60]   M. I. A. Lourakis and A. A. Argyros, 'SBA: A software package for generic sparse bundle adjustment,' *ACM Trans. Math. Softw.*, vol. 36, no. 1, 2009, Article 2, March 2009, 30 pages, doi: 10.1145/1486525.1486527.

[61]   M. I. A. Lourakis and A. A. Argyros, 'OpenCV wrapper for the sba sparse bundle adjustment library,' https://aur.archlinux.org/packages/cvsba/

[62]   A. Kenneth Levenberg, 'Method for the solution of certain non-linear problems in least squares,' *Quarterly of Applied Mathematics*, vol. 2, no. 2, pp. 164–168, 1944, (5 pages), Brown University.

[63]   A. Ranganathan, 'The Levenberg–Marquardt Algorithm,' https://sites.cs.ucsb.edu/~yfwang/courses/cs290i_mvg/pdf/LMA.pdf, 8th June 2004.

[64]   N. Sunderhauf and P. Protzel, 'Towards Using Sparse Bundle Adjustment for Robust Stereo Odometry in Outdoor Terrain,' In *Proceedings of Towards Autonomous Robotic Systems TAROS06*, Guildford, UK, 2006, pp. 206–213.

[65] P. Ozog and R. M. Eustice, 'On the importance of modeling camera cali-
      bration uncertainty in visual SLAM,' *Proceedings – IEEE International
      Conference on Robotics and Automation*, May 2013, doi: 10.1109/
      ICRA.2013.6631108.

[66] N. J. Higham, 'Cholesky factorization,' *WIREs Computational Statistics*,
      vol. 1, no. 2, pp. 251–254, 2009, doi: 10.1002/wics.18.

[67] M. L. A. Lourakis and A. A. Argyros, 'Is Levenberg–Marquardt the most
      efficient optimization algorithm for implementing bundle adjustment?,'
      Tenth IEEE International Conference on Computer Vision (ICCV'05),
      vol. 1, 2005, pp. 1526–1531, vol. 2, doi: 10.1109/ICCV.2005.128.

[68] C. Wu, S. Agarwal, B. Curless and S. M. Seitz, 'Multicore bundle
      adjustment,' *CVPR*, vol. 2011, pp. 3057–3064, 2011, doi: 10.1109/
      CVPR.2011.5995552.

[69] S. Agarwal, N. Snavely, S. M. Seitz, and R. Szeliski, 'Bundle Adjustment in
      the Large,' https://homes.cs.washington.edu/~sagarwal/bal.pdf

[70] M. I. A. Lourakis, 'Bundle Adjustment Gone Public,' Institute of Computer
      Science, Foundation for Research and Technology – Hellas. PRCV Colloquium
      Prague 2011, http://users.ics.forth.gr/~lourakis/sba/PRCV_colloq.pdf.

[71] M. Pierrot Deseilligny and I. Clery, 'APERO: an open source bundle
      adjusment software for automatic calibration and orientation of set of ima-
      ges,' *International Archives of the Photogrammetry, Remote Sensing and
      Spatial Information Sciences*, vol. XXXVIII-5/W16, 2011, ISPRS Trento
      2011 Workshop, 2–4 March 2011, Trento, Italy.

[72] K. Konolige, 'Sparse bundle adjustment.' British Machine Vision
      Conference, 2010.

[73] G. Briskin, A. Geva, E. Rivlin, and H. Rotstein, 'Estimating pose and motion
      using bundle adjustment and digital elevation model constraints,' *IEEE
      Transactions on Aerospace and Electronic Systems*, vol. 53, no. 4, pp. 1614–
      1624, 2017, doi: 10.1109/TAES.2017.2667819.

[74] R. Hänsch, I. Drude, O. Hellwich, 'Modern methods of bundle adjustment on
      the GPU,' *ISPRS Annals of the Photogrammetry, Remote Sensing and
      Spatial Information Sciences*, vol. III-3, 2016, pp.43–50, June 2016, doi:
      10.5194/isprs-annals-III-3-43-2016.

[75] B. Laurent, *Traitement d'Images et de Vidéos avec OpenCV 3 en C++*,
      ISBN-13: 978-2822705813, D-BOOKER éditions, 2017.

[76] S. Brahmbhatt, *Practical OpenCV*, ISBN-13: 978-1430260790, Apress, 2013.

[77] S. Sumikura, M Shibuya, and K Sakurada, 'OpenVSLAM: A Versatile Visual
      SLAM Framework.' In *Proceedings of the 27th ACM International Conference
      on Multimedia (MM'19)*, 2019, Association for Computing Machinery, New
      York, NY, USA, pp. 2292–2295. doi: 10.1145/3343031.3350539.

[78] S. Bianco, G. Ciocca, and D. Marelli, 'Evaluating the performance of
      structure from motion pipelines,' *Journal of Imaging*, vol. 4, no. 8, 98, 2018,
      https://doi.org/10.3390/jimaging4080098.

[79] Meshroom Release 0.1: https://readthedocs.org/projects/meshroom-manual/
      downloads/pdf/latest/

202   *Virtual reality and light field immersive video technologies*

[80] https://commons.wikimedia.org/wiki/File:Meshroom.png.

[81] L. Maier-Hein, P. Mountney, A. Bartoli, *et al.*, 'Optical techniques for 3D surface reconstruction in computer-assisted laparoscopic surgery,' *Medical Image Analysis*, vol. 17, no. 8, pp. 974–996, 2013, ISSN 1361-8415, doi: 10.1016/j.media.2013.04.003.

[82] S. Painer, 'Variation Based Dense 3D Reconstruction Using Photometric Invariants from Monocular Mini-Laparoscopic Sequences,' https://www.springer.com/cda/content/document/cda_downloaddocument/Figures_Painer_Sven_OnlinePlus.pdf?SGWID=0-0-45-1558070-p179444492, Springer Fachmedien Wiesbaden, 2015.

[83] Y. Furukawa and J. Ponce, 'Accurate camera calibration from multi-view stereo and bundle adjustment,' *2008 IEEE Conference on Computer Vision and Pattern Recognition*, pp. 1–8, 2008, doi: 10.1109/CVPR.2008.4587681

[84] W. Fang and L. Zheng, 'Distortion correction modeling method for zoom lens cameras with bundle adjustment,' *J. Opt. Soc. Korea,* vol. 20, pp. 140–149, 2016.

[85] T. Dang, C. Hoffmann, and C. Stiller, 'Continuous stereo self-calibration by camera parameter tracking,' *IEEE Transactions on Image Processing*, vol. 18, no. 7, pp. 1536–1550, 2009, doi:10.1109/TIP.2009.2017824.

[86] L. Bonde, A. Brumfield, and Y. Yuan. 'Error Minimization in 3-Dimensional Model Reconstruction Using Sparse Bundle Adjustment and the Levenberg-Marquardt Algorithm on Stereo Camera Pairs,' *Midwest Instruction and Computing Symposium*, 2014.

[87] C. Kurz, T. Thormählen, and H. P. Seidel, 'Bundle Adjustment for Stereoscopic 3D.' In: Gagalowicz A., Philips W. (eds) *Computer Vision/Computer Graphics Collaboration Techniques. MIRAGE 2011*. Lecture Notes in Computer Science, vol. 6930. Springer, Berlin, Heidelberg. 2011, doi: 10.1007/978-3-642-24136-9_1.

[88] S. Ji, Z. Qin, J. Shan, and M. Lu, 'Panoramic SLAM from a multiple fisheye camera rig,' *ISPRS Journal of Photogrammetry and Remote Sensing*, vol. 159, pp. 169–183, 2020.

[89] C. Albl, *PanCam Bundle Adjustment*, Master Thesis, Luleå University of Technology, 2011.

[90] Y. Li, Y. Cai, D. Wen, and Y. Yang, 'Optimization of radial distortion self-calibration for structure from motion from uncalibrated UAV images,' *2016 23rd International Conference on Pattern Recognition (ICPR)*, 2016, pp. 3721–3726, doi: 10.1109/ICPR.2016.7900213.

[91] C. Stamatopoulos, 'Orientation and Calibration of Long Focal Length Cameras in Digital Close-Range Photogrammetry,' PhD thesis, The University of Melbourne, 2011.

[92] V. Devecseri, L. Raj, R. T. Fekete, 'Comparison of different multiple camera calibration methods,' *XV International PhD Workshop*, OWD2013, 19–22 October 2013.

[93]   A. Karakottas, N. Zioulis, A. Doumanglou, *et al.*, 'Xr360: A Toolkit for Mixed 360 and 3d Productions,' *2020 IEEE International Conference on Multimedia and Expo Workshops (ICMEW)*, 2020, pp. 1–6, doi: 10.1109/ICMEW46912.2020.9105984.

[94]   www.UGOsansH.com.

[95]   R. Mur-Artal, J. M. M. Montiel, and J. D. Tardós, 'ORB-SLAM: a versatile and accurate monocular slam system,' *IEEE Transactions on Robotics*, vol. 31, no. 5, pp. 1147–1163, 2015, doi: 10.1109/TRO.2015.2463671.

[96]   M. Nitsche, 'Appearance-based teach and repeat navigation method for unmanned aerial vehicles,' Universidad de Buenos Aires Facultad de Ciencias Exactas y Naturales Departamento de Computación, 2016.

[97]   C. Pingyuan, Y. Fuzhan, and C. Hutao, 'Research on Autonomous Navigation of Lunar Rovers for the Moon Exploration,' *2006 IEEE International Conference on Robotics and Biomimetics*, 2006, pp. 1042–1047, doi: 10.1109/ROBIO.2006.340372.

[98]   S. B. Goldberg, M. W. Maimone and L. Matthies, 'Stereo vision and rover navigation software for planetary exploration,' *Proceedings, IEEE Aerospace Conference*, 2002, p. 5, doi: 10.1109/AERO.2002.1035370.

[99]   J. N. Maki, J. F. Bell III, E. Kenneth, *et al.*, 'The Mars Exploration Rover engineering cameras,' *Journal of Geophysical Research E: Planets,* vol. 108, no. E12, 2003, doi: 10.1029/2002JE002038.

[100]   B. Godard, F. Budnik, G. Bellei, P. Muñoz, and T. Morley. 'Multi-arc Orbit Determination to determine Rosetta trajectory and 67P physical parameters,' *International Symposium on Space Flight Dynamics*, 2016.

[101]   G. Arantes, E. M. Rocco, I. M. da Fonseca, and S. Theil, 'Far and proximity maneuvers of a constellation of service satellites and autonomous pose estimation of customer satellite using machine vision,' *Acta Astronautica*, vol. 66, nos. 9–10, pp. 1493–1505, 2010, ISSN 0094-5765, doi: 10.1016/j.actaastro.2009.11.022.

[102]   K. Di, Y. Liu, B. Liu, M. Peng, and W. Hu, 'A self-calibration bundle adjustment method for photogrammetric processing of Chang 'E-2 stereo lunar imagery,' *IEEE Transactions on Geoscience and Remote Sensing*, vol. 52, no. 9, pp. 5432–5442, 2014, doi: 10.1109/TGRS.2013.2288932.

[103]   J. Schneider, 'Visual Odometry and Sparse Scene Reconstruction for UAVs with a Multi-Fisheye Camera System,' Universitäts- und Landesbibliothek Bonn, 2019.

[104]   D. Fox, *Sebastian Thrun, and Wolfram Burgard Probabilistic Robotics*, ISBN: 9780262201629672, MIT Press, August 2005.

[105]   P. Słowak, and P. Kaniewski, 'LIDAR-based SLAM implementation using Kalman filter,' *Proceedings Volume 11442, Radioelectronic Systems Conference*, 2019; 114420N, 2020, doi: 10.1117/12.2564818.

[106]   G. Grisetti, R. Kümmerle, C. Stachniss, and W. Burgard, 'A tutorial on graph-based SLAM,' *IEEE Intelligent Transportation Systems Magazine*, vol. 2, no. 4, pp. 31–43, 2010, doi: 10.1109/MITS.2010.939925.

[107]   F. Fraundorfer and D. Scaramuzza, 'Visual odometry : Part II: matching, robustness, optimization, and applications,' *IEEE Robotics & Automation Magazine*, vol. 19, no. 2, pp. 78–90, 2012, doi: 10.1109/MRA.2012.2182810.

[108]   M. Pollefeys, D. Nistér, J. M. Frahm, *et al.*, 'Detailed real-time urban 3D reconstruction from video,' *Int J Comput Vis.*, vol. 78, pp. 143–167, 2008, doi: 10.1007/s11263-007-0086-4.

Chapter 12

Towards 6DoF with image-based rendering

In previous chapter, we have seen how we can perform a 6DoF VR navigation by representing the scene in a point cloud format. In the present chapter, we will rather use an image-based approach, interpolating the images from various camera views into a virtual view that can be presented to the user. Though this process is based on images only, the inclusion of depth images transforms the data into an implicit point cloud (or even mesh) format, very well handled by the 3D graphics pipeline of the Graphical Processing Unit (GPU), cf. Chapter 3.

12.1 Introduction

The philosophy of image-based rendering (IBR) consists in avoiding any explicit 3D reconstruction of the scene, in contrast to point clouds we have covered in previous sections: all the views that give the feeling of immersion and/or free navigation should be natively present in the content representation.

For instance, stereograms, as in the example of Figure 12.1, are a typical IBR instantiation: lenticular lenses project a couple/dozen of images in various directions, in such a way that the spectator standing in a comfort zone in front of the stereogram will capture the correct stereoscopic pair of images to perceive the scene in 3D, without wearing stereo glasses [1]. Of course, this cannot be shown in the static images that have been captured from such stereogram in Figure 12.1, but one can nevertheless observe that there are parallax changes, for example the varying distance between the front bag and eagle badge in Figure 12.1(d)–(f).

How such a stereogram is created is fully explained in [2]. The main idea is that each pixel underneath one lens corresponds to a specific projection direction, so that crossing light rays representing the same pixel over various viewing directions provide the perception of a 3D point in space, as shown in Figure 12.2(a) for two viewing directions (stereoscopy) and Figure 12.2 (b) for five. A nice video prototype of such principle with even more views projected from the front to a diffusive screen has been developed in [1].

Today, we call these light field displays because they emit 'the field of light' that surrounds us, but decades ago, these were called autostereoscopic displays [3]. They were by then fashionable, and even considered for 3D cinema theatres, cf. [4], but like stereoscopic 3D cinema, they did not get a great success. For small single-user displays, however, there seem a to be somewhat a revival of these light field displays [5]. Of course, projecting all these images from a screen having a small form factor is really an engineering challenge. Therefore, such displays often impose a constraint that

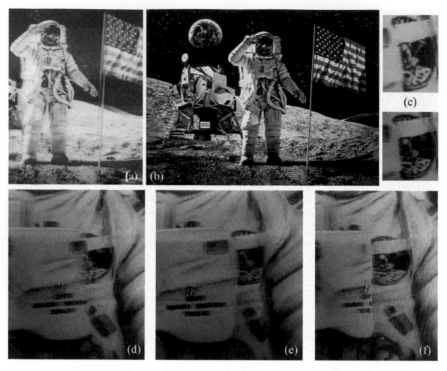

Figure 12.1   *Stereogram (a) from artistic image (b) from David Penfound with different views on the scene to give an illusion of parallax, as exemplified in (c) to (f) on Apollo's 11 badge showing the colourful eagle. (b) Courtesy: David Penfound ©*

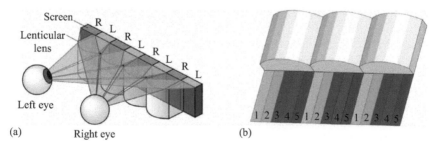

Figure 12.2   *Lenticular screen with creating two views (a) and five views (b) in horizontal parallax only. Reproduced from Public Domain resources (a) from [6] and (b) from [7]*

parallax is only visible in the horizontal direction; the one in which our eyes (and brain) perceive depth. They are then called horizontal parallax only (HPO) light field displays. A professional product example is shown in Figure 12.3, where one clearly observes different perspective views from different viewing positions.

Figure 12.3   Large light field display. Courtesy: ETRO-VUB, Vrije Universiteit Brussel

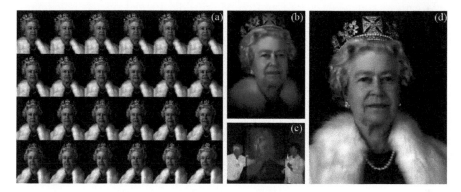

Figure 12.4   Input views (a) for creating the holographic stereogram of Queen Elizabeth II (b,c) and a stereoscopic anaglyph print-out (d). Reproduced from [8]

Of course, a VR application with synthetic content would rather use a point cloud, but when one only has a couple of pictures of the scene insufficient to apply a full 3D reconstruction, as in Section 11.4.1, then IBR is the only option left. The question to ask is whether IBR provides sufficient quality? After all, the structure of an object may look very different from one viewpoint to another, and can image warping deal with that correctly?

Moreover, even though the views look very similar with only slight perspective changes from one view to the next, it does not mean that a simple image warp can go from one view to the next correctly. An image warp will indeed miss all occlusions and disocclusions that may occur when background objects disappear behind or appear from behind a foreground object. IBR is therefore much more than just a couple of images that are warped to create all other images in-between. To have a correct rendering, all the views should be correctly captured and restored. This can be a painful process when increasing the number of views to a few hundreds of them, like in the example of Figure 12.4, a holographic stereogram of Queen Elizabeth II, made by Rob Murray in 2004 for her jubilee [9–12].

By abuse of language, this is often called a hologram, but in fact, it is a stereogram where the refractive lenses (the ones used by photographers, but in a smaller form factor) have been replaced by diffractive lenses to create the same effect as in a stereogram, but at much higher density, typically 400 to 800 different views over the viewing range. We will return to the various holographic modalities in Section 12.8 to make the reader understand their differences; let us now rather study the impact of these hundreds of input views on the acquisition setup. If instead of hundreds of views, only a dozen would be needed, the setup would be simple: just use one camera per view to render, a bit like the first MIT stereograms, back in the 1990s [13]. But things get a little bit more involved when hundreds of views are needed.

Reference [14] recommends that when a scene is at 1 m distance, the camera that is capturing the scene should be displaced mm by mm from one view to the next for obtaining a good IBR of the holographic stereogram. This calls for a camera setup with a single camera sliding on a rail, as Rob Murray did in making the hologram of Figure 12.4. Indeed, for such a small inter-camera distance, it is impossible to physically put various cameras side by side to capture the scene in one shot. Of course, the sliding camera approach calls for a perfectly static scene during the full acquisition time, which may represent several seconds. The obvious question now rises: 'Can't we apply a trick to increase the inter-camera distance such that we may capture the scene in a single, instantaneous shot?'. If the answer to this question is positive, then we may use a synchronized camera array to capture the scene in one shot, even though it might be highly dynamic and rapidly changing. The answer to this question lies in an extension of the Nyquist sampling theorem, and its relation to depth acquisition, which will lead to the concept of depth image-based rendering (DIBR). More details will be given in Section 12.7.2; for now, we take for granted that DIBR is possible with a limited number of cameras positioned at least a couple of centimetres (cm), or even tens of cm away from each other. In such settings, we can compare images from different cameras and fuse them to give an illusion of perspective changes when moving the virtual viewpoint. Let us first introduce some preparatory concepts, explained in the following sections.

12.2   Finding relative camera positions

12.2.1   *Epipolar geometry*

The concept of epipolar geometry is important in any application using more than one camera: it is the cornerstone for extracting the camera extrinsics, that is their relative poses, without which it would not be possible to somehow fuse or extract information from multiple cameras.

In the setup of Figure 12.5, two cameras capture the scene from different viewpoints. A 3D point P in space is projected into the 2D image planes of both cameras: point P_1 in the first camera, point P_2 in the second camera. Inversely, one can reconstruct point P in space by triangulation: first draw the rays R_1 and R_2 that connect points P_1 and P_2 to the camera centres C_1 and C_2, then find the intersection point of R_1 and R_2, which will be point P.

As a matter of terminology, the plane connecting P, C_1 and C_2 (and hence also passing through P_1 and P_2) is called the epipolar plane (EP). Taking another 3D point

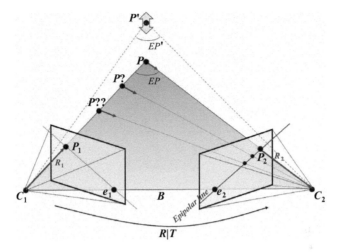

Figure 12.5 Epipolar geometry observing a point P from two cameras

P' lying slightly above P creates another epipolar plane, represented in Figure 12.5 as EP'. The epipolar planes EP and EP' share a common baseline B, connecting the two camera centres C_1 and C_2. Observe how this baseline B is fixed. Moreover, it intersects the two image planes in points e_1 and e_2, which are called epipoles. They also have an important meaning in epipolar geometry, as we will see later.

Having set up this geometrical framework, the question now raises whether there are some physical invariants that might help us solve some correspondence problems. For instance, having the projection point P_1 in the first camera plane, where might the corresponding projection point P_2 lie in the second camera plane? This is not a trivial question, but – as we will see in a minute – the answer lies in epipolar geometry.

To answer this question, one must be aware that we do not have any knowledge of the exact position of the original 3D point P in space; actually, this is something we are looking for. We know, however, that its projection in the first camera is point P_1, and that P should be somewhere on the ray R_1, since this is also the ray that projects P to P_1 in the first camera. Where exactly P is lying on this ray R_1 is not known (represented by question marks in the figure); it will depend on its depth, which again is unknown. Nevertheless, what we do know is that – for whatever position of P on R_1 – a corresponding projection in the second camera will appear. By visual inspection of Figure 12.5, we even observe that all these hypothetical projections will appear somewhere on a line: the projection line of R_1 into the second camera's image plane. This line in the second camera is called the epipolar line, corresponding to P_1 in the first camera.

Summarized, we have now found a relationship between a point in the first camera, and where the corresponding point in the second camera might lie according to the physics of image perspective projection: it must lie somewhere on the epipolar line. This is an important geometrical invariant that gives us the possibility to restrict our search area for point P_2 to a single epipolar line. In the next section, we will construct the formula corresponding to this line.

Meanwhile, observe that the epipolar line depends on the position of point P_1 in the first camera: when P_1 goes up (because point P in space goes up to P', for instance), so will its ray R_1, as well as its projection into the second image. A remarkable characteristic is that all these epipolar lines intersect each other in the epipole e_2. Indeed, whatever the inclination of the epipolar plane EP on which ray R_1 and its projection – the epipolar line – lie, it always turns around the baseline B, with its epipole e_2 being the spinning point for all epipolar lines in the second camera.

Of course, a similar story holds when choosing P_2 in the second camera as the starting point and searching for the corresponding epipolar line in the first camera. Epipolar geometry is hence somewhat symmetric between cameras.

Box 12.1:   Nonlinear epipolar geometry

Epipolar geometry does not always yield linear equations. For instance, think of cylindrical projection cameras where the image is not projected onto a plane like with pinhole cameras, but rather onto a cylinder. Drawing the figure that tells how a point P will be projected onto two cylindrical projection cameras will reveal sine waves as epipolar lines. When capturing the surroundings with a fisheye camera, epipolar conics will be formed, cf. [15].

Interestingly, linear cameras can still give something else than pinhole cameras. For instance, satellite images follow an affine epipolar geometry, not a perspective projection, since all their projective rays are almost parallel. The reader is referred to [16,17] for more insights.

12.2.2   Rotation and translation from the essential and fundamental matrices

Knowing the basic principles of epipolar geometry, we now proceed in finding the rotation R and translation T from Figure 12.5. R and T are in fact the transformations needed to go from the left camera coordinates to the right one. Inversely, to go back from the right camera to the left one, we apply the inverse rotation, which corresponds to the transposed matrix (the matrix is orthonormal, hence inverse and transpose are equal), and the inverse translation, which is the translation with a minus sign. By definition of the epipolar plane, point P_1 lies in the same plane as the translation vector T (or its inverse $-T$). Likewise, point P_2 – and also the one turned with a rotation towards the coordinates of the left camera, that is $R^t.P_2$ – lies in the same plane as the translation vector T. P_1, P_2 (after rotation) and T are hence coplanar [18–21], which we are now going to express mathematically.

Note that the cross product of T and P_2 is a vector that is orthogonal to the epipolar plane holding P_1, P_2 and T. We can thus express their coplanarity by saying that P_2 (after rotation with R^t) is perpendicular to $(T \times P_2)$, by claiming that their scalar product is zero:

$$\overline{(R^t \cdot P_2)} \cdot \overline{(T \times P_1)} = 0 \tag{12.1}$$

We now replace the scalar product notation by the corresponding column vector notation, which requires to add a transpose in the first factor:

$$(R^t \cdot P_2)^t \cdot (T \times P_1) = 0 \tag{12.2}$$

where P_1 and P_2 are 2D points (in images), but expressed in their 3D space coordinates, with the z-coordinate equal to the focal length f in the pinhole camera model:

$$P_i = \begin{pmatrix} x_i \\ y_i \\ f \end{pmatrix} \tag{12.3}$$

The transpose of a product is the product of transpose of its factors; hence we obtain

$$P_2^t \cdot R \cdot (T \times P_1) = 0 \tag{12.4}$$

The cross-product between vectors is now transformed into the cross matrix of the first vector multiplied by the second one. We so obtain:

$$P_2^t \cdot R \cdot (T_{[\times]} \cdot P_1) = 0 \tag{12.5}$$

with

$$T_{[\times]} = \begin{pmatrix} 0 & -T_z & T_y \\ T_z & 0 & -T_x \\ -T_y & T_x & 0 \end{pmatrix} \tag{12.6}$$

Rearranging the brackets in (12.5) yields:

$$P_2^t \cdot (R \cdot T_{[\times]}) \cdot P_1 = 0 \tag{12.7}$$

which clearly couples points P_1 and P_2 (their 3×1 column vectors from (12.3)) together, through a simple equation:

$$P_2^t \cdot E \cdot P_1 = 0 \tag{12.8}$$

where E is a 3×3 matrix, called the essential matrix, which is the product of R and T.

Note that a similar expression holds between P_1 and P_2 in the opposite order. Indeed, taking the transpose of (12.8), one obtains:

$$P_1^t \cdot E^t \cdot P_2 = 0 \tag{12.9}$$

which holds the transpose of the essential matrix, thus also inversing the order of (and transposing) the R and T matrices of the essential matrices in (12.7). In fact, which camera is taken as the reference, and where the rotations and translation refer to, has an influence on the exact shape of the essential matrix (the transpose or not). In practice, this is a delicate issue in numerical stability, and since anyway decomposing E into its rotation and translation matrices R and T involves four different possibilities to verify [22], we do not further go into the details of the forward or backward referencing issues of R and T; just keep in mind that in practice one must be careful.

The mathematical derivations so far assumed that the pinhole cameras were perfect with the principal point perfectly in the centre of the image. When this is not true, the essential matrix E is replaced by the fundamental matrix F that holds the intrinsic matrices K_1 and K_2 of both cameras, and thus also the focal length that is now absorbed into F. We finally obtain:

$$\begin{aligned} P_2^t \cdot F \cdot P_1 &= 0 \\ F &= K_2^t \cdot E \cdot K_1 \end{aligned} \qquad (12.10)$$

which is literally the fundamental equation used in epipolar geometry.

Knowing the essential or fundamental matrix, one can find R and T by a singular value decomposition (SVD) of the essential matrix, as explained constructively in [22]. Here we just give the main ideas, without focusing on the forward or backward referencing interpretation issues mentioned before.

The SVD of E can be written as

$$E = U \cdot \Sigma \cdot V^t \qquad (12.11)$$

where Σ holds two identical, non-zero eigenvalues (without proof), which allows to find R and T as one of the four possible configurations (cf. forward or backward references of R and T) to be [23,24]:

$$\begin{aligned} T_{[\times]} &= U \cdot (\pm W) \cdot \Sigma \cdot U^t \\ R &= U \cdot (\pm W)^{-1} \cdot V^t \end{aligned} \qquad (12.12)$$

where

$$W = \begin{pmatrix} 0 & \pm 1 & 0 \\ \mp 1 & 0 & 0 \\ 0 & 0 & 1 \end{pmatrix}$$

Finding the rotation and translation separately is clearly more difficult than estimating the essential or fundamental matrix they originate from. Quaternions well representing rotations might help in this endeavour, as shown in [25,26].

As a final remark, finding explicitly R and T individually is often not really needed, as will be shown in the next section. It can, however, be useful when one wants to rectify the images of two cameras, that is transform them such that they are virtually taken from two perfectly parallel cameras. In that case, we might take half of the rotation R to be applied on both cameras in opposite directions to bring the cameras parallel to each other (other methods exist). This is equivalent to applying a homography on the images, a subject we have encountered previously in Section 8.2 of Chapter 8. More details can be found in good registration/rectification tutorials with source code, for example, see [27–29]. Furthermore, the OpenCV library provides some useful functions with this functionality, like findFundamentalMat, stereoRectify and stereoRectifyUncalibrated.

12.2.3 Epipolar line equation

Thanks to the fundamental matrix equation, we can find the equation of the epipolar line. Remember that it is expressed in homogeneous coordinates, where we can arbitrarily choose the w-coordinate to be one (the other two coordinates will then directly correspond to the physical coordinates), yielding in simple matrix form:

$$
\begin{pmatrix} x_2 \\ y_2 \\ 1 \end{pmatrix}^t \cdot \begin{pmatrix} f_{11} & f_{12} & f_{13} \\ f_{21} & f_{22} & f_{23} \\ f_{31} & f_{32} & f_{33} \end{pmatrix} \cdot \begin{pmatrix} x_1 \\ y_1 \\ 1 \end{pmatrix} = 0 \tag{12.13}
$$

Filling in numerical values for the coordinates of a chosen point P_1, the last two matrices of (12.1) will correspond to numerical values; let us represent them by F_x, F_y and F_z, obtaining:

$$
\begin{pmatrix} x_2 \\ y_2 \\ 1 \end{pmatrix}^t \cdot \begin{pmatrix} F_x \\ F_y \\ F_z \end{pmatrix} = 0 \tag{12.14}
$$

$$
\begin{pmatrix} x_2 & y_2 & 1 \end{pmatrix} \cdot \begin{pmatrix} F_x \\ F_y \\ F_z \end{pmatrix} = 0 \tag{12.15}
$$

$$
F_x \cdot x_2 + F_y \cdot y_2 + F_z = 0 \tag{12.16}
$$

which clearly exhibits a linear relationship between the (x,y) 2D coordinates of point P_2, corresponding to a straight line. This is the epipolar line equation, which – as said in the previous section – does not need to explicitly separate the rotation R and translation T from the essential or fundamental matrix.

Equation (12.10) also provides the equation of the epipole e_2, after a simple interpretation. Since for any point P_1 the same epipole e_2 is obtained (here we replace P_2 by e_2 in (12.10)), the (x_1, y_1) coordinates do not matter, ending up in the equation for the epipole:

$$
F \cdot e_2 = 0 \tag{12.17}
$$

12.2.4 Extrinsics with checkerboard calibration

Chapter 4 already presented some camera calibration principles, but these were merely focused on its intrinsics. In a multi-camera setup, it may be useful to also know the relative camera poses, that is the rotations and translations required to move from one camera view to the neighboring camera. This process is also called camera registration, because one 'registers' the relative position of the camera, compared to a reference coordinates system.

Registration is typically done with epipolar geometry and a checkerboard. Checking how the corner points undergo perspective transformations in the various camera views, it is possible to find the rotation and translations required to go from

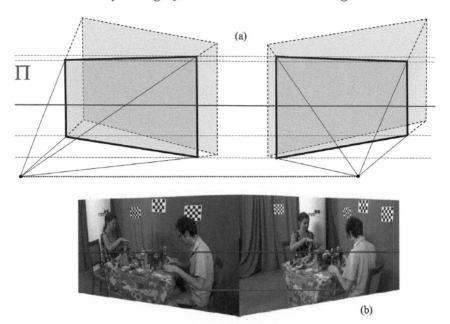

Figure 12.6   Camera rectification with a plane Π cutting the view frustums (a) and
features on the same horizontal line in the rectified images (b),
courtesy: Poznan University of Technology, Poland

the checkerboard's position to the respective camera positions. In Section 8.6, we have already seen a similar method for pose estimation using homographies, which are the 2D projective transformations corresponding to the equations in 3D epipolar geometry. In a similar way, we obtain the results of Figure 12.6.

Once the registration is done, it is also possible to 'rectify' the image to create a new set of images that all have respective, horizontal epipolar lines, as if they were taken by perfectly aligned cameras with identical intrinsics and parallel optical axes. Inversely rotating and translating the camera views will indeed bring their respecting views virtually aligned along the z-axis of the central checker-board. Even stronger, according to Section 8.4, it is not even required to have a checkerboard: the DLT and RANSAC algorithms allow to efficiently track a set of points in space (hence, not necessarily lying on a planar surface) to be able to perform these operations solely with the real scene content. This is called self-calibration.

Box 12.2:   Rectification in 3D cinema

The rectification process makes a lot of sense when using stereo cameras, because it is then much easier to perform the stereo matching along horizontal lines, as will be explained in a large part of the following sections.

Rectification is also very helpful in 3D cinema, where a stereo rig captures the scene, but nothing guarantees that the stereo cameras are well aligned. Even worse, when changing the focal length of the cameras (e.g. for zooming) it might happen that cameras that were originally perfectly aligned optically, suddenly lose this alignment, for instance, the left image might be positioned a bit lower than the right image. If nothing is done, showing this pair of images to spectators will cause a lot of eyestrain and even heavy pain. Therefore, in 3D cinema shooting, there is often a need to do rectification either during acquisition with a closed-loop control system [30] or in the post-processing stages.

12.2.5   *Extrinsics with sparse bundle adjustment*

We have seen in Section 11.3 how sparse bundle adjustment (SBA) allows one to find the camera poses while reconstructing the scene in 3D. Often, SBA is used mainly for the former, where a crude camera calibration is refined by matching features used in SBA. The application of PhotoTourism [31,32] uses SBA for this purpose, while only allowing rapid transitions from one camera view to the next. To be able to go one step further in also rendering intermediate views, special view synthesis methods must be used, as we will explain in the next sections. For this, we first need to talk about depth estimation.

12.2.6   *Depth estimation*

Depth estimation is a family of techniques where instead of sensing the depth with a light source, the depth is estimated by comparing various images of the scene taken from different viewpoints. To simplify our discussion, we assume that a single camera is moved along a line, with its objective perfectly perpendicular to this line. This may be obtained by simple image processing known as rectification. In such conditions, objects close to the camera will move more than background objects when jumping from one camera view to the next one; this is called disparity. The next sections will provide various methods of estimating that pixel disparity.

12.2.7   *Stereo matching*

The most straightforward technique of depth estimation consists of comparing two images, as we humans do with our eyes: the difference between the left and right eye images reveals the disparity. The estimated disparity is then driven from the match between pixels or neighborhoods thereof over these two images. To ease the matching problem, the image pair is calibrated and rectified, so that matching features lie on the same horizontal line over the two images. However, for image pairs that are not rectified, the matching point will not be necessarily on the same line, but rather follow epipolar lines, as we will explain in Section 12.2. The basic matching principles, however, will not change over these two configurations, as long as 'we follow the lines' we just spoke of.

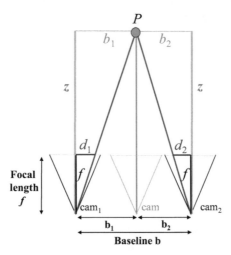

Figure 12.7   Relation between depth z and disparity d

Once we find matching features, their relative displacement called the disparity d can be estimated, out of which one can deduce the depth z, as shown in Figure 12.7, according to

$$d = b\frac{f}{z} \tag{12.18}$$

where f is the focal length and b is the distance between the cameras' optical centres, called the baseline. Here, for simplicity, we show three cameras, the middle one being a virtual camera with an optical axis pointing straight to a point P of interest in space.

Equation (12.18) is easily obtained by observing at the left side in Figure 12.7 two triangles that are similar, with sides (b_1, z) and (d_1, f), respectively, yielding:

$$\frac{b_1}{z} = \frac{d_1}{f} \tag{12.19}$$

Likewise, we find similar triangles with sides (b_2, z) and (d_2, f), yielding:

$$\frac{b_2}{z} = \frac{d_2}{f} \tag{12.20}$$

Expressing the b_i values as a function of the d_i values, we obtain

$$b_1 = \frac{z}{f} \cdot d_1 \tag{12.21}$$

$$b_2 = \frac{z}{f} \cdot d_2 \tag{12.22}$$

After summing left and right sides, we get:

$$(b_1 + b_2) = \frac{z}{f} \cdot (d_1 + d_2) \qquad (12.23)$$

which, by definition of the disparity, yields (12.18).

Clearly, depth and disparity are inverse proportional to each other. This is an important feature to keep in mind.

12.2.8   Depth quantization

Let us for now assume we have found the disparity of a point (or many points) in space, by matching the left-right image pair pixels, in a magical way. The solution will always somehow involve rays that are traced from the camera centre, through the pixel, to the point in space, yielding the very regular pattern shown in Figure 12.8 (here shown for half of the camera's field of view and mirrored symmetrically). Obviously, whatever disparity estimation is used, the N levels of uniform quantization in disparity expressed as an integer number of pixels ($d = 1$ pixel, 2 pixels, 3 pixels, etc.) will lead to a non-uniform quantization of the corresponding depth levels. For instance, the curve S_1 that corresponds to a surface in bird's eye view is so far in the background that any point on this curve/surface will not cause any additional pixel shift between camera A and camera B, even if we bend and displace S_1, as long as it stays within the top horizontal band of Figure 12.8. In general, each feature within a horizontal band ΔZ will always be allocated to a single depth value.

If we look at the curve/surface S_2, we observe it passes through various bands, indicated by a colour difference. Thus, S_2 will get different depth values; in a sense,

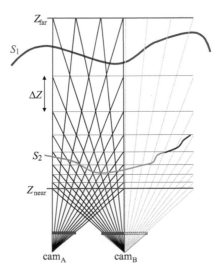

Figure 12.8   Non-uniform depth quantization [33]

its depth profile is more precise. This is also what happens in the human visual system, where we can see subtle depth differences between foreground objects, while beyond 3 or 10 m it starts to become difficult to see depth differences without other cues, like motion parallax [34].

To account for this inverse proportional behaviour of depth quantization (in line with (12.18)) between the z_{near} and z_{far} depth planes, depth values are often represented in the following way [33]:

$$Z(d) = \frac{1}{\frac{d}{N-1}\left(\frac{1}{z_{\text{near}}} - \frac{1}{z_{\text{far}}}\right) + \frac{1}{z_{\text{far}}}} \tag{12.24}$$

where the $1/Z$ terms express the transformation of depth Z to disparity d, transforming a non-uniform depth distribution into a uniform distribution of disparities over N layers.

In fact, very often, people speak about depth, while they actually mean disparity. In passive depth estimation techniques (with depth sensing with light), disparity is king. Remember that in depth sensing, it was rather the depth that was king.

12.2.9   Stereo matching and cost volumes

Let us now take the example of Figure 12.9 where we have a scene with a house, a garden and the sun in bird's eye view in (a) and in frontal view in (b), to see how we can actually perform a stereo matching that will yield the disparity values of all pixels. The garden being hidden behind the house, we cannot see it in the frontal views. That is why we only see the house and the sun in Figure 12.9(b).

We are now going to really estimate the disparity for each pixel in the image, comparing somehow the left-right image pair. Since the sun is at infinity in the background, its true disparity (which we seek) is zero, hence the sun is not moving from the left to the right image. This will be an important clue to find its disparity in the estimation process. In contrast, the house is lying in the foreground, so it must have a non-zero disparity. The reader can easily verify that when one jumps from the left camera to the right camera, the foreground objects move in the opposite direction in the image, resulting in the house being moved to the left in Figure 12.9(b).

Let us now try to find the disparity of the top of the roof. One would think this is an easy challenge: we take the colour of that pixel (here red) and we seek for the same colour at the same height in the other image. Doing so, however, one might find another pixel of the same colour, not belonging to the roof at all, and hence mistakenly extracting the corresponding disparity... that would be completely wrong. To overcome this problem, instead of looking for the same pixel colour over the two images, one rather uses the pixel colour and its surrounding context, expressed in the colour of its neighbouring pixels. This is shown in Figure 12.9(b), where not only the roof top is observed, but also the surrounding pixels, effectively creating an $N \times N$ (here, 3×3, but in practice, it is often equal to 5×5) window around the pixel under test.

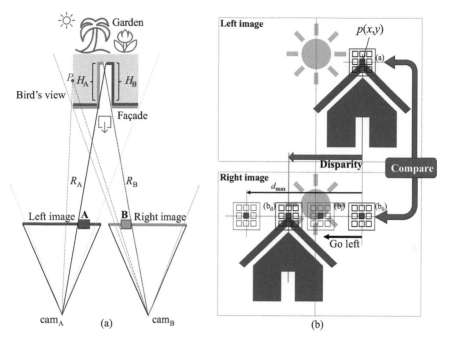

Figure 12.9   A scene with a house, a garden and the sun in bird's eye view (a) and in frontal view (b) looking through two cameras

For the rooftop, we start from pixel p at coordinates (x,y) in the left image, take a surrounding 3×3 window of pixels, and this is the pixel cluster we will compare with the pixels of the right image, to estimate the disparity of pixel p. A simple approach is to test various disparity candidates one after the other, until we find the right one. We do this by first assuming that the disparity might be equal to zero, in which case the same pixel cluster must be found in the right image at exactly the same position. This is represented by the 3×3 window at position (b_0) in the bottom image of Figure 12.9 (b). We compare this window of pixels with the one in the left image at the top of Figure 12.9(b) ... and we observe no match: in the left image we see the top of the roof; in the right image we are in blue sky. Consequently, our assumption that the disparity is zero was wrong. We hence continue our search by now assuming that the disparity would be one. We thus shift the pixel window one pixel to the left in the right image, and we compare again the windows (a) and (b_1). Again, there is no match. We thus continue our adventure, moving again the pixel window one more pixel to the left, and again, and again, each time matching the windows (a) and (b_i). After a while, we finally find the window (b_d) that matches well with (a), and so conclude that the pixel p has the corresponding disparity d, that is the number of times we had to move one pixel to the left in the right image in order to match the windows in the left and right images. Of course, the disparity must stay below a maximum disparity d_{max}, expected in the image and corresponding to the Z_{near} value in Figure 12.8. Repeating this process for each pixel in the left image, comparing it with candidate pixel windows in the right image, we end up in estimating the disparity for each pixel.

The interested reader remains with the open question which metrics we use to match the pixels in the respective windows of Figure 12.9(b). One may use cross-correlation or any other comparative metric for the surroundings of the left and right pixels. Here are some popular measures often used in stereo matching: *sum of absolute differences* (SAD), *sum of squared differences* (SSD), *normalized SSD* (NSSD) and *normalized cross correlation* (NCC):

$$SAD(x,y) = \sum_{x,y \in W} |I_R(x,y) - I_L(x - d, y)| \qquad (12.25)$$

$$SSD(x,y) = \sum_{x,y \in W} (I_R(x,y) - I_L(x - d, y))^2 \qquad (12.26)$$

$$NSSD(x,y) = \sum_{x,y \in W} \left(\frac{I_R(x,y) - I_L(xd,y)}{\sum_{x,y \in W} (I_R(x,y) - I_L(x,y))^2} - \frac{I_R(x,y) - I_L(x - d, y)}{\sum_{x,y \in W} (I_R(x,y) - I_L(x - d, y))^2} \right)^2 \qquad (12.27)$$

$$NCC(x,y) = \frac{\sum_{x,y \in W} (I_R(x,y) - I_L(x,y))(I_R(x,y) - I_L(x - d, y))}{\sqrt{\sum_{x,y \in W} (I_R(x,y) - I_L(x,y))^2 (I_R(x,y) - I_L(x - d, y))^2}} \qquad (12.28)$$

where I_R and I_L are the intensity value of a pixel at the coordinate of (x,y) in right and left images, respectively. Symbol d is the disparity value that is the solution we are seeking. The region where the similarity measure is calculated is represented by W.

We are stressing again that for finding the disparity of a pixel in the left image, we need to evaluate the matching cost on various windows in the right image, positioned from candidate disparity 0 to $d_{\max}$. Therefore, in Figure 12.10, each pixel $p(x,y)$ has various depth or disparity candidates d_i that are represented along the depth axis in Figure 12.10(b). Doing this for all pixels creates the cost volume of Figure 12.10(b). When looking at one specific pixel, the curve obtained along its d-direction indicates the match between the pixels (x_l,y) and $(x_r,y) = (x_l\text{-}d,y)$ for that specific value of the candidate disparity d. The minimum along the curve corresponds to the best match between the left and right pixel under test and the corresponding d-value is kept as the estimated disparity of the pixel (x_l, y). This minimum operation is performed over all pixels, finding the disparity of all pixels, and equivalently their depth.

Mathematically, we aim at finding the parameter value d that minimizes the matching cost that has been selected from the table above, yielding:

$$d(x,y) = \text{argmin 'MATCHING-COST-FUNCTION'} (x,y,d) \qquad (12.29)$$

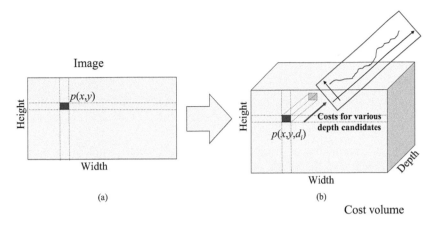

Figure 12.10 Cost volume in stereo matching

It is a winner-takes-all (WTA) approach that is equivalent to a likelihood-based solution, that is maximizing likelihood (ML). After the minimization process, estimating the disparity over all pixels, additional refinement filters can be applied to further smooth the estimated depth. Such refinements can be done by using usual image filters to remove the noise or based on checking the reliability of each disparity [35]. In the latter case, the reliability check can be performed by projecting the right view to the left view, measuring their difference. If the difference is larger than a threshold, we can eliminate those disparities, that are labelled as unreliable or possibly as occluded regions, as explained in the next section.

Box 12.3: Parallelization needs

Parallelization is an important issue in stereo matching because many operations are involved. For instance, stereo matching on HD images ($1{,}920\times1{,}080$ pixels) using a window size of 5×5 pixels and a disparity ranging from 0 to 255 (256 levels of disparity/depth, which corresponds to an 8-bit depth quantization), would require $(1{,}920\times1{,}080)\times(5\times5)\times256 = 13.3\times10^9$ operations, that is 13 billion operations. With a processor of 4 GHz and assuming that each operation would need only 1 clock cycle (probably it will need more), we would need 3 to 4 s of execution time for a single-frame stereo matching in a left-right image pair. Considering that video streams have a minimum frame rate of 25 fps, a speed up with a factor of 100 is needed to achieve real-time processing of an HD stereo video stream. Parallelization is often unavoidable for real-time applications.

For parallelization purposes, note that we can traverse the cost volume of Figure 12.10 in a different way than choosing a specific pixel and then searching over all its candidate d-values. Indeed, we might fix a candidate disparity value d first, and then traverse all pixels, before continuing with another candidate disparity value d'. This traversal will go slice by slice in constructing the cost volume, before starting the minimum operation along the z-direction. Such an approach provides parallelization opportunities: calculate each slice of the cost volume with a different thread, so that the d-slices are calculated in parallel (if no dependencies are introduced due to priors).

12.2.10 Occlusions

So far, we have explained how to handle left-to-right stereo matching. Would there be any difference in the result when handling the right-to-left stereo matching scenario? In most image regions, the depth estimation results should be comparable; however, around object silhouettes, one might encounter so-called occlusions: these are regions that are visible in one image but not in the other image of the stereo pair, as shown with the point P in Figure 12.9(a): it is visible in Cam_A; however, the ray from Cam_B's centre to point P is intersected by the left facade, hence gets invisible in Cam_B. This is called an occlusion. Other occlusions occur in Figure 12.9(a) around the central open door of the house. Both cameras see the facade of the house, but ray R_A in Cam_A shows that the left region H_A when looking through the door inside the house is kept hidden (hence the abbreviation H) and invisible in Cam_A, which only sees the right region H_B as the partial image A when looking through the door. Likewise, region H_A remains hidden in Cam_A but is visible as the partial image B in Cam_B. For these occlusion cases, since we have only information in one of the images, the matching process with the cost function approach will fail over there. In fact, the system itself will provide numerical values for the cost function, and still a minimization will be possible, but the actual visual results will be garbage. One simple way to detect this situation is exactly to perform a left-to-right and a right-to-left stereo matching and then evaluate where their results are consistent (except their inversed sign). In these regions, we obtain a reliable depth map. However, in the inconsistent regions, we probably will rather be in an occlusion scenario. Occlusions can thus quite reliably be detected as inconsistencies between the left-to-right and right-to-left stereo matching results [36].

12.2.11 Stereo matching with adaptive windows around depth discontinuities

Object silhouettes can also cause another issue in the $N \times N$ window matching process: the incorrect assumption of an almost constant depth in the window. Indeed, the window was used to better match two pixels and their surroundings for a specific candidate disparity value, but this hides the underlying constraint that the disparity should be constant in the window. If not, then a region of the window has a disparity d and another region has a disparity d' (different from d), which should be handled separately using another candidate disparity value d' during the window matching.

The most straightforward way to get out of this dilemma is to detect object edges in the window, and split the window into two (or more) regions: one with candidate disparity d and the other with another disparity d' that is yet unknown. Only the pixels corresponding to the former candidate disparity d are then

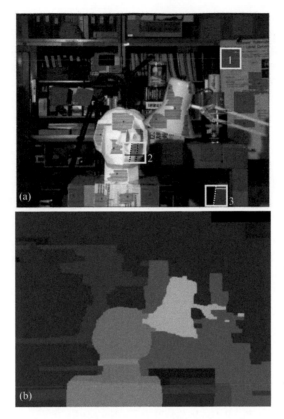

Figure 12.11: *Adaptive windows by cutting squares into sub-regions (a), yielding the disparity map of (b)*

considered in the matching cost. Such stereo matching approaches include gradients (border detection) and bilateral filters (filters taking borders into account). An example of this approach is given in Figure 12.11(a), where the matching window 1 at the top-right is clearly not split, matching window 3 at the bottom-right is split in two, and matching window 2 in the face of the statue is split in many separate regions, with only the centre one taken into account for finding the disparity of the central pixel, yielding eventually the disparity map of Figure 12.11(b). Reference [37] provides open source and mathematical explanations of a similar stereo matching process. Other features than edges and gradients can be used in this window splitting process [36,38–42]. A general overview of feature-based matching algorithms can be found in [43]. Matching based on segmentation together with hierarchical feature-based matching is further proposed in [44], and [45] uses multiple window sizes per region to perform stereo matching.

12.2.12 Stereo matching with priors

The interested reader understands little by little that stereo matching – though simple in its main principles – hides many 'hand-crafted tricks' to make things work sufficiently well as to obtain reasonable disparity maps, like the one in Figure 12.11(b). Such a disparity map is certainly not perfect – for instance, the two arms of the lamp are missing – but it looks reasonably well, following most object silhouettes quite well.

In practice, any real-world object will exhibit similar disparity values for nearby pixels within the same object, and this is an observation that has not yet been translated into something useful to exploit in stereo matching. We can therefore add an additional trick in our stereo matching suite by adding a regulation term (known as a prior) to the cost function (likelihood) of (12.29) that forces the minimization to follow the disparity values that already have been estimated before the pixel we are currently estimating. This is equivalent to the framework of a maximum posterior (MAP) estimation, formulated as follows:

$$d(x,y) = argmin f_{\text{Likelihood}}(x,y,d) + \lambda f_{\text{Prior}}(d, d_{\text{previous}}) \tag{12.30}$$

where $f_{\text{Liklihood}}$ is the matching cost function, and f_{Prior} is the regulation term to smooth the estimated depth (given the already estimated disparity in the close neighbourhood). The coefficient λ is normally less than 1 and experimentally set (yet another empirical trick) according to the image or locally in the region. In an MAP-based solution, one prior function that is often used is

$$f_{\text{Prior}} = \lambda \sum_{j \in \mathcal{N}} |d - d_j| \tag{12.31}$$

where d_j is refers to the disparity of the pixels in region W_p as shown in Figure 12.12 that shows a neighbourhood of $2 \times 6 + 4$ pixels, with the latter fourth pixel being the one for which the disparity is being evaluated.

The numbered horizontal arrows indicate the order in which all image pixels are handled. In this example, all pixels over the scanlines prior to scanline 8, as well as all previous pixels of scanline 8 itself have been handled and hence can be used as a priori in the window W_p for evaluating the current pixel p. Since the current pixel lies in the roof of the house, all window pixels in that same roof will give some prior information to guide the disparity estimation of the current pixel under test. Note that, in this example, many

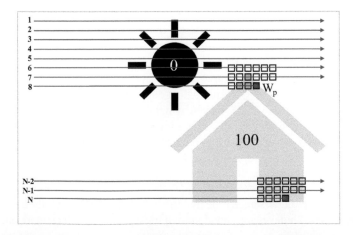

Figure 12.12   Neighbouring pixels in region W_p for defining priors

pixels within window W_p fall outside the roof, and have therefore a totally other disparity (from the sky), which will wrongly steer the disparity estimation process. However, over scanlines N-2, N-1 and N, we see that the window stays well within the facade of the house, therefore reinforcing its true disparity over the corresponding pixels.

What we learn from this example of Figure 12.12 is that priors can be helpful in the disparity/depth estimation, but that they should be used with care. Here, probably, it would be wiser to use a window W_p that is shape-adaptive, a bit like in Figure 12.11 to weigh the priors intelligently.

We will see in Section 12.4 another approach that will be more effective in using priors, trying to find the best compromise between the segments in the colour image and the disparity.

Box 12.4: View synthesis

View synthesis is a subject we will encounter further in this chapter but let us give a glimpse of what it might be once we have a disparity map. Figure 12.13 shows the main principles.

Starting from a left and right image, the disparity map is estimated; it corresponds to the middle image with disparity numbers given in the objects. In this example, the sun has a disparity of zero, and the house has a disparity of 100.

Suppose now that we want to create a viewpoint to the house that is exactly in the middle between the left and the right image. All we have to do is to displace all objects with half of their disparities between the left and right image, here zero for the sun and 50 for the house, yielding the synthesized mid-view at the bottom of Figure 12.13.

Of course, in practice, things are a bit more complicated than this. Indeed, starting from the left image and displacing its pixels with half their disparity, we will end up with a region at the right of the image where no pixels are left; these

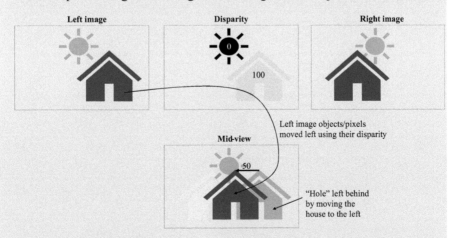

Figure 12.13   The view synthesis process creating a mid-view between a left and a right image by estimating disparity and displacing pixels with half of their disparity to create the mid-view

are the pixels of the original position of the house in the left image. Somehow, these 'unpainted pixels' should be filled. The easiest way is to repeat the mid-view synthesis starting from the right image, in which the right region has been left unaltered, therefore overlaying the unpainted pixels.

12.2.13   Uniform texture regions

Note that uniform texture regions, that is extended regions with a uniform colour (or even a regular pattern) fail in finding depth accurately, because various candidate disparities will lead to almost the same matching results in their pair of windows. Stereo matching has thus the disadvantage to work only in textured regions but compared to active depth sensing (which works well in uniform scene regions) it reaches much higher depth map resolutions, since the depth map has the same resolution as the colour images used in the stereo matching process.

To get the best out of the two worlds, some active depth sensing devices (the subject of Section 11.2 of Chapter 11) are projecting an irregular pattern (in infrared, hence invisible to the human eye) onto the scene, allowing accurate stereo matching. In fact, these devices are more stereo matching devices than active light emitting devices, though they are nevertheless often categorized in the active depth sensing category. The random dot pattern that is projected on the scene has the advantage that locally, on each tangential plane in the scene, the cross-correlation (one often used matching criterion in stereo matching) of the dot pattern (from the left image) with itself (from the right image) is the auto-correlation of random dots, which is known to be a delta function, that is one for the right disparity displacement d, zero elsewhere, as shown in Figure 12.14. This is a simple trick to make

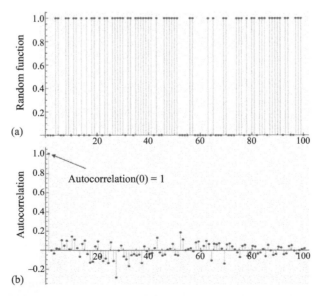

Figure 12.14   Autocorrelation of a random signal (a) gives a delta function (b)

stereo matching work properly, also within untextured regions [46]. It requires nevertheless a lot of post-filtering to obtain good results [47].

Box 12.5: NASA stereo

Since the 1960s, NASA has developed stereo matching software that has been extensively used in the Apollo missions to the moon. This software has always been maintained, and is now a very mature open source [48]. We highly recommend having a closer look at it. In fact, in the Apollo 15-17 missions, there was a payload in the command capsule for capturing stripes of the moon surface. The system was foreseen to take a stripe forward under an angle of 22.5° and then a little later the same region was captured backward under the same angle, cf. Figure 12.15. This allowed them to make stereo captures complementing the laser pulse height measurements of Box 11.1.

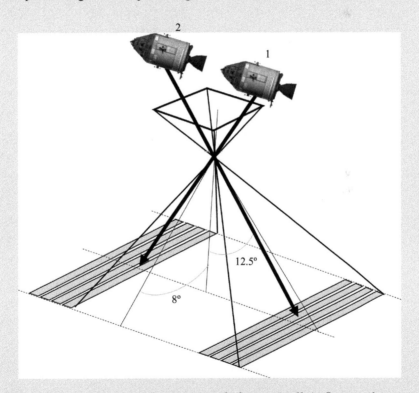

Figure 12.15   Stereo matching approach during Apollo's fly-over the moon. Reproduced from [49]

Interestingly, the software also performs 3D rendering of the moon surface, but this is not an OpenGL implementation; it is NASA's own implementation of an orthographic rasterization (approximation of a perspective transformation under the optics focal lengths used in the equipment), indicating that it is similar, yet different from OpenGL's (up to a term 0.5 to take the midpoint of each pixel). This is also worth a closer look.

Finally, since the rendering is close to orthographic, the epipolar lines are almost parallel and the fundamental matrix has zero coefficients in its upper-left 2×2 part. Under these conditions, homographies degenerate into affine transformations, with some equivalences, as explained in [50].

12.2.13.1   Different resolution input pairs

Let us consider a stereo pair that is not uniform in terms of sampling density, and we want to perform stereo matching and find dense correspondences between them. In this case, we expect to have correspondences per pixel. One simple solution to make them uniform is to up-sample them to have a similar resolution. However, if both views do not have similar aspect ratio, the matching cannot perform in all regions. Moreover, up-sampling an image introduces new artefacts, and consequently it may cause degradation in the accuracy of stereo matching.

Therefore, we need a method that can find accurate and dense correspondences, while being independent of dissimilarities (resolutions, field of views and their optical axes configuration) among views is the best solution.

To overcome such dissimilarities without up-sampling, the method in [51] proposed changing the coordinate sampled pixels at each view to a common coordinate. In other words, this approach projects all pixels at both views to camera coordinate. Now, the projected samples are observed in a common coordinate while the sampling densities are still different.

In [51] for the similarity measure between correspondences, coefficients of a quadratic polynomial [52] at each pixel for both views are compared. The comparison of the polynomials' coefficients is used for the estimation of dense displacement. Note that polynomial expansion is originally developed for estimation of displacement in the video, where the displacement is mainly small. However, when the correspondences between two stereo views have large spatial displacement, such modelling using polynomial expansion cannot perform well. To overcome this problem, [51] proposed a multi-resolution analysis for the detection of dense correspondences between views.

By this approach, we can expect that the polynomial expansion method can estimate a dense displacement between two views, independent of differences in their resolutions, field of views and their optical axes configuration.

12.2.13.1.1   *Polynomial expansion for stereo matching*

The heterogeneous multi-camera system [53] that was developed by Nagoya University, Japan is an example of the capturing scenarios when we need such an approach for estimation among views. To simplify the process, we consider the case when two views have different resolutions and fields of views. Other differences such as frame rate and bit-depth per pixel can be further investigated.

A flowchart of this method when only resolutions and field of views are different is shown in Figure 12.16. In the flowchart, Camera (1) has low resolution with narrow field of view, whereas Camera (2) has a higher resolution and wider field of view. Normally, the colour camera responses are different. To reduce this brightness difference (consequently improve the matching efficiency), it is recommended to perform histogram equalization [54]. Other steps of the process in Figure 12.16 are described in the following.

12.2.13.1.2   Projection from image to camera coordinate

In this step, the two input views are projected from the image coordinate to the camera coordinate [55], using the intrinsic parameters of cameras, as given in (12.32). The reason for this coordinate transform is to simply get rid of the dissimilarity between two views, that is resolution and field of view:

$$\begin{bmatrix} x \\ y \\ 1 \end{bmatrix} = \begin{bmatrix} f_x & 0 & c_x \\ 0 & f_y & c_y \\ 0 & 0 & 1 \end{bmatrix}^{-1} \begin{bmatrix} u \\ v \\ 1 \end{bmatrix} \tag{12.32}$$

where image coordinate is (u, v) and camera coordinate is (x, y). f_x and f_y are focal lengths in pixel. c_x and c_y are the principal points in image coordinates. Figure 12.16 illustrates two images with different sampling densities and field of views, in the same coordinate and scale, after the projection using intrinsic camera parameters.

In this projection, one should manually define the same corresponding point in both images for having zero displacement, that is the disparity map. Pixels in the camera coordinates are placed according to the pixel with zero displacement.

Thanks to this coordinate transformation, we can estimate the correspondence between pixels in two cameras and in the same scale, independent of their sampling density, field of view and their optical axes configuration. Note that for large

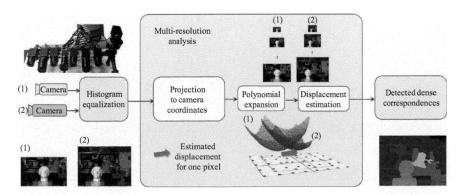

Figure 12.16   Flowchart of the polynomial expansion stereo method

displacement, the block size used for polynomial expansion should be at least as large as the maximum displacement. The polynomial estimated by pixels of a large area will not have an accurate model. Therefore, multi-resolution analysis will be a good solution.

12.2.13.1.3   Approximation by Continuous Quadratic Polynomial

In this step, each pixel with a continuous quadratic polynomial [52] is estimated, given the neighbourhood pixels or block, as formulated in (12.33):

$$f(x,y) = [x\ y]A\begin{bmatrix}x\\y\end{bmatrix} + b\begin{bmatrix}x\\y\end{bmatrix} + c \tag{12.33}$$

where A, b and c are symmetric matrix, a vector and scaler, respectively. They are approximated by a weighted least square fitting of the pixel's intensity in the block [52] for polynomial expansion. $f(x, y)$ is pixel intensity at (x, y) which is approximated by a continuous quadratic polynomial, as illustrated in Figure 12.16. Note that x and y are non-integer values at camera coordinate. In the following, we explain how the corresponding pixels are detected by the approximated quadratic polynomials.

12.2.13.1.4   Estimation of displacement

Given pixels at (x_1, y_1) of Camera (1) and Camera (2), a block in the camera coordinate is defined. In the block, the number of pixels is different in Camera (1) and Camera (2), due to the difference in sampling densities of the input cameras, while the coordinates are the same. Therefore, the approximated neighbourhood by a quadratic polynomial in two cameras with different sampling densities or field of views are comparable for the estimation of the displacement. Hence, the polynomial expansion is scale-invariant. For the pixel at (x_1, y_1) of Camera (1) and Camera (2), the coefficients of two polynomials can be derived, that is (A_1, b_1, c_1) and (A_2, b_2, c_2), respectively. These coefficients are used for estimating the displacement $(\Delta x, \Delta y)$:

$$(x_1, y_1) \Longleftrightarrow (x_1 + \Delta x, y_1 + \Delta y) \tag{12.34}$$

Details of the process are explained in [51]. The displacement $(\Delta x, \Delta y)$ is estimated as expressed in (12.35):

$$\begin{pmatrix}\Delta x\\\Delta y\end{pmatrix} = \left(\sum_{(x,y)\in\mathcal{N}(x_1,y_1)} A^T A\right)^{-1} \sum_{(x,y)\in\mathcal{N}(x_1,y_1)} A^T b \tag{12.35}$$

where $A(x_1, y_1)$ and $\Delta b(x_1, y_1)$ are given in (12.36) and (12.37):

$$A(x_1,y_1) = \frac{1}{2}(A_1(x_1,y_1) + A_2(x_1,y_1)) \tag{12.36}$$

$$\Delta b(x_1,y_1) = -\frac{1}{2}(b_2(x_1,y_1) - b_1(x_1,y_1)) \tag{12.37}$$

respectively. The estimated displacement of the correspondences between cameras is in both x and y directions. $N(x, y)$ corresponds to the search area where polynomials are compared, and it is constant in all layers. This estimation explained above, can be iteratively repeated. In the first iteration ($i = 0$), the quadratic polynomials for pixel at the position (x_1, y_1) of Camera (1) that is the same pixel to pixel at (x_1, y_1) and Camera (2) in the camera coordinate are approximated, and the displacement is estimated by (12.35). The result of the estimation provides displacement ($\Delta x_i, \Delta y_i$).

In the second iteration ($i = 1$), polynomials of pixel at (x_1, y_1) of Camera (1), and pixel at ($x_1 + \Delta x_i, y_1 + \Delta y_i$) of Camera (2) are approximated, and then the displacement is estimated. This iteration can be performed until the results converge. According to the results in [51], three to five iterations are recommended.

12.2.13.1.5 Multi-resolution analysis

Since the approximation by quadratic polynomials is used for the estimation of displacement, the block size for this approximation shall be large enough to cover the largest disparity. Meanwhile, the displacement estimation proposed in [52] is originally for motion estimation in the video sequence where the displacement is not as large as the disparity in multiview images. To handle the estimation of large displacement, multi-resolution analysis can be used.

For estimation of displacement by multi-resolution analysis, firstly, we prepare a pyramid of multi-resolution images for maximum k layers, as shown in Figure 12.16. In this pyramid, the image at the bottom layer $l = 0$ is the original size, and images in a higher layer are down-sampled by order of r in both x and y directions. Therefore, the pixel at (x, y) in bottom layer $l = 0$ is corresponding to the pixel ($x/r^k, y/r^k$) at the highest layer $l = k$. The down-sampling process may consist of some filtering such as bilinear filtering.

The multi-resolution analysis is started from the highest layer where the displacement is estimated as ($\Delta x_k, \Delta y_k$). This result is used for estimation in a lower layer $l = k - 1$. Therefore, in the lower layer, $l = k - 1$ quadratic polynomial for pixel ($x_1/r^{k-1}, y_1/r^{k-1}$) and pixel ($x_1/r^{k-1} + r\Delta x_k, y_1/r^{k-1} + r\Delta y_k$) are approximated and the displacement ($\Delta x_{k-1}, \Delta y_{k-1}$) is estimated. In general, the corresponding pixels at layer l can be expressed as (12.38) and (12.39):

$$\left(\frac{x_1}{r^l}, \frac{y_1}{r^l}\right) \Leftrightarrow \left(\frac{x_1}{r^l} + \sum_{t=l}^{k} r^{t-1}\Delta x_t, \frac{y_1}{r^l} + \sum_{t=l}^{k} r^{t-1}\Delta y_t\right) \tag{12.38}$$

for layer l and

$$(x_1, y_1) \Leftrightarrow \left(x_1 + \sum_{t=l}^{k} r^t \Delta x_t, y_1 + \sum_{t=l}^{k} r^t \Delta y_t\right) \tag{12.39}$$

for layer 0. This process continues until the lowest layer and the displacement is output. Note the number layers in multi-resolution analysis is an important parameter for this stereo matching and dependent on the resolution of the views. Also, it is worth knowing that in the explained stereo matching, the sum of absolute differences (SAD) of the coefficients from polynomial expansion is used as the measure to find the best match pixels. This solution can be formulated differently and solved through more sophisticated approaches, such as graph-cut.

12.2.14   *Epipolar plane image with multiple images*

Taking many precautions into account, stereo matching already gives good results, but one understands that using more than two images will most probably give even better results. One of these methods is the Epipolar plane image (EPI) approach, with a seminal paper back in the late 1980s [56], which uses many equidistant and parallel camera views (possibly obtained after rectification) to find the disparity. Its genesis is shown in Figure 12.17, where lateral views from a scene are stacked one after the other as in (e), creating a horizontal (perpendicular) slice as shown in (f), which slopes give an indication of the depth of each object.

Let us explain in more detail how this works, following the example of the scene represented in the top part of Figure 12.17; it represents a star object that is at infinity and a partial circle in the foreground. Four camera views are shown in the top row (a), with the partial circle moving stepwise to the left for each new camera view to the right. Since all cameras are presumed rectified and equidistant, the partial circle moves always with the same step, its disparity – represented by the

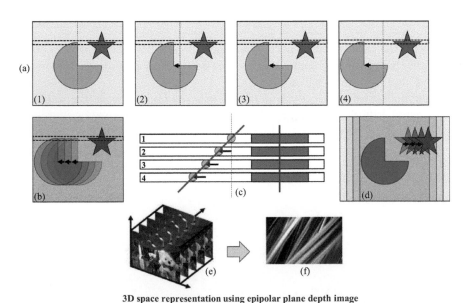

3D space representation using epipolar plane depth image

Figure 12.17   (a) Four 2D projections of a scene, with alignment on the background object (b) and foreground object (d). (c) shows the genesis of the epipolar plane image lines, with the example of (e) yielding de lines of (f)

bold arrow – compared to the previous camera view. The vertical dashed mid-line in each view better shows the relative displacement.

Since the star is lying at infinity, it does not move (has no disparity) from one image to the next; hence, its horizontal arms, for instance, stay at exactly the same position over all images in the horizontal dashed band shown in the images (1) to (4). Consequently, putting all images over each other to align the star as in Figure 12.17(b) results in the partial circle undergoing three horizontal shifts, each represented by the bold black arrow. If we would, however, like to align the partial circle, as in (d), then it would be the star that is shifted to the right. In general, overlaying the images with stepwise shifts to the left or the right (and/or top to bottom if we would have a 2D array of images) allows that some objects with a disparity equal to the shift are getting sharp, while all others get blurred because they exhibit replicates. This phenomenon is further shown in the examples of Figure 12.18, with the arrows indicating where the objects get in focus. A posteriori software refocusing some parts of plenoptic camera images depending on the objects' depth works exactly on the same principle.

Coming back on how an EPI image is built, we take one horizontal line in each image and track how all features are evolving from one image to the next. In the example of Figure 12.17, let us take the horizontal dashed band in (a) and (b) as being the line of interest (we assume its height is very small, that is the size of a pixel) and let us first follow what happens with the two horizontal arms of the star that lie in that band; we observe that from one camera to the next, this region does not move. This is represented by its vertical mid-line in Figure 12.17(c).

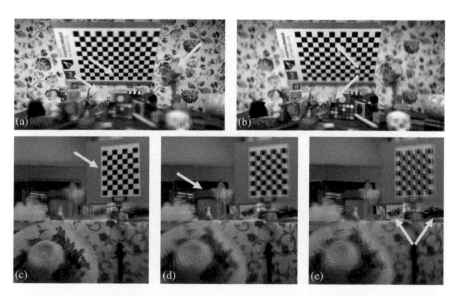

Figure 12.18   Performing slight shift operations as in (b,d) allows to focus on foreground or background objects, as indicated by the arrows for two example scenes (a,b) and (c,d,e)

We now move on by tracking how the upper point of the partial circle is moving in that same horizontal dashed band, when jumping from one camera view to the next. Since this point is moving one step further to the left over a distance equal to its disparity, we end up in the diagonal line in Figure 12.17(c). The larger the disparity of the point, the more this line is inclined towards the horizontal direction. Hence, the slope of this slanted line is a measure for the corresponding point's disparity, and thus also for its depth (inverse of disparity). This explains all the slanted lines one sees in Figure 12.17(f): each line is a point (from the scene) that moves over its disparity to the left when jumping from one camera view to the next (equidistant) one. The horizontal top border of Figure 12.17(f) is one line in the scene with points having various colours, while the vertical axis corresponds to the camera number. Clearly, points in the foreground of the scene follow an EPI-line that is more slanted than points in the background. The latter can in an extreme case even represent a point at infinity, in which case it will create a vertical EPI-line in Figure 12.17(f).

There is another information that this EPI reveals: the occlusions. Indeed, a background point following its more vertically oriented EPI-line than a point in the foreground, when moving downward in Figure 12.17(f), we come at one point in time to a situation where the two EPI-lines cross each other. At that exact position, that is in that specific camera view, the background point hides behind the foreground point, hence gets occluded. This happens for instance at the light-blue EPI line at the top-left of Figure 12.17(f). Interestingly, at the far bottom-left of the image, we see that this EPI-line appears back from behind a large, slanted region of lines. Here, the background point gets disoccluded, becoming again visible. In summary, crossing points over EPI-lines represent either occlusions or disocclusions, which are both much more easily determined in an EPI than in the left-to-right and right-to-left stereo matching refinement stage of Section 12.2.9.

In general, the more camera views are available, the more continuous the lines in Figure 12.17(f) become. Indeed, there is only a discrete number of pixels along such lines: one for each camera view. If one would capture the scene with let us say only half a dozen of camera views, the EPI image will be severely subsampled, as exemplified in Figure 12.19(c) compared to (b). It will then become very difficult to estimate the EPI lines' orientation and determine their slopes and occlusions/disocclusions correctly. For instance, the slopes d_3 and d_3' of two adjacent pixels might get mixed up, ending up in the same slope d_3' for both in Figure 12.19(c), wrongly discarding the red-green dashed line slope d_3. The EPI is thus a powerful tool, but it requires many images to be applied on, which is not always practical. There exist nevertheless good implementations as presented in [57].

12.2.15   Plane sweeping

Plane sweeping is another method following the principles of Figure 12.17, without explicitly building up the EPI. As the name suggests, a plane is swept over the scene, like a slice in the depth cost volume. This plane corresponds to a candidate depth, and one must check whether the corresponding pixels one sees over the various camera views are indeed lying in this depth plane or not.

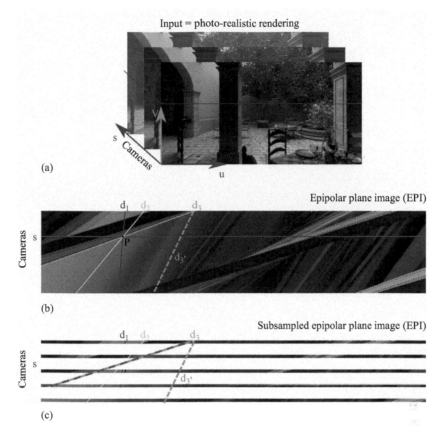

Figure 12.19   A scene (a), its Epipolar Plane Image (b) and a subsampled version (c)

To better explain the process, the example of Figure 12.20 represents in (a) the two depth layers of the objects already encountered in Figure 12.17, while (b) shows all the candidate depth layers that will be tested. We start by checking whether the objects are lying in depth layer d_0, a foreground depth that apparently lies much in front of the first object, the partial circle. For this front depth layer, a large disparity vector is expected, represented in Figure 12.20(c) by the large top arrows. If this disparity vector were true, the matching windows used in stereo matching (and by extension over multiple images, here) would be repetitively displaced over this large disparity vector over the successive views, as shown in the top row d_0 of (c). Clearly, these matching windows hold very different information over the various views, which is an indication that the proposed disparity vector is incorrect. This is not surprising, since we know from Figure 12.17 that the disparity vector is much smaller, actually as small as the one displayed in the bottom row d_2 of Figure 12.20(c). We thus must test another candidate depth layer d_i with $i \neq 0$. After having tested d_1, which also does not provide satisfactory results, we test

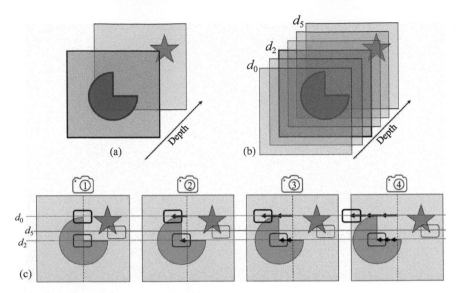

*Figure 12.20   A scene with two objects at different depth layers (a), on which
various candidate depth layers are tested (b), with their
corresponding matching windows in (c) for three candidate depth
layers d_0, d_2 and d_5*

depth layer d_2. There, we find that all pixels of the partial circle object – and in
particular its centre point surrounded by a matching window, as shown in
Figure 12.20(c) – will undergo a shift that is equal to the disparity of the corresponding depth layer d_2, over successive views. The content over these matching
windows clearly coincides and hence indicates that the centre point of the partial
circle has indeed depth d_2. The same reasoning holds for all other points of the
partial circle, leading to the conclusion that the partial circle has depth d_2.

The matching at depth layer d_2 for the partial circle does, however, not hold for
the star in the background. Therefore, the candidate depth layer d_2 is not valid for
the star. We therefore continue the search over more candidate depth layers until all
pixels in the image have been allocated a depth layer. In the case of the star, the
matching windows will not hold corresponding information until we reach the
depth layer with zero disparity, here d_5. For this candidate depth, the matching
windows correspond to the position given by the thin rounded window at row d_5 in
Figure 12.20(c), here shown around the bottom-right arm of the star. The content of
these matching windows matches perfectly, hence the candidate depth layer (here
with disparity zero) is correct for that arm of the star. Likewise, it will also be
correct for all other pixels in the star.

In summary, plane sweeping is indeed the process of sweeping over successive
candidate depth layers, checking for each of them whether the corresponding disparity yields matching windows holding equivalent information over the object
pixels.

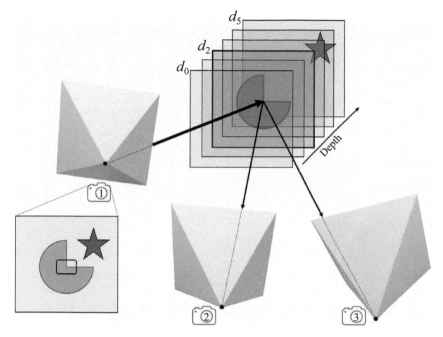

Figure 12.21   Plane sweeping for non-parallel cameras with one camera window (1) being unprojected to the candidate depth layer, followed by a reprojection towards the other camera views (2, 3)

The process explained in Figure 12.20 clearly only holds when the camera views are equidistant and perfectly rectified; only then we can shift the matching windows accordingly. For an irregular camera setup like in Figure 12.21, it is much more difficult to find in which orientations the various matching windows must be put. Nevertheless, if we know the exact position and orientation of each camera, the process of matching windows can be mimicked by taking one camera view as the reference, comparing it with all others. In that case, we start in the example of Figure 12.21 with camera 1 and define a window of interest, here for example the rectangular region around the centre of the partial circle object. This region is projected towards the candidate depth layer, here d_2 (that will yield the correct depth) following the rays starting at the camera centre and traversing each pixel under test of camera 1. Of course, be aware that this operation requires a depth and that we have assumed here that the depth is d_2, but at this point in the process, we cannot know whether that assumption is correct or not. To verify that, we project the point obtained from camera 1 and lying on depth layer d_2 towards all other camera views, here cameras 2 and 3. Each pixel pix_1 within the region of interest (matching window) from camera 1 will thus end up – after back- and forth projection – in pixels pix_2 and pix_3 of respectively cameras 2 and 3, and we can so evaluate the matching cost, here for instance with the absolute value of differences, that is $|pix_2\text{-}pix_1|+|pix_3\text{-}pix_1|$. This process is repeated over all pixels within the matching window of camera 1, adding all these matching costs together into a total matching cost. In essence, instead of a stereo matching between two cameras, we here calculate the matching cost from one camera to the cluster of all other cameras. We do not need to perform a rectification; only a registration is needed for knowing the exact position and orientation of the camera views. Consequently, the plane sweeping uses matching concepts of stereo matching, but extends them to multiple camera views without the need of rectification as in the EPI approach. Therefore, plane sweeping can be a remarkably effective approach to find pixel depths that are consistent over all camera views. Nevertheless, in practice, the results cannot be considered perfect yet, therefore some refinement methods as explained in the next section are often added.

12.3   Graph cut

Graph cut is a technique that categorizes pixels, that is, gives them a label, based on an energy or cost function that must be minimized. Adjacent pixels in an image are connected through a graph with weights that are taken into the energy function to minimize [58–60]. How these weights are chosen will be explained later. For now, just keep in mind that the technique is called graph 'cut' because the energy minimization will correspond to a cut of the graph in two sets with the minimized energy corresponding to the sum of weights over the cut [61]. Also be aware that graph cut is an iterative process that leads to a high computational load, hence acceleration strategies have been studied in [62–66].

In literature [58,67], you may find that graph cut is related to the max flow problem of finding the maximum flow through a network of pipes, each having a flow capacity given by the corresponding weight in the graph [68]. A source (let us say of water) is connected to one side of the graph, while a sink is connected to the other side. The sum of weights over the cut that will maximally cut the graph in two corresponds to the maximum flow (of water) that can go through the network of pipes. Therefore, minimizing the cost in the image processing problem by graph cut is equivalent to finding the cut having the maximum flow through the graph cut's weights. Once the cut is found, the image pixels still connected to the source get a specific meaning, while the other set of pixels has the opposite meaning, in the same way as the source has the opposite meaning of the sink. In the explanations given in the remainder of the section, we will mainly focus on the minimum cut problem, not on the maximum flow, though both are equivalent.

Figure 12.22 shows the generic architecture of the graph related to the image. Starting from neighbouring pixels p and q in an image (a), and using the terminology in [69], the horizontal dimension of the graph is built up of t-links, each representing a disparity cost. In the vertical dimension (as well as orthogonally to the sheet of paper), pixels are interconnected by n-links that express a constraint between them. The values allocated to these t- and n-links uniquely define the energy function to minimize, while the minimal cut through all these links, cf. the dashed line in Figure 12.22(b), will tell us which disparities to assign to each pixel,

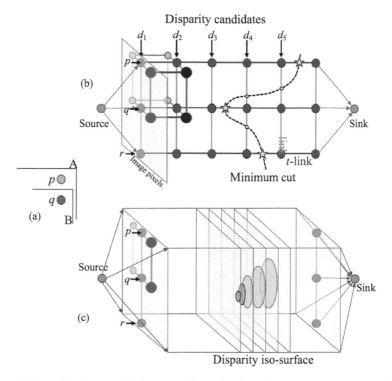

Figure 12.22   *Graph cut with focus on the behaviour for three pixels p, q and r (a). Construction of the graph (b) and the final result after cut minimization (c)*

cf. the star markers. In this example, pixel p will get disparity d_5, pixel q disparity d_3 and pixel r disparity d_4. Note that the minimum cost does not only involve these t-link values indicated by stars, but also n-link values corresponding to the small, highlighted circles on the dashed line. Applying such minimization cut over all pixels of the image creates disparity iso surfaces, as in Figure 12.22, which will delimit the object's disparity profile.

We will show some examples of such construction in the remainder of this section and will evaluate two specific situations depicted in Figure 12.22(a): one where the pixels p and q are lying in the same object, here represented by the border A, and one where the two pixels are lying at each side of the border of an object, here represented by the scenario B. The two pixels have a very similar colour, for example p has an intensity value of 248, while q has an intensity of 250. The gradient between these two pixels is hence equal to two, a value that we will encounter very often in the example pictures below. The rationale of these two scenarios A and B is that when two pixels have very similar value while being at both sides of an object border, the chances are high they have a different disparity, one pixel being in a foreground object and the other in the background. Said differently, when pixels have similar intensity values, as well as similar disparity values, they are most probably belonging to the same object, hence belonging to scenario A.

We now proceed with a critical aspect in the graph cut minimization, that is the definition of the energy function that will be minimized. Many different models exist in the literature, but they all share the same general principle of defining a first cost for assigning a disparity label d_p to a pixel p, and a second cost expressing the dissimilarities between adjacent pixels p and q, yielding equations such as [70]:

$$E(d) = \sum_p C_p(d_p) + \lambda \cdot \sum_{p,q} u_{p,q} \cdot \left[1 - \delta(d_p - d_q)\right] \tag{12.40}$$

where $E(d)$ is the global energy function to minimize. It is understood that d does not represent a single value, but rather a 'field', that is the collection of all disparity values over all pixels. When a subscript is added to d, for example d_p, then we assign this disparity value d to a specific pixel p.

In [61], we should say straight away that the second term has already been adapted from literature, adding a δ function (returns one when its argument is zero, otherwise returns zero) to clearly express the idea that if the disparities d_p and d_q are different for two adjacent pixels p and q, the second term in [61], comes into action, putting $u_{p,q}$ forward, somehow differentiating scenarios A and B above. The $u_{p,q}$ function will typically incur a high cost when the neighbouring pixels p and q are very different. A gradient function corresponding to the difference of colours or intensities is a very good candidate. A side note is that this function should behave in the same way when p and q are interchanged, hence we take its absolute value, transforming (12.40) as follows:

$$E(d) = \sum_p C_p(d_p) + \lambda \cdot \sum_{p,q} |I_p - I_q| \cdot \left[1 - \delta(d_p - d_q)\right] \tag{12.41}$$

where I_p and I_q are the pixel intensities of neighbouring pixels p and q, respectively (in our example of the A and B scenarios, this is 248 and 250, respectively), while λ indicates how much weight we give to the second term of (12.41). Observe that this term is zero when we give the same disparity value (often we speak about labels) to p and q, while it is equal to the intensity gradient (its absolute value, further amplified with the weight factor λ) when different disparity values/labels are assigned to neighbouring pixels p and q. This second term therefore corresponds to the vertical n-links in Figure 12.22(b), which will often be cut during the graph cut minimization approach. In fact, such n-link cut corresponds to assigning a different disparity label to the pixels p and q, with an additional cost equal to their intensity difference, being two in our examples. It corresponds to scenario B where the pixels belong to different objects, expressed by their colour difference/gradient at one of the object borders. The gradient cost is then added to the energy that is then more difficult to minimize, perfectly expressing the idea that crossing an object border should be avoided, favouring scenario A over B, unless their disparities are different. We thus clearly feel that the n-links tighten neighbouring pixels together as if connected with a string, telling the minimization process that they should be kept together within a reasonable limit; if the string is too much stretched, then it breaks (a string that breaks is equivalent to avoiding its cut in the energy minimization).

The first term in (12.41) corresponds to the cost of assigning a disparity to each pixel p. Again, it is the sum over all pixels, hence it is one single-valued function to minimize. Nevertheless, each term of that function is a cost that we have encountered previously in stereo matching and plane sweeping: it is the matching cost for a single pixel p. If no second term in (12.41) appears, that is $\lambda = 0$, then minimizing each pixel's matching cost (the depth dimension in Figure 12.10(b)) will also minimize the sum of these contributions and hence the total energy. This is exactly what happens in the top graph of Figure 12.23: the minimum cut line with value 4 is also the one that cuts each horizontal line of t-links at their respective minimum. Note that the n-links have no impact since $\lambda = 0$, hence we have represented them as very thin dashed lines without any value, while the t-links have a thickness that is proportional to their weight. In all other graphs we will show further on, thicker t- and n-links only show the region of interest in the graph; their exact weight is indicated by the value in their vicinity.

The bottom graphs of Figure 12.23 show some examples for various values of λ (the n-links) and t-links. When each individual pixel's matching cost function (each contribution in the first term of (12.41)) reaches the ideal minimum of zero, then the matching is considered as being perfect and whatever the value of λ, the n-links will never be cut to reach the minimum energy, cf. the bottom-left graph in Figure 12.23. However, when the individual matching cost functions of each pixel do not reach the ideal zero-valued minimum, for example 3 for pixel p and 1 for pixel q, then the global energy might still be minimized while crossing an n-link, like in the example of the bottom-right graph in Figure 12.23. Here, we reach a minimum cut of energy-value 5, while still reaching the minima in each matching

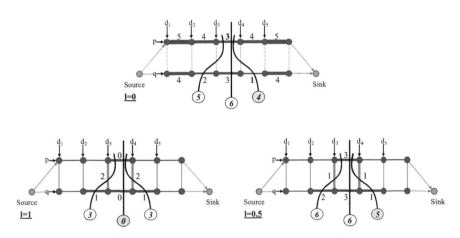

*Figure 12.23 Graph cut examples with small λ-value and/or low-valued cost
 functions*

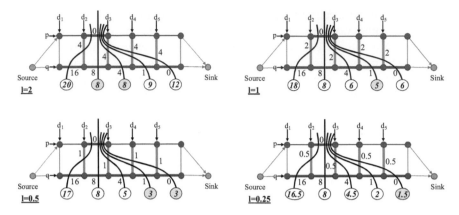

Figure 12.24   Graph cut examples with varying λ-value

cost function of each pixel individually. The interested reader may verify that if λ would be increased to a value of one (or higher), the vertical n-link values of 1 would become 2 (or higher), changing the picture. We will explain this phenomenon in more detail in the other example of Figure 12.24.

Figure 12.24 shows the influence of varying λ, which changes the values of the vertical n-links. This has an impact on the minimum cut, which value is indicated by the numbers in the highlighted circles, and hence also on which disparity labels are assigned to which pixel. In this figure, we also assume that pixel p achieves the ideal minimum matching cost of zero at disparity d_2, hence will probably be allocated this value (we say 'probably', because there might be another t-link in p that has also value zero, in which case another disparity label is equally probable). Pixel q has matching costs that gradually decrease (16, 8, 4, 1) to zero, this latter being again the ideal match, hence suggesting that the minimum cut would most likely also fall on this t-link edge … but, as Figure 12.24 shows, this is often not true at all. Indeed, with high values of λ, the vertical n-links incur a high cost in the total energy, so cutting them is not a wise choice. For instance, in the top-left graph, the minimum cut of value 8 is reached with the vertical cut over t-links only (there is another candidate minimum cut of the same value 8, just at its right side). The more λ decreases, the less the vertical n-links prevent a minimum cut through them, eventually ending for $\lambda = 0.25$ to the exact same disparity labelling as if the matching cost of each pixel would be followed individually. This example clearly shows the impact of adding a linking constraint between neighbouring pixels in finding the disparities that are eventually assigned to each of them.

Of course, the examples we presented so far are only taking two adjacent pixels into account. In practice, the minimum cut should go over all the pixels, further influencing the pixel labelling. For instance, in the top-left example of Figure 12.24, there are two minimum cut candidates of value 8 over the two pixels p and q. It is clear that a third-row pixel will further select between both options … and actually between all options: it might well be that the distribution of t-links costs in this third row drastically changes the picture, leading to a totally different minimum cut. Eventually, the graph cut corresponds to a global optimization, not a local one. This makes graph cut very appealing in a large range of applications, for example in image segmentation [71], RANSAC outlier detection and structured light depth sensing [5]. In the remainder of the section, we will rather focus on the use of a binary graph cut for depth estimation.

12.3.1 The binary graph cut

What we explained so far with respect to graph cut included all possible disparity labels of interest, which has a large impact on the memory footprint and the implementation complexity in general. Therefore, many implementations (e.g. the one in next section) rather target a binary disparity labelling process as shown in Figure 12.25, where one label tells that the pixel of interest has indeed that specific disparity we selected upfront. The other label tells that it does not have that selected disparity at all; which disparity value it then has precisely is determined in a later phase. For an extensive explanation of binary graph cuts, the interested reader is referred to [72].

In the context of depth estimation, this binary graph cut is obtained in two phases: the first one consists in holding only the front and rear planes of Figure 12.22(b), yielding Figure 12.25(a), and then put these two remaining planes into one another to reach Figure 12.25(b). The minimum cut is then represented by the dashed line and all grey arrow connections from the source to the pixels and from the pixels to the sink are then split over two groups: one assigned to the source with label d_1; another assigned to the sink not having label d_1. These remaining connections are represented by the thick black arrows in Figure 12.25(b).

With respect to the plane sweeping process of Figure 12.20(b) or Figure 12.21, all image pixels will now be split over the ones that will be part of the candidate plane (the source, labelled d_1), and the others that are not part of the candidate

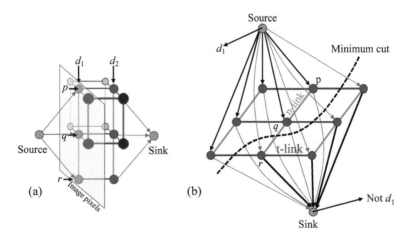

Figure 12.25   *From the general graph cut approach, retain two planes (a) that are merged in obtaining a binary graph cut (b)*

plane (the sink, labelled 'not d_1'). To do that, the cost function to use is the stereo matching cost accumulated over all corresponding camera views in the plane sweeping process. We do this for each depth plane candidate, from the largest depth plane (background) to the smallest (foreground). If in this process of going from one depth plane to the next a pixel gets two depth values to be allocated, we will favour the one that creates the smallest cost, which is most probably the one causing the largest disparity, because foreground pixels are more probable than background pixels in this probabilistic optimization approach (the graph cut is related to Random Markov Fields [73] that we will not further examine mathematically, here, but that somehow give a probabilistic framework that results in guaranteeing some important convergence features of graph cut [58,59]).

12.4   MPEG reference depth estimation

The MPEG standardization committee has worked for the last decade in the domain of immersive video, which supports 3DoF and 6DoF applications. To enable the latter, there is a need for fully accurate depth estimation software, which was developed under the name Depth Estimation Reference Software (DERS). More details on the historical evolution can be found in [74]. Here we only give a flavour of what it achieves.

DERS was developed to find depth values per pixel. It works with a combination of plane sweeping and graph cut as explained in the previous section. It provides very high-quality results with as little as (half) a dozen of input camera views, yielding the intermediate results of Figure 12.26(a) and (b), corresponding to

Figure 12.26   Graph cut layer by layer applied on the ULB ToysTable test scene (a,b), with different DERS results (c,d) under various parameter settings

various slices in the plane sweeping. Figure 12.26(c) and (d) shows the final depth map result once the graph cut has completely converged. The sharpness of the object silhouettes depends on the parameters settings, expressed as different visual results over Figure 12.26(c) and (d).

The price to pay for such high-quality results, however, is that it is a slow process requiring one to 10 min per frame processing on a high-end computer, even though the processing has been simplified to the binary graph cut approach of the previous section. A more in-depth study on DERS complexity is given in [75].

Recently, to increase the processing speed, DERS was extended to a super-pixel version [76], called Immersive Video Depth Estimation (IVDE), using clusters of pixels instead of individual pixels. Each super-pixel is somehow obtained through a segmentation process, with the assumption that all its pixels are part of an approximately planar surface. More details can be found in [77].

Other methods to increase the speed of the graph cut have been proposed by segmenting the graph into subgraphs, running the minimization by processing all of them in parallel [78]. Doing so, the intense workload from DERS can be reduced considerably with one order of magnitude in the execution time, while achieving up to two orders of magnitude memory footprint gains [79].

12.5   Depth estimation challenges

Despite the long history of research in depth estimation, it remains a challenging research topic, for instance with respect to the colour response of two cameras, and non-Lambertian objects.

When a scene is captured from two different angles, even when using identical cameras, the histogram of the captured images will be most likely different. This dissimilarity reduces the accuracy of the disparity estimation. To overcome this issue, there are basically two general approaches. One is to colour correct the images [80] before performing the disparity estimation, and the other approach is to perform an internal colour correction within the estimation process, for example, see [78].

The other main challenge is estimation of the disparity for non-Lambertian objects. Such objects are either reflective or transparent; therefore, the light rays captured from different angles may highly vary. In these conditions, the cost metrics used in matching various images [e.g. (12.1–12.7)] will most probably fail. Consequently, depth estimation in these circumstances will also fail. Non-Lambertian depth estimation remains indeed challenging and is not covered in this textbook.

Finally, the view synthesis process explained in the following sections heavily relies on high resolution and good quality depth maps, where each pixel is assigned a depth value. Unfortunately, by the very nature of light propagation with slight divergence (diffraction) of light rays is unavoidable, the resolution of such depth sensing devices often remains below the one of the colour image and video acquisition: while colour images nowadays easily achieve resolutions of 2k $(1,920 \times 1,080$ pixels) or even 4k $(3,640 \times 2,160$ pixels), depth sensing devices hardly reach half or even one-fourth of this resolution. Using them in DIBR, without any special measures (e.g. increasing their effective resolution with super-resolution techniques) would result in awfully bad results. Consequently, DIBR often presumes that the depth has been estimated, rather than sensed, though strictly speaking both methods can be applied. We will even give a visual comparison in Section 12.7.8, showing that depth sensing can be competitive.

12.6   6DoF view synthesis with depth image-based rendering

DIBR [81] is an alternative technique to the full 3D reconstructions described in Chapter 11: images are transformed to emulate the effect of perspective changes for a new camera pose, instead of rendering the fully 3D modelled scene with OpenGL. Figure 12.27 shows its main building blocks, using depth estimation (b) and view synthesis ((c)–(e)), the latter being continuously performed in real-time for all user's head positions.

Section 12.7.2 already shows the importance of depth in this process from a theoretical sampling point of view. In the current section, we will rather show a variety of practical techniques that can perform the DIBR rendering itself, often referred to as view synthesis, since a virtual view is synthesized from a couple of other viewpoints to the scene.

The methods proposed in this section are quite new and have been brought to maturity thanks to the recent MPEG-I standardization activities. Nevertheless, we cannot claim that these methods are completely novel, since premises existed

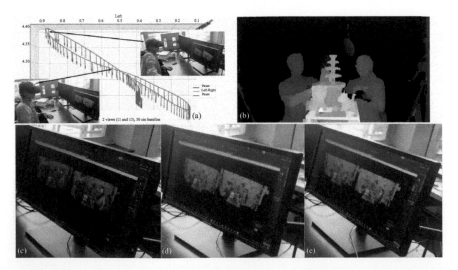

Figure 12.27   Four captured viewpoints and their depth maps are estimated offline (b). They allow to generate any viewpoint to the scene (c)–(e), while the person is moving (a)

already in the 1990s, for example, see [82]. Some aspects that are related to what we call today light fields are exposed in [82], besides other interesting 2.5D rendering topics.

12.6.1   Morphing without depth

If no depth is given, the only option one has for synthesizing new viewpoints is to use 2D warping, which corresponds to stretching the image regions so that they gradually transform from one picture to another, or equivalently from one camera pose to another. This is called morphing or warping, and the first time in history this was applied for commercial purposes was in the 'Black and White' video clip of Michael Jackson, a famous singer of the twentieth century [83], showing a continuous morphing from one actor to another, but always from the exact same camera pose.

Such an approach has been used in [84] for interpolating various views of a scene, captured with cameras that are quite far apart from each other. In general, however, one should not expect too many miracles with this approach when applied to new camera poses. Distortions will indeed easily appear, especially at object silhouettes where occlusions and disocclusions are supposed to occur in physical reality but do not become visible when using 2D images only. However, when depth images are given (and therefore, they should be estimated, prior to any DIBR action), then more intelligent DIBR view synthesis techniques are used to synthesize new virtual views to the scene, as explained in all further sections of this chapter.

12.6.2   Nyquist–Whittaker–Shannon and Petersen– Middleton in DIBR view synthesis

In this section, we will investigate under which conditions we may reduce the number of cameras to capture the scene, or more precisely, we may increase the distance between two adjacent cameras safely, without jeopardizing the quality of the image-based rendering (IBR). We will see that depth plays an important role, impacting the spectrum of the involved images. The discussion we expose here gives some insights on features that an optimal DIBR view synthesis may provide; it is not a recipe for doing view synthesis in practice, which will be discussed further in the next sections.

Let us first remind the reader of an important theorem in signal processing: the Nyquist–Shannon sampling theorem. It basically states that when a continuous time signal has a spectrum (i.e. its Fourier Transform) that has a maximum frequency f_{max}, one may safely digitally sample the signal at sample frequency $f_{sample} = 2 \times f_{max}$, without jeopardizing its time domain reconstruction. However, if one samples at a sampling rate $f_{sample} < 2 \times f_{max}$, like in Figure 12.28(b) and (c), then all frequencies above $f_{sample}/2$ (so, up to f_{max}) will be folded back in the spectrum. These frequencies will be wrongly reconstructed in the time domain, and the signal will become distorted, also known as aliasing.

In practice, Nyquist–Shannon tells us that we must sample in the time domain sufficiently rapidly, that is with time samples separated over not more than

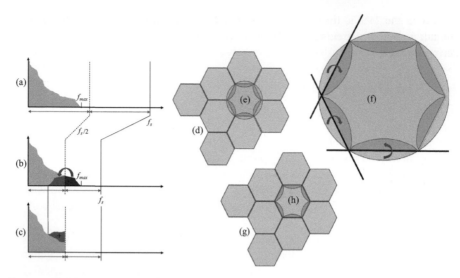

Figure 12.28   Spectrum of a 1D signal (a) and spectral fold-back due to too low sampling frequency (b), leading to a wrong spectrum (c). In 2D, the spectrum is arranged in a (here hexagonal) lattice (d,g), where the (here circular) response (e) is folded back as in (f) over the lattice (g), obtaining the final aliased spectral response (h)

$1/(2f_{max}) = \frac{1}{2} \times 1/f_{max}$, where f_{max} is the guaranteed maximum frequency in the signal by applying an appropriate (analogue) filtering, cutting off all frequencies above f_{max}. The continuous time domain signal $x(t)$ can then be reconstructed with the Whittaker–Shannon interpolation formula from the discrete samples $x[nT]$ (square brackets are used to indicate it is a discrete signal):

$$x(t) = \sum_{n=-\infty}^{+\infty} x[nT] \cdot sinc\left(\frac{t - nT}{T}\right) \tag{12.42}$$

where T is the sampling period, and the sinc function is given by

$$sinc(\tau) = \frac{\sin \tau}{\tau} \tag{12.43}$$

A similar theorem exists in 2D, aka the Petersen–Middleton sampling theorem [85,86], dating back from the 1960s. There are some slight differences with Nyquist–Whittaker–Shannon, though they are not essential in understanding the theorem. For instance, instead of having horizontal and vertical sampling points on a rectangular grid, also a non-rectangular so-called lattice can be followed, as shown with the hexagonal lattice at the right of Figure 12.28. The spectral folding phenomenon of Figure 12.28(b) and (c) in a 1D signal, corresponds now – for a 2D signal – to folding along the lattice cell boundaries, as shown in Figure 12.28(f).

Since various lattices can be chosen, the reconstruction is not necessarily unique; it is up to the designer to choose one, but for the one chosen there will be a unique associated reconstruction formula for the 2D signal, here an image with two spatial dimensions. Most often, instead of having a sinc reconstruction function, however, a multi-dimensional signal will use a Bessel or Hankel reconstruction kernel, which resembles a sinc, but with different zero-crossings. More details can be found in the original paper from Petersen and Middleton [85].

After this little reminder about Nyquist–Whittaker–Shannon and Petersen–Middleton sampling, let us see how this can be applied in the field of IBR. For simplicity, let us take a camera array with equal distance between the cameras, all pointing forward to the scene and being parallel to each other, as shown in Figure 12.29. With a 2D camera array, the position of the cameras is given by coordinates (s,t), while each camera image plane is represented by the (u,v) coordinates. This is actually the parallel planes 4D light field representation (s,t,u,v) often followed in literature [87].

Interestingly, we have already encountered a subset of this representation in the EPI images of Section 12.3.8, repeated here in Figure 12.29(b). Instead of a 2D camera array, however, we only have a one-dimensional coordinate s, dropping out the coordinate t. Moreover, the EPI image was only one horizontal slice of the stack (b), selecting the same row over all images, hence ending up with a constant value for v and a free coordinate for u. The EPI image has thus only two of the four coordinates, here s and u, where u is the horizontal dimension representing one row

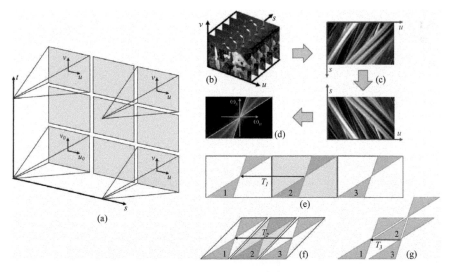

Figure 12.29   Camera array (a) with parametrization (s,t) and (u,v). A horizontal slice through the images stacked in (b) yields the EPI image of (c) and its spectral response (d). Various lattices (e–g) allow reduction of the spectral intervals, hence increases the spatial sampling period in the s (and t) coordinate

in each camera, and s is the vertical dimension, stepping from one camera to the next. Note that the s-coordinate increases downward in the conventional EPI representation; flipping the image vertically as in Figure 12.29(c) brings it back to the conventional 2D coordinate axes (u,s). Its 2D Fourier transform is shown in Figure 12.29(d), clearly showing predominant directions, which are roughly speaking perpendicular to the slope directions in Figure 12.29(c). The peculiar shape of the spectrum in Figure 12.29(d) plays an important role in sampling the scene to be captured by a limited number of cameras, as we will directly show.

We first wish to express the spectrum in any camera s as a function of what we observe along the line u in the very first camera, used as a reference, therefore holding the subscript 0 in Figure 12.30. To do so, we look for the relationship between the coordinate u in any camera s, compared to the coordinate u_0 in the reference camera. For any point P at depth z seen by the reference camera 0 and any camera s, visual inspection of Figure 12.30 shows that:

$$b_0 = z \cdot \tan \theta_0$$
$$b = -z \cdot \tan \theta$$
\hfill (12.44)

where the minus sign in the second equation comes from the fact that the angle θ is by convention positive to the right of the z-axis and negative to its left, while the distance b is by definition positive. The minus sign corrects this discrepancy.

The sum of the left sides of (12.44) corresponds to the distance between a camera s and the reference camera, yielding:

$$s = z \cdot (\tan \theta_0 - \tan \theta)$$
\hfill (12.45)

Multiplying both sides by the focal length f of the cameras, we obtain

$$f \cdot s = z \cdot (f \cdot \tan \theta_0 - f \cdot \tan \theta) = z \cdot (u_0 - u)$$
\hfill (12.46)

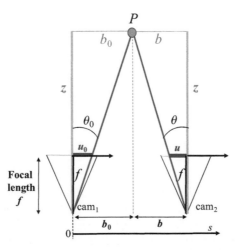

Figure 12.30:   Relation between s and u parameters in the pinhole camera model

Hence, since each coordinate u is equal to f times the tangent of the inclusive angle, we obtain from (12.46):

$$u_0 = u + \frac{f}{z} \cdot s \tag{12.47}$$

This is a simple, yet important equation that will link any camera s to the reference camera 0, and where we already see that the depth z is playing an important role.

If the scene is Lambertian, the pixel with a luminance $l(u_0, 0)$ in camera 0, emanating from point P, will be seen with exactly the same colour in camera s, yielding for its luminance:

$$l(u, s) = l(u_0, 0) \tag{12.48}$$

By combining (12.47) and (12.48) in computing the spectrum $L(\omega_u, \omega_s)$ of the image s along spatial frequencies ω_u and ω_s, using the 2D Fourier transform, we obtain [88–93]:

$$L(\omega_u, \omega_s) = \int\!\!\!\int_{-\infty}^{\infty} l(u, s) \cdot e^{-j(\omega_u \cdot u + \omega_s \cdot s)} du \cdot ds$$

$$L(\omega_u, \omega_s) = \int\!\!\!\int_{-\infty}^{\infty} l(u_0, 0) \cdot e^{-j(\omega_u \cdot u + \omega_s \cdot s)} du \cdot ds$$

$$L(\omega_u, \omega_s) = \int\!\!\!\int_{-\infty}^{\infty} l\left(u + \frac{f}{z} \cdot s, 0\right) \cdot e^{-j(\omega_u \cdot u + \omega_s \cdot s)} du \cdot ds \tag{12.49}$$

$$L(\omega_u, \omega_s) = \int_{-\infty}^{\infty} l(u, 0) e^{-j\omega_u \cdot u} du \cdot \int_{-\infty}^{\infty} e^{-j\left(\omega_s - \frac{f}{z}\omega_u\right) \cdot s} ds$$

$$L(\omega_u, \omega_s) \cong L_0(\omega_u) \cdot \delta\left(\omega_s - \frac{f}{z}\omega_u\right)$$

where $L_0(\omega_u)$ is the spectral response in camera 0 along coordinate ω_u, and δ is the delta function that is one when its argument is zero, and zero otherwise.

Equation (12.50) shows that the spectrum in any camera at coordinate s is completely governed by the generic line equation:

$$\omega_s - \frac{f}{z}\omega_u = 0 \tag{12.50}$$

with a slope that depends on the z-coordinate of the point P under test.

Therefore, the (ω_u, ω_s)-Fourier transform of the (u,s) EPI image of Figure 12.29 must have a predominant orientation along the line given by (12.50). For a scene with constant depth z, this is a single diagonal line. A real scene may be divided into several depth layers, between a minimum depth $z = z_{\min}$ and a maximum depth $z = z_{\max}$. We will then not find a single diagonal line, but a multitude of diagonal lines, all passing through the origin, as shown in Figure 12.29(d), which gives the main trend one may find in the Fourier transform of the EPI: a tilted bow tie alike spectrum, with lines that are somewhat orthogonal to the EPI lines (high frequencies come mostly of the sudden jumps between adjacent lines in the EPI, hence are oriented perpendicularly to the EPI lines).

Interestingly, [89] provides derivations when the cameras are not necessarily parallel, and there, Bessel and Hankel functions appear explicitly when reconstructing the images from their spectral response (recall that in 2D Petersen–Middleton, these functions appear instead of the sinc function in the 1D signal case), which keeps in many cases this bow-tie alike structure also.

When also adding texture variations [93], as well as aperture settings of a real camera [88], one shows that some vertical lines may appear in this bow tie spectrum, sometimes even beyond the bow tie region itself. Nevertheless, its spectral response stays well within the rectangular zone of Figure 12.29(e), so that one may apply a rectangular lattice structure along with the 2D Petersen–Middleton sampling theorem, which will hence follow two times the Nyquist–Shannon sampling grid, one per dimension. Thus, the rectangular lattice structure gives a safe margin to determine the aliasing-free sampling. This might, however, not be the best sampling approach, since we lose a lot of space T_1 between the bow tie spectra that are repeated periodically in reconstructing the signal, that is the EPI image.

This is a very important observation because it enables one to improve the lattice structure to be used in the 2D Petersen–Middleton sampling theorem. As shown in Figure 12.29(f) and (g), we can move various bow tie regions such that they overlap each other's rectangular boundaries, however, without any overlap in their lattice bow tie structures themselves, drastically reducing T_1 to T_2 or T_3. This penetration factor depends on how the bow tie spectra are tiled in the lattice, and visual inspection of Figure 12.29(e)–(g), the total surface of one tile in the 2D lattice is considerably reduced, hence increasing the sampling period (the inverse of the frequencies) that still preserves perfect signal/image reconstruction. Note that downshifting the middle bow tie halfway down – as permitted by the 2D Petersen–Middleton sampling theorem – yields large gains.

Therefore, while the Nyquist–Shannon theorem recommends a large f_{max} value, and hence a large sampling frequency, Figure 12.29(e)–(g) suggests that the effective f_{max} to be applied with the 2D Petersen–Middleton lattice structure is much smaller, requiring a much smaller sampling frequency. Though in practice it is very difficult to make precise spectral calculations, the estimated order of magnitude sampling gain may be sufficient to go from the 1 mm inter-camera distance for a scene 1 m away (a recommendation followed for making holograms [14]) to 10 mm inter-camera distance instead. Some more mathematical derivations can be found in [94]. If additionally, the scene is not 1 m away from the cameras, but 3 m away, then this inter-camera distance may even increase with an additional factor 3, allowing a distance of 30 mm, that is 3 cm between adjacent cameras. With machine vision cameras not more than 2.5 cm wide, this bow-tie spectrum story yields perspectives to have a practical camera array setup rather than using a 1 mm steps sliding camera rail, without jeopardizing the final quality of the IBR rendering. A simulator for dimensioning a camera setup can be found in annex *C* of [95]. Of course, now, IBR should rather be referred to as a DIBR approach, because of the presence of depth layers that drastically lower the sampling constraints. Therefore, it is DIBR that is used in practice when applying image-based approaches for VR.

Now we know that DIBR is the process to follow, let us make abstraction of the Fourier transforms of the 2D Petersen–Middleton theorem, and find DIBR approaches that directly work on the images, even taking care of occlusions/disocclusions that were not explicitly addressed in Petersen–Middleton. This will be covered in the remainder of this chapter.

12.6.3   Depth-based 2D pixel to 3D point reprojections

Multi-view-video-plus-depth (MVD) representation is commonly used for DIBR view synthesis. Using the colour-plus-depth data, synthesizing free-viewpoint images [81,96–101] is a straightforward approach. The process is as simple as back-projecting image pixels to 3D space using per-pixel depth information and then projecting them back to 2D from the chosen virtual viewpoint or camera pose. This process is often referred to as 3D warping [102], very different from the 2D warping previously mentioned.

Figure 12.31 shows an example where a view (a) is reprojected in this way, using its depth map (not shown) to create the new viewpoint (b). Evidently, there are many regions in (b) that were not visible in (a) and hence are painted black. For instance, the statues and tower are only partially rendered in Figure 12.31(b), but this is not surprising, since after all, we cannot expect to see behind the corners of (a) to create (b).

Therefore, in the view synthesis process, multiple views with their corresponding depth maps are used. Those so-called reference views are then 3D warped to the perspective pose of the virtual view (this is called a forward projection, cf. [103]), where there is no physical camera present; we therefore also refer to it as a virtual camera.

Figure 12.32 shows an example with one, three and seven reference views used in creating the virtual camera view. In the case of only one reference view, we clearly see the same effect as in Figure 12.31, creating a kind of shadow effect around the silhouette of the person. This region was occluded in the reference view but got disoccluded in the virtual camera view, and hence appears as black. Also note that there are many small holes that appear in the image.

In fact, in the former back-and-forth projection operations, it might happen that two pixels in the first reference view are projected to the same pixel in the new, virtual view. In this case, only the pixel in the foreground – the one with the smallest depth value, seen from the virtual view – is retained; the other is discarded. Moreover, pixels that are lying on the integer pixel grid of a reference view (pixels are positioned at integer coordinates in the image) do not necessarily project on an integer position in the virtual camera. This creates these little holes that often appear as cracks, as in the example of Figure 12.33 where the virtual camera is positioned a bit to the right and perfectly parallel to the single reference view. In

Figure 12.31   DIBR for a video game, creating view (b) from (a) and its depth map. Reproduced from [104]

this case, it is simpler to perform the de-projection and re-projection operation by moving each pixel to the left over a distance proportional to its disparity, the inverse of its depth, as JPEG-PLENO is proposing [105]. Foreground pixels will be moved to the left more than background objects, and over one scanline of the image, we obtain the situation depicted in Figure 12.33: some background pixels along the left silhouette of the baby get hidden or occluded behind a foreground region. At the right side of the baby's silhouette, however, some pixels get no colour at all; we say they get disoccluded, that is they appear, while they were originally not visible. Of course, because no colour was allocated to them – even not in the original image – they are left blank, creating a white disoccluded region.

Besides these large disocclusion regions, we see narrow cracks inside the baby's body, mainly in the face, the chest and the legs. We also see little cracks in the background. All these come from rounding to an integer position in the image, instead of keeping the exact, highly accurate floating-point value. In JPEG-PLENO, these little cracks are removed by applying a median filter, which works well for small baseline scenarios with little shifts from one camera view to the next. For large baselines, however, larger holes may appear, which can be filled either by enlarging the pixels or by interconnecting the pixels by triangles that will

Figure 12.32   Effect of increasing the number of input cameras in the final rendering with 1 (a), 3 (b), 5 (c) and 7 input views (d)

Figure 12.33   Small disocclusions appear during view synthesis

get processed by the OpenGL pipeline, stretching and squeezing them depending on the pixel displacements, as shown in Figure 12.34.

Figure 12.34 shows how pixels in an input view (a) are unprojected with the depth map to 3D space (b), followed by a reprojection to the virtual view (c).

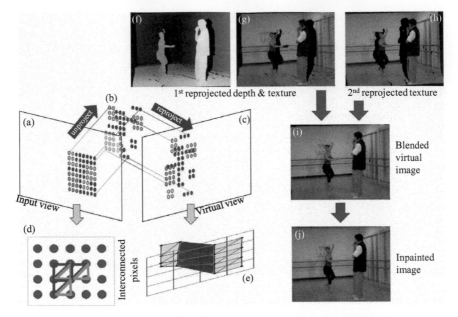

Figure 12.34   Un- and reprojecting an input view (a,d) through 3D space (b) to create a virtual view (c,e). Reprojections on a couple of input views (g,h) with depth map (f) yield a blended virtual image (i) that is further inpainted (j)

Interconnecting the input pixels with triangles (d), the un- and reprojection operations will yield the corresponding virtual view triangles in (e), handling most of the cracks correctly for whatever the camera orientation. Large disocclusions, however, will remain unfilled (or have elongated triangles that are clearly unwanted and will be discarded as further explained in Section 12.7.7).

With a virtual view in the centre of the two input views, all disocclusions will be filled by one or the other reprojected input view since they counteract each other. For instance, in Figure 12.34, the reprojected input view (g) at the left of the wanted virtual view position (*i,j*) will create mostly disocclusions at the right object borders, also visible in the reprojected depth map (f) which is involved in the process. An input camera view at the right side of the wanted virtual view position will be un- and reprojected, creating disocclusions at the left side of the objects/persons, as shown in (h). Merging – or using the more scientific term 'blending' – the images (g) and (h), creates the virtual image (i) that corresponds to a virtual camera position somewhere between the left and right camera input views.

In practice, instead of only filling the disoccluded space with the pixels of the other reprojected input view, as shown in the (g,h)–(i) blending in Figure 12.34, one can just blend both views fully, adjusting the blending factor with the number of relevant pixels that are blended [106]. This blended view might still have some small disoccluded regions, depending on the camera positions and the number of input camera views involved. With only a couple of cameras there is a high chance of remaining disocclusions that must be handled by a so-called inpainting (j), which fills in the holes with plausible colours. The interested reader is referred to [107] for more details about inpainting in general, and [109] for its application to the ballet dancer sequence shown in Figure 12.34.

12.6.4 Splatting and hole filling

From the examples of the previous section, it is clear that large disocclusions can only be addressed properly by putting a sufficient number of cameras all around the scene so that almost everything that gets disoccluded can be filled with known data coming from another reference view. If then, there are still remaining disocclusions that are small, inpainting [107] will take care of filling everything up with 'plausible content'; let us say, a reasonable extrapolation of the object borders. In practice, however, one should not rely too much on inpainting, because this is a process that may well fail and on which the user has no control.

For the other little cracks that remain in the image, it is clear from Figure 12.32 and Figure 12.33 that increasing the size of each coloured pixel, without scaling up the image, will already provide good results.

As already explained in Section 11.4.2, there exists in 3D graphics rendering another approach, called splatting, that is very similar: a disk is put around each point in space, so that the 2D projections of these disks overlap on the image plane of the virtual camera, automatically creating a full image. Note that these disks are oriented in the direction of the normal in each point, which can be calculated from the depth map associated with each reference view in the DIBR framework. The disks projected as ellipses on the 2D image give a more pleasant visual result than just enlarging each pixel uniformly on the 2D image space, and at the same time closes all holes.

12.6.5 Super-pixels and hole filling

An approach often followed in computer vision is the use of super-pixels; these are micro-segments that cluster neighbouring pixels having similar characteristics together. The advantage is that all pixels of each super-pixel are handled all together as one entity, as if it were a unique, albeit irregularly shaped splat. Consequently, the number of cracks to fix is drastically reduced, and the inpainting process (if any) is simplified [109,110]. Of course, the question raises on how to best create these super-pixels.

The method in [111] over-segments the image into super-pixels without taking any depth information into account. Tezuka *et al.* [112,113] create super-pixels by segmentation based on simple linear iterative clustering (SLIC) [114]. In this method, super-pixels are appropriately spaced using diamond tiling.

Many researchers have further tried to solve the problems of cracks by applying filtering techniques on the depth maps prior to 3D warping. Mao *et al.* [115,116] proposed filling cracks based on a method that is initially proposed for adaptive depth coding [118]. They have further improved their approach in [119] using a graph signal processing method [126]. Methods in [81,99,109,112,114,117,118,120–125,127] perform depth smoothing after 3D warping. Generally speaking, methods that perform depth smoothing introduce artefacts and are therefore not recommended.

Other methods use both colour and depth information, for example, see [113,128–131] and [132] through a K-means-based interpolation method, creating arbitrary shaped super-pixels, with typical results shown in Figure 12.35.

When the virtual view pose is physically far from the reference views, especially when they are limited in their number, 3D warping might produce large disocclusion holes, difficult to handle. In these conditions, super-pixels really show their merits, as shown in Figure 12.36 for various scenarios (colour and/or depth).

Figure 12.35   Synthesized virtual viewpoints

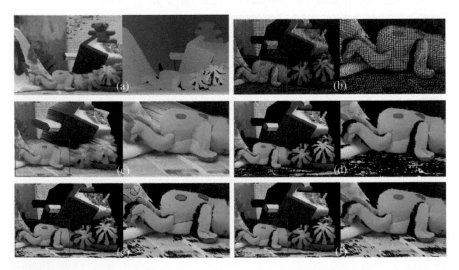

Figure 12.36   Comparison of view synthesis using naïve 3D warping, without (b) or with all 3D points connected (c), versus super-pixel based, when the super-pixel segmentation is applied for depth segmentation (d), colour segmentation (e) or both (f). The reference view and depth map are given in (a)

12.6.6   Depth reliability in view synthesis

From the discussion of Section 12.3.5, some regions in the depth maps may be unreliable, especially around boundaries. This is particularly true for sensed depth maps with flying points around boundaries, but also estimated depth maps using matching windows crossing the object boundaries with highly discontinuous depth values, hence causing spurious depth boundaries. Moreover, if the depth map is estimated or sensed from another viewpoint than the colour reference views, one has to perform a reprojection of the depth map to the camera view, which will cause some additional cracks, as shown in Figure 12.37(a,b). Simple median filtering as in [129] can handle the situation of Figure 12.37(a), but flying points are more challenging to handle. As this may cause severe artefacts during the view synthesis, it is recommended to determine whether the depth values are reliable, especially at object boundaries where depth discontinuities occur.

There are several reliability-based view synthesis methods which handle boundary artefacts caused by depth errors. Kauff *et al.* [130] used the consistency crosscheck with disparity maps to detect mismatches. An alternative strategy is to treat all boundaries or depth discontinuities as unreliable areas. Reference [131] first proposed solving the boundary artefacts by rendering boundaries separately from other areas. A two-layer boundary representation is used for a matting algorithm where boundaries along depth discontinuities are extracted. References [134] and [135] improve the boundary extraction via a Canny edge detector [136]. They split boundary areas into a foreground and a background layer. The foreground regions are first projected to the virtual view. The background boundaries are considered as unreliable areas, but since they are projected after the foreground layer is considered as reliable, most of the background unreliable boundaries are hidden away by the reprojected foreground layer. References [39,137] followed a

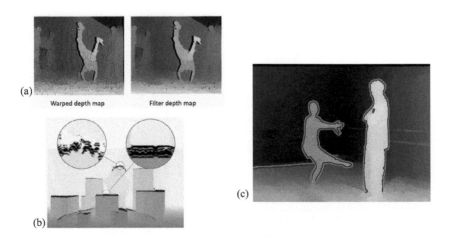

Figure 12.37   Depth filtering, warping the depth maps (a,b) and indicating reliable and unreliable pixels (c)

similar approach, while [38] used a split-patch search method to recover boundaries. In [40], Zhao *et al.* refrained from the usage of unreliable pixels by enforcing texture-depth alignment. An example of their boundary reliability results is shown in Figure 12.37(c).

12.6.7   MPEG-I view synthesis with estimated depth maps

From all previous methods, the MPEG-I standardization committee has selected two methods, one is the splatting of Section 11.4.2 and the other one is a new, fairly simple, yet effective method, summarized in Figure 12.38. An efficient implementation thereof based on the OpenGL rendering pipeline can be found in the reference software suite of the MPEG immersive video coding standard [138–140], aka the reference view synthesis (RVS) module. The interested reader can also find a demo on [141]. A demo player, extending the well-known VLC player [142] with depth maps, has also been provided by one of the participating companies.

In essence, each reference view holds both a colour image and its depth map. Knowing the depth of each pixel, they are all pushed into space – called de- or un-projection – where they form locally the 3D shape of the object as a partial point cloud. Afterwards, they are projected back in the direction of the wanted virtual camera pose, effectively synthesizing a new virtual view. Up to this point, the method is hardly different from the process outlined in Section 12.6.3.

However, instead of just letting each pixel be processed independently of its neighbours, every adjacent triplet of pixels is now connected by a triangle [101], letting the fragment shader in the graphical processing unit (GPU) do all necessary interpolations to fill in any gaps that would occur, cf. Section 3.3. This solves all problems of holes and cracks encountered in Sections 12.7.3–12.7.5.

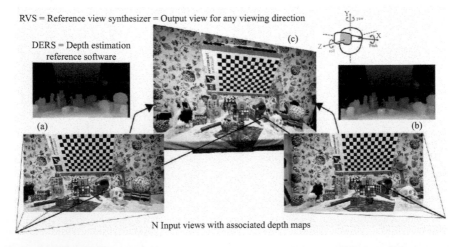

Figure 12.38   View synthesis by un- and re-projecting pixels from a given view to a virtual view

A side effect is that disocclusion areas will then most likely be filled in with coloured triangles that are horizontally stretched, somehow unwillingly inpainting the missing area. Though being a fully automatic operation, the visual result of Figure 12.39 is clearly not aesthetic. Therefore, to overcome this unwanted inpainting operation, triangles are cut (effectively discarded) in regions with large depth discontinuities, which typically occur around object silhouettes. The interested reader is referred to [143] for more details, yielding the large aesthetic improvement from left to right in Figure 12.39.

One possible condition to cut the triangle is when it is too elongated, for example with one side larger than 15 pixels. Many different detection criteria exist, as shown in Figure 12.40, one being the detection of sudden changes in the normal direction. Calculating normals is perfectly possible since the depth in each point is known through the depth maps. From Figure 12.40, options (b) and (d) are probably the most promising, with respectively the orientation of the normal and finding long elongated triangles, to decide whether a triangle should be cut or not. Interestingly, seminal work on view synthesis [144,145], back to the late 1990s, was already mentioning these kinds of challenges to address ... and 25 years later, we are still busy developing them. Since then, many different approaches have been proposed to solve this elongated triangle problem, for example with adaptive blending techniques [146,147], some using deep learning methods, like in [148–154], with a comparative study given in [155,156]. Every day, they are new deep learning papers suggesting view synthesis improvements, mostly focusing on these disocclusion problems, but often they are restricted to rather small movements around the objects of interest; nevertheless, providing stunning results, for example, see [157,158]. Clearly, there is still a long way to go for finding the optimal solution for all application scenarios.

Figure 12.39   Elongated triangles (left) can be removed by cutting triangles away when there is a too large depth discontinuity (right)

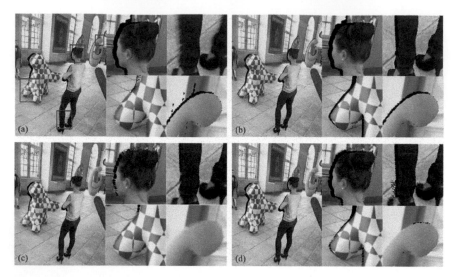

Figure 12.40:   Detection of object boundaries in various ways: (a) depth variations, (b) normal orientations, (c) long triangle side and (d) long elongated triangle

12.6.8   MPEG-I view synthesis with sensed depth maps

In view of the disocclusion challenges exposed in Figure 12.40 and the deceiving results obtained for point clouds with depth sensing devices, great care was taken in the previous section to estimate, rather than sense, high-quality depth maps before performing the view synthesis. This depth estimation process comes with a high compute cost and consequently jeopardizes real-time performances in VR applications. It may therefore be interesting to consider lidar depth sensing, as shown in Figure 12.41. Its bottom row shows view synthesis results for the midpoint between two camera views that are 10 cm apart, using an estimated depth map and a L515 lidar sensed depth map, respectively. Though the lidar depth map has some artefacts due to its reprojection from its capturing position to the colour camera position, cf. the transition from (a) to (c), the view synthesis results look visually close to the one obtained with a high-quality estimated depth map. The attentive reader will observe that some object borders are thinner with the lidar approach, cf. the right side of cubes 2, 7 and 9 in Figure 12.41(e), but the overall quality of the synthesized view looks sufficiently appealing to consider depth sensing as a future exploration in view synthesis.

12.6.9   Depth layered images – Google

In previous sections, we have seen how triplets of pixels form triangles that altogether form a mesh covering the image. This texture mesh takes care of filling small cracks

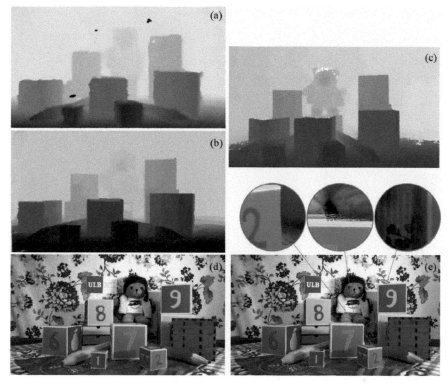

Figure 12.41: Lidar sensed depth map (a), compared to DERS (b), before reprojection to a camera viewpoint (c). View synthesis results with DERS (d) and lidar (e)

that occur during the de- and re-projection operations in the view synthesis. Though this mesh is one complete structure, some of its triangles may get too elongated at object boundaries in disocclusion areas. The corresponding triangles are then discarded, which is an operation that could have been done in the original texture mesh, there where large depth discontinuities occur. Depth-layered images [106], finding its roots in the 1990s [159], are exactly doing that: instead of having one full image with many depth regions, all regions with approximately the same depth are put together in one depth layer. The original camera image is hence split over various depth layers, each having a textured mesh covering some parts of the input image. In the end, each camera view is split over depth layered images, as shown in Figure 12.42.

Note that with some pre-processing, it is possible to have two successive depth layers with texture regions that are overlapping somewhat. This has the advantage that in the de- and re-projection operations with a virtual viewpoint a bit sidewise from the camera viewpoint, disocclusions will not suddenly become black, but will rather take a hidden texture portion of the next depth layer. In this way, disocclusions are partly handled in a pre-processing phase, rather than entirely in the

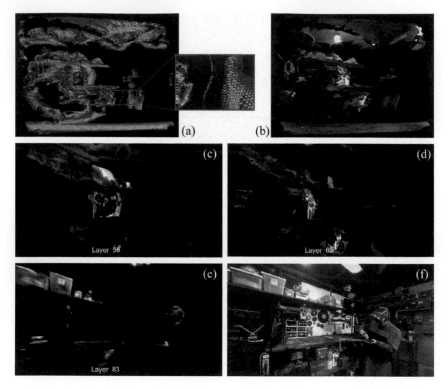

*Figure 12.42:   Depth-layered images with meshes per layer (a) and corresponding
texture (b). Three layers are shown in (c)–(e) with the final
obtained result in (f). Courtesy: Google LLC*

post-processing rendering phase, which is execution time critical. The price to pay,
however, is how the pre-processing phase should be done, which may be somewhat
ill-posed and is certainly a time-consuming process (off-line). The interested reader
is referred to [160] for a neural network-based solution to this challenge.

Noteworthy, with multiple depth layers, the compression of DLI images might
also become challenging. A first attempt [161] was proposed in the MPEG framework,
in the early years 2000, and the reader active in today's MPEG-I point cloud coding
(PCC) might find some similarities. Also in the MIV counterpart, the compression of
multi-plane images (MPI), very closely related to DLI, has been addressed; it is actually a sub-family (called profile in MPEG jargon) of MIV. Compression aspects will be
further discussed in Chapter 15 and are therefore left aside at this point in the textbook.

Finally, it is believed that DLI can handle intrinsically non-Lambertian scenes
well, for example, see [159]. This, however, requires multiple depth maps, for
example one for the diffusive (Lambertian) materials, another one for the reflective
and transparent materials. This is yet another challenge to address in future work.
One interesting approach using EPI images is presented in [162].

12.7 Use case I: view synthesis in holographic stereograms

Besides the obvious use case of VR where various viewpoints to the scene must be synthesized and rendered instantaneously, holographic stereograms may also benefit from DIBR technology.

We already encountered the glasses-free stereogram in Section 12.1 under the name of the lenticular display. It is a device that projects parallax images in a dozen of directions, so that the viewer's eyes may capture two of these images for a stereoscopic viewing experience without the need to wear stereo glasses. The directional images are interleaved, overlayed with thin lenticular lenses taking care that the right image is projected in the right direction. The interested reader is referred to [2] for optical considerations, as well as how to post-process photos of a scene (i.e. perspective corrections with homography transformations) for visualization through a lenticular display. In fact, lenticular displays project only a limited number of views, typically a dozen, so in practice, one can easily capture all these views manually, even with a simple photographic camera.

If one wants a denser stereogram with hundreds of viewing directions (typically 400 to 800), there is a need to go for diffractive lenses instead of lenticular, refractive ones, leading to holographic stereograms where pixels are replaced by hogels (holographic elements), a kind of super-pixel that holds all information for the hundreds of viewing directions. In essence, each a super-pixel is made of superposed diffractive gratings, one for each viewing direction [163]. Once the angular colour information in each super-pixel is known, the grating can be calculated by a 2D Fourier transform. Counter-intuitively, such super-pixel or hogel is very tiny, typically 250 or 500 μm in size (yes, a fraction of a mm), with smaller hogels yielding holograms of higher visual quality. Relatively modest holographic printers [164] yield very high-quality printouts [165] with good eye accommodation [166], and electronic tabletop holographic displays designs are shown in [167]. More details can be found in [108], and some intuition on how holograms work, as well as their hogel sizes can be found in the two boxes: Box 12.6 and Box 12.7.

Box 12.6: Analogue holograms and eye accommodation

Undoubtedly, holograms store directional light information, otherwise one would not see parallax changes when moving left or right in front of a hologram. In this sense, holograms are an instantiation of light fields, though they are more than that, holding also phase information that plays an important role in the interference phenomena that are at the basis of holograms.

As shown in Figure 12.43, holograms can be recorded by capturing an interference pattern between a reference laser beam and a reflection thereof onto the object to record, for example, see [168]. For each point in space, such interference pattern looks like circular rings that amplitude modulate the light that will pass through when illuminating the hologram with laser light or

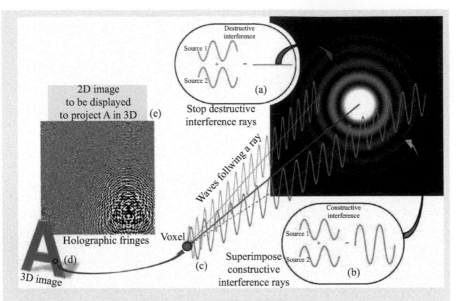

Figure 12.43   Hologram interference pattern with constructive (a) and destructive interference (b) creating voxels (c) and a projected 3D image in space (d). The holographic fringes look like (e)

white led light. In an extreme case, these pixels are just switched on or off, which we will assume here for simplicity, without loss of generality. All pixels that are switched on propagate coherent laser light such that a gigantic amount of little, imperceptible light waves reinforce themselves, creating a tsunami of light in each point in space where they are in phase, cf. Figure 12.43(b) and (c). At the same time, with the same pixels switched on, the electromagnetic light rays that are statistically not in phase destructively interfere, keeping the corresponding points in space unlit or very dimmed. The same pixel on the hologram hence contributes to all points in space in a statistical way, sometimes constructively, sometimes destructively. Of course, when pixels are analogue, they are not just switched on or off, hence the interference pattern provides a plethora of amplitude modulations in the light intensity of the points projected into 3D space. This provides continuous tone variations of the 3D object the viewer will perceive.

Note that – thanks to the interference approach in holograms – there exist strangely enough regions in front and behind the lit object points, where no light is observed; the interference there is destructive. This provides something unique to holograms: the eye of the human observer will always focus on the light points in space, not on the pixels of the hologram plane, as was the case for lenticular sheets. Holograms therefore confer so-called eye accommodation and vergence (EAVE), as if one would look at a real object in space, though here it has become a virtual object.

Figure 12.44   Hologram captured with a plenoptic camera (a) focus changing over various regions (b)

Figure 12.44 shows a visual example of the ability to focus correctly on each object in the scene at will. A hologram is illuminated and captured by a plenoptic camera, which has the ability – in contrast to conventional cameras – to refocus a posteriori using software computational imaging techniques, rather than having to adjust the objective lens to a specific depth of focus, once and for all. Observe how the image region around the mouse pointer comes into focus when selecting it as the region of interest, while all other regions get blurred. The exact same phenomenon occurs in our eyes, but this time in 'hardware', with the eye lenses refocusing on the object of interest at will. The dense light field VR goggles of Figure 10.9(b) also sustain eye accommodation along the same working principles.

Box 12.7:   Digital holograms

As for the analogue holograms of the previous section, digital holograms are a specific implementation of light field displays, which for technological reasons (their sub-micron pixel sizes) are often restricted to static rendering. Their working principle of a digital hologram is similar to analogue holograms: an interference phenomenon in space creates tsunamis of point lights, which all together represent the 3D object in space. Interestingly, the digital hologram is computed following the exact opposite light travelling direction of the analogue hologram: given the points in space to lit, calculate the Fresnel light propagation and determine how many light rays hit each pixel in phase. If this number is higher than a threshold, switch on the pixel, otherwise switch it off. Note that here we use binary pixels, resulting already in good-quality holograms; generalization to more bits per pixel is straightforward. In practice, two or three bits per pixel is better, but more is often unnecessary [169,170]. Obviously, in order to allow two adjacent light rays in Figure 12.43 to be in different phases when reaching a point in space, their travel length difference should be in the order of half the wavelength of light, that is roughly ¼ µm, which also imposes the pixel pitch to be in the same order of magnitude. Moreover, to spread out the light rays of each pixel like a wavefront in all directions – a necessary condition to obtain interference from light rays of different pixels – diffractive optics (i.e. the diffractive rings and dot patterns in Figure 12.43) impose also the pixels to be no larger than the wavelength. This explains why large field-of-view holograms have such a high pixel density, in the order of a couple of thousands of so-called line pairs per mm, which leads to many billions – not millions – of pixels in a digital hologram. Furthermore, since the printing of a hologram is an opto-chemical process with practical inaccuracies by nature, the grain size in the photographic emulsion should be even smaller, typically around 5 to 50 nm [171].

At first sight, the hundreds of views required for a holographic stereogram cannot come from just a dozen of pictures during a photo-shoot session anymore; there is clearly a need for a more professional setup. One approach is to use a camera sliding with a step motor on a rail, so that one picture is taken every mm, a setup recommended in [14]. Another approach is to use view synthesis to create hundreds of views from only a dozen (or less) of pictures taken from the scene. This is exactly the approach we have followed; it opens the door to a more democratic use of holograms using consumer photographic devices.

Figure 12.45 shows an example of the Blender classroom scene printed as a holographic stereogram, using only four input views to the scene, out of which all other 800 views are estimated through the DIBR techniques explained in previous sections; more specifically, the RVS view synthesis explained in Section 12.7.7. Except for the large disocclusion behind the desk, for which no information is visible

Figure 12.45   Holographic stereogram of the Blender classroom scene (left) with the closest corresponding Blender views (right). Courtesy: OSA Applied Optics

from the four camera views to fill it up (only inpainting techniques [107], beyond the scope of this textbook can handle this appropriately), the scene is rendered very well with high details. This amazing result, obtained with only four input views (in contrast with 64×64 images in [173]), nevertheless hides a little secret: each of the input views must be accompanied by its depth map at very high quality, otherwise the Nyquist–Shannon/Petersen–Middleton sampling conditions would not be met, resulting in a very bad holographic image quality. The Blender classroom scene being synthetic, its depth maps can easily be computed when preparing the input views.

The hologram of Figure 12.46, however, corresponds to a real scene from which a dozen of pictures have been taken to estimate the depth maps with DERS. Afterwards, RVS has been used to synthesize hundreds of views from again only four input views. Technical details can be found in [174]. Note that the hogel size is here 500 μm, that is half mm, which starts to become visible as a perceptible raster grid. Nevertheless, the quality is very satisfactory.

At the time of writing, we have become aware that LitiHolo is kickstarting the production of holographic printers, also using multiple input views. We are eager to see how our respective technologies might be combined.

12.8   Use case II: view synthesis in integral photography

Integral photography is an extension of HPO stereograms by also allowing vertical parallax, creating a full parallax representation of the scene. The technology used here is not based on interference fringes; it is rather a kind of lenticular lens as in Section 12.1 but extended to 2D, hence made of microlenses that project the various

Figure 12.46   Two views to a holographic stereogram synthesized with DERS
and RVS. Courtesy: OSA Applied Optics

views in different directions towards the user. Figure 12.47 shows an example from
[175] where a real scene is captured from a sparse set of viewpoints (only one is
shown in the figure), out of which all the viewpoints for the integral photography
representation are synthesized. These viewpoints are interleaved to create the image
that will be put underneath a microlens sheet, as shown in Figure 12.47(b). To create
this image, [175] has used a method that is close to the shearlet transform of
[176–178] where the bow-tie spectral responses of Figure 12.29 are tightly interleaved. It is also a DIBR method, but that partially works in the Fourier domain with
depth estimation in the EPI image. Further details can be found in [175].

12.9   Difference between PCC and DIBR

In previous chapters, we have addressed the issue of representing visual volumetric
data in an appropriate format to enable 6DoF navigation, adding geometry information – 3D object shape or depth maps – for enabling the reconstruction of any
viewpoint to the scene. Even in the DIBR approach, the underlying data format
intrinsically contains a point cloud, captured from a limited number of viewpoints,
which are de- and re-projected to new virtual viewpoints.

The main difference between DIBR and the explicit point cloud format is that
in DIBR, the point cloud is not constructed by a global optimization on all input
views – like photogrammetry and its SBA algorithm would do – but rather by local,
surrounding projection operations on partial point clouds, obtained by pushing
pixels of only these input views into 3D space using their depth information. This
process has the advantage that not applying a global optimization overcomes
smoothing which would wipe out local details, like fur and hair. In DIBR, on the
contrary, such details are maintained, as long as adjacent views participating in the
de- and re-projections remain coherent between each other, which is a relatively
weak constraint related to the inter-view coherence of depth maps and a satisfactory

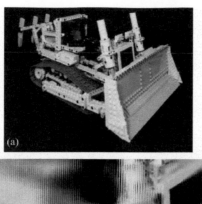

*Figure 12.47   One view of a real scene (a) and its integral photography image (b).
Courtesy: Lode Jorissen, PhD, UHasselt, Belgium*

camera calibration. We even showed in the previous section that DIBR provides remarkable results in stereographic holograms, which are the main type of holograms one can find in the market nowadays. DIBR, therefore, represents an exceptionally good alternative to full 3D reconstruction whose details would otherwise have to be reproduced with bump maps and particle systems [179].

Let us remind the reader that in the DIBR approach, implicit meshing was added to the 2D image pixels for obtaining automatic interpolation for little holes and cracks filling (severe disocclusions must still be covered by inpainting). We may therefore loosely state (this is really a philosophical interpretation; not a scientific equivalence) that DIBR is therefore not only implicitly a point cloud; it may also be regarded as a regularly meshed point cloud.

References

[1]   https://gl.ict.usc.edu/Research/PicoArray/PicoArray_2013E-Tech_864x486_30fps.mp4.

[2]   Y. Weissman. *'Lenticular imaging: Theory and practice'*. Pop3dart, 2018.

[3]   N. A. Dodgson. Autostereoscopic 3D displays. *IEEE Xplore Computer*. 2005;38(8):31–36. doi: 10.1109/MC.2005.252.

[4]   W. Funk. 'History of autostereoscopic cinema'. *Proceedings*. Volume 8288: Stereoscopic Displays and Applications XXIII; 82880R. 2012. doi: 10.1117/12.909410.

[5]   E. Thomas, and E. Potetsianakis (TNO). Beyond the VR HMD, ISO/IEC JTC 1/SC 29/WG 2 m56003. Online – January 2021.

[6]   https://commons.wikimedia.org/wiki/Category:Lenticular_printing#/media/File:Parallax_barrier_vs_lenticular_screen.svg.

[7]   https://commons.wikimedia.org/wiki/Category:Lenticular_printing#/media/File:Lenticular-Stereogram.jpg.

[8]   R. Munday, 'A holographic portrait of Queen Elizabeth II', https://av.tib.eu/media/21304?portal-locale=en.

[9]   R. Munday. 'A holographic portrait of Queen Elizabeth II'. *Proceedings of the 7th International Symposium on Display Holography, OpTIC Technicum*, St Asaph in North Wales, UK, 2006.

[10]   R. Munday. 'A holographic portrait of Queen Elizabeth II'. https://av.tib.eu/media/21304, doi: 10.5446/21304.

[11]   R. Munday. 'Queen Elizabeth II'. http://rob-munday.com/account-of-her-majesty-queen-elizabeth-ii-portrait-shoots.html.

[12]   LEVINE hologram expo: Chris Levine, Lightness of Being, ARCHEUS/POST-MODERN. www.archeus.com, 2010.

[13]   M. W. Halle, S. A. Benton, M. A. Klug, and J. S. Underkoffler, 'The generalized holographic stereogram'. *Proceedings*. Vol. 1461, Practical Holography V. 1991.

[14]   G. Saxby, and S. Zacharovas. *Practical Holography*. CRC Press, 2017, ISBN 978-1138455719.

[15]   T. Svoboda, T. Pajdla, and V. Hlaváč 1998. 'Epipolar geometry for panoramic cameras'. In: Burkhardt H., and Neumann B. (eds). Computer Vision – *ECCV 1998. Lecture Notes in Computer Science*, Vol. 1406. Berlin, Heidelberg: Springer. doi: 10.1007/BFb0055669.

[16]   Affine Epipolar Geometry. www.cse.iitd.ernet.in/~suban/vision/affine/node8.html.

[17]   Satellite Epipolar Rectification. lunokhod.org/?p=1206, 2013.

[18]   B. K. P. Horn. Recovering baseline and orientation from essential matrix. https://people.csail.mit.edu/bkph/articles/Essential.pdf, January 1990.

[19]   Essential matrix. https://en.wikipedia.org/wiki/Essential_matrix.

[20]   K. Schindler. Mathematical foundations of photogrammetry. In *Handbook of Geomathematics*. doi: 10.1007/978-3-642-27793-1_63-1, January 2014.

[21]   T. Moons, L. Van Gool, and M. Vergauwen, *3D Reconstruction from Multiple Images: Part 1: Principles*, Now Foundations and Trends, 2010.

[22]   R. Hartley, and A. Zisserman. *Multiple View Geometry in Computer Vision*. Cambridge: Cambridge University Press, 2004.

[23]   D. Nister. 'An efficient solution to the five-point relative pose problem'. *Proceedings of 2003 IEEE Computer Society Conference on Computer Vision and Pattern Recognition*. 2003. pp. II-195. doi: 10.1109/CVPR.2003.1211470.

[24]   D. Scaramuzza, and F. Fraundorfer. Visual odometry: Part I – The first 30 years and fundamentals. *IEEE Robotics and Automation Magazine*. 2011; 18(4):80–92.

[25]   K. Fathian, J. Jin, S.-G. Wee, D.-H. Lee, Y.-G. Kim, and N. R. Gans. Camera relative pose estimation for visual servoing using quaternions. *Robotics and Autonomous Systems*. 2018;107:45–62. doi:10.1016/j.robot.2018.05.014.

[26]   K. Fathian, J. P. Ramirez-Paredes, E. A. Doucette, J. W. Curtis, and N. R. Gans. QuEst: A quaternion-based approach for camera motion estimation from minimal feature points. *IEEE Robotics and Automation Letters*. 2018;3(2):857–864. doi: 10.1109/LRA.2018.2792142.

[27]   A. Fusiello. Tutorial on Rectification of Stereo Images. Università di Udine, Italia, 1999.

[28]   P. Monasse. 'Quasi-Euclidean epipolar rectification.' *Image Processing*. IPOL. 2011. Online. 2011-09-13. doi: 10.5201/ipol.2011.m_qer.

[29]   L. Moisan, P. Moulon, and P. Monasse. Fundamental matrix of a stereo pair, with a contrario elimination of outliers. *Image Processing*. 2016; 6: 89–113. doi:10.5201/ipol.2016.147.

[30]   S. Heinzle, P. Greisen, D. Gallup, *et al*. 2011. Computational stereo camera system with programmable control loop. *ACM Trans. Graph.* 2011. 30(4), Article 94: 10 pages. doi: 10.1145/2010324.1964989.

[31]   N. Snavely, S. M. Seitz, and R. Szeliski. 2006. Photo tourism: Exploring photo collections in 3D. *ACM Trans. Graph.* 2006;25(3):835–846. doi: 10.1145/1141911.1141964.

[32]   M. Shawn. 3D reconstruction from multiple images. https://cvgl.stanford. edu/teaching/cs231a_winter1415/prev/projects/CS231a-FinalReport-sgmccann. pdf.

[33]   K. J. Oh, and Y. S. Ho. 'Non-linear bi-directional prediction for depth coding'. in: Muneesawang P., Wu F., Kumazawa I., Roeksabutr A., Liao M., and Tang X. (eds). *Advances in Multimedia Information Processing – PCM 2009. PCM 2009. Lecture Notes in Computer Science*, Vol. 5879. Berlin, Heidelberg: Springer; 2009. doi:10.1007/978-3-642-10467-1_46.

[34]   J. H. Schwartz, and B. L. Krantz. *Sensation and Perception*. SAGE Publications. ASIN: B010WHKFH8, https://isle.hanover.edu/Ch07Depth Size/Ch07MotionParallaxIllus.html.

[35]   K. P. Aditya, V. K. Reddy, and H. Ramasangu. Enhancement technique for improving the reliability of disparity map under low light condition. *Procedia Technology*, 2014;14:236–243. doi:10.1016/j.protcy.2014.08.031.

[36]   S. W. Hasinoff, S. B. Kang, and R. Szeliski. Boundary matting for view synthesis, *Computer Vision and Image Understanding*, 2006;103(1): 22–32.

[37]   P. Tan, and P. Monasse. Stereo disparity through cost aggregation with guided filter. *Image Processing On Line*, 2014;4: 252–275. doi:10.5201/ ipol.2014.78.

[38]   A. Criminisi, and A. Blake. The SPS algorithm: Patching figural continuity and transparency by split-patch search, *IEEE Conference on Computer Vision and Pattern Recognition*, 2004;1: 342–349.

[39] C. Lee, and Y.S. Ho. Implementation of Boundary Noise Removal for View Synthesis, ISO/IEC JTC1/SC29/WG11, coding of moving pictures and audio, M16064 (2009).

[40] Y. Zhao, C. Zhu, Z. Chen, D. Tian, and L. Yu. Boundary artifact reduction in view synthesis of 3D video: From perspective of texture-depth alignment, broadcasting, *IEEE Transactions*, 2011;57(2): 510–522.

[41] L. Yang, T. Yendo, M. P. Tehrani, T. Fujii, and M. Tanimoto. Artifact reduction using reliability reasoning for image generation of FTV, *Journal of Visual Communication and Image Representation*, 2010;21(5–6): 542–560.

[42] L. Yang, T. Yendo, M. P. Tehrani, T. Fujii, and M. Tanimoto. View synthesis using probabilistic reliability reasoning for FTV, *The Journal of The Institute of Image Information and Television Engineers,* 2010;64 (11):1671–1677.

[43] L. Yang, T. Yendo, M. P. Tehrani, T. Fujii, and M. Tanimoto. Error supression in view synthesis using reliability reasoning for FTV, *IEEE 3DTV-CON*, pp. 1–4, 2010.

[44] L. Yang, T. Yendo, M. P. Tehrani, T. Fujii, and M. Tanimoto. Probabilistic reliability based view synthesis for FTV, *Image Processing (ICIP), 2010 17th IEEE International Conference*, 1785–1788 (2010).

[45] Y. Han, W. Liu, X. Huang, S. Wang, and R. Qin. Stereo dense image matching by adaptive fusion of multiple-window matching results. *Remote Sensing*, 2020;12(19):3138. doi: 10.3390/rs12193138.

[46] L. Keselman, J. I. Woodfill, A. Grunnet-Jepsen and A. Bhowmik. Intel(R) RealSense(TM) Stereoscopic Depth Cameras. *2017 IEEE Conference on Computer Vision and Pattern Recognition Workshops (CVPRW)*, 2017, pp. 1267–1276, doi: 10.1109/CVPRW.2017.167.

[47] A. Grunnet-Jepsen, and D. Tong. Depth Post-Processing for Intel® RealSense™ D400 Depth Cameras, Revision 1.0.2, https://dev.intelrealsense.com/docs/depth-post-processing.

[48] Ames Stereo Pipeline Documentation Release 2.7.0, https://stereopipeline.readthedocs.io/en/latest/.

[49] D. Baker. 'Haynes NASA Moon Missions 1969–1972 (Apollo 12, 14, 15, 16 and 17) Operations Manual: An Insight into the Engineering, Technology and Operation of NASA's Advanced Lunar Flights'. J H Haynes & Co Ltd, 2019.

[50] D. Barath, and L. Hajder. 'Novel ways to estimate homography from local affine transformations'. *VISIGRAPP*, Vol. 3: VISAPP, 434–445 (2016).

[51] K. Shibata, M. Panahpour Tehrani, K. Takahashi, and T. Fujii. 'Estimation of dense displacement by scale invariant polynomial expansion of heterogeneous multi-view images', *IEICE Transactions ED*, pp. 2048–2051, 2017, E100-D, No. 9, doi:10.1587/transinf.2016PCL0008.

[52] G. Farneback. 'Two-frame motion estimation based on polynomial expansion'. *Proc. of SCIA*, pp. 363–370, 2003.

[53] K. Shibata, M. P. Tehrani, K. Takahashi, and T. Fujii. Time-space interpolation for multiview image synthesis. IMPS, P-3-03, 2015.

[54] R. C. Gonzalez and R. E. Woods, *Digital Image Processing* (3rd ed.), Prentice-Hall, Englewood Cliffs, NJ, 2008.

[55] Z. Zhang. Flexible camera calibration by viewing a plane from unknown orientations. *Proceedings of the Seventh IEEE International Conference on Computer Vision*, pp. 666–673, 1999.

[56] R. C. Bolles, H. H. Baker, and D. H. Marimont Epipolar-plane image analysis: An approach to determining structure from motion. *International Journal of Computer Vision,* 1987;1: 7–55. doi:10.1007/BF00128525.

[57] Y. Sun and L. Yu. Light field virtual view rendering based on EPI-representations. *ZTE Communications*, 2016;14(3):55–59.

[58] Y. Boykov, O. Veksler, and R. Zabih. Fast approximate energy minimization via graph cuts. *IEEE Transactions on Pattern Analysis and Machine Intelligence*, 2001;23(11): 1222–1239. doi:10.1109/34.969114.

[59] Y. Boykov and V. Kolmogorov. An experimental comparison of min-cut/max-flow algorithms for energy minimization in vision. *IEEE Transactions on Pattern Analysis and Machine Intelligence*, 2004;26(9): 1124–1137. doi:10.1109/TPAMI.2004.60.

[60] V. Kolmogorov and R. Zabih. What energy functions can be minimized via graph cuts? In *Proceedings of the 7th European Conference on Computer Vision-Part III (ECCV'02)*. 2002. Springer-Verlag, Berlin, Heidelberg, 65–81.

[61] W. J. Cook, W. H. Cunningham, and W. R. Pulleyblank. Alexander Schrijver, *Combinatorial Optimization*, 1997.

[62] H. S. Özsaraç, FPGA implementation of graph cut method for real time stereo matching, Master Thesis, Middle East Technical University, 2010.

[63] D. Kobori and T. Maruyama. An acceleration of a graph cut segmentation with FPGA. *22nd International Conference on Field Programmable Logic and Applications (FPL)*, 2012, pp. 407–413, doi: 10.1109/FPL.2012.6339137.

[64] I. Daribo, Z. Garrett, Y. Takaya, and H. Saito. 'Accelerating live graph-cut-based object tracking using CUDA.' IntechOpen, 2011. doi: 10.5772/15719.

[65] P. Narayanan and V. Vineet. 'CUDA cuts: Fast graph cuts on the GPU'. In *2008 IEEE Computer Society Conference on Computer Vision and Pattern Recognition Workshops (CVPR Workshops)*, Anchorage, AK, 2008, pp. 1–8. doi: 10.1109/CVPRW.2008.4563095.

[66] Y. Peng, L. Chen, F. Ou-Yang, W. Chen, and J. Yong. JF-cut: A parallel graph cut approach for large-scale image and video. *IEEE Transactions on Image Processing*, 2015;24(2): 655–666. doi:10.1109/TIP.2014.2378060.

[67] J. Yuan, E. Bae, and X. Tai. A study on continuous max-flow and min-cut approaches. In *2010 IEEE Computer Society Conference on Computer Vision and Pattern Recognition*, 2010, pp. 2217–2224, doi: 10.1109/CVPR.2010.5539903.

[68] S. Roy and I. J. Cox. A maximum-flow formulation of the N camera stereo correspondence problem. *Proceedings of the International Conference on Computer Vision*, pp. 492–499, 1998.

[69]   A. Zureiki, M. Devy, and R. Chatila. Stereo matching and graph cuts. In *Stereo Vision*, A. Bhatti (ed.), IntechOpen; 2008. doi: 10.5772/5888.

[70]   Y. Boykov, O. Veksler, and R. Zabih. *Markov random fields with efficient approximations. Proceedings of the 1998 IEEE Computer Society Conference on Computer Vision and Pattern Recognition (Cat. No. 98CB36231)*, pp. 648–655, 1998, doi: 10.1109/CVPR.1998.698673.

[71]   J. Jiang. Image Segmentation with Graph Cuts, https://julie-jiang.github.io/image-segmentation/.

[72]   J. Yuan, E. Bae, X. C. Tai, *et al.* A spatially continuous max-flow and min-cut framework for binary labeling problems. *Numer. Math.* 2014;126:559–587. doi:10.1007/s00211-013-0569-x.

[73]   L. E. Sucar, *Probabilistic Graphical Models: Principles and Applications,* Springer Nature Switzerland AG, 2021.

[74]   Summary on MPEG-I Visual Activities, Serial Number 19737, ISO/IEC JTC 1/SC 29/WG 04 N0007 October 2020, Online.

[75]   J. Sancho, G. Vazquez, M. Chavarrías, C. Sanz, and E. Juárez. Holographic Vision for Immersive Tele-Robotic OperatioN, HoviTron, deliverable D2.1: Test conditions and refactorization. H2020-ICT-2019-3, Grant Agreement no. 951989, December 2020.

[76]   W. Daolei, and K. B. Lim. Obtaining depth maps from segment based stereo matching using graph cuts, *J. Vis. Commun. Image R.* 2011;22:325–331.

[77]   Dawid Mieloch, Depth Estimation in Free-Viewpoint Television, PhD Thesis, Poznań University of Technology.

[78]   https://gitlab.com/mpeg-i-visual/ivde

[79]   Manual of Immersive Video Depth Estimation 3, Serial Number 20010, ISO/IEC JTC 1/SC 29/WG 4 N0058, January 2021, Online.

[80]   M. P. Tehrani, A. Ishikawa, S. Sakazawa, and A. Koike. Iterative colour correction of multicamera systems using corresponding feature points. *Journal of Visual Communication and Image Representation,* 2010;21(5–6):377–391.

[81]   C. Fehn. Depth-image-based rendering (DIBR), compression and transmission for a new approach on 3DTV. *SPIE USA*, 2004;5291: 93–104.

[82]   D. Scharstein, *View Synthesis Using Stereo Vision*, Springer-Verlag, Berlin Heidelberg, 1999, doi: 10.1007/3-540-48725-5.

[83]   'History of computer animation (CGI): Michael Jackson – Black Or White (1991)'. https://computeranimationhistory-cgi.jimdofree.com/michael-jackson-black-or-white-1991/.

[84]   T. Gurdan, M. R. Oswald, D. Gurdan, and D. Cremers. Spatial and temporal interpolation of multi-view image sequences. *German Conference on Pattern Recognition*, 2014.

[85]   D. P. Petersen, and D. Middleton. Sampling and reconstruction of wave-number-limited functions in N-dimensional euclidean spaces. *Information and Control*, 1962;5(4):279–323. doi: 10.1016/S0019-9958(62)90633-2.

[86]   J. C. Burton. End-to-end analysis of hexagonal vs. rectangular sampling in digital imaging systems. Ph.D. Dissertation. College of William and Mary, USA. Order Number: UMI Order No. GAX94-03277, 1993.

[87] C. Zhang, and T. Chen, A survey on image-based rendering—representation, sampling and compression, *Signal Processing: Image Communication*, 2004;19(1):1–28. doi: 10.1016/j.image.2003.07.001.

[88] Analysis, Acquisition, and Processing of Light Field for Computational Photography: http://chiakailiang.org/papers/thesis.pdf.

[89] C. Chen and D. Schonfeld. Geometrical plenoptic sampling. *2009 16th IEEE International Conference on Image Processing (ICIP)*, 2009, pp. 3769–3772, doi: 10.1109/ICIP.2009.5414363.

[90] C. Zhu, H. Zhang, Y. Y. Qiuming Liu, and H. Su. Frequency analysis of light field sampling for texture information. *Optics Express,* 2020;28 (8):11548–11572. doi: 10.1364/OE.383606.

[91] J.-X. Chai, X. Tong, S.-C. Chan, and H.-Y. Shum. Plenoptic sampling. *Proceedings of the 27th Annual Conference on Computer Graphics and Interactive Techniques (SIGGRAPH'00)*. ACM Press/Addison-Wesley Publishing Co., Reading, MA, 2000, pp. 307–318. doi: 10.1145/ 344779.344932.

[92] H.-Y. Shum, S.-C. Chan, and S. B. Kang. *Image-Based Rendering.* Springer, Berlin, 2011.

[93] C. Gilliam, P. L. Dragotti, and M. Brookes. On the spectrum of the plenoptic function. *IEEE Trans Image Process,* 2014;23(2):502–516. doi: 10.1109/TIP.2013.2292363. PMID: 26270905.

[94] Z. Lin, and H.-Y. Shum. On the number of samples needed in light field rendering with constant-depth assumption. *Proceedings IEEE Conference on Computer Vision and Pattern Recognition*, 2000, doi: 10.1109/ CVPR.2000.855873.

[95] M. Diebold. *Light-Field Imaging and Heterogeneous Light Fields: Orientation estimation and 3D Reconstruction.* AV Akademiker verlag, 2017.

[96] Y. Mori, N. Fukushima, T. Yendo, T. Fujii, and M. Tanimoto. View generation with 3D warping using depth information for FTV. *Signal Process. Image Commun.*, 2009;24:65–72.

[97] L. Yang, M. Panahpour Tehrani, T. Fujii, and M. Tanimoto. High-quality virtual view synthesis in 3DTV and FTV. *3D Research*, 2011;2(4):1–13.

[98] ISO/IEC JTC1/SC29/WG11: View synthesis algorithm in View Synthesis Reference Software 2.0 (VSRS2.0), in MPEG Doc. M16090, Lausanne, 2009, pp. 1–5.

[99] M. P. Tehrani, T. Tezuka, K. Takahashi, and T. Fujii. Free-viewpoint image synthesis using superpixel segmentation. *APSIPA Transactions on Signal and Information Processing*, 2017;6:e5. doi: 10.1017/ATSIP.

[100] D. Bonatto, S. Fachada, and G. Lafruit. RaViS: Real-time accelerated View Synthesizer for immersive video 6DoF VR. *IS&T Electronic Imaging*, San Francisco, California, USA, January 2020.

[101] S. Fachada, D. Bonatto, A. Schenkel, and G. Lafruit. Depth image based view synthesis with multiple reference views for virtual reality. *2018 – 3DTV-Conference: The True Vision – Capture, Transmission and Display of 3D Video (3DTV-CON)*, 2018, pp. 1–4, doi: 10.1109/3DTV.2018.8478484.

[102]   Y. Mori, N. Fukushima, T. Yendo, T. Fujii, and M. Tanimoto. View generation with 3D warping using depth information for FTV. *Signal Process. Image Commun.*, 2009;24:65–72.

[103]   F. Dufaux, B. P. Popescu, and M. Cagnazzo. *Emerging Technologies for 3D Video: Creation, Coding, Transmission and Rendering.* Wiley–Blackwell, New York, 2013.

[104]   Max Planck Institute for Intelligent Systems, http://sintel.is.tue.mpg.de/downloads.

[105]   ISO/IEC FDIS 21794-2(E), Information technology — Plenoptic image coding system — Part 2: Light field coding, ISO/IEC JTC1/SC29/WG01, 2021.

[106]   V. Jantet, Layered depth images for multi-view coding, ENS-Cachan Bruz and INRIA Rennes, https://tel.archives-ouvertes.fr/tel-00758301v2/file/jantet-12-PhD.pdf, Thesis, 2012.

[107]   C. Guillemot and O. L. Meur. Image inpainting: overview and recent advances. *IEEE Signal Processing Magazine*, 2014;31(1):127–144. doi: 10.1109/MSP.2013.2273004.

[108]   P.-A. Blanche, *Optical Holography: Materials, Theory and Applications,* Elsevier, Amsterdam, 2019.

[109]   I. Daribo and B. Pesquet-Popescu. Depth-aided image inpainting for novel view synthesis, in *IEEE International Workshop on Multimedia and Signal Processing*, Saint-Malo, France, October 2010, pp. 167–170.

[110]   C. Lee and Y. S. Ho. Boundary filtering on synthesized views of 3D video, in *Int. Conf. on Future Generation Communication and Networking Symposia*, 2008, pp. 15–18.

[111]   P. Buyssens, M. Daisy, D. Tschumperlé, and O. Lézoray. Superpixel-based depth map inpainting for RGB-D view synthesis, in *2015 IEEE Int. Conf. on Image Processing (ICIP)*, Quebec City, QC, 2015, pp. 4332–4336.

[112]   T. Tezuka, M. Panahpour Tehrani, K. Suzuki, K. Takahashi, and T. Fujii. View synthesis using superpixel based inpainting capable of occlusion handling and hole filling, in *Picture Coding Symp. (PCS)*, 2015, pp. 124–128.

[113]   T. Tezuka, K. Takahashi, and T. Fujii. 3D visualization from view plus depth data using superpixel representations, in *Int. Workshop on Smart Info-Media Systems in Asia*, pp. 198–200, 2013.

[114]   A. Radhakrishna. SLIC superpixels compared to state-of-the-art super-pixel methods. *IEEE Trans. Pattern Analysis Machine Intelligence*, 2012; 34:2274–2282.

[115]   Y. Mao, G. Cheung, A. Ortega, and Y. Ji. Expansion hole filling in depth-image-based rendering using graph-based interpolation, in *IEEE Int. Conf. on Acoustics, Speech and Signal Processing*, Vancouver, Canada, May 2013, pp. 1859–1863.

[116]   Y. Mao, G. Cheung, and Y. Ji. Image interpolation during DIBR view synthesis using graph Fourier transform, in *3DTV-Conf. 2014*, Budapest, Hungary, July 2014, pp. 1–4.

[117]   W. Mark, L. Mcmillan, and G. Bishop. Post-rendering 3D warping, in *Proc. Symp. I3D Graphics*, 1997, pp. 7–16.

[118] G. Shen, W.-S. Kim, S. K. Narang, A. Ortega, J. Lee, and H. Wey. Edge-adaptive transforms for efficient depth map coding, in *IEEE Picture Coding Symp.*, Nagoya, Japan, December 2010, pp. 566–569.

[119] Y. Mao, G. Cheung, and Y. Ji. On constructing z-dimensional DIBR-synthesized images. *IEEE Trans. Multimedia*, 2016;18(8):1453–1468.

[120] L. Zhang, and W. J. Tam. Stereoscopic image generation based on depth images for 3D TV. *IEEE Trans. Broadcasting*, 2005;51:191–199.

[121] W. Y. Chen, Y. L. Chang, S. F. Lon, L. F. Ding, and L. G. Chen. Efficient depth image-based rendering with edge dependent depth filter and interpolation, *Proc. of IEEE Int. Conf. on Multimedia and Expo*, 2005, pp. 1314–1317.

[122] Y. K. Park, K. Jung, Y. Oh, *et al.*. Depth-image-based rendering for 3DTV service over T-DMB. *Signal Process. Image Commun.*, 2009;24:122–136.

[123] Y. Horng, Y. Tseng, and T. Chang. Stereoscopic images generation with directional Gaussian filter, in *Proc. of ISCAS*, 2010, pp. 2650–2653.

[124] P. Lee. Nongeometric distortion smoothing approach for depth map pre-processing. *IEEE Trans. Multimedia*, 2011;13(2):246–254.

[125] D. Tian, P. Lai, P. Lopez, and C. Gomila. View synthesis techniques for 3D video, in *SPIE, Applications of Digital Image Processing XXXII*, vol. 7443, 2009, pp. 1–11.

[126] O. Lezoray, and L. Grady (Editors). *Image Processing and Analysis with Graphs: Theory and Practice,* 1st edition. CRC Press, Boca Raton, FL, 2012.

[127] ISO/IEC JTC1/SC29/WG11. View synthesis algorithm in View Synthesis Reference Software 2.0 (VSRS2.0), in MPEG Doc. M16090, Lausanne, 2009, pp. 1–5.

[128] M. Schmeing, and X. Jiang. Faithful disocclusion filling in depth image based rendering using superpixel-based inpainting. *IEEE Trans. Multimedia*, 2015;17(12):2160–2173.

[129] D. Min, D. Kim, S. Yun, and K. Sohn. 2D/3D freeview video generation for 3DTV system. *Signal Processing: Image Commun.,* 2009;24(1–2):31–48.

[130] P. Kauff, N. Atzpadin, C. Fehn, M. Müller, O. Schreer, A. Smolic, and R. Tanger. Depth map creation and image-based rendering for advanced 3DTV services providing interoperability and scalability. *Signal Processing: Image Commun.,* 2007;22(2):217–234.

[131] C. L. Zitnick, S. B. Kang, M. Uyttendaele, S. Winder, and R. Szeliski. High-quality video view interpolation using a layered representation, *SIGGRAPH'04*, 2004;23(3):600–608.

[132] M. P. Tehrani, T. Tezuka, K. Takahashi, and T. Fujii. Free-viewpoint image synthesis using superpixel segmentation. *APSIPA Transactions on Signal and Information Processing*, 2017;6:e5. doi:10.1017/ATSIP.

[133] S. Roy and I. J. Cox. A maximum-flow formulation of the N-camera stereo correspondence problem. In *Proceedings of the Sixth International Conference on Computer Vision (ICCV'98)*. IEEE Computer Society, USA, 492, 1998.

[134] A. Smolic, K. Müller, K. Dix, P. Merkle, P. Kauff, and T. Wiegand. Intermediate view interpolation based on multiview video plus depth for advanced 3D video systems. *Proceedings of the International Conference on Image Processing*, 2008, pp. 2448–2451.

[135] K. Müller, A. Smolic, K. Dix, P. Kauff, and T. Wiegand. Reliability-based generation and view synthesis in layered depth video. *International Workshop on Multimedia Signal Processing*, 34–39 (2008).

[136] Canny edge detector: J. Canny. A computational approach to edge detection. *IEEE Transactions on Pattern Analysis and Machine Intelligence*, 1986;PAMI-8(6):679–698. doi: 10.1109/TPAMI.1986.4767851.

[137] C. Lee, and Y. S. Ho. Boundary filtering on synthesized views of 3D video. *FGCNS'08: Proceedings of the 2008 Second International Conference on Future Generation Communication and Networking Symposia*, 2008, pp. 15–18.

[138] https://gitlab.com/mpeg-i-visual/rvs

[139] https://gitlab.com/mpeg-i-visual/tmiv

[140] https://mpeg-miv.org/

[141] https://lisaserver.ulb.ac.be/rvs/

[142] B. Salahieh, M. Chen, M. Dmitrichenko, and J. Boyce. Immersive video playback of HEVC bitstream on Intel GPU. ISO/IEC JTC 1/SC 29/WG04/ m55800, January 2021.

[143] D. Bonatto, S. Fachada, S. Rogge, A. Munteanu, and G. Lafruit. Real-time depth video based rendering for 6-DoF HMD navigation and light field displays. *IEEE Access*, 2021;9:146868–146887. doi: 10.1109/ACCESS.2021. 3123529.

[144] T. Kanade, P. Rander and P. J. Narayanan. Virtualized reality: constructing virtual worlds from real scenes. *IEEE MultiMedia*, 1997;4(1):34–47. doi: 10.1109/93.580394.

[145] D. Scharstein. Stereo vision for view synthesis. *Proceedings CVPR IEEE Computer Society Conference on Computer Vision and Pattern Recognition*, pp. 852–858, 1996, doi: 10.1109/CVPR.1996.517171.

[146] S. Kwak, J. Yun, J. Y. Jeong, W.-S. Cheong, and J. Seo. Ray-based blending weight for 6DoF view synthesis, ISO/IEC JTC1/SC29/WG11 MPEG2020/m54409, June 2020, Online.

[147] Y. J. Jeong. Light-field rendering in the view interpolation region without dense light-field reconstruction, *Journal of Physics: Conference Series*, Volume 1098, *2018 2nd International Conference on Computer Graphics and Digital Image Processing (CGDIP 2018)*, 27–29 July 2018, Bangkok, Thailand.

[148] B. Mildenhall, P. P. Srinivasan, R. Ortiz-Cayon, *et al.* 'Local Light Field Fusion: Practical View Synthesis with Prescriptive Sampling Guidelines,' SIGGRAPH 2019, arXiv:1905.00889.

[149] J. P. Peter Hedman, T. Price, J.-M. Frahm, G. Drettakis, and G. Brostow. Deep blending for free-viewpoint image-based rendering. *ACM Trans. Graph.*, 2018;37(6). Article 257 (November 2018), 15 pages. doi: 10.1145/ 3272127.3275084.

[150] R. Martin-Brualla, N. Radwan, M. S. M. Sajjadi, J. T. Barron, A. Dosovitskiy, and D. Duckworth, 'NeRF in the Wild: Neural Radiance Fields for Unconstrained Photo Collections,' Conference on Computer Vision and Pattern Recognition, 2021, arXiv:2008.02268.

[151] B. Mildenhall, P. P. Srinivasan, M. Tancik, J. T. Barron, and R. Ramamoorthi. 'Ren Ng, NeRF: Representing Scenes as Neural Radiance Fields for View Synthesis,' arXiv:2003.08934.

[152] S. Lombardi, T. Simon, J. Saragih, G. Schwartz, A. Lehrmann, and Y. Sheikh. Neural volumes: Learning dynamic renderable volumes from images. *ACM Transactions on Graphics (SIGGRAPH 2019)*, 2019;38(4). Article 65, doi: 10.1145/3306346.3323020.

[153] S.-H. Sun, M. Huh, Y.-H. Liao, N. Zhang, and J. J. Lim. Multi-view to novel view: Synthesizing novel views with self-learned confidence. *Proceedings of the 15th European Conference on Computer Vision*, 2018.

[154] S. H. Sun, M. Huh, Y. H. Liao, N. Zhang, and J. J. Lim. Multi-view to novel view: Synthesizing novel views with self-learned confidence. In: Ferrari V., Hebert M., Sminchisescu C., Weiss Y. (eds) *Computer Vision – ECCV 2018. Lecture Notes in Computer Science*, vol. 11207, 2018. Springer, Cham. doi:10.1007/978-3-030-01219-9_10.

[155] D. Yue, M. S. Khan Gul, M. Bätz, J. Keinert and R. Mantiuk. A benchmark of light field view interpolation methods. *2020 IEEE International Conference on Multimedia and Expo Workshops (ICMEW)*, pp. 1–6, 2020, doi: 10.1109/ICMEW46912.2020.9106041.

[156] G. Riegler, and V. Koltun. Free view synthesis. In: Vedaldi A., Bischof H., Brox T., Frahm J. M. (eds) *Computer Vision – ECCV 2020. Lecture Notes in Computer Science*, vol. 12364, 2020. Springer, Cham. doi:10.1007/978-3-030-58529-7_37.

[157] M.-L. Shih, S.-Y. Su, J. Kopf, and J.-B. Huang. '3D Photography using Context-aware Layered Depth Inpainting,' Conference on Computer Vision and Pattern Recognition, 2020, arXiv:2004.04727.

[158] N. K. Kalantari, T.-C. Wang, and R. Ramamoorthi. Learning-based view synthesis for light field cameras. *ACM Trans. Graph.* 2016;35(6). Article 193 (November 2016), 10 pages. doi: 10.1145/2980179.2980251.

[159] D. Lischinski, and A. Rappoport. Image-based rendering for non-diffuse synthetic scenes. In: Drettakis G., Max N. (eds) *Rendering Techniques'98. EGSR 1998. Eurographics*, 1998. Springer, Vienna. doi:10.1007/978-3-7091-6453-2_28.

[160] J. Flynn, M. Broxton, P. Debevec, *et al.* DeepView: View synthesis with learned gradient descent. *2019 IEEE/CVF Conference on Computer Vision and Pattern Recognition (CVPR)*, 2019, pp. 2362–2371, doi: 10.1109/CVPR.2019.00247.

[161] L. Levkovich-Maslyuk, A. Ignatenko, A. Zhirkov, *et al.* Depth image-based representation and compression for static and animated 3-D objects. *IEEE Transactions on Circuits and Systems for Video Technology*, 2004;14(7):1032–1045. doi:10.1109/TCSVT.2004.830676.

[162] S. Wanner, and B. Goldluecke. Reconstructing reflective and transparent surfaces from epipolar plane images. In: Weickert J., Hein M., Schiele B. (eds) *Pattern Recognition. GCPR 2013. Lecture Notes in Computer Science*, vol. 8142, 2013. Springer, Berlin, Heidelberg. doi:10.1007/978-3-642-40602-7_1.

[163] A. Bulanovs. 'Principles of Recording Image-Matrix Holographic Stereogram,' Daugavpils University, Latvia, 2015.

[164] D.-K. Kang, M. A. Rivera, J. J. Báez-Rojas, and M.-L. Cruz-López. New fully functioning digital hologram recording system and its applications. *Optical Engineering*, 2010;49(10):105802. doi:10.1117/1.3497068.

[165] H. I. Bjelkhagen. Super-realistic-looking images based on colour holography and Lippmann photography, *Proceedings Volume 4737, Holography: A Tribute to Yuri Denisyuk and Emmett Leith*; (2002). doi: 10.1117/12.474952.

[166] J. Nam, M. Park, and S. Shin. Accommodation-dependent holographic images quality evaluation based on human visual system. In *Imaging and Applied Optics Congress*, The Optical Society (Optical Society of America, 2020), paper HTh4H.7.

[167] J. Kim, Y. Lim, K. Hong, *et al.* Electronic tabletop holographic display: Design, implementation, and evaluation. *Appl. Sci.,* 2019;9(4):705. doi: 10.3390/app9040705.

[168] A. Sarakinos, A. Lembessis, and N. Zervos. A transportable system for the in situ recording of color Denisyuk holograms of Greek cultural heritage artifacts in silver halide panchromatic emulsions and an optimized illuminating device for the finished holograms. *J. Phys.: Conf. Ser.,* 415 012024 (2013), doi: 10.1088/1742-6596/415/1/012024.

[169] P. W. M. Tsang, T.-C. Poon, and W. K. Cheung. Intensity image-embedded binary holograms. *Applied Optics*, 2013;52(1):A26–A32. doi:10.1364/AO.52.000A26.

[170] T. J. Naughton, J. B. Mc Donald, Y. Frauel, and B. Javidi. Efficient compression of digital holograms for Internet transmission. *The 15th Annual Meeting of the IEEE Lasers and Electro-Optics Society*, doi: 10.1109/LEOS.2002.1133904.

[171] J. Hong. Holographic printing: Technologies and requirements. In *JPEG Pleno Holography Workshop*, ITU-T/CICG, Geneva, Switzerland, March 2019.

[172] S. M. Muddala. Free view rendering for 3D video edge-aided rendering and depth-based image inpainting. Department of Information and Communication Systems, Faculty of Science, Technology and Media Mid Sweden University, Doctoral Thesis No. 226, Sundsvall, Sweden, 2015.

[173] J. Jurik, T. Burnett, M. Klug, and P. E. Debevec. Geometry-corrected light field rendering for creating a holographic stereogram. *CVPR Workshops*, 2012

[174] S. Fachada, D. Bonatto, and G. Lafruit. High-quality holographic stereogram generation using four RGBD images. *Applied Optics*, 2021;60(4): A250–A259. Online meeting.

[175] L. Jorissen. Wide baseline view interpolation for light field displays and transparent light field display design. Dissertation for the degree of Doctor of Philosophy in Computer Science at Hasselt University, 2021.

[176] S. Vagharshakyan, R. Bregovic, and A. Gotchev. Light field reconstruction using shearlet transform. *IEEE Transactions on Pattern Analysis and Machine Intelligence,* 2018;40(1):133–147. doi: 10.1109/TPAMI.2017. 2653101.

[177] E. Sahin, S. Vagharshakyan, J. Mäkinen, R. Bregovic, and A. Gotchev. Shearlet-domain light field reconstruction for holographic stereogram generation. *2016 IEEE International Conference on Image Processing (ICIP),* 2016, pp. 1479–1483, doi: 10.1109/ICIP.2016.7532604.

[178] S. Vagharshakyan, R. Bregovic, and A. Gotchev. Image based rendering technique via sparse representation in shearlet domain. *2015 IEEE International Conference on Image Processing (ICIP),* 2015, pp. 1379–1383, doi: 10.1109/ICIP.2015.7351026.

[179] L. Quan, and T. Kanade. *Image-Based Modeling.* Springer-Verlag, New York, 2010.

Chapter 13

Multi-camera acquisition systems

Inspired by human vision (stereo vision), 3D imaging has found its way in different fields. To capture dynamic 3D content, the data acquisition system must be extended from a single camera to a stereo camera or even a multi-camera system. They can acquire a large amount of 3D scene information with cameras put all around the scene. On the other hand, so-called plenoptic cameras, which are the acquisition counterpart of integral photography displays. In essence, a sheet of microlenses transforms the image of the scene into a multitude of tiny images that are captured by the camera sensor. Post-processing software can then fuse all these tiny images into high-resolution images with parallax and all kinds of special effects like refocusing on any portion of the image without having to reshoot the scene multiple times. All this is made possible with so-called plenoptic imaging that we will briefly survey in this chapter. Let us first start with more conventional approaches using two or more conventional cameras.

13.1 Stereo vision

With a pair of eyes, humans can observe the world in 3D. Therefore, setting up a pair of cameras, one should be able to see the world in 3D after combining the information from both views. One simple solution is to have two cameras (Figure 13.1) with similar intervals of human eyes, and each camera view directly fed to a display in front of our eyes, for example a head-mounted display (HMD). However, if we want to reconstruct the 3D scene with depth of field on a single display, we need to simulate the process humans naturally do in the brain. In a stereo pair of images captured by two cameras, a point in 3D space is not located in a similar coordinate of the imaging sensor. In the other world, the relative position of a projected point on two imaging sensors is dependent on the depth of the same point in the 3D space. In order to extract the depth of the field from the stereo camera planes, we need to find points that are similar in two different images. This process is called stereo matching which has already been discussed in Section 12.2. In general, the recommended camera interval (baseline) for a stereo camera to observe the real world is similar to the human eye distance. However, depending on the application, the camera interval can be variable. Stereoscopy has a long history and is a well-studied topic.

Figure 13.1   Stereo camera and stereo vision [1]

13.2   Multiview vision

To extend the field of view in 3D, we either need to move around to capture the scene from different angles but in different time stamps, or increase the number of cameras that capture our desired scene sufficiently from different angles. Similar to stereo vision, the concept of extracting depth of field can be extended from two cameras to multiple cameras, while the matching algorithm to detect the correspondences among views will be more complex. Multiview camera array can be set up in several configurations (baseline and viewing angle). The number of cameras and complexity of 3D reconstruction (depth of field) has a trade-off. Since horizontal parallax is natural for the human eye, camera arrays on a line or arc are most common. However, there are also many ways to capture for having horizontal parallax that can add more degrees of freedom. There have been many examples of capturing with multi-camera.

Several acquisition systems to capture a 3D scene by multiple cameras have been developed [2–5]. Figure 13.2 shows the '100-camera system' [2,3] of Nagoya University. This system consists of one host-server PC and 100 client PCs (called 'nodes') connected to each camera. The host PC generates a synchronization signal and distributes it to all of the nodes. This system is capable of capturing not only high-resolution video with 30 fps but also recording analogue sound signals of up to 96 kHz. The camera setting is flexible. MPEG test sequences 'Rena', 'Pantomime', 'Champagne_tower' and 'Dog'. Other sequences, 'Kendo' and 'Balloons' were taken using the same system with only nine cameras while the actors are moving (Figure 13.3).

The Université Libre de Bruxelles (ULB) [4] captured a video dataset with a 3×5 camera array. Each camera is a 4k micro-studio Blackmagic cameras (3,840 × 2,160 pixels @ 30 fps, i.e. 2,160p30 format) connected to a rack of dedicated Blackmagic lossless recording units, using DaVinci Resolve Multiview recording software, as shown in Figure 13.4.

13.2.1   Geometry correction for camera array

For geometry correction, one approach is the camera calibration-based rectification method [6]. While many geometric methods have the limitation of the number of cameras, this method is designed for a multi-camera setup. The outline of our

Figure 13.2 100 camera capturing system (Arc, 1D, and 2D). Courtesy of Nagoya University (1,024×768, 30 fps)

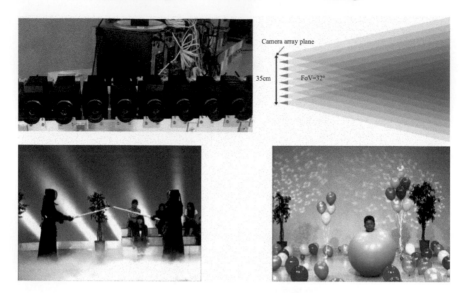

Figure 13.3   Moving camera array. Courtesy of Nagoya University –
1,024×768, 30 fps

correction method is as follows. First, all camera parameters, that is intrinsic and extrinsic parameters, are calibrated [7] and lens distortions are removed during this process. Second, an ideal camera array is fitted by PCA (principal component analysis) as shown in Figure 13.5. Finally, we can correct homographies by computing the relationship between ideal projection and the real captured image. Note that this geometrical correction does not need camera intrinsic and extrinsic parameters in an explicit form that is used for rectification in stereo (two or three) camera setups. However, it can provide the camera parameters in complete form, unlike the non-metric rectification methods that perform correction after capturing without camera calibration.

13.2.2   Colour correction for camera array

Basically, colour correction in a multi-camera system can be done either by adjusting the parameters (gain level, brightness level, etc.) or by image processing. A common correction approach is to self-calibrate each camera using an automatic gain and white balance adjustment. The result of this method varies, depending on what part of the scene is viewed by each camera. Considering the assumption of fixed illumination throughout all viewpoints (i.e. the Lambertian condition where light rays from the corresponding colours are the same), we prefer an approach that performs colour correction using image processing techniques.

The image processing techniques for colour correction [8–24] of multi-camera systems are generally divided into two categories, which are colour correction using a colour pattern board [9,10] and colour correction without colour pattern board [12–24]. The correction approach using a colour pattern board [12,13] can

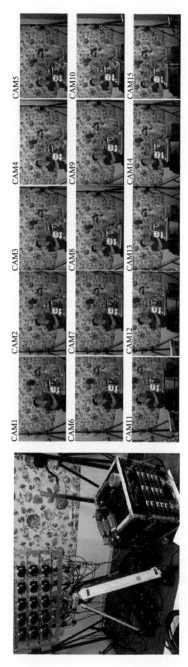

Figure 13.4 *Studio setup with 3×5 camera array, and example of 3×5 views. Courtesy of Université Libre de Bruxelles [4]*

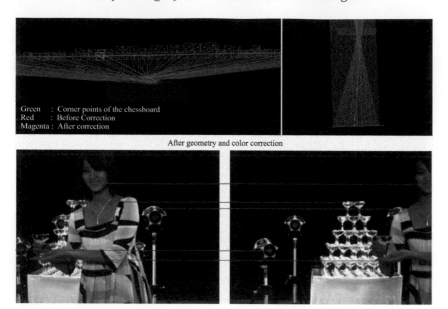

Green   : Corner points of the chessboard
Red   : Before Correction
Magenta : After correction

After geometry and color correction

Figure 13.5   Correction of geometry and colour differences. Courtesy of Nagoya University [25]

achieve the average colour intensity among viewpoints. However, due to limitations of this approach, it is not suitable for large areas, outdoor situations, and sparse multi-camera systems. Alternatively, the colour correction methods without colour pattern boards [12–22] are more popular, since they can be performed after capturing, and applied to any situation, for example indoor and outdoor. However, using these methods, the average colour intensity cannot be achieved after colour correction.

Furthermore, the correction methods without colour pattern board [12–22] can be classified into illumination-based [8–12,17–22] and feature-based [13–16,23,24] approaches. Despite the nonlinear characteristic of colour intensities, the illumination-based approach is easy to implement and basically linear transformations are derived for correction transformations. While the process is applied to multi-camera systems, however, this approach is not considering the geometrical characteristics of multi-camera systems. Therefore, feature-based approaches are developed that are further improved by estimating nonlinear colour transformations using the geometrical characteristics of multi-camera systems. In general, methods belonging to the colour correction without colour pattern board equalize colour intensities in all viewpoints to be similar to one viewpoint as the reference. Therefore, the average colour intensities cannot be mainly achieved.

For colour correction, generally, our method minimizes the total error from the target colour space. Colour correspondence maps are initially obtained by using a 'Macbeth' colour chart. To obtain a matched colour vector, we have to capture the

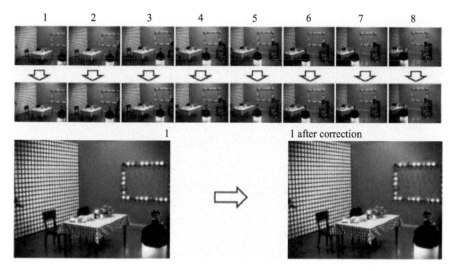

Figure 13.6   Colour correction by dynamic programming (iteration-based). [24]

colour pattern at different exposure times. Then, we can obtain a colour correction matrix which minimizes the error using iteration-based optimization. The iteration stops when the amount of error becomes small. This approach keeps the consistency of colours in all cameras, unlike correction methods that mostly focus on the relationship between the nearest two cameras. In these methods, even if the colour distance among neighbourhood cameras is sufficiently small, the distance between cameras at end to end might be large, because errors at each camera are accumulating. To tackle this problem in [24], an iteration-based method for colour correction of camera array is proposed that optimizes for the most uniform colour responses among views, using dynamic programming. This colour correction starts from any camera on the array sequentially, following a certain path, for pairs of cameras, until it reaches the starting point, and triggers several iterations. The iteration stops when the correction applied to the images becomes small enough. The process is entirely automatic. An example of correction using this method is shown in Figure 13.6.

13.3   Plenoptic imaging

Unlike stereoscopy and multi-camera arrays that are inspired by the human eye, plenoptic imaging has been inspired by insects, for example bee eyes, cf. Figure 13.7. Plenoptic or 3D holoscopic imaging, first proposed by Nobel laureate in Physics, G. M. Lippmann in 1908 [27], relies on the use of a series of microlenses – a microlens array (MLA) – at the picture surface to create the impression of depth and provide the user with full motion parallax without requiring special glasses. The process uses an array of small spherical microlenses, known as a 'fly's eye' lens array or MLA, to both record and display the 3D holoscopic image [28].

Figure 13.7   Plenoptic camera 2.0 (Raytrix [26]) and the Lenslet image

Using an image captured by a plenoptic camera, one can refocus images at different depths, and reconstruct images with viewpoint changes, which facilitates its application to chromatography, 3D reconstruction, depth estimation and digital refocusing. Since the multi-view are rendered from LL image, developing efficient coding tools for LL images/videos can directly benefit the quality of applications related.

Through the MLA, Lenslet data are captured by plenoptic cameras. Generally, there are two types of optical architecture of plenoptic cameras, that is plenoptic camera 1.0 and plenoptic camera 2.0. Their optical architectures are shown in Figure 13.8. Different from plenoptic camera 1.0, which inserts a microlens array at the image plane of the main lens, plenoptic camera 2.0 is a relay imaging system by inserting a microlens array behind the image plane of the main lens to re-image the object. So, the plenoptic camera 2.0 is also called 'focused plenoptic camera'. Lytro 1.0 and Lytro Illum (i.e. went out of business) are typical plenoptic camera 1.0 and RayTrix cameras [26] belong to plenoptic camera 2.0. The optical architecture introduces differences and similarities in the LL data captured. As the instances shown in Figure 13.8, both of them consist of a number of macro-pixels, that is the circular regions, each of which corresponds to the pixels recording the lights going through microlens. Since plenoptic camera 2.0 reimages the image at the main lens's image plane, each macro-pixel shows a micro-image of the imaging target, as shown in Figure 13.8, while the macro-pixels acquired by plenoptic camera 1.0 provide only the angular information.

The microlens may be hexagonally packed to improve the fill-factor or rectangularly packed to facilitate the data rendering. The packing method is directly reflected by the macro-pixel arrangement.

13.3.1   Processing tools for plenoptic camera

Here, we explain the required processing units for a plenoptic camera. The camera calibration for such cameras is normally performed by the SDK that is commercially sold with the camera, for example RayTrix. This SDK outputs the physical distances and location of the micro-lenses in the microlens array (MLA), corresponding to the dimension of the image sensing (CCD).

The captured content by plenoptic camera is LL format. A Lenslet image that is captured by a plenoptic camera that consists of light rays from different angles,

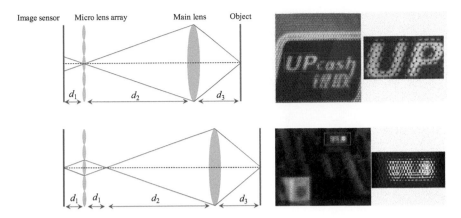

Figure 13.8 *(Top) Optical configuration of plenoptic camera 1.0 and LL image –*
partial magnification; and (bottom) optical configuration of
plenoptic camera 2.0 and LL image – partial magnification,
respectively

therefore, a LL image contains the 3D information of the scene. Hence, it can be
converted to multiview images that can be captured by an array of cameras [24,29–35].
The conversion tool converts the LL content into Multiview video. Note that by conversion from LL to Multiview (MV) data format, some data may be lost. Depending on
the process, the conversion can be invertible or not.

13.3.2 Conversion from Lenslet to Multiview images for plenoptic camera 1.0

The overall flow of conversion from LL to MV is shown in Figure 13.9. First, the
raw image of each frame is exported from the camera for pre-processing. Pre-
processing is performed using the Light Field Toolbox v0.4 [37]. After
Devignetting and Demosaicing, the coloured raw image is achieved, which is an
RGB 4:4:4 8-bit RAW colour image. Since the LL spacing in the raw image may be
a non-integer multiple of pixel pitch, *Rotation and Scaling* is performed to align
macro-pixels to an orthogonal integer pixel grid. Since interpolation may be performed during scaling, the resolution of the aligned LL image is a bit larger than the
raw image. Using a frame in a sequence captured by Lytro, Figure 13.10(a) shows
the aligned LL image. *Slicing* will slice the aligned LL image into a 4D light field,
which is an invertible conversion. By this step, the invertible conversion from LL to
MV is completed. Figure 13.10(b) shows the central sub-aperture image generated
by invertible conversion from the LL image in Figure 13.10(a). The *Resampling*
process afterwards is used to convert the hexagonally sampled data to an orthogonal grid by 2D interpolation and to provide the multiview (sub-aperture) images
with the same width-to-height ratio as the aligned LL image. This process is a non-
invertible conversion. Figure 13.10(c) shows the central view of multi-view (sub-
aperture) images generated by non-invertible conversion from the LL image in

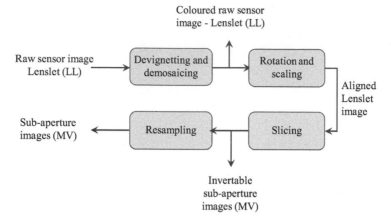

Figure 13.9   The overall flow chart of data conversion from LL to MV. Adapted
from [36] – also see http://plenoptic.info/pages/sub-aperture.html

Figure 13.10(a). Figure 13.10(d) shows the generated sub-aperture images for the LL
image in Figure 13.10(a). Each frame in the sequence will go through the process to
convert the LL data to MV data.

13.3.2.1   Conversion tool for plenoptic camera 1.0

Conversion tool from Lenslet to Multiview is provided (modified based on Light
Field Toolbox v0.4 by Tsinghua University) [36,39]. This tool is for Plenoptic 1.0
cameras. This tool includes two versions: non-invertible version and invertible
version. The data converted by the invertible tool can be converted back to the LL
data. The conversion tools for invertible and non-invertible can be found in [36,39].

13.3.2.2   Conversion from Lenslet to Multiview video for
plenoptic Camera 2.0

This tool is used in MPEG-I visual standardization as a reference tool, namely
Reference Lenslet Convertor (RLC) [29–35]. The optical system of a multi-focused
plenoptic camera (MFPC), that is Plenoptic 2.0, is more complicated compared
to that of an ordinary plenoptic camera, for example the Lytro (Plenoptic 1.0).
Despite the effectiveness, MFPCs are not often utilized. The main reason is that
the MFPCs are difficult to handle due to their complicated optical system.
Figure 13.8 shows the optical system in a focused plenoptic camera (FPC), that is
plenoptic 2.0.

In an FPC such as the RayTrix camera, the imaging plane of the main lens is in
front of the microlens array (MLA). This makes it possible to acquire high-density
directional rays, and as a result, it is possible to acquire an LF with a higher spatial
resolution than the number of microlenses used.

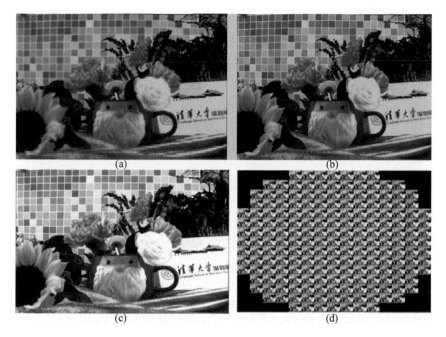

Figure 13.10 (a) Aligned LL image of a frame, (b) the central view of invertible conversion, (c) the central view of non-invertible conversion and (d) generated multiview (sub-aperture) images. Courtesy of Tsinghua Shenzhen International Graduate School

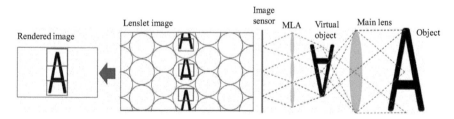

Figure 13.11 Diagram of rendering image from a raw image captured by a focused plenoptic camera

The RayTrix camera, that is MFPC, combines three types of microlenses with different foci. Due to the complicated optical system in the RayTrix, we need a sophisticated rendering process to generate a high-quality LF. The straightforward rendering method is to extract not a pixel but a patch with a fixed size from each image of a microlens, as shown in Figure 13.11. However, using a fixed patch size causes severe artefacts as shown in Figure 13.12. We need to adaptively adjust the patch size to solve the problem,

Figure 13.12   Rendering artefacts

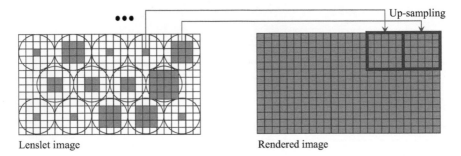

Figure 13.13   Rendering image at particular point using suitable patch sizes

but few studies have addressed this problem. The methodology to render an LF is not sufficiently sophisticated for FPC [40], especially for MFPC. Nagoya University proposed a processing method (Reference Lenslet content Convertor – RLC) [29–35,37], and release the source code, for MPEG standardization and academic purposes.

This method is inspired by the Laplacian-based method. By computing the Laplacian of all viewpoint images, we are able to robustly estimate the patch size. Figure 13.13 illustrates how different patch sizes are selected and up-sampled for rendering a viewpoint. A novel integrating method is proposed [29,30] for three sets of multi-view images with different focal lengths produced from the multi-focus plenoptic camera. The averaging method can efficiently reduce the rendering artefacts while simultaneously causing blurring of textures. To avoid this problem, we introduce a weighted averaging method.

There are three sets of multi-view images, each converted from one type of MLA; each multi-view image is focused on a particular depth according to the focal length. Moreover, information of suitable patch size can also be interpreted as depth information. Therefore, this method weights each multi-view image depending on the lens type.

The multi-view images have clear texture due to weighting, while the weighting causes artefacts when an unreliable patch size, for example patch sizes estimated from low-frequency regions, is used. This method solves this problem by applying a blending process of two multi-view image sets integrated with averaging and weighted averaging. The patch size is unreliable when it is estimated from low-textured or occluded regions.

Figure 13.14   (Left) Result without post-processing on rendered multiview video and (right) result with post-processing. Courtesy of Nagoya University

13.3.2.3   Pre-/post-processing

The conversion tool has several pre- and post-processing steps [33] that are summarized here:

1.   Demosaicing function to process Bayer images.
2.   Gaussian filter on a raw image before conducting patch size estimation. Therefore, patch size estimation becomes more accurate.

Colour correction: Sometimes the colour of multi-view images generated from the raw image lacks fidelity. Therefore, we added colour correction and gamma correction to adjust colour and brightness. Figure 13.14 shows the comparison with and without post-processing. After post-processing, the rendered multiview video has an equalized colour response.

13.3.2.4   Temporal consistency

In order to render MV images from raw images captured by the focused Plenoptic camera, patch size estimation (equivalent to depth estimation) is conducted. However, sometimes the contents in raw image are almost the same (e.g. background regions) in consequent frames, and the estimated patch size has significant fluctuations, which leads to temporal inconsistency of multi-view videos. To tackle this issue, the following two methods can be considered.

Method 1: Energy function with a penalty

The first method is very straightforward, adding a penalty to the energy function, as shown in (13.1):

$$K_t(i,j) = \arg\min_k \sum_{s,t \in S,T} (E_k(i,j) + \lambda|k - K_{t-1}(i,j)|) \tag{13.1}$$

Here, $K_t(i,j)$ is the suitable patch size for the (i,j)-th microlens of frame t, k means a patch size ($k \in \{k_{\min}, \ldots, k_{\max}\}$), the $E_k(i,j)$ is the average value of the

Laplacian of patch boundaries for the (i,j)-th microlens of frame t, and the λ represents the coefficient of penalty.

The patch size of initializing frame is estimated by (13.2) [33]:

$$K_t(i,j) = \arg \min_k \sum_{s,t \in S,T} E_k(i,j) \tag{13.2}$$

Method 2: Gaussian filter on EdgeSumMap

The second proposed method is applying a Gaussian on EdgeSumMap, as shown in (13.3):

$$K_t(i,j) = \arg \min_k \text{Gaussian} \left[\sum_{s,t \in S,T} E_k(i,j) \right] \tag{13.3}$$

Here, $[\sum_{s,t \in S,T} E_k(i,j)]$ represents the EdgeSumMap and Gaussian $[\bullet]$ is the Gaussian filter.

References

[1] https://vision.middlebury.edu/stereo/data/.

[2] M. Tanimoto, T. Fujii, and N. Fukushima, '1D parallel test sequences for MPEG-FTV', ISO/IEC JTC1/SC29/WG11 M15378, Archamps, France, April 2008.

[3] M. Tanimoto, T. Fujii, M. P. Tehrani, M. Wildeboer, N. Fukushima, and H. Furihata, 'Moving multiview camera test sequences for MPEG-FTV', ISO/IEC JTC1/SC29/WG11 M16922, October 2009, Xian, China.

[4] S. Fachada, D. Bonatto, A. Schenkel, M. Teratani, G. Lafruit, '[MPEG-I Visual] ULB proposal of new test sequences for Windowed-6DoF', ISO/IEC JTC1/SC29/WG11 MPEG2018/m43460, July 2018, Ljubljana, Slovenia.

[5] M. Teratani, T. Senoh, B. Kroon, *et al.*, 'Overview of MPEG-I Visual Test Materials', ISO/IEC JTC1/SC29/WG11 MPEG2020/ N19489, July 2020, Online.

[6] M. Tanimoto, T. Fujii, and N. Fukushima, 'Adjusting method for multi view image; color and geometry correction for MPEG-FTV test sequences', ISO/IEC JTC1/SC29/WG11 M15379, Archamps, France, April 2008.

[7] Z. Zhang, 'A flexible new technique for camera calibration', Technical Report, MSR-TR-98-71, Microsoft Research, Microsoft Corporation, December 2, 1998.

[8] A. Ilie, and G. Welch, 'Ensuring colour consistency across multiple cameras', *ICCV05*, 2005, pp. II: 1268–1275.

[9] N. Joshi, B. Wilburn, V. Vaish, M. Levoy, and M. Horowitz, 'Automatic colour calibration for large camera arrays', UCSD CSE Technical Report, CS2005- 0821, 2005.

[10] F. Shao, G. Jiang, M. Yu, and K. Chen, 'A content-adaptive multi-view video colour correction algorithm', in *Proceedings of the ICASSP 2007*, Hawaii, USA, April 2007, pp. I-969–I-972.

[11] K. Yamamoto and U. James, 'Colour calibration for multi-camera system without colour pattern board', Monash University, DECSE Technical Report MECSE-4- 2006.

[12] K. Yamamoto, T. Yendo, T. Fujii, M. Tanimoto, and D. Suter, 'Colour correction for multi-camera system by using correspondences', in *Proceedings of the SIGGRAPH2006*, Poster, USA, 2006.

[13] K. Yamamoto, T. Endo, T. Fujii, M. Tanimoto, and D. Suter, 'Colour correction for multiple-camera system by using correspondences', *Journal of the Institute of Image Information and Television Engineers (ITE)*, vol. 61, no. 2, pp. 213–222, 2007.

[14] K. Yamamoto, M. Kitahara, H. Kimata, *et al.*, 'Multiview video coding using view interpolation and color correction', *IEEE Transactions on Circuits and Systems for Video Technology*, vol. 17, no. 11, pp. 1436–1449, 2007.

[15] K. Yamamoto and R. Oi, 'Colour correction for multiview video by minimizing energy of view networks', *Proceedings of the Workshop on Multi-Dimensional and Multi-View Image Processing, ACCV'07*, MM-O-02, November 2007, pp. 9–16.

[16] K. Yamamoto and R. Oi, 'Color correction for multi-view video using energy minimization of view networks', *International Journal of Automation and Computing*, vol. 5, no. 3, pp. 234–245, 2008.

[17] U. Fecker, M. Barkowsky, and A. Kaup, 'Improving the prediction efficiency for multi-view video coding using histogram matching', in *Proceedings of the PCS2006*, P2-16, 2006.

[18] Y. Chen, J. Chen, and C. Cai, 'Luminance and chrominance correction for multiview video using simplified colour error model', in *Proceedings of the PCS2006*, P2-17, 2006.

[19] Y. L. Lee, J. H. Hur, D.-Y. Kim, *et al.*, 'H.264/AVC-based multi-view coding (MVC)', Sejong, Korea, ISO/IEC JTC/SC29/ WG11 M12871, 2006.

[20] K. Sohn, Y. Kim, J. Seo, J. Yoon, C. Park, and J. Lee, 'H.264/AVC-compatible multi-view video coding', ISO/IEC JTC1/SC29/WG11 M12874, 2006.

[21] Y. Su, P. Yin, C. Gomila, J. H. Kim, P. L. Lai, and A. Ortega, 'Thomson's response to MVC CfP', Shanghai, China, ISO/IEC JTC1/SC29/WG11, 2006.

[22] S. J. Kim and M. Pollefeys, 'Robust radiometric calibration and vignetting correction,' *IEEE Transactions on Pattern Analysis and Machine Intelligence*, vol. 30, no. 4, pp. 562–576, 2008.

[23] S. J. Kim and M. Pollefeys, 'Radiometric alignment of image sequences', in *Proceedings of the of CVPR 2004*, I-645-I-651, 2004.

[24] M. P. Tehrani, A. Ishikawa, S. Sakazawa, and A. Koike, 'An iterative color correction of multicamera system using corresponding feature points', *Journal of Visual Communications and Image Representation*, vol. 21, pp. 377–391, 2010.

[25] M. Tanimoto, M. P. Tehrani, T. Fujii, and T. Yendo, 'Free-Viewpoint TV', *IEEE Signal Processing Magazine*, vol. 28, no. 1, pp. 67–76, 2011. doi:10.1109/MSP.2010.939077.

[26]   https://raytrix.de/.

[27]   G. Lippmann, 'Épreuves réversibles donnant la sensation du relief', *Académie des Sciences*, vol. 146, no. 9, pp. 446–451, 1908.

[28]   JCT3V-C0210, '3D Holoscopic Video Test Material', FP7 3D VIVANT Consortium, 2013.

[29]   M. P. Tehrani, S. Fujita, W. Ouyang, K. Takahashi, and T. Fujii, '3D imaging system using multi-focus plenoptic camera and tensor display', *Proc. International Conference on 3D Immersion (IC3D2018)*, Brussels, Belgium, 2018.

[30]   S. Fujita, S. Mikawa, M. P. Tehrani, K. Takahashi, and T. Fujii, 'Extracting multi-view images from multi-focused plenoptic camera', *Proc. IWAIT-IFMIA 2019*, Singapore, 2019.

[31]   M. P. Tehrani, S. Mikawa, Y. Kobayashi, S. Fujita, K. Takahashi, and T. Fujii, '[MPEG-I Visual] development of a 3D imaging system using light field camera and tensor display', ISO/IEC JTC1/SC29/WG11, M41244, Torino, Italy, July 2017.

[32]   M. Teratani, S. Fujita, W. Ouyang, K. Takahashi, and T. Fujii, '[MPEG-I Visual] Conversion tool – Raytrix data to multiview video', ISO/IEC JTC1/ SC29/ WG11, M44731, Macao, SRA China, October 2018.

[33]   M. Teratani, W. Ouyang, and T. Fujii, '[MPEG-I Visual] Temporal consistency algorithms for reference lens', ISO/IEC JTC1/SC29/WG11, m49668, Gothenburg, Sweden, July 2019.

[34]   M. Teratani and T. Fujii, 'Manual of Reference Lenslet Content Convertor (RLC 0.3)', ISO/IEC JTC1/SC29/WG11, N18567, Gothenburg, Sweden, July 2019.

[35]   http://www.fujii.nuee.nagoya-u.ac.jp/multiview-data/.

[36]   https://dgd.vision/Tools/LFToolbox/.

[37]   RLC 1.0 Git. https://gitlab.com/mpeg-dense-light-field/rlc.

[38]   M. Teratani and X. Jin, 'Activity Report on Dense Light Fields', ISO/IEC JTC1/ SC29/WG04, MDS20008_WG04_N00056, Online, January 2021.

[39]   https://www.mathworks.com/matlabcentral/fileexchange/49683-light-field-toolbox-v0-4.

[40]   S. Wanner, J. Fehr, B. Jaahne, 'Generating EPI representations of 4D light fields with a single lens focused plenoptic camera', In: G. Bebis *et al.* (eds) *Advances in Visual Computing*. ISVC 2011. Lecture Notes in Computer Science, vol. 6938. Springer, Berlin, Heidelberg, 2011. doi: 10.1007/978-3-642-24028-7_9.

Chapter 14

3D light field displays

There are various ways to display the captured three-dimensional (3D) information based on the display devices. Those display devices can be separated into two groups. The first group is the display devices that are used in 2D visual systems such as conventional 2D display or television. The other group includes a special display device designed for 3D visual systems. Among many excellent works, the following 3D immersive displays and systems are introduced.

14.1   3D TV

MERL developed a 3D TV prototype system [1] with real-time acquisition, transmission and 3D display of dynamic scenes. It is a distributed, scalable architecture to manage the high computation and bandwidth demands. The system consists of an array of cameras, clusters of network-connected PCs, and a multi-projector 3D display. Multiple video streams are individually encoded and sent over a broadband network to the display. The 3D display shows high-resolution (1,024×768) stereoscopic colour images for multiple viewpoints without special glasses. The system is implemented with rear-projection and front-projection lenticular screens (Figure 14.1).

14.2   Eye vision

The system was proposed by Carnegie Mellon University (CMU) and called 'Eye Vision' [2] (Figure 14.2). It involves shooting multiple video images of a dynamic event, such as a football game, from multiple cameras placed at different angles. The video streams from these cameras are combined by computer and the resulting images reach viewers in a format that will make them feel as if they are flying through the scenes. The action at the game was captured by more than 30 cameras, each positioned some 80 feet above the field at Raymond James Stadium in Tampa, Florida. Each camera, with computer-controlled zoom and focus capabilities, was mounted on a custom-built, robotic pan-tilt head, which could swing the camera in any direction at the command of a computer. These camera heads were controlled in concert so that cameras pointed, zoomed and focused at the same time on the same spot on the field, where a touchdown or fumble occurred.

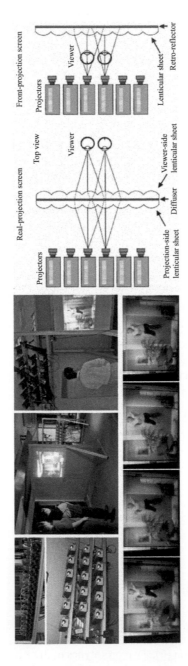

Figure 14.1   3DTV prototype. Courtesy of MERL

For this modelling technology to achieve its full impact, the set of captured, multiple video images must be processed beyond the playback. The detailed geometrical information about a scene is extracted by a computer, which enables a person to choose how to view a scene, even from a perspective that was not shot by any camera. To bring this concept to life, CMU built a '3D room' [3] equipped with more than 50 video cameras, and experimented by filming people involved in a variety of sports activities (Figure 14.2).

14.3 Surface light field system

The system was proposed by Intel [4] and called 'Surface Light Field System'. A light field parameterized on the surface offers a natural and intuitive description of the view-dependent appearance of scenes with complex reflectance properties. To enable the use of surface light fields in real-time rendering, a compact representation suitable for an accelerated graphics pipeline is needed. The approximated light field data is processed by partitioning it over elementary surface primitives and factorizing each part into a small set of lower-dimensional functions. After acquisition, it can be further compressed using standard image compression techniques leading to extremely compact data sets that are up to four orders of magnitude smaller than the input data. Finally, an image-based rendering method and light field mapping are used that can visualize surface light fields directly from this compact representation at interactive frame rates on a personal computer.

A total of NI ($200 < NI < 400$) images is captured with a handheld digital camera in the prototyped system [4]. The object is placed on a platform designed for the purpose of automatic registration. The outcome of this process is a set of NI images captured from known vantage points in 3D space. The object geometry is computed using a structured lighting system (explained in Section 11.3.2) consisting of a projector and a camera. The projector is used to project a translating stripped pattern onto the object. Between 10 and 20 scans are taken to completely cover the surface geometry of the object. Between two consecutive scans, the object is rotated in front of the camera and projector by about 20°. The individual scans are automatically registered together in the object reference frame using the same grid corners previously used for image registration. The resulting cloud of points (approx. 500,000 points) is then fed into mesh editing software to build the final triangular surface mesh. Since the same calibration platform is used for both image and geometry acquisition, the resulting triangular mesh is naturally registered to the camera images.

14.4 1D-II 3D display system

The system was proposed by Toshiba [5,6] and called '1D Integral Imaging (1D-II 3D Display System'. The II method is based on the integral photography (IP) method proposed by M. G. Lippmann [7]. Two prototypes of 3D PC-based display system are developed, which have 20.8 and 15.4 inches of diagonal size, using one-dimensional integral imaging. Horizontal resolution of 300 with 32 parallaxes in 20.8-inch type

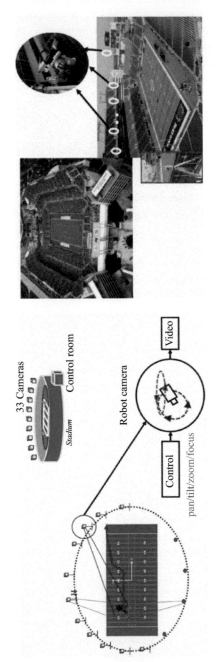

Figure 14.2   Eye Vision. Courtesy of CMU [2]

and 18 parallaxes in 15.4-inch type were developed thanks to the adoption of a mosaic pixel arrangement of the display panel. These prototypes have a wide viewing area and a viewer can observe 3D images with continuous motion parallax. By using lenticular sheets, these prototypes can also display the same bright images as an ordinal display in spite of having many parallaxes. Plug-ins for creating 3D images for computer graphics software are also developed. In the prototype of 15.4-inch, movies of computer graphics contents and real-time interaction are demonstrated.

14.5 Integral photography

NHK developed integral 3D television using an ultra-high-definition imaging system [8]. The system uses a device having 7,680 pixels in the horizontal direction and 4,320 pixels in the vertical direction for each of the red, green and blue channels. A lens array comprising 400 lenses is configured in the horizontal direction and one comprising 250 lenses is configured in the vertical direction. The system is designed to ensure a maximum spatial frequency of 11.3 cycles/degree and a viewing angle of 24° when the display is observed from three times the display height. The setup has simultaneously maintained the balance between the maximum spatial frequency and the viewing angle by shortening the focal length of the elemental lens while narrowing the pitch of the elemental lens (Figure 14.3).

14.6 Real-time free viewpoint television

The system was proposed by Nagoya University [9–12] and called 'Free viewpoint TV (FTV)'. In the FTV system, one user can freely control the viewpoint position of

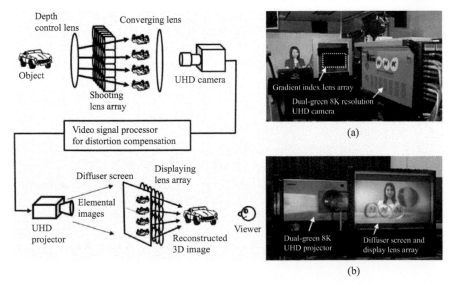

Figure 14.3 Integral photography (IP). Courtesy of NHK

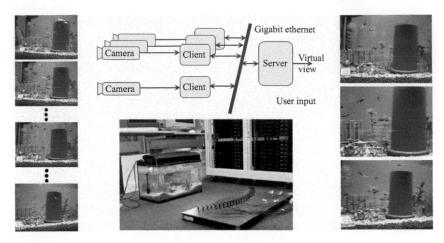

*Figure 14.4   The FTV system hardware configuration. Courtesy of Nagoya
University [14]*

any dynamic real-world scene. It uses an image-based rendering method based on the
ray-space concept. The system includes 16 client's nodes with a server node computer. Each node is a PC cluster powered by Intel Pentium III 800 MHz CPU with
256 Mbyte RAM. Each PC is a general-purpose PC that has an image capturing board
mounted in a PCI bus. A Gigabit Ethernet connects sensor node PCs with a central
node PC. Three camera configurations were installed on the FTV system. One is
16 cameras mounted on a line with 2-cm distance between each with 11 fps (frame per
second), another configuration consists of a 2D camera array on a plane with 2-cm
distance between each in x and y directions with 7 fps, and one-dimensional cameras
with 11 fps, which are set with 3° (20 mm) intervals on an arc-array. The closest
object is considered to be about 35-cm away from the camera's plane. In this system,
the colour images are of size 160 × 120 pixels. This system does not need any special
hardware such as a special computer or depth sensor. The user requests the viewpoint
from the server side (Figure 14.4).

14.7   SMV256

A new super multi-view (SMV) display system that enables the number of views to
be increased has been developed by Tokyo University of Agriculture and
Technology [13]. All 3D images generated by multiple multi-view flat-panel displays are superimposed on a common screen using a multi-projection system. The
viewing zones of the flat-panel 3D display are produced in the pupils of the projection lenses and then imaged to the observation space by a screen lens. Sixteen
flat-panel 3D displays having 16 views were used to construct an SMV display
having 256 views. The 3D resolution was 256×192 pixels. The screen size was
10.3 inches. The horizontal interval of the viewing zones was 1.3 mm (Figure 14.5).

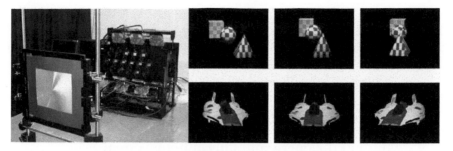

Figure 14.5   Super multi-view (SMV) display. Courtesy of Tokyo University of Agriculture and Technology [13]

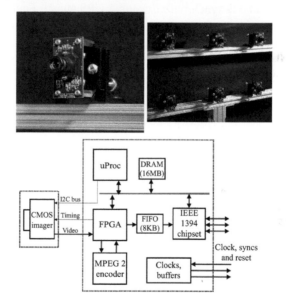

Figure 14.6   Individual LFVC and LFVC system, and LFVC basic diagram. Courtesy of Stanford University [16]

14.8   Light field video camera system

In this system, the system designing approach and the display rendering algorithms are carried in a very different approach. The system was proposed by Stanford University [15] and called 'Light Field Video Camera System' (Figure 14.6).

In this system, the special cameras called the 'Light Field Video Camera' (LFVC) are used to construct a camera array. The LFVC consists of multiple CMOS imagers, each providing 640×480-pixel RGB resolution at 30 frames per second. Custom-built driver boards enable online pre-processing as well as MPEG-2 compression of each video stream. At 5 MB/s per camera, up to 60 MPEG-encoded video streams can be streamed to one PC via the IEEE1394 High Performance Serial Interface Bus where the data are stored on a SCSI hard drive. The LFVC cameras and their basic block diagram are shown in Figure 14.6. The array system is formed as 3×2 camera array using six LFVCs. The camera heads are aligned in parallel. Each camera node is connected to the other and a host PC via an IEEE 1394 High Speed Serial Bus. To keep the cameras synchronized, a common clock signal is distributed to all of the cameras. A reset signal and two general purpose triggers are also routed to all camera nodes. The system is based on a small 3×2 camera array, which leads to a simple hardware requirement. However, in the rendering step, extra processing steps are required.

14.9   Multipoint camera and microphone system

Nagoya University developed 100 cameras and 400 microphones system [17–22]. The acquisition system is synchronized using a GPS signal. Each camera and four microphones are connected to a node which is a personal computer. All nodes are connected in cascade configuration. The system is able to generate free viewpoint video and free listening points being synchronized. The free viewpoint synthesis is based on a DIBR approach (cf. Chapter 12) (Figure 14.7).

14.10   Walk-through system

KDDI Research has developed a 3D system allowing walk-through experience [23–29]. The captured data are inward and around the scene. In this system, each object in the scene is extracted from all viewpoints and the corresponding background. A dense circular ray-space [29] is generated for each object in the scene, that is a local ray-space. Combined with the warped background, the walk-through video visualizer chooses the corresponding local ray-space to synthesize the corresponding viewpoints (Figure 14.8).

14.11   Ray emergent imaging (REI)

NICT has developed a light field display [30–33]. The capturing system consists of 64 cameras. The DIBR method is used to synthesize virtual viewpoints among actual camera viewpoints to have a sufficient number of views corresponding to the requirement of the display. The compression of the data is based on a method, presented in [31]. Ray emergent imaging (REI) [33,34] is fed by about 200 full HD images per frame to compete with conventional HDTV or current 3D cinema. Users have a natural 3D depth impression without using special glasses. The viewpoint can be freely chosen by relocating in front of the display, as if we relocate in front of a real object. Such life-sized objects as humans and cars can be fit or rendered in the 16:9, 200-inch large screen display. The REI provides dense and fluid horizontal motion parallax and limited the flipping effects appear in the observed images (Figure 14.9).

14.12   Holografika

The capturing system for this system is similar to the REI display. HoloVizio [35,36] by Holografika shows 3D images in which spatial points of the image are

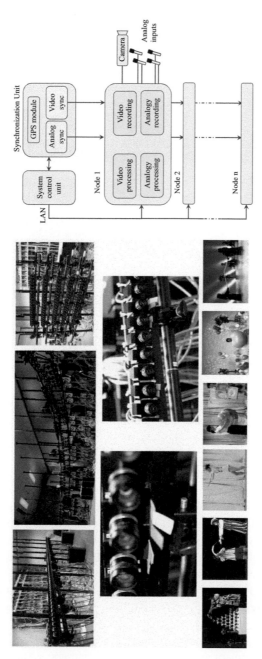

Figure 14.7   100 cameras and 400 microphones system. Courtesy of Nagoya University [14]

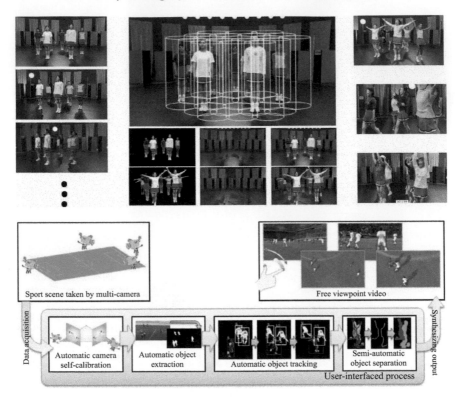

Figure 14.8   Walk-through system. Courtesy of KDDI Research

addressed individually. Therefore, the position of the displayed 3D object does not depend on the viewing position but it remains fixed in space. The system's main specifications are 180° FOV and continuous motion parallax (Figure 14.10).

14.13   Light field 3D display

Samsung developed a projection-based 300-Mpixel light-field display that has a 100-inch screen and a 40° viewing angle [37]. The projector configuration is modified to achieve a high-quality 3D image, by analysing the luminance characteristics of the display and optimizing the design to minimize the variation in the brightness of projected images (Figure 14.11).

14.14   Aktina Vision

NHK reported two different capture-to-display systems. The capturing system can be an integral UHD camera or dense multiview camera system (Table 14.1, Figure 14.12). The display is called Akitna Vision [38] which is based on multiple projectors and 3D screen with a narrow diffusion angle.

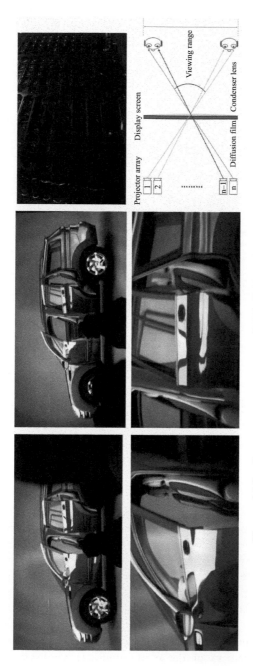

Figure 14.9   Ray emergent imaging (REI) [33] and courtesy of NICT [41]

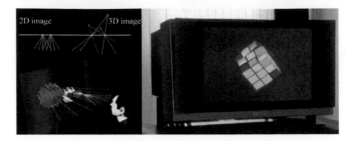

Figure 14.10   HoloVizio. Courtesy of Holografika [35]

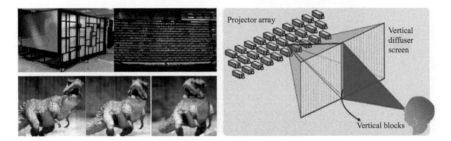

Figure 14.11   Light field 3D display [37]

Table 14.1.   Specifications of high-definition 3D display (Aktina Vision)

Number of viewpoints	350
Resolution (pixels × pixels)	768 × 432
Viewing angle (degree × degree)	H 35.1, V 4.7

14.15   IP by 3D VIVANT

Plenoptic or 3D holoscopic imaging, first proposed by G. M. Lippmann in 1908 [7], relies on the use of a series of micro-lenses at the picture surface to create the impression of depth and provide the user with full motion parallax without requiring special glasses. The process uses an array of small spherical micro-lenses, known as a 'fly's eye' lens array, to both record and display the 3D holoscopic image [39]. At the display side, this array is designed so that when viewed from different angles, different images will be visible. This happens because, for a given direction, only one pixel from each micro-image is visible by the user. This technology can be used for creating 3D images on a flat panel display. If motion pictures are considered, instead of still images, this results in 3D holoscopic video. At the capture side, the operation is basically the same, but the micro-lens array is applied to the sensor (Figure 14.13).

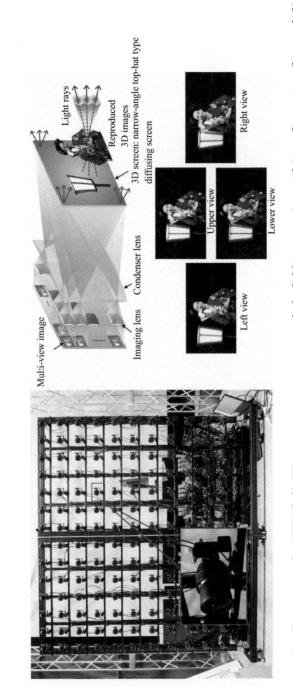

Figure 14.12   Aktina vision by NHK (left) HD camera array to capture light field images; (top-right) configuration; (bottom-left) multi-view images; and (bottom-right) displayed 3D images from different viewpoints. Courtesy by NHK [38]

Figure 14.13   IP. Courtesy of 3D VIVANT [45]

14.16   Projection type IP

This 3D display system [40] implements 3D/2D convertible features in the projection-type integral imaging by using a concave half mirror array. The concave half mirror array has the partially reflective characteristic of the incident light. And the reflected term is modulated by the concave mirror array structure, while the transmitted term is unaffected. With such unique characteristics, 3D/2D conversion or even the simultaneous display of 3D and 2D images is also possible. Experiments verified the 3D/2D conversion and the display of 3D image on 2D background with the fabricated prototype. This system can be useful for the 3D industry such as the 3D theatres (Figure 14.14).

14.17   Tensor display

This type of display is newly emerging, and such an approach uses a stack of a few semi-transparent layers [42,43]. The tensor display [44], developed by MIT, is a family of compressive light field displays comprising all architectures employing a stack of time-multiplexed, light-attenuating layers illuminated by uniform or directional backlighting (i.e., any low-resolution light field emitter). The light field emitted by an N-layer, M-frame tensor display can be represented by an Nth-order, rank-M tensor. Using this representation, a unified optimization framework is used, based on non-negative tensor factorization (NTF), encompassing all tensor display architectures. In Figure 14.15, the display prototype is configured as a three-layer display, and different displayed viewpoints.

14.18   Multi-, plenoptic-, coded-aperture-, multi-focus- camera to tensor display system

The system was developed by Nagoya University [46–59]. It is an end-to-end system where a real 3D scene captured by a multi-view camera can be reproduced in 3D on a prototyped tensor display. The main contribution lies in the data conversion method using image-based rendering, by which a set of sufficiently dense light field data, which is required for high quality displaying of a 3D scene, is generated from a sparser set of data that can be captured by the multi-view camera,

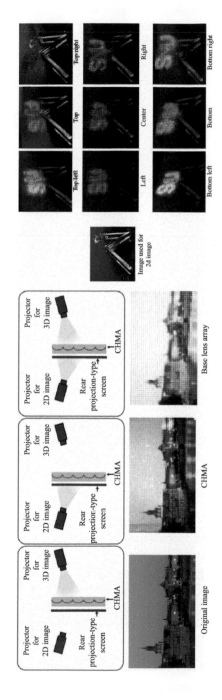

Figure 14.14   Projection type IP. Courtesy of Seoul National University display [40]

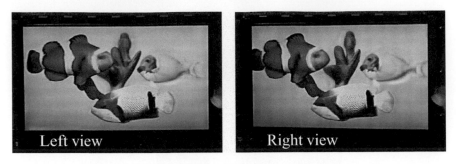

Figure 14.15   Tensor display. Courtesy of MIT [44]

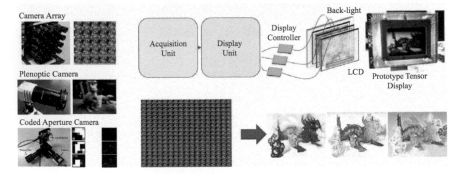

Figure 14.16   End-to-end 3D system using multi-camera, plenoptic camera, codec aperture camera and prototyped tensor display. Courtesy of Nagoya University [63]

or plenoptic camera, or codec aperture camera [60,61]. The system can also be fed with a single viewpoint but multi-focused images [54] In all acquisition scenarios, the captured data is converted to multiview images. If the multiview images in the acquisition side are not sufficiently dense, aliasing is observed in the display [58]. Therefore, at the display side, a dense multiview images is synthesized using image-based rendering approach (cf. Chapter 12). The densely synthesized multiview images can then be converted to the multilayer pattern to be fed to the display using an analytical method or machine learning approaches [47] (Figure 14.16).

14.19   360° light field display

The system contains a set of rendering techniques for an autostereoscopic light field display that is able to present interactive 3D graphics to multiple simultaneous viewers, 360° around the display [62]. The display consists of a high-speed video projector, a spinning mirror covered by a holographic diffuser, and FPGA circuitry to decode specially rendered DVI video signals. The display uses a standard programmable graphics card to render over 5,000 images per second of interactive 3D graphics, projecting 360° views with 1.25° separation up to 20 updates per second (Figure 14.17).

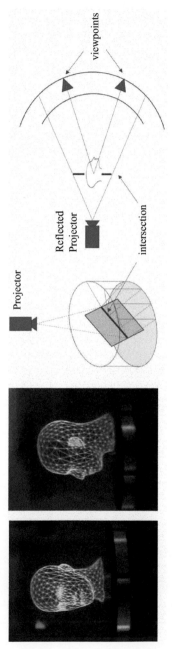

Figure 14.17   360° LFD. Courtesy of USC [64]

14.20   360° mirror scan

It is worth mentioning that there are other attempts to capture in 3D with a special capturing system, for example, parabolic mirrors and a high-speed camera, such as the 360° mirror-scan ray capturing system [65] shown in Figure 14.8. This system uses two parabolic mirrors. Incident rays that are parallel to the axis of a parabolic mirror gather at the focus of the parabolic mirror. Hence, rays that come out of an object placed at the focus of the lower parabolic mirror gather at the focus of the upper parabolic mirror. Then, the real image of the object is generated at the focus of the upper parabolic mirror and a rotating slope mirror scans rays at the focus of the upper parabolic mirror. Finally, the image from the aslope mirror is captured by a high-speed camera. By using this system, we can capture all-around convergent views of an object.

In the 360° mirror-scan ray capturing system, the captured images have distortion caused by the parabolic mirror optics and rotation-distortion caused by the rotation of the aslope mirror. To compensate for these, simple 2D image transformation should be done for each frame of the high-speed camera (Figure 14.18).

14.21   Seelinder

The Seelinder [66] display has two spinning cylinders, one inside the other. The outer cylinder is a parallax barrier that has a series of vertical slits spinning rapidly while the inner cylinder spins slower in the opposite direction with a series of one-dimensional LED arrays on its surface. If the slit width of the outer cylinder is sufficiently small, the light through the slit becomes a thin flux, whose direction is scanned rapidly by the spinning of the outer cylinder. By synchronously changing the intensity of each LED in the arrays to the spinning, rays of different directions have different colours with time-multiplexing. Moreover, the inner cylinder also rotates slowlier, and the LED

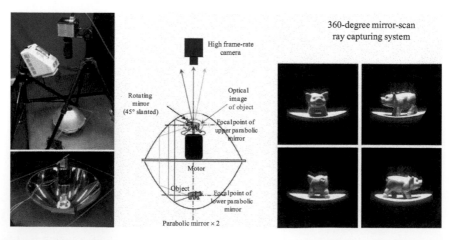

Figure 14.18   360° mirror-scan ray capturing systems. Courtesy of Nagoya University [14]

array's position is a little different when the next slit comes, and so rays are shot to each direction from each position. In this way, a cylindrical light field display is realized and can be displayed (Figure 14.19).

14.22   Holo Table

A portable 360° viewable 3D display, 'Holo- Table', was developed [67]. It displays more than 500 views with 1,024×768 pixels at 30–60 fps. The feature of this display is not only the large number of views but also the high density of views. Because of these features, users can see a 3D scene from any direction with smooth motion parallax (Figure 14.20).

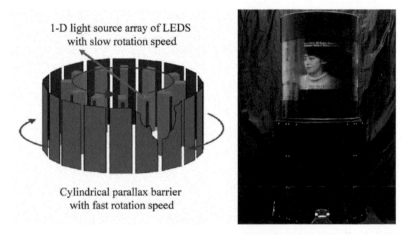

Figure 14.19   Seelinder. Courtesy of Nagoya University and The University of Tokyo [66]

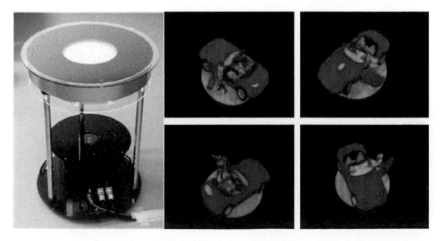

Figure 14.20   Holo Table. Courtesy of Holy Mine [67]

14.23   fVisiOn

The fVisiOn [68,69] is a novel glasses-free tabletop 3D display, that is, floating virtual 3D objects appearing on a flat tabletop surface. The developed novel technique can float standing 3D images on a blank flat tabletop surface, and allows multiple viewers to observe the 3D from omnidirectional 360° in seated conditions. It is designed to be a friendly interface for multiple users for varied tabletop tasks by featuring our glasses-free method and observation style. For a generation of the 3D images, fVisiOn employs a newly developed special optical device as a screen and a series of micro projectors arranged circularly. The combination of those devices reproduces a light field in a certain volume on the table. The entire 3D imaging mechanism is installed underneath the table. The fVisiOn can display virtual 3D images besides printed documents and physical mock-ups. This primal prototype can float the 3D images of a height of approximately 5 cm on the tabletop surface like a centrepiece in the centre of the table (Figure 14.21).

14.24   Use cases of virtual reality systems

The use cases [70,71] described below may be developed based on different capturing systems, such as multi-camera or plenoptic imaging systems.

14.24.1   Public use cases

Multi-camera systems are commercially affordable. Therefore, public use cases are expected to be developed based on such systems. Several use cases, such as *Virtual Stadium, Theme Park, Future Cinema, Virtual EXPOs, Virtual Restaurant/Café/ Bar and Digital Signage*. For example, in sports events, the number of fans in the stadiums is limited to the number of seats. The famous games are normally broadcasted but the fans who were successful to watch the match have the privilege to enjoy more than those who watch the game on a 2DTV. Therefore, one may consider using the current technology and provide a nearly similar experience to the fans on the other side of the world.

During the Olympic games or Football World Cups, many stadiums all over the world remains empty. As explained above, large 3D displays such as REI [34] or fVision [70] can be placed over the ground of a playground and project the same content of a game in another stadium. This might seem very fictionist but given all available technologies from capture to display, we can realize a *virtual stadium* in the near future (Figure 14.22).

14.24.2   Professional use cases

For such applications, depending on the requirements of an application, either multi-camera or plenoptic systems can be used as capturing devices. Authorities may use virtual reality technologies to provide higher/safer quality of life, such as *Robotics, Safety issue in Human and robot interaction, Monitoring and Visualization, Video Contents Editing, Industry Inspection, Security and Law*

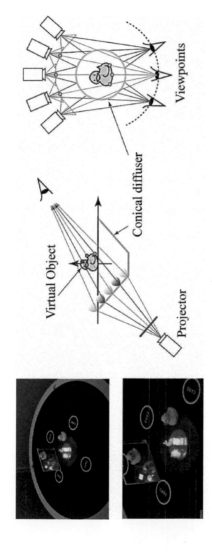

Figure 14.21 fVisiOn [72] and courtesy of NICT [74]

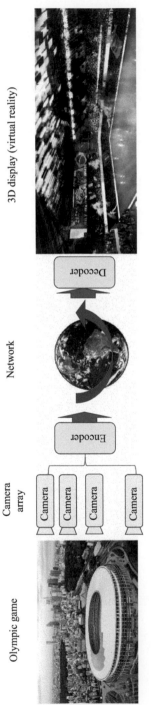

Camera array

Olympic game

Network

3D display (virtual reality)

Encoder

Decoder

Camera

Camera

Camera

Camera

Figure 14.22 Public use case for Sport Events [74,75]

Figure 14.23   Professional use case: remotely operating robots in space or hazard environments [76]

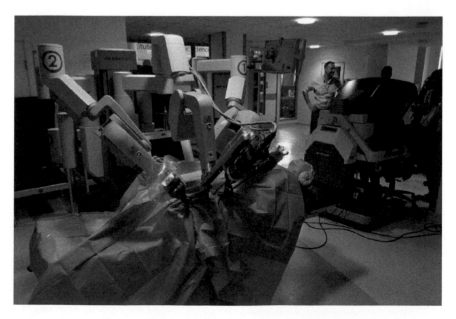

Figure 14.24   Medical use case: surgery [78]

Enforcement and Product Design. For example, in the case of robotics, recent advancement in Telecommunication (e.g., 5G) enables us to make robots more involved in our operations. In order to operate remotely with a realistic sense of 3D space in real time, a full chain of 3D vision systems of the robots has become the centre of interest in this field. Robot operation areas normally are limited to close objects, and therefore, plenoptic cameras with the capability of acquiring a depth of field (DoF) are a very efficient way to handle such applications (Figure 14.23) [77].

14.24.3   Scientific use cases

Such use cases [78] can facilitate progress in different fields of science, such as *Astronomy, Geographic Information Systems and Medicine*. For instance, currently, remote surgery is nearly possible, but the viewing device is HMD and if the doctor is not trained to use such a system, his valuable experience cannot save the life of a person on another side of the world. A high-quality 3D display, with HRI would be more natural and can be used for such an application. Meanwhile, light-field microscopes can be designed by applying the plenoptic imaging technique. Combined with processing algorithms, high-resolution 3D structures can be visualized for close tissues, which is beneficial for medical treatment (Figure 14.24).

References

[1]   W. Matusik and H. Pfister, "3D TV: A scalable system for real-time acquisition, transmission and autostereoscopic display of dynamic scenes," *ACM SIGGRAPH*, vol. 23, no. 3, pp. 814–824, 2004.

[2]   https://www.youtube.com/watch?v=Bse7YXWdP-c.

[3]   H. Saito, S. Baba, M. Kimura, S Vedula, and T. Kanada, "Appearance-based virtual view generation of temporally-varying events from multi-camera images in the 3D room," *Proc. on 3-D Imaging and Modeling*, 1999.

[4]   W. Chao Chen, J. Y. Bouguet, M. H. Chu, and R. Grzeszczuk, "Light field mapping: Efficient representation and hardware rendering of surface light fields". *ACM Transactions on Graphics*, vol. 21, no. 3, pp. 447–456, 2002.

[5]   K. Taira, S. Yanagawa, H. Kobayashi, Y. Yamauchi, and Y. Hirayama, "Development of 3-D display system using one-dimensional integral imaging method," *Proc. of 3D Conf.*, Tokyo, Japan, 2004. (in Japanese).

[6]   T. Saishu, K. Taira, R. Fukushima, and Y. Hirayama, "Distortion control in a one-dimensional integral imaging autostereoscopic display system with parallel optical beam groups," *Proc. of SID*, Seattle, USA, 2004.

[7]   G. Lippmann, , "La photographie integrale," *Comptes-Rendus Academie des Sciences*, vol. 146, pp. 446–451, 1908.

[8]   J. Arai, F. Okano, M. Kawakita, *et al.*, "Integral three-dimensional television using a 33-megapixel imaging system," *Journal of Display Technology*, vol. 6, no. 10, pp. 422–430, 2010.

[9] M. P. Tehrani, T. Fujii, and M. Tanimoto, "The adaptive distributed source coding of multi-view images in camera sensor networks," *IEICE Transaction on Fundamentals of Electronics, Communication and Computer Sciences, vol. E88-A*, no. 10, pp. 2835–2843, 2005.

[10] P. N. Bangchang, M. P. Tehrani, T. Fujii, and M. Tanimoto, "Realtime system of free viewpoint television," *The Journal of the Institute of Image Information and Television Engineers (ITE)*, vol. 59, no. 8, pp. 63–70, 2005.

[11] M. P. Tehrani, M. Droese, T. Fujii, and M. Tanimoto, "Distributed source coding architecture for multi-view images" *The Journal of the Institute of Image Information and Television Engineers (ITE)*, vol. 58, no. 10, pp. 1461–1464, 2004.

[12] M. P. Tehrani, P. N. Bangchang, T. Fujii, and M. Tanimoto, "The optimization of distributed processing for arbitrary view generation in camera sensor networks," *IEICE Transaction on Fundamentals of Electronics, Communication and Computer Sciences*, vol. E87-A, no. 8, pp. 1863–1870, Aug. 2004.

[13] Y. Takaki and N. Nago, "Multi-projection of lenticular displays to construct a 256-view super multi-view display," *Optics Express*, vol. 18, no. 9, pp. 8824–8835, 2010.

[14] M. Tanimoto, "FTV (free-viewpoint television)," *APSIPA Transactions on Signal and Information Processing*, vol. 1, E4, 2012.

[15] B. Goldlucke, M. Magnor, and B. Wilburn, "Hardware accelerated dynamic light field rendering," *International Workshop on Vision, Modeling, and Visualization*, 2002.

[16] B. S. Wilburn, M. Smulski, H.-H. Kelin Lee, and M. A. Horowitz, "Light field video camera," *Proc. SPIE 4674*, 2001.

[17] M. P. Tehrani, K. Niwa, M. N. Fukushima, *et al.*, "3DAV integrated system featuring arbitrary listening-point and free viewpoint generation," *IEEE 10th Workshop on Multimedia Signal Processing*, Cairns, QLD, Australia, 2008, pp. 855–860, doi: 10.1109/MMSP.2008.4665193.

[18] M. P. Tehrani, Y. Hirano, T. Fujii, S. Kajita, K. Takeda, and K. Mase, "An integrated audio-visual viewer for a large scale multipoint cameras and microphones," *Proc. International Workshop on Advance Image Technology*, IWAIT, Bangkok, 2007.

[19] M. P. Tehrani, Y. Hirano, T. Fujii, S. Kajita, K. Takeda, and K. Mase, "Arbitrary listening-point generation using sub-band representation of sound wave ray-space," *2006 IEEE International Conference on Acoustics Speech and Signal Processing Proceedings*, Toulouse, France, 2006, doi: 10.1109/ICASSP.2006.1661332.

[20] T. Fujii, K. Mori, K. Takeda, K. Mase, M. Tanimoto, and Y. Suenaga, "Multipoint measuring system for video and sound – 100-camera and microphone system," *2006 IEEE International Conference on Multimedia and Expo*, Toronto, ON, Canada, 2006, pp. 437–440, doi: 10.1109/ICME.2006.262566.

[21] M. P. Tehrani, Y. Hirano, T. Fujii, S. Kajita, K. Takeda, and K. Mase, "The sub-band sound wave ray-space representation," *Proc. International Workshop on Advance Image Technology*, IWAIT 2006, S9-1, pp. 291–296, 2006.

[22] M. P. Tehrani, Y. Hirano, T. Fujii, *et al.*, "The sound wave ray-space," *2005 IEEE International Conference on Multimedia and Expo*, Amsterdam, Netherlands, 2005, doi: 10.1109/ICME.2005.1521622.

[23] M. P. Tehrani, A. Ishikawa, S. Naito, S. Sakazawa, and A. Koike, "Iterative colour correction of multicamera system using corresponding feature points," *Journal of Visual Communications and Image Representation*, vol. 21, no. 5–6, pp. 377–391, 2010.

[24] M. P. Tehrani, A. Ishikawa, S. Naito, S. Sakazawa, and A. Koike, "A precise detection of moving objects in video," *The Journal of the Institute of Image information and Television Engineers (ITE)*, vol. 63, no. 11, pp. 84–94, Nov. 2009.

[25] A. Ishikawa, M. P. Tehrani, S. Naito, S. Sakazawa, and A. Koike, "Free viewpoint video generating method for walk-through experience," *IEICE Transactions D, vol. J92-D*, no. 6, pp. 854–867, 2009

[26] A. Ishikawa, M. P. Tehrani, S. Naito, S. Sakazawa, and A. Koike, "Walk-through in free viewpoint video generation," *Magazine of IMAGE LAB*, vol. 19, no. 4, pp. 48–52, 2008.

[27] A. Ishikawa, M. P. Tehrani, S. Naito, S. Sakazawa, and A. Koike, "Free viewpoint video generation for walk-through experience using image-based rendering," *Proc. of ACM Multimedia 2008*, Vancouver, Canada, 2008.

[28] M. P. Tehrani, A. Ishikawa, S. Naito, S. Sakazawa, and A. Koike, "Enhanced Multiple Local Ray-spaces Method for Walk-through View Synthesis," *2008 Second International Symposium on Universal Communication*, Osaka, Japan, 2008, pp. 206–209, doi: 10.1109/ISUC.2008.12.

[29] M. Tanimoto, M. P. Tehrani, T. Fujii, and T. Yendo, "Free-Viewpoint TV," *IEEE Signal Processing Magazine*, vol. 28, no. 1, pp. 67–76, 2011.

[30] M. P. Tehrani, A. Ishikawa, M. Kawakita, N. Inoue, and T. Fujii, "A hybrid representation for multi-view images," *2012 3DTV-Conference: The True Vision – Capture, Transmission and Display of 3D Video (3DTV-CON)*, Zurich, Switzerland, 2012, pp. 1–4, doi: 10.1109/3DTV.2012.6365445.

[31] M. P. Tehrani, A. Ishikawa, M. Kawakita, N. Inoue, and T. Fujii, "Synthesis error compensated multiview video plus depth for representation of multiview video," *IEEE International Conference on Acoustics, Speech, and Signal Processing (ICASSP)*, pp. 890–894, Florence, Italy, 2014.

[32] M. P. Tehrani, A. Ishikawa, M. Kawakita, N. Inoue, and T. Fujii, "Compression of multi-view images using hybrid representation for 200-inch 3D display," *Proc. IWAIT 2013*, pp. 498–503, 2013.

[33] https://www.youtube.com/watch?v=NiaInndP1S0.

[34] S. Iwasawa, M. Kawakita, and N. Inoue, "REI: An automultiscopic projection display," *Proc. 3DSA 2013*, Selected paper 1, 2013.

[35] http://www.holografika.com/.

[36] https://www.youtube.com/watch?v=3oX-aOJMX34.

[37] J. Lee, J. Park, D. Nam, S. Young Choi, D. Park, and C. Y. Kim, "Optimal projector configuration design for 300-Mpixel light-field 3D display," *Optics Express*, vol. 21, pp. 26820–26835, 2013.

[38] H. Watanabe, N. Okaichi, T. Omura, M. Kano, H. Sasaki, and M. Kawakita, "Aktina vision: Full-parallax three-dimensional display with 100 million light rays," *Scientific Reports*, vol. 9, 17688, 2019.

[39] JCT3V-C0210: 3D Holoscopic Video Test Material, FP7 3D VIVANT Consortium, 2013.

[40] J. Hong, Y. Kim, S. G. Park, *et al.*, "3D/2D convertible projection-type integral imaging using concave half mirror array," *Optics Express*, vol. 18, no. 20, pp. 20628–20637, 2010.

[41] National Institute of Information and Communications Technology, https:// www.nict.go.jp/en/pdf/copy_of_NICT_NEWS_1111_E.pdf.

[42] S. Suyama, H. Takada, and S. Ohtsuka, "A direct-vision 3-D display using a new depth-fusing perceptual phenomenon in 2-D displays with different depths," *IEICE Transactions on Electronics*, vol. 85, no. 11, pp. 1911–1915, 2002.

[43] D. Lanman, M. Hirsch, Y. Kim, and R. Raskar, "Content adaptive parallax barriers: Optimizing dual-layer 3D displays using low-rank light field factorization," *ACM Transactions on Graphics*, vol. 29, no. 6, pp. 1–10, 2010.

[44] G. Wetzstein, D. Lanman, M. Hirsch, and R. Raskar, "Tensor displays: Compressive light field synthesis using multilayer displays with directional backlighting," *ACM Transactions on Graphics*, vol. 31, no. 4, pp. 1–11, 2012.

[45] https://cordis.europa.eu/project/id/248420.

[46] K. Sakai, K. Takahashi, T. Fujii, and H. Nagahara, "Acquiring dynamic light fields through coded aperture camera," *European Conference on Computer Vision 2020 (ECCV2020)*, Springer Lecture Notes in Computer Science, vol. 12364, pp. 368–385, 2020.

[47] Y. Inagaki, Y. Kobayashi, K. Takahashi, T. Fujii, and H. Nagahara, "Learning to capture light fields through a coded aperture camera," *European Conference on Computer Vision (ECCV2018), Springer Lecture Notes in Computer Science*, vol. 11211, pp. 431–448, 2018.

[48] K. Sakai, Y. Inagaki, K. Takahashi, T. Fujii, and H. Nagahara, "CFA handling and quality analysis for compressive light field camera," *ITE Transactions on Media Technology and Applications*, vol. 9, no. 1, pp. 25–32, 2021.

[49] Y. Yagi, K. Takahashi, T. Fujii, T. Sonoda, and H. Nagahara, "Designing coded aperture camera based on PCA and NMF for light field acquisition," *IEICE Transactions on Information and Systems*, vol. E101-D, no. 9, pp. 2190–2200, 2018.

[50] Y. Yagi, K. Takahashi, T. Fujii, T. Sonoda, and H. Nagahara, "PCA-coded aperture for light field photography," *IEEE International Conference on Image Processing (ICIP)*, pp. 3031–3035, Poster, China National Convention Center, Beijing, China, 2017.

[51]   K. Maruyama, K. Takahashi, and T. Fujii, "Comparison of layer operations and optimization methods for light field display," *IEEE Access*, vol. 8, pp. 38767–38775, 2020.

[52]   K. Maruyama, Y. Inagaki, K. Takahashi, T. Fujii, and H. Nagahara, "A 3-D display pipeline from coded aperture camera to tensor light-field display," *IEEE International Conference on Image Processing (ICIP)*, pp. 1064–1068, 2019.

[53]   K. Takahashi, Y. Kobayashi, and T. Fujii, "From focal stack to tensor light-field display," *IEEE Transactions on Image Processing*, vol. 27, no. 9, pp. 4571–4584, 2018.

[54]   Y. Kobayashi, K. Takahashi, and T. Fujii, "From focal stacks to tensor display: A method for light field visualization without multi-view images," *Proc. IEEE International Conference on Acoustics, Speech and Signal Processing (ICASSP2017)*, New Orleans, USA, 2017.

[55]   Y. Kobayashi, S. Kondo, K. Takahashi, and T. Fujii, "A 3-D display pipeline: Capture, factorize, and display the light field of a real 3-D scene," *ITE Transactions on Media Technology and Applications*, vol. 5, no. 3, pp. 88–95, 2017.

[56]   K. Takahashi, Y. Kobayashi, and T. Fujii, "Displaying real world light fields using stacked LCDs," The 23rd International Display Workshops in conjunction with Asia Display 2016, *DES4/3D8 - 1*, pp. 1300–1303, invited talk & Innovative Demonstration Session (I-DEMO), Fukuoka, Japan, 2016.

[57]   T. Saito, Y. Kobayashi, K. Takahashi, and T. Fujii, "Displaying real-world light-fields with stacked multiplicative layers: requirement and data conversion for input multi-view images," *Journal of Display Technology*, vol. 12, no. 11, pp. 1290–1300, 2016.

[58]   K. Takahashi, T. Saito, M. P. Tehrani, and T. Fujii, "Rank analysis of a light field for dual-layer 3D displays," *IEEE International Conference on Image Processing (ICIP), NEW-P1.4*, Poster, Quebec City, Canada, 2015.

[59]   T. Saito, K. Takahashi, M. P. Tehrani, and T. Fujii, "Data conversion from multi-view cameras to layered light field display for aliasing-free 3D visualization," *IS&T/SPIE Electronic Imaging, Stereoscopic Displays and Applications XXVI*, Paper 9391-42, San Francisco, USA, 2015.

[60]   H. Nagahara, C. Zhou, T. Watanabe, H. Ishiguro, and S. K. Nayar, "Programmable aperture camera using LCoS," *European Conference on Computer Vision*, Springer, pp. 337–350, 2010.

[61]   T. Sonoda, H. Nagahara, and R. Taniguchi, "Motion-invariant coding using a programmable aperture camera," *IPSJ Transactions on Computer Vision and Applications*, vol. 6, pp. 25–33, 2014.

[62]   A. Jones, I. McDowall, H. Yamada, M. Bolas, and P. Debevec, "Rendering for an interactive 360° light field display," *ACM Transactions on Graphics*, vol. 26, no. 3, pp. 40–es, 2007.

[63]   https://www.fujii.nuee.nagoya-u.ac.jp/research-e.html.

[64] A. Jones, I. McDowall, H. Yamada, M. Bolas, and P. Debevec, "An interactive 360° light field display," *ACM SIGGRAPH 2007 emerging technologies (SIGGRAPH '07)*. Association for Computing Machinery, New York, NY, USA, pp. 13–es, 2007.

[65] K. K. Manoh, T. Yendo, T. Fujii, and M. Tanimoto, "Ray-space acquisition system of all-around convergent views using a rotation mirror," *Proc. SPIE 6778, Three-Dimensional TV, Video, and Display VI*, 67780C, 2007 https://doi.org/10.1117/12.740689.

[66] T. Yendo, T. Fujii, M. Tanimoto, and M. P. Tehrani, "The Seelinder: Cylindrical 3D display viewable from 360 degrees," *Journal of Visual Communication and Image Representation*, vol. 21, no. 5–6, pp. 586–594, 2010.

[67] http://www.holymine3d.com/prod/prod03.html.

[68] S. Yoshida, "fVisiOn: Glasses-free tabletop 3D display to provide virtual 3D media naturally alongside real media," *Proc. SPIE 8384, Three-Dimensional Imaging, Visualization, and Display* 2012, 838411 (1–9), 2012.

[69] S. Yoshida, "fVisiOn: 360-degree viewable glasses-free tabletop 3D display composed of conical screen and modular projector arrays," *Optics Express*, vol. 24, no. 12, pp. 13194–13203, 2016.

[70] M. P. Tehrani, T. Senoh, M. Okui, *et al.*, "Proposal to consider a new work item and its use case - REI: An ultra-multiview 3D display," ISO/IEC JTC1/SC29/WG11/m30022, 2013.

[71] M. Teratani, X. Jin, and G. Lafruit, "[MPEG-I-Visual] use case and application scenario for dense light field" ISO/IECJTC1/SC29/WG02, m56260, Online, 2021.

[72] S. Yoshida, S. Yano, and H. Ando, "fVisiOn: glasses-free tabletop 3D display observed from surrounding viewpoints of 360°," *Journal of the National Institute of Information and Communications Technology*, vol. 57, nos. 1/2, pp. 73–82, 2010.

[73] https://ucri.nict.go.jp/fvision/.

[74] https://fr.wikipedia.org/wiki/Nouveau_stade_olympique_national.

[75] https://www.theguardian.com/sport/2017/jun/15/stadiums-future-holograms-drones-fan-experience.

[76] https://en.wikipedia.org/wiki/Robotic_arm.

[77] M. Lingenauber, K. H. Strobl, N. W. Oumer, and S. Kriegel, "Benefits of plenoptic cameras for robot vision during close range on-orbit servicing maneuvers," *IEEE Aerospace Conference*, 2017, pp. 1–18, doi: 10.1109/AERO.2017.7943666

[78] https://en.wikipedia.org/wiki/Da_Vinci_Surgical_System.

Chapter 15

Visual media compression

As it has been shown in several use cases (cf. Chapters 13 and 14), 3D content has found its application scenarios and recently reached to users. These days, end users can enjoy 3D content in the home stereoscopic (glasses-based) display or head-mounted display, thanks to existing transmission and compression standards. In the progress of virtual reality, we expect that in near future users can enjoy 3D content with a wider view angle using multi-view displays (more than 20% and up to 50% of views). Such displays add a narrow view angle but users can enjoy 3D content without any special glasses. In the future, we expect that 3D displays with larger parallax (100 views) will be available for the end user. Such displays can create a true virtual reality with a large viewing angle, and can provide individual viewing experiences to all viewers based on the location where they watch the content. All these experiences are to some extent ready to be delivered to users, but still the bandwidth to transmit such a huge amount of data remains challenging. Here the compression techniques show their importance.

The transmission or storage of 3D content is generally similar to the transmission of 2D content in the video-based system. It means that the 3D data can be transmitted through a common communication channel, such as the Internet or wireless channel. However, the 3D information of a scene is usually a lot larger than the 2D information of the same scene. Thus, compression is compulsory. One should be aware that compression is not just a process of binarization. Compression is the process of removing redundancies that can be recovered at the user side, and even discarding some information that has little impact on the visual perception. In the following, we will review different compression technologies based on different representations of the 3D data.

During the last couple of decades, many codec alternatives have been proposed. Some have been proposed in competing standardization committees, some even in competing subgroups of the same committee. This explains the plethora of video codecs that exist, from open-source initiatives to highly efficient, though overly complex video codecs with intellectual property ruled through patent pools. Fortunately, most committees are following similar rules to compare the relative merits of video codecs. Simply stated: first evaluate the codec objectively, then confirm with subjective evaluation through user tests under strict test viewing conditions, which we will not further discuss here. The objective evaluation, however, is interesting because it can basically be performed by any skilled individual.

The basic idea of the objective evaluation is to start from an uncompressed video test sequence (standardization committees have a few dozens of them), compress and decode it with the video codec under test, and then compare the quality of the decompressed video with the original, uncompressed one through an objective metric. Typically, the objective metric is PSNR, which stands for peak signal to noise ratio, averaging the squared difference between all pixels of the original and decoded images. PSNR is most easily defined via the mean squared error (MSE). Given a noise-free $m \times n$ monochrome image I and its noisy approximation K, MSE is defined as

$$\text{MSE} = \frac{1}{mn} \sum_{i=0}^{m-1} \sum_{j=0}^{n-1} |I(i,j) - K(i,j)|^2$$

The PSNR (in decibel – dB) is defined as

$$\begin{aligned} \text{PSNR} &= 10 \log_{10} \left(\frac{\text{MAX}_I^2}{\text{MSE}} \right) \\ &= 20 \log_{10} \left(\frac{\text{MAX}_I}{\sqrt{\text{MSE}}} \right) \\ &= 20 \log_{10}(\text{MAX}_I) - 10 \log_{10}(\text{MSE}) \end{aligned}$$

Here, MAX_I is the maximum possible pixel value of the image. When the pixels are represented using 8 bits per sample, this is 255. For B bits per sample, MAX_I is $2^B - 1$. The common value for B is 8 bits.

Assessments in VR applications cannot be precise when the virtual image is synthesized nearly perfectly, but with some pixel shift. For instance, the immersive video PSNR (IV-PSNR) is defined as [1,2]. IV-PSNR is a PSNR-based objective quality metric adapted for immersive video applications. Compared to PSNR, two major modifications were added: the corresponding pixel shift and the global colour difference. The corresponding pixel shift eliminates the influence of a slight shift of objects' edges caused by reprojection errors. Global colour difference reduces the influence of different colour characteristics of different input views. IV-PSNR for colour component c is defined as follows:

$$\text{IV-PSNR}(c) = 10 \cdot \log \left(\frac{\text{MAX}^2}{\text{IVMSE}(c)} \right)$$

where MAX is the maximum value of the color component (e.g. 255 for 8-bit video) and IVMSE is the mean of the squared error:

$$\text{IVMSE}(c) = \frac{1}{W \cdot H} \sum_{y=0}^{H-1} \sum_{x=0}^{W-1} \min_{\substack{x_R \in [x-\text{CPS}, x+\text{CPS}] \\ y_R \in [y-\text{CPS}, y+\text{CPS}]}} (c_T(x,y,c) - c_R(x_R, y_R, c) + \text{GCD}(c))^2$$

where W and H are width and height of the image, $c_T(x,y,c)$ and $c_R(x,y,c)$ are values of color component c in the position (x,y) in the test image and the reference image, respectively, CPS is the maximum corresponding pixel shift between reference and test image, and GCD is the global colour difference for component c:

$$\text{GCD}(c) = \max\left(\frac{1}{W \cdot H} \sum_{y=0}^{H-1} \sum_{x=0}^{W-1} (c_R(x,y,c) - c_T(x,y,c)), \text{MUD}(c)\right)$$

where MUD(c) is the maximum unnoticeable difference for colour component c.

IV-PSNR is calculated separately for each frame of the sequence. In the end, the mean IV-PSNR value is returned. The IV-PSNR quality metric is based on PSNR; therefore, the higher the number, the better is the quality. Both metrics are explicitly pixel-wise with little consideration of human visual system (HVS) centric aspects that should be more in line with subjective evaluations.

Whichever of these metrics (or others) is used, the video quality evaluation will change the quantization parameter Q, which itself has a direct impact on the bitrate – typically in the range of Megabits per second (Mbps), expressed in the horizontal axis of Figure 15.1 – and the quality of the decoded video, expressed in dB for PSNR in the vertical axis of Figure 15.1.

Clearly, the higher the quantization parameter Q, the larger the tolerated error margin is for all quantized information; hence, the more lossy compression and decreased quality will appear at lower bitrates. Figure 15.1 shows the typical trend of the quality-bitrate curve: a steep increasing curve at increasing bitrates (left), ending up in a saturation zone (right) where quality hardly increases at higher bitrates. In general, a video is considered of high quality at a PSNR of 35 dB and excellent quality at 45 dB or higher. A PSNR of 30 to 35 dB is still good. However, below a PSNR of 30 dB, the quality of the video might start to be worryingly low (it nevertheless depends on the exact viewing conditions).

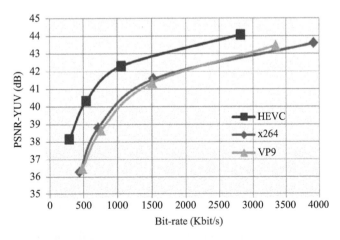

Figure 15.1   *Typical quality-bitrate figure in video codecs – R-D curves of HEVC, H.264/MPEG-AVC: an open-source x264 encoder, and VP9 encoders by Google®*

15.1   3D video compression

3D video represents a huge amount of information – more than for 2D video – to be streamed through the network. Compression of the video stream hence becomes mandatory, with compression performances that should be at least as good as for 2D video. Therefore, the paradigm that has been followed in MPEG-I is to reuse existing 2D video codecs, while applying a pre-processing step on the 360 videos or multiview video, so that it shows its most favourable characteristics for good compression performance. In general 3D content can be either stereo video or multiview video or 360 panoramas. A *backward compatible* solution for compression of 3D video content allows transmission of video too. The *backward compatibility* has been an important requirement for any new codec in the standardization society.

Having this in mind and back to video content, for compression of 3D video formats (with backward compatibility), multiview video coding (MVC) was standardized as an extension of H.264/MPEG-4 advanced video coding (AVC). Note that H.264/MPEG-4 AVC [3,4] was originally standardized for compression of video content and the extension of the same standard was utilized for multiview video content. In MVC standard, the idea of temporal prediction in time domain (in H.264/MPEG-4 AVC) was extended to predict the disparity between two given views, namely disparity-compensated prediction. By utilizing this we can exploit inter-view dependency, and as result, the MVC can compress the multiview video with better efficiency than compressing each of the views in multiview video independently, that is, simulcast compression. Despite the fact MVC is efficient, but for a given quality of video, the bit rate is linearly proportional to the number of compressed views [5]. This makes the MVC not suitable for transmission of multiview video.

While MVC as an extension of AVC has been developing, the same group of experts worked in parallel to improve the AVC codec and as the result, high-efficiency video coding (HEVC) standard was officially approved by ITU-T in 2013, as H.265, that is, ISO/IEC 23008-2 (MPEG-H Part 2). This standard was jointly developed by ITU-T Visual Coding Experts Group (VCEG), and ISO/IEC Moving Picture Expert Group (MPEG) [6]. In comparison with AVC, HEVC can achieve 50% gain in bit rate when these standards are subjectively assessed [7]. Similar to MVC which is an extension of H.264/MPEG-4 AVC, MV-HEVC was developed based on HEVC as an extension of HEVC. Furthermore, MV-HEVC extended to utilize depth information in MVD data format in interview predication and 3D-HEVC has been developing.

Note that race to improve the coding efficiency of video is still ongoing in the standardization society, and currently a new codec, namely versatile video coding (VVC) [8,9] is being investigated for standardization, jointly by VCEG and MPEG. Recently, neural network (NN), and machine learning (ML) techniques have also found its way in the compression field and MPEG now investigating such tools in their standards. In the following, we briefly review compression of 3D video in different formats, starting with the image and video compression.

15.1.1   Image and video compression

In this section, we will provide a brief review of the basics of image video coding, so that the reader can better understand the remainder of the chapter. It is, however, not our intention to revisit all technologies that have been developed in JPEG – Joint Photographic Experts Group or in MPEG – the Moving Picture Experts Group – a worldwide committee that (besides other similar committees) has since more than three decades explored and standardized most video codecs that have flooded the multimedia market, since then. Though there are subtle historical and technical differences between all these codecs (beyond the scope of this book), we may nevertheless state that since the very first version of this long series of codecs, the basic principles of video coding or compression have remained unchanged: the encoder finds similarities between adjacent frames in the video stream, and only transmit the core and vital signalling information to recover the frames in the decoder.

In the framework of image/video compression, transformation and prediction are the two main core tools. Figure 15.2 shows the module of JPEG coding [10,11] that consists of transform followed by quantization and entropy coding. In a JPEG codec, the image is initially partitioned into non-overlapped blocks (each block has the size of 8x8 pixels). The reason for dividing into blocks is because in a block the probability of change in texture is low and therefore compression can be high – most probably. This transformation transfers the image signal in a 2D block to the frequency domain: the block-DCT [12–14]. Based on the hypothesis of having blocks with low texture, we can quantize them in frequency domain with low loss in the amount of information. Furthermore, the quantized block in zigzag scanned to be converted to a 1D stream, followed by DPCM and entropy coding, such as run-length, Huffman or athematic coding [15–17].

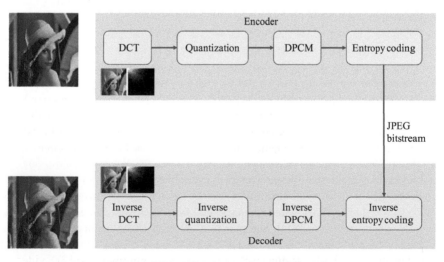

Figure 15.2   JPEG encoder and decoder

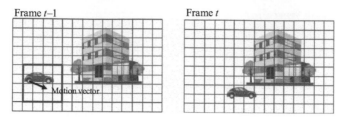

Figure 15.3   Motion vector for video compression

Unlike JPEG, a video codec has an intra-prediction [18] capability to recon-struct blocks in spatial domain from neighbouring blocks (Figure 15.3). By utiliz-ing motion estimation [19–21] to find the similar block (as prediction), significant coding gains are achieved in video prediction (Figure 15.3). Additionally, loop filter or deblocking filters are used to reduce the artefacts caused by block-based compression [21–30]. In video compression standards, such techniques are used, for example, MPEG-2, H.264/MPEG-4 AVC [32] and HEVC [33], MV-HEVC, 3D-HEVC, VVC – versatile video coding (VVC), also known as H.266, ISO/IEC 23090-3 [8,9] MPEG-I Part 3 and future video coding (FVC).

The main building blocks of a video codec as shown in Figure 15.4 are: a discrete cosine transform (DCT), a quantizer (Q), a motion estimation (ME) and an entropy coder (EC). All, except the last one, induce some information losses to increase the compression ratio – that is, the ratio of the original file size with the compressed file size – to two orders of magnitude. This loss is, however, imper-ceptible (or hardly perceptible) by the human eye, hence this 'lossy compression' is actually 'visually lossless'. The Entropy Coder module, however, does a lossless compression of the vital information that comes out of the pipeline, reaching a compression ratio typically below a factor two. It may be compared to the zip utility one uses on his/her PC to reduce a file size.

To achieve higher compression ratios with an additional order of magnitude, the motion estimation (ME) module will estimate how the various 8x8 pixels blocks of one frame are moved around to best match the next frame in the video sequence. These block translations are represented by motion vectors, which are also quantized and transmitted through the network, to the decoder. Note that these moved blocks do not completely cover the next frame – some gaps remain – and moreover, they do not necessarily coincide with the 8x8 pixels block grid of that next frame. Therefore, the difference between the moved blocks and the original frame blocks is calculated, aka the residue. With the previous I-frame, the motion vectors and the residue, one can reconstruct the next frame at the decoder. It is referred to as a P-frame since it has been 'predicted' (P) from the previous I-frame. The motion estimation and residue process of a P-frame further reduces the amount of information to transmit, and it is hence these P-frames that lead to higher compression ratios.

To be complete, an even higher compression ratio up to two orders of mag-nitude (including the additional factor of two with the compression from the EC) can be obtained with so-called B-frames or Bidirectional frames. Unlike P-frames

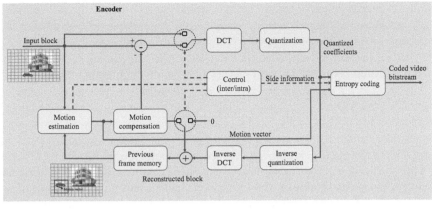

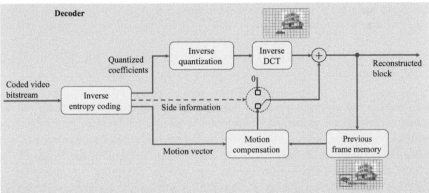

Figure 15.4   Video compression encoder and decoder

that are predicted from previous I-frames only, B-frames are back- and forth-predicted from either I-frames or P-frames, which themselves are predicted in a chain reaction from I-frames. B-frames can hence not be predicted instantaneously from incoming video frames; there is a need to buffer sufficient frames so that the B-frame has all information from a 'future' frame for performing its bidirectional prediction. This buffering process always induces latencies between the coding and decoding process. When you look at a live program where a close-up of the speaker is visible on a TV-screen behind his/her back, you may notice a big delay between his/her live mimics and the TV-screen's image. This delay reflects the B-frame latencies induced by the required buffering process to access data 'from the future'; a time shift transforms this future moment towards the present.

The interested reader may wonder why there is a feedback loop. Note that the reverse (bottom) part of the loop does exactly the opposite of the forward (top) part of the loop, to recover the predicted frame, including the lossy quantization that yields higher compression; it is this predicted frame – and not a theoretical one that must be used in calculating the residue image. This is an important aspect in practical codecs: with many P-frames following an I-frame, residue images are cumulated over all these P-frames, which would otherwise end up with a completely erroneous 'cumulated residue' image, with the encoder drifting away from the decoder. Adding the bottom part of the loop – effectively a copy of the decoder's process into the encoder – ensures that the drift is discarded.

We will stop here with the general introduction of a coding process; after all, we only want to provide the high-level aspects thereof to the reader. Of course, a video codec nowadays is much more complex than the general picture given here: during more than three decades, hundreds of experts have fine-tuned all parameters of the codec, ending up in subtle variations of the basic principles shown in Figure 15.4. For example, various pixel blocks sizes are allowed instead of a single 8x8 pixels size (albeit at a slightly higher signalling cost to indicate to the decoder which block size has been used at the encoder), various chrominance subsampling schemes (the human eye is less sensitive to the colour information than the luminance from early black and white television sets), etc.

15.2   MPEG standardization and compression with 2D video codecs

The interested reader might ask how all these coding and rendering modules are put together to create an end-to-end processing pipeline in existing products. One should be aware that video coding (including immersive video) is covered by the MPEG standardization committee, while any 3D rendering is in the hands of the Khronos group, which amongst others has standardized OpenGL. A product like an immersive video 3D renderer in a set-top-box will hence always cover various standardization committees. They stay in liaison, but they are nevertheless independent, hence a product designer must follow a multi-disciplinary approach to be able to implement the full pipeline.

Additionally, one has also to well-understand that a standard does not cover everything a product designer needs. For instance, the MPEG standard mainly covers the video bitstream format; this is the normative part of the standard. The committee also provides access to a reference software decoder which tells how the packets in the bitstream are typically used to recover the video; it is only one possible decoder implementation, out of many that can all be compliant with the video bitstream format. In fact, this reference software is called the 'test model' in the standardization committees, because it is used to 'test' (cross-check) whether the standard specification is complete. Typically, a first tester will create a bitstream with the encoder part of the software (be aware that the encoder is always informative, in the sense that anybody can make a totally different implementation, as long as the bitstream is compliant to the format defined by the standard). A second tester will use this bitstream and decode it with the decoder part of the reference software to check whether he can recreate the original sequence of images in the video. The reference software is thus indeed rather a test software and only a specific implementation of the standard. It does not guarantee that all operation modes that the standard foresees are really, fully implemented.

In the remaining sections, we will gradually build up a 3D immersive codec, using 2D video codecs, starting with 3DoF functionalities, and ending up in 6DoF functionalities. Let us start with a simple codec for 360 video using a cubemap.

15.2.1   Cubemap video

The video compression community has worked for more than 30 years with 2D video footage, hence, using video compression tools for immersive video requires some adjustments. A team was set up within the immersive video standardization committee of MPEG-I to add some tools to existing video codecs so that they can be used for 360 video. Their activities were put under the so-called OMAF umbrella, which stands for Omnidirectional Media Application Format. The team basically concentrated on how to transform 360 video into a rectangular video representation format that can be handled by a conventional video coder.

Though we know that a spherical or cylindrical video can be unwrapped into a 2D format, cf. Section 9.2.2, the team also considered that rendering any curved surface in a 3D player might be technically challenging. After all, OpenGL was developed with planar, triangular patches for a reason: it highly simplifies the rasterization stage in the OpenGL pipeline, avoiding overloading the graphics card. For this very reason, OMAF favoured polyhedral surfaces – including the cubemap – for the representation of 360 video.

To compress the video onto a cubemap, one can unfold the cube towards 2D, with the cross-based representation of Figure 15.5 being the straightforward approach. Unfortunately, this does not give a rectangular video, unless one would compress each face of the cubemap separately, which is not recommended because the codec hardware in graphics cards and processors can only instantiate a limited number of video streams simultaneously. Therefore, reshuffling the faces of the cube as in Figure 15.5(b) to obtain a perfect rectangle, is more appropriate. Also note that the cube's face images can never create a continuous image when shuffled together; there will always be borders between two completely different

Figure 15.5   Unfolding the cubemap (a) for better video compression using a rectangular map (b). Reproduced under a Creative Commons license from [34]

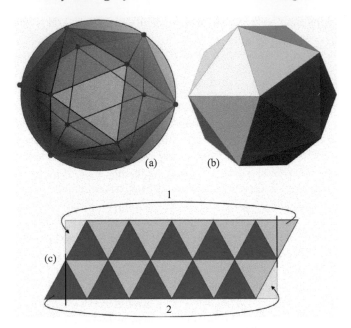

Figure 15.6   Approximating a sphere with polyhedral maps (a,b), and unfolding and rearranging these for better video compression (c). Reproduced under a Creative Commons license (a) from [35] and (b) from [36]

sub-images in the video stream cf. the orange border, which has a detrimental impact on the video coding performances. Nevertheless, rotating the images appropriately can reduce the number of discontinuities.

The same reasoning is applied for non-cubical mappings, for example the icosahedron mapping of Figure 15.6. Here too, sub-image rotations and partial triangle reshuffling, cf. Figure 15.6(c), are applied to obtain the smoothest possible rectangular 2D image. The so-obtained video stream will reach better performances than in the presence of image discontinuities. OMAF has reviewed a long list of polyhedral mappings as recommendations for worldwide standardization [37].

At the end of the day, in a product implementation of let us say a set-top box with decoder, one will have to parse the incoming compressed video stream to find back the various packets, followed by the actual decoding of these packets that are interpreted for reconstruction of the I, P and B-frames. The output of this process is a 2D video that must be mapped onto a polyhedral dome that the VR user will visualize from a specific point of view. This process is supported by OpenGL, but it is the set-top box implementer that has the responsibility to develop this functionality since MPEG is not providing such 3D visualization tool, while Khronos only provides the OpenGL framework for 3D rendering, not the 3D player itself. A system designer that creates a 3D player on a set-top box for 360 immersive video has therefore to do much more than waiting for the standards to roll out and compile their software tools.

15.2.2   Multiview video and depth compression (3D-HEVC)

Since the focus of this chapter is on compression of MVD data format for transmission of a 3D video content, we will continue with the 3D-HEVC [38]. The extended version of high efficiency video coding (HEVC), namely 3D-HEVC is for compression of 3D video in the format of multiview video plus depth. This extension includes disparity-compensated prediction, inter-view motion parameter, and inter-view residual prediction for coding of the dependent multiview video. For multiview depth, a new intra-coding mode, a modified motion compensation, motion vector coding, and concept of motion parameter are included. The encoder optimizes the rate-distortion trade-off based on the quality control of the novel view between the existing view in the multiview video. The coder is compatible so that the bit stream, 2D video, stereo video, and of course multiview video plus depth can be decoded. 3D-HEVC evolution based on objective and subjective assessment demonstrates about 20% gain in comparison with multiview-HEVC (MV-HEVC), and nearly 50% gain when we compare it with HEVC simulcast.

As mentioned earlier, this extension of HEVC is backward compatible and scalable so that it can decode any subset of MVD, that is, a video, stereo video, or multiview video. This codec is composed of parallel codecs (HEVC for video and depth) that interact to improve the coding gain. Figure 15.7 shows the structure of 3D-HEVC. The presented 3D video coding (3DVC) extension of HEVC was developed for depth-enhanced 3D video formats, ranging from conventional stereo video (CSV) to multiview video plus depth (MVD) with two or more views.

By using an independent codec (HEVC), we can satisfy backward compatibility (Figure 15.7). This encoder consists of basic elements – spatial prediction in a frame, temporal motion-compensated prediction between frames, transform coding of the prediction residual, and entropy coding. For a detailed discussion on

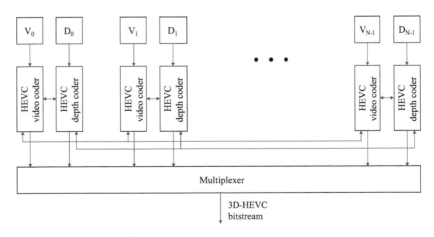

Figure 15.7   Encoder of 3D-HEVC with inter-view and inter-component prediction. The coder can compress N independent views and their associated depth

individual tools of HEVC and the coding performance, readers are referred to [7] and [39]. An overview of HEVC can be found in [33].

The extension of HEVC design consists of the following tools:

- Dependent views are encoded using disparity-compensated prediction, inter-view motion prediction and inter-view residual prediction.
- The depth maps are encoded using intra coding modes, motion compensation – motion vector coding, and motion parameter inheritance.
- The rate distortion optimization is based on the quality of the block-wise synthesized view distortion.

Note that 3D-HEVC can imbed a decoder-side renderer based on DIBR for generating the required number of display views at user side. Below some of the new tools that are added to HEVC are briefly explained, while readers are encouraged to read more detailed references on HEVC [33], MV-HEVC and 3D-HEVC [38] for details.

15.2.2.1   Motion- and disparity-compensated prediction (MCP and DCP)

It is inspired from motion-compensated prediction (MCP) in the video codec which has also initially been introduced in H.264/MPEG-4 AVC. For the same coded views at different frame or time instances, MCP is an inter-picture prediction process. On the other hand, if we utilize the coded pictures of other views but at the same frame or time instance, DCP is equivalent to inter-picture prediction. In this extension, the syntax used in the decoding process remains the same when using either motion- or disparity-compensated prediction. In this extension, only high-level syntax is modified.

15.2.2.2   Inter-view motion parameter prediction

Since multiview videos in MVD are captured from a scene but in different angles, the similarity among views is high. Therefore, the motion parameters among multiview video should have similar characteristics to motion among consecutive frames (Figure 15.8). Several researchers challenged this hypothesis and some methods proposed for depth-based inter-view prediction of motion parameters such as motion vectors have been studied [40–43].

Note that in Figure 15.8, the assumption is that the multiview video is rectified and the depth map has only horizontal shift, that is, disparity d, between blocks in two views, that is, $X_R(u_R, v_R)$ and $X_L(u, v)$. Symbols u and v refer to the centre of the block.

15.2.2.3   Inter-view residual prediction

Originally, a residual prediction was introduced in HEVC for predicting the motion between two reconstructed residual images after motion compensation in consecutive frames. This concept was extended to the reconstructed residual inter-view motion parameter prediction and it is called inter-view residual prediction. Again, for details, we invite interested readers to study HEVC review references.

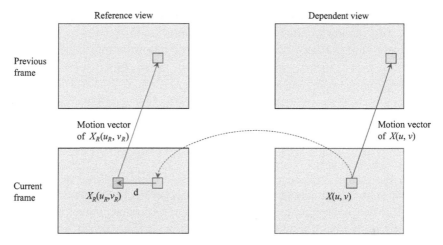

Figure 15.8   Motion vector correspondences between a block in a current picture of a dependent view, and an already coded reference view, using the disparity vector d from a depth map estimate

15.2.2.4   Depth map coding

Since a depth map is similar to an image to some extent, there are some differences such as sharp edges and large areas with constant intensity [44]. In general, for the compression of depth maps, intra-prediction, motion-compensated prediction, disparity-compensated prediction, and transform coding for the coding of the video pictures can be utilized. Due to some differences, it is worth concentrating on the differences with video as it enhance the compression schemes for depth map, by utilizing other techniques such as wavelet coding [45,46], mesh-based depth coding [47], sub-sampling of depth data [48], non-rectangular block partitioning for depth maps – wedgelet or platelet coding [49,50], and edge chain coding [51]. Hence, to adapt with the multiview depth map video, a new intra coding using so-called depth modelling modes have been developed. Motion-compensated prediction and motion vector coding methods also changed to adopt with the coding of depth maps. A depth-coding mode that utilizes the block partitioning and motion data from the associated video component was developed. For the rate distortion optimization of depth coding, the synthesized images using decoded depth maps are used to adjust the coding parameters for optimal compression.

15.2.3   Dense light field compression

Light field data normally refers to a large and dense number of views from a scene. For example, 25×25 viewpoints of a single image with a resolution of 640×480 is about 553 MB and if the same number of views of each 4k×2k is about 15 GB. There has been a lot of research to compress such data based on techniques we briefly explained for 3D-HEVC by disparity compensation [52–54] and geometry estimation [55], and enabling random access coding. On the other hand, based on plenoptic theory [56], a new type of camera developed that is commercially available [57], namely plenoptic camera. Plenoptic cameras are a new imaging device that can acquire 3D content. A plenoptic camera can capture the light field image in a shot. In plenoptic camera, through a microlens array (MLA), real-world is captured from multiple angles – cf. Chapter 13. This camera can acquire not only spatial light information but also angular light information. Since the data captured by a plenoptic camera contains essential 4D light field information, it should have larger data (less redundancy) than an image acquired by a traditional 2D camera. Hence, a novel and efficient compression method is essential for plenoptic cameras to promote their use cases.

Among different approaches for compression of data captured by plenoptic, use of MV codec remains as an anchor for comparison and comparison with novel methods that can efficiently compress in Lenslet (LL) format. Therefore, most of the research in this field is concentrated on how redundancy can be exploited in light fields when it is in LL format. In order to investigate the different approaches, MPEG standardization activities on this topic have categorized the compression scheme for better understanding and investigation of tools that exist for such research. Based on the available conversion tools and data format, we can perform several compression configurations.

15.2.3.1   Compression formats

Depending on the data format (LL or MV), two methods to investigate compression tools can be defined, as follows. As shown in Figure 15.9, we aim at compressing MV video data formats data without any conversion back to a LL format. The MV video can be either captured densely or be converted from LL video captured by a plenoptic camera. In this compression, the quality assessment is performed in the MV domain using PSNR.

According to Figure 15.10, one aims at compressing the LL video data format without any conversion to the MV video format. However, to evaluate the compression performance, the quality assessment is performed in MV domain to be consistent with the compression in MV format.

15.2.3.2   Existing tools for Lenslet data coding

Some existing coding tools in HEVC screen content coding extension (HEVC-SCC) [58] present superior efficiency in coding LL data. Also, HEVC-SCC

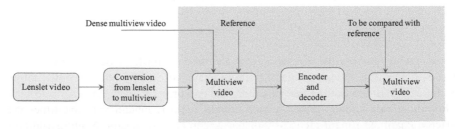

Figure 15.9   Compression of dense light field in multiview video format

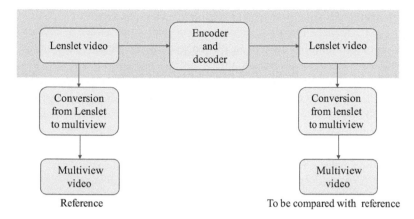

Figure 15.10   Compression of dense light field in Lenslet video format

supports non-4:2:0 colour formats, for example 4:4:4 and 4:2:2, which may benefit coding the LL data. So, the starting point of the compression for LL data coding is HEVC-SCC [19]. The HEVC screen content coding extension (HEVC-SCC) is developed based on HEVC version 1 [33] and HEVC range extensions (HEVC-RExt) [59]. Thus, it inherits the coding structure and coding tools of HEVC version 1 and HEVCRExt. HEVC-SCC also maintains backward compatibility to HEVC version 1 and HEVC-RExt [58].

HEVC-SCC introduces a new coding unit (CU) mode in addition to the conventional intra and inter modes, referred to as intra block copy (IBC). When a CU is coded in IBC mode, the prediction units (PU) of this CU find similar reconstructed blocks within the same picture. IBC can be considered as 'motion compensation' within the current picture. IBC is a coding tool similar to inter-picture prediction. The main difference is that in IBC, a predictor block is formed from the reconstructed samples (before application of in-loop filtering) of the current picture. IBC is performed at the PU level and is treated as an inter-PU. Specifically, using the inter mode design, the current picture can also be used as a reference picture for IBC. When a PU's reference picture is the current picture, it means that its prediction is performed from the reconstructed samples, before in-loop filtering in the encoder, of the current picture, which corresponds to the original IBC design. In order to decide whether to use IBC mode for a CU, a rate-distortion (RD) cost is calculated for the CU. Block matching (BM) is performed at the encoder to find the optimal BV for each prediction unit. Depending on the size of the PU, the three types of candidate BVs are evaluated.

Recently, MPEG has started new activities on Lenslet video coding (LVC) based on recent compression evidence provided to MPEG [59–66]. These activities in the near future aim to bring new tools for compression such content. The new tools under investigation will utilize inter and intra redundancy in the time and space domain. The main focus of this new codec will be mostly on industrial and scientific use cases, such as robotics and plenoptic microscopy, respectively.

15.3   Future challenges in 2D video compression

Before continuing with our endeavour for 3D immersive video coding, let us first give a glimpse of a new promising field in video coding: deep learning with neural networks. Such video coding techniques utilize deep learning and the HEVC framework, which seriously challenges the state-of-the-art video coding performance. Due to its potential, recently experts in the standardization committees are investigating potential standards for video coding based on neural networks. However, for a more detailed review, we refer the interested readers to [31].

Inspired by research on neuroscience and mathematics, the concept of neural networks (NN) was born. As in the human brain, a neural network consists of multiple layers of units with simple processing capability, called neurons (perceptrons). Neurons interact with each other via a connection. The connection transmits a signal from one neuron to the other with some weighting factor. In other words, the activated neuron is activated from previously activated neurons. To have non-linearity, activation functions are applied to all intermediate layers in the network [67,68]. Figure 15.11 shows the architecture of a simple neural network – one input layer, one output layer and multiple hidden layers, each of which contains various numbers of neurons.

In the early 1960s [69], the learning process was introduced and analysed for simple perceptions. Later a back-propagation procedure [70,71] was proposed during the 1970s and 1980s that was inspired by the chain rule derivative of training objectives. This process was proposed to solve the training problem of several layers of neurons, that is, multi-layer perceptron (MLP). The stochastic gradient descent with backpropagation procedure is normally used to train the multi-layer structure but they are computationally expensive and may lead to a local minimum. However, in [72] back in 1990, parameter-sharing for MLP was proposed. This method is a simple version of a CNN that was applied for specific

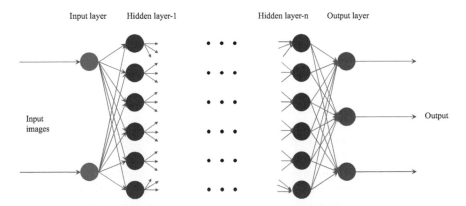

Figure 15.11   An illustration for neural network with one input layer, one output layer and multiple hidden layers, each of which contains various number of neurons

tasks, for example, document recognition. This method made the training possible for large-scale neural networks.

Note that compression is computationally expensive because the process is sequential that limits usage of the parallel computational platform, such as GPU. Also, each tool in the rule-based compression is acting relatively individually that limits the improvement in compression efficiency, compared with a compression scheme that is able to optimize the whole process. Here, we can understand the urge for having an alternative technology, like a neural network, that can be applied for image and compression.

Neural networks have found their significance in image compression and video compression since the late 1987 [73] and 1989 [74], respectively. It has rapidly been evolving in recent years after it has been recognized by the video coding standardization society. The reader is referred to following references for the use of neural networks in compression.

- Multi-layer perceptron (MLP)-based image coding [75–85]
- Random neural network-based image coding [86–89]
- Convolutional neural network-based coding [89–98]
- Recurrent neural network-based coding [99–103]
- Generative adversarial network-based coding [104–107]
- Intra prediction techniques using neural networks [108–120]
- Neural network-based inter prediction [121–133]
- Neural network-based quantization and entropy coding for video coding [134–138]
- Neural network-based loop filtering [139–153]
- New video coding frameworks based on neural network [154–157]
- Optimization techniques for image and video compression using neural network [158–160]

There are, however, some remaining challenges in using neural networks for image and video compression. To mention some of the potentials, we can refer to content adaptivity of neural networks. In other words, we can optimize the performance of neural networks for specific types of content. Another advantage can be in the prediction process within the codec. By neural network-based codec, we can improve the coding efficiency because it can refer to far distance blocks in the intra or inter-view predictions. We also can indicate that neural networks not only can compress the visual content but also the features that are most meaningful for machine vision analysis.

Therefore, compression of features of an image or video can be a new challenge in the field of image or video codec when the content is supposed to be delivered for machine vision analysis rather than human. Another unmatured topic is rate-distortion (RD) optimization in neural networks when a diverse content of image/video is compressed. In other words, we need a multiple network training and adaptivity switching mechanism to obtain the best RD solution. Finally, it is the computational cost which is an obstacle in the development of image and video compression using neural networks. Therefore, the complexity of the network versus the required processing time and memory should be well studied to achieve the highest possible compression rate. This is related to RD optimization tasks that should be optimized considering the computational cost too.

Clearly, there are promising frameworks for compression of image and video, in addition to many challenging topics. However, the high efficiency of prediction and compact representation of the compression for image and video signals with high coding gain, and possibility to deploy them in parallel hardware architecture made this field more interesting, not only for industry but also for academia.

15.4 MPEG codecs for 3D immersion

This section is devoted to the latest advances in MPEG video coding for 3D immersive applications, referred as MPEG-I, where 'I' stands for Immersion/ Immersive. At the time of finalizing this textbook (end of 2021), the publication of the MPEG-I standards was still in press, therefore, we will only present the high-level aspects of how coding of 3D content for 6DoF applications is handled in the upcoming standard. It is made of a suite of coding tools, referred to as Video Point Cloud Coding (V-PCC), MPEG Immersive Video (MIV) and Visual Volumetric Video Coding (V3C), where the latter is the umbrella that encompasses V-PCC and MIV with a single bitstream format. Let us see how this differs from the 3D coding tools that have been presented so far.

In Section 15.2, the mindset to obtain 3D coding was to start with regular 2D video codecs that each code one view to the scene, possibly (not necessarily, though it is highly recommended) exploiting the interview dependencies to reach higher compression. The caveat of this approach is that instead of transmitting one high-resolution image to the decoder in the set-top box, a multitude of such images must be transmitted, increasing the pixel rate accordingly. Unfortunately, hardware implementations of codecs (e.g. on the 3D graphics card or GPU) always put a limit on the number of pixels per second that can be processed.

The approach chosen in V-PCC, MIV and V3C to overcome this constraint is to discard redundant image segments and packing the remaining ones in an intelligent way – like in a Tetris game – so that the essential information to send stays within acceptable limits with respect to the pixel rate. This approach has been initiated in the point cloud coding exposed in the next section, but it has really been pushed to its ultimate capabilities in the immersive video coding of Section 15.4.2. We will now have a closer look at how this all works.

15.4.1 Point cloud coding with 2D video codecs

In the following, we will constantly play on the ambiguity between point clouds, meshes and underlying colour and depth images to ask ourselves the question how we best obtain compression for visual volumetric data. If everything can eventually be brought back to meshes, it looks reasonable to think that compression of meshes is the way to go. Recently, initiatives like Google Draco based on EdgeBreaker

[161,162] have brought rather good lossy compression performances for mesh objects with 15–30 bits per transmitted vertex for a 3D object with little quality degradation [163,164]. However, compared to what video coders can achieve nowadays for 2D images – that is, 0.04 bits per pixel for HEVC, and even 0.02 bits per pixel in the new VVC codecs – one feels that 3D object coding remains a challenge. The main reasons lie in (1) the vertex mesh connectivity, which is expensive to code, and (2) the difficulty to exploit temporal redundancy between the successive positions of moving vertices.

The MPEG-I immersive media standardization committee proposed first an alternative approach, where instead of directly coding the 3D object as a collection of interconnected 3D vertices, its 2D projections are coded with conventional video codecs [165]. This technique is remarkably similar to the approach that one would directly apply in DIBR: code all views and their depth maps into one or more video streams, exploiting somehow the inter-view redundancy, both spatially and temporally.

Figure 15.12 shows the main ingredients of this approach. The object is surrounded by a cube in (a), then orthographically projected onto each of its faces in (b, c) (note that orthographic projection does not cause perspective downscaling) with segmentations that cover regions that have some 'flatness' in (d). These segments are collected in a so-called atlas shown in Figure 15.12 (f), using a 'Tetris packing' that overall reduces the size of the image to code. At the same time, also the distance between the objects' points and the cube faces is recorded – point by point – into depth maps, also added to the atlas (g). Efficiently packing and coding

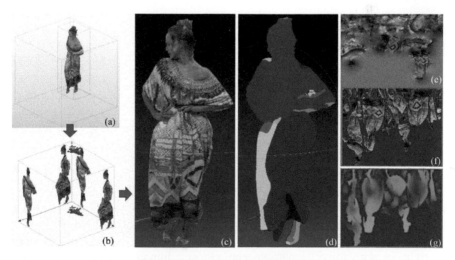

Figure 15.12   *Coding a 3D object (a) with its 2D projections (b). One projection of a point cloud (c), and its segmentation in depth patches (d,g) and texture patches (f). Smoothing the latter (e) creates smoother textures for better compression*

the texture and depth map segments of Figure 15.12 allows an unambiguous reconstruction of the 3D point cloud at the client side. The crux in 3D coding is how to do all this in an 'efficient' way from the point of view of coding?

Note that the segments of Figure 15.12 (f) have sharp boundaries, which are difficult to preserve with lossy video coding: at low to moderate bitrates, they will somewhat smooth out, which will be directly visible in the reconstructed 3D object, after decoding. Therefore, MPEG-I recommends the pre-processing of these segments to become 'coding friendly'. One may avoid sharp edges by extending and diluting the textures when moving outward, as shown in the transition from Figure 15.12(f) to (e); such dilution can be obtained by successively filtering and down/up-sampling the pixels. This inherent smoothing operation will be favourable to the video coding process, but it requires that one can easily find back where the original segments were positioned, while discarding all smoothing extensions. Therefore, a so-called occupancy map is introduced (not shown), indicating which pixel belongs to an original segment and which not. Since such occupancy map is binary, its coding can be efficiently done with arithmetic coding.

In summary, the segments of Figure 15.12 (e/f) and (g) are forming images ready to be processed by any conventional 2D video codec, and some peripheral pre-processing. At the decoder, the equivalent steps are followed in reverse order: first decode, then select the segments that really contribute to an object, after which the object is reconstructed as a 3D puzzle from these segments, put at the right spatial distance using the decoded depth maps.

At this point, we have been able to code and decode back a point cloud, based on some pre- and post-processing and conventional 2D video codecs. Nothing guarantees that this point cloud is dense enough to obtain a visually appealing rendering result. It might be needed to do some splatting, or even reconstruct a 3D mesh to guarantee that all holes are filled. Interestingly, such 3D mesh reconstruction can be done at the decoder-only, without having to transmit the 3D mesh connectivity we know is so expensive in bitrate. If the 3D mesh reconstruction from the decoded point cloud is reproducible, meshing can be done at the decoder only. In practice, however, this is rarely recommended since it remains a quite heavy processing step.

The final question is how much bitrate is required to send each 3D point cloud or mesh object? With as much as six object projections to send, we may end up with bit rates much higher than the 10 Mbps used in high-definition TV broadcasting. With the dynamic point clouds transmitted at 30 fps in the MPEG-I explorations, bitrates of 25 Mbps to 50 Mbps per object, and sometimes even more than 100 Mbps for high quality transmission can be expected. This is one order of magnitude more important than in high-definition TV broadcasting, but probably an exaggerated figure within future 5G applications that will run on tablets or smartphones with lower resolution requirements; future will tell. Anyway, preliminary studies have shown that at lower bitrate transmission (<20 Mbps) with UHTV viewing, it is probably better to use the 3D mesh reconstruction approach, while beyond 50 Mbps point clouds with minimal splatting provide more satisfactory visual results [160].

15.4.2 MPEG immersive video compression

The depth-image-based rendering (DIBR) approach uses multiple camera views and associated depth maps (one per view; not a single global depth map over all views), out of which any viewpoint to the scene can be reconstructed with the techniques presented in Sections 12.6.3–12.6.9.

With respect to the coding of these views, it would be wise to use a so-called 'multiview video codec, such as MV-HEVC' that does not only find spatial and temporal correspondences or redundancies over a single view but also over various views in the multiview video. However, since the cameras are not necessarily parallel, their views undergo perspective transformations when jumping from one camera view to the next, and this drastically reduces the correspondences found with block matching techniques. In the end, during the experimental explorations in the MPEG-I coding committee (the reader is referred to [166] for a summary of the MIV activities), such multiview codec approach has been abandoned in favour of transmitting one or more reference views (and transmitting much less pixels to reach a much lower pixel rate), as well as the slight differences – mostly dis-occlusions – between the input views and the reference views.

The easiest way to explain this process of disocclusion transmission is to take the example of multiple cameras looking from the surface of a sphere outward to the scene, as in Figure 15.13. Such setup will allow to create a 360° panoramic view for 3DoF VR experiences, as explained in Chapter 9: all camera views are projected to a spherical central view, yielding the equirectangular projection (ERP) image of Figure 15.14(c). This will be the single reference view, in this example, combining all camera views.

*Figure 15.13   Capturing a scene from central cameras will exclude some
occlusions behind the persons and objects (in purple)*

Figure 15.14   Multiple cameras looking outward (a,b) with a reconstructed central
view (c) and the disocclusion areas (d,e) coded in an atlas, together
with their depth information (f) [167], courtesy: InterDigital

It may look counter-intuitive, but in doing so, we have lost vital information
that would allow us to support 6DoF navigation with freedom of movement within
the sphere that physically carries the cameras. Indeed, with the user leaving the
centre of the sphere, for example by moving forward towards one of the surrounding cameras, the user should be able to partially see regions behind the
scene's objects, touching the extreme border of the camera's field of view. These
are disocclusions not captured in the 360° panoramic ERP reference view, mostly
because the reprojection to the very centre of the sphere has artificially reduced the
viewing zone. Interpreted differently, in overlapping regions of adjacent camera
views some contradictory information is present (disocclusions from different sides
of the object) and discarded to create a seamless stitched image.

At the end of the day, disocclusions that get exposed when the user moves
outside the spherical centre should be captured separately; these are the patches
collected in a so-called atlas, cf. Figure 15.14(d, e, f). With all this information, it is
now possible to completely synthesize any viewpoint within the sphere, enabling a
6DoF experience within this volume, delimited by the physical camera setup. In
general, good view synthesis results can only be expected well within the convex
hull of the cameras, probably not outside this volume.

With this approach, bitrates of 50-100 Mbps have been observed at 30 fps on
the test data set used in MPEG-I for immersive video, which typically includes a
dozen of UHD camera views per sequence [168]. This is in the same order of
magnitude as with point cloud coding, with the difference that this includes all
objects in the scene, while with point cloud coding such figures arise for each
single object. It is nevertheless premature to conclude the bitrate figures of one or

the other technology since in general test sequences used in codec explorations are very peculiar to trigger various exceptional coding conditions. We may expect more favourable results with real content, but this will also be highly influenced by steady technological fine-tuning that gradually, but inevitably, will occur when such new coding technology appears on the market. This will, however, not modify the data file or streaming format of immersive video sequences, as established by the MPEG-I standardization committee [169].

15.4.3   Visual volumetric video coding

The previous two sections have shown astonishing similarities between point cloud coding and DIBR video coding using both 2D textures, 2D depth maps, various projections, atlases, and video codecs to properly transmit all this information to a client's device. Consequently, the MPEG-I standardization committee has identified the 'common denominator' between both technologies, packaged into the OpenV3C software library [170,171], where 'V3C' stands for visual volumetric video-based coding. This library fully replaces the original V-PCC, or video-based point cloud coding. Its API supports plug-ins for DIBR immersive video modules that function slightly differently than in point cloud coding. Eventually, OpenV3C will support both point cloud coding and DIBR coding, with portions of the processing distributed to CPUs, GPUs (graphical processing units) and other dedicated processing modules.

15.4.4   Compression for light field displays

The basic principles of lenticular and light field displays, as well as holographic stereograms have been introduced in Chapter 12, with concrete implementations described in Chapter 14. Such displays project hundreds of images in various directions to the viewer, allowing him/her to watch a movie stereoscopically, without wearing glasses. Moreover, as shown in Chapter 10 for light field HMDs, such displays also provide correct eye accommodation and vergence, that is, holographic vision. There is hence clearly a need to have proper codecs supporting such displays.

Figure 15.15 [172] shows the evolution of the required pixel rate (right vertical axis) and bitrate (mostly uncompressed; left vertical axis) for multiview displays that steadily improve over the years (more projected views), eventually leading to the dense light field displays that start to enter the market today. Around 2020, point B in the graph represents a 30-inch full parallax light field display with 30° field of view, which would require at 30 fps a pixel rate of 250 Gpix/s. Using only Multiview coding techniques where all the views would be compressed with HEVC each, delivering a compression of 0.04 bits/pixel, a total bitrate of 10 Gbps would be expected, which is impossible to sustain over most networks. For instance, broadband Internet would in 2015 reach theoretically 300 Mbps (point A), which extrapolated to 2020 reaches around 1 Gbps, far below the required 10 Gbps. This clearly suggests the need for even better compression techniques than HEVC ... and MIV of Section 15.4.2 is clearly a good candidate for this, though at the time of

354 Virtual reality and light field immersive video technologies

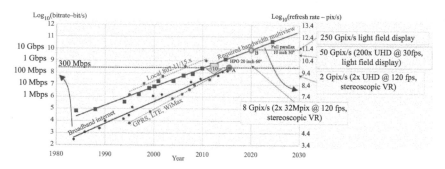

Figure 15.15   Evolution over the years for the required pixel rate of light field displays (upper solid line and right vertical axis), compared to the available bitrate over various networks (lower solid line and left vertical axis). Reproduced with permission from [172] © IEEE

writing this textbook, no clear figures of its compression performance can be provided for such high-quality light field displays. This is something to be investigated in future MPEG-I experiments.

The advantage in using MIV for light field display coding is that the content to be transmitted is often captured from non-parallel cameras, which MIV can perfectly handle. A standard like JPEG-PLENO's light field coding [173] that is also based on DIBR principles requires that all the content must first be rectified (as if the capturing cameras would have been ideally parallel) since the reconstruction of missing views is solely based on translating reference views' pixels based on their disparity (no un-projection and re-projection as in MIV for non-parallel cameras). This may be a burden, though strictly speaking not a major obstacle that cannot be overcome. Still, the way to select reference views will remain important for drastically reducing the bitrate with state-of-the-art 2D image codecs. The interested reader is referred to [174] for a more in-depth comparison between the various light field coding approaches recently developed, including JPEG-PLENO and MIV.

At the end of the day, data transmission bitrates for light field displays will most probably remain prohibitively high for some years to come, hence having a large light field display at home for movie watching will probably not become mainstream for some time. However, VR light field HMDs for holographic vision, as presented in Section 10.4, might come on the market soon. Indeed, even though their frame rate is often higher (120 fps), their total number of pixels and finally their pixel rates are much lower, hence also their required bitrate. According to Figure 15.15, a reasonable spec with a pixel rate below 10 Gpix/s would yield a bitrate around 300 Mbps, which is easily sustainable with a good USB wired connection. Since an HMD is often used locally connected to a PC, for example for 3D gaming using preloaded content on a hard disk, standards like MIV and JPEG-PLENO will easily serve light field HMDs well. Preliminary studies suggest that high-quality VR applications using MIV technology would require 25 Mbps, a figure much lower than the 300 Mbps suggested above.

References

[1] Adrian Dziembowski, 'Software manual of IV-PSNR for Immersive Video' ISO/IEC JTC 1/SC 29/WG 11, N19495, July 2020.

[2] https://gitlab.com/mpeg-i-visual/ivpsnr.

[3] Advanced Video Coding for Generic Audiovisual Services, Standard ISO/ IEC JTC 1, March 2012.

[4] S. Shimizu, M. Kitahara, H. Kimata, K. Kamikura, and Y. Yashima, 'View scalable multiview video coding using 3-D warping with depth map'. *IEEE Trans. on Circuits and Systems for Video Technology*, vol. 17, no. 11, pp. 1485–1495, 2007.

[5] P. Merkle, A. Smolic, K. Müller, and T. Wiegand, 'Efficient prediction structures for multiview video coding'. *IEEE Trans. on Circuits and Systems for Video Technology*, vol. 17, no. 11, pp. 1461–1473, 2007.

[6] Text of ISO/IEC DIS 23008-2: High Efficiency Video Coding, Standard ISO/IEC JTC1/SC29/WG11, July 2012.

[7] J.-R. Ohm, G. J. Sullivan, H. Schwarz, T. K. Tan, and T. Wiegand, 'Comparison of the coding efficiency of video coding standards – Including high efficiency video coding (HEVC)'. *IEEE Trans. on Circuits and Systems for Video Technology*, vol. 22, no. 12, pp. 1669–1684, 2012.

[8] 'Information technology — Coded representation of immersive media — Part 3: Versatile video coding'. International Organization for Standardization. Retrieved 16 February 2021.

[9] https://www.iso.org/standard/73022.html.

[10] G. K. Wallace, 'Overview of the JPEG (ISO/CCITT) still image compression standard'. In *Image Processing Algorithms and Techniques*, vol. 1244. International Society for Optics and Photonics, Bellingham, WA, pp. 220–234, 1990.

[11] G. K. Wallace. 'The JPEG still picture compression standard'. *Communications of the ACM*, vol. 34, no. 4, pp. 30–44, 1991.

[12] H. Andrews and W. Pratt. 'Fourier transform coding of images'. *Proc. Hawaii Int. Conf. System Sciences*, pp. 677–679, 1968.

[13] W. K. Pratt, J. Kane, and H. C. Andrews. 'Hadamard transform image coding'. *Proceedings of the IEEE*, vol. 57, no. 1, pp. 58–68, 1969.

[14] N. Ahmed, T. Natarajan, and K. R. Rao. 'Discrete cosine transform'. *IEEE Trans. on Computers*, vol. 100, no. 1, pp. 90–93, 1974.

[15] D. A. Huffman. 'A method for the construction of minimum-redundancy codes'. *Proceedings of the IRE*, vol. 40, no. 9, pp. 1098–1101, 1952.

[16] S. Golomb. 'Run-length encodings (Corresp.)'. *IEEE Trans. on Information Theory*, vol. 12, no. 3, pp. 399–401, 1966.

[17] I. H. Witten, R. M. Neal, and J. G. Cleary. 'Arithmetic coding for data compression'. *Communications of the ACM*, vol. 30, no. 6, pp. 520–540, 1987.

[18] J. Lainema, F. Bossen, W.-J. Han, J. Min, and K. Ugur. 'Intra coding of the HEVC standard'. *IEEE Trans. on Circuits and Systems for Video Technology*, vol. 22, no. 12, pp. 1792–1801, 2012.

[19] Y. Taki, M. Hatori, and S. Tanaka. 'Interframe coding that follows the motion'. *Proc. Institute of Electronics and Communication Engineers Japan (IECEJ)*, p. 1263, 1974.

[20] A. Netravali and J. Stuller. 'Motion-compensated transform coding'. *Bell System Technical Journal*, vol. 58, no. 7, pp. 1703–1718, 1979.

[21] J.-L. Lin, Y.-W. Chen, Y.-W. Huang, and S.-M. Lei. 'Motion vector coding in the HEVC standard'. *IEEE Journal of Selected Topics in Signal Processing*, vol. 7, no. 6, pp. 957–968, 2013.

[22] M. Naccari and F. Pereira. 'Adaptive bilateral filter for improved in-loop filtering in the emerging high efficiency video coding standard'. in *IEEE Picture Coding Symposium (PCS)*, pp. 397–400, 2012.

[23] X. Zhang, R. Xiong, W. Lin, J. Zhang, S. Wang, S. Ma, and W. Gao. 'Low-rank-based nonlocal adaptive loop filter for high-efficiency video compression'. *IEEE Trans. on Circuits and Systems for Video Technology*, vol. 27, no. 10, pp. 2177–2188, 2017.

[24] S. Ma, X. Zhang, J. Zhang, C. Jia, S. Wang, and W. Gao. 'Nonlocal in-loop filter: The way toward next-generation video coding?' *IEEE Multi-Media*, vol. 23, no. 2, pp. 16–26, 2016.

[25] C.-Y. Tsai, C.-Y. Chen, T. Yamakage, *et al.* 'Adaptive loop filtering for video coding'. *IEEE Journal of Selected Topics in Signal Processing*, vol. 7, no. 6, pp. 934–945, 2013.

[26] X. Zhang, R. Xiong, S. Ma, and W. Gao. 'Adaptive loop filter with temporal prediction'. in *IEEE Picture Coding Symposium (PCS)*, pp. 437–440, 2012.

[27] X. Zhang, S. Wang, Y. Zhang, W. Lin, S. Ma, and W. Gao. 'High-efficiency image coding via near-optimal filtering'. *IEEE Signal Processing Letters*, vol. 24, no. 9, pp. 1403–1407, 2017.

[28] P. List, A. Joch, J. Lainema, G. Bjontegaard, and M. Karczewicz. 'Adaptive deblocking filter'. *IEEE Transactions on Circuits and Systems for Video Technology*, vol. 13, no. 7, pp. 614–619, 2003.

[29] A. Norkin, G. Bjøntegaard, A. Fuldseth, *et al.* 'HEVC deblocking filter'. *IEEE Transactions on Circuits and Systems for Video Technology*, vol. 22, no. 12, pp. 1746–1754, 2012.

[30] K. Andersson, M. Zhou, and G. Van der Auwera. 'HEVC deblocking filter'. *IEEE Trans. on Circuits and Systems for Video Technology*, vol. 22, no. 12, pp. 1746–1754, 2012.

[31] S. Ma, X. Zhang, C. Jia, Z. Zhao, S. Wang, and S. Wang. 'Image and video compression with neural networks: A review'. *IEEE Transactions on Circuits and Systems for Video Technology*, vol. 30, no. 6, pp. 1683–1698, 2020.

[32] T. Wiegand, G. J. Sullivan, G. Bjontegaard, and A. Luthra. 'Overview of the H.264/AVC video coding standard'. *IEEE Trans. on Circuits and Systems for Video Technology*, vol. 13, no. 7, pp. 560–576, 2003.

[33] G. J. Sullivan, J. Ohm, W.-J. Han, and T. Wiegand. 'Overview of the high efficiency video coding (HEVC) standard'. *IEEE Trans. on Circuits and Systems for Video Technology*, vol. 22, no. 12, pp. 1649–1668, 2012.

[34]   E. Persson, 'Field skyboxes,' https://opengameart.org/content/field-skyboxes

[35]   https://commons.wikimedia.org/wiki/Category:Icosahedron#/media/File: Icosa%C3%A8dre_sph%C3%A8re.jpg

[36]   https://commons.wikimedia.org/wiki/Category:Icosahedron#/media/File: Zeroth_stellation_of_icosahedron.svg

[37]   Text of ISO/IEC FDIS 23090-2(E), Information technology — Coded representation of immersive media — Part 2: Omnidirectional Media Format, ISO/IEC JTC1/SC29/WG03, 2021.

[38]   K. Müller, H. Schwarz, D. Marpe, *et al.* '3D high-efficiency video coding for multi-view video and depth data'. *IEEE Transactions on Image Processing*, vol. 22, no. 9, pp. 3366–3378, 2013, doi: 10.1109/TIP.2013.2264820.

[39]   T. K. Tan, A. Fujibayashi, Y. Suzuki, and J. Takiue. '[AHG 8] objective and subjective evaluation of HM5.0'. *Joint Collaborative Team on Video Coding*, San Jose, USA, Tech. Rep. JCTVC-H0116, Feb. 2012.

[40]   X. Guo, Y. Lu, F. Wu, and W. Gao. 'Inter-view direct mode for multiview video coding'. *IEEE Trans. on Circuits and Systems for Video Technology*, vol. 16, no. 12, pp. 1527–1532, 2006.

[41]   J. Konieczny and M. Domanski. 'Depth-based inter-view prediction of motion vectors for improved multiview video coding'. in *Proc. IEEE True Vis., Capture, Transmission Display 3D Video*, Tampere, Finland, Jun. 2010, pp. 1–4.

[42]   H.-S. Koo, Y.-J. Jeon, and B.-M. Jeon. 'Motion skip mode for MVC'. *ITU-T and ISO/IEC JTC1*, Hangzhou, China, Tech. Rep. JVT-U091, Oct. 2006.

[43]   H. Schwarz, C. Bartnik, S. Bosse, *et al.* '3D video coding using advanced prediction, depth modeling, and encoder control methods'. in *Proc. Picture Coding Symp.*, Krakow, Poland, May 2012, pp. 1–4.

[44]   K. Müller, P. Merkle, and T. Wiegand. '3D video representation using depth maps'. *Proc. IEEE, Special Issue 3D Media Displays*, vol. 99, no. 4, pp. 643–656, 2011.

[45]   I. Daribo, C. Tillier, and B. Pesquet-Popescu. 'Adaptive wavelet coding of the depth map for stereoscopic view synthesis'. in *Proc. IEEE Int. Workshop Multimedia Signal Process.*, Cairns, Australia, Oct. 2008, pp. 34–39.

[46]   M. Maitre and M. N. Do. 'Shape-adaptive wavelet encoding of depth maps'. in *Proc. Picture Coding Symposium*, Chicago, IL, USA, May 2009, pp. 1–4.

[47]   S.-Y. Kim and Y.-S. Ho. 'Mesh-based depth coding for 3D video using hierarchical decomposition of depth maps'. in *Proc. IEEE Int. Conf. Image Process.*, San Antonio, TX, USA, Sep. 2007, pp. V-117–V-120.

[48]   K.-J. Oh, S. Yea, A. Vetro, and Y.-S. Ho. 'Depth reconstruction filter and down/up sampling for depth coding in 3-D video'. *IEEE Signal Process. Lett.*, vol. 16, no. 9, pp. 747–750, 2009.

[49]   P. Merkle, Y. Morvan, A. Smolic, D. Farin, K. Müller, P. H. N. de With, and T. Wiegand. 'The effects of multiview depth video compression on multi-view rendering'. *Signal Process., Image Communication*, vol. 24, nos. 1–2, pp. 73–88, 2009.

[50]   Y. Morvan, D. Farin, and P. H. N. de With. 'Platelet-based coding of depth maps for the transmission of multiview images'. *Proc. SPIE*, vol. 6055, p. 60550K, 2006.

[51]   I. Daribo, G. Cheung, and D. Florencio. 'Arithmetic edge coding for arbitrarily shaped sub-block motion prediction in depth video compression'. in *Proc. IEEE Int. Conf. Image Process.*, Orlando, FL, USA, Oct. 2012, pp. 1541–1544.

[52]   M. Magnor and B. Girod. 'Data compression for light-field rendering'. *IEEE Trans. on Circuits and Systems for Video Technology*, vol. 10, no. 3, pp. 338–343, 2000.

[53]   A. Jagmohan, A. Sehgal, and N. Ahuja. 'Compression of lightfield rendered images using coset codes'. in *Signals, Systems and Computers, 2004. Conference Record of the Thirty-Seventh Asilomar Conference on*, vol. 1. IEEE, 2003, pp. 830–834.

[54]   B. Girod, C.-L. Chang, P. Ramanathan, and X. Zhu. 'Light field compression using disparity-compensated lifting'. in *Multimedia and Expo, 2003. ICME'03. Proceedings. 2003 International Conference on*, vol. 1. IEEE, 2003, pp. I–373.

[55]   X. Zhu, A. Aaron, and B. Girod. 'Distributed compression for large camera arrays'. *IEEE Workshop on Statistical Signal Processing*, Piscataway, NJ, 2003, pp. 30–33.

[56]   M. Levoy and P. Hanrahan. 'Light field rendering'. in *Proceedings of the 23rd Annual Conference on Computer Graphics and Interactive Techniques*. ACM, New York, 1996, pp. 31–42.

[57]   https://raytrix.de/

[58]   J. Xu, R. Joshi, and R. A. Cohen. 'Overview of the emerging HEVC screen content coding extension'. *IEEE Trans. on Circuits and Systems for Video Technology*, vol. 26, no. 1, pp. 50–62, 2016.

[59]   J. Boyce, J. Chen, Y. Chen, *et al.* 'Edition 2 draft text of high efficiency video coding (HEVC), Including Format Range (RExt), scalability (SHVC), and multi-view (MV-HEVC) extensions'. *18th JCT-VC meeting, Sapporo, Japan*, document JCTVC-R1013, Jul. 2014.

[60]   F. Dai, J. Zhang, Y. Ma and Y. Zhang, 'Lenselet image compression scheme based on subaperture images streaming'. *Image Processing (ICIP), 2015 IEEE International Conference on*, Quebec City, QC, 2015, pp. 4733–4737.

[61]   C. Perra. 'Lossless plenoptic image compression using adaptive block differential prediction'. in *2015 IEEE International Conference on Acoustics, Speech and Signal Processing (ICASSP)*. IEEE, Piscataway, NJ, 2015, pp. 1231–1234.

[62]   Y. Li, M. Sjostrom, R. Olsson, and U. Jennehag. 'Coding of focused plenoptic contents by displacement intra prediction'. *IEEE Trans. on Circuits and Systems for Video Technology*, vol. 26, no. 7, pp. 1308–1319, 2016.

[63]   Y. Li, M. Sjostrom, R. Olsson, and U. Jennehag. 'Scalable coding of plenoptic images by using a sparse set and disparities'. *IEEE Transactions on Image Processing*, vol. 25, no. 1, pp. 80–91, 2016.

[64] Y. Li, M. Sjöström, R. Olsson and U. Jennehag. 'Scalable coding of plenoptic images by using a sparse set and disparities'. *IEEE Transactions on Image Processing*, vol. 25, no. 1, pp. 80–91, 2016, doi: 10.1109/TIP.2015.2498406.

[65] J. Chen, and L. P. Chau. 'Light field compressed sensing over a disparity-aware dictionary'. *IEEE Trans. on Circuits and Systems for Video Technology*, vol. 27, no. 4, pp. 855–865, 2017.

[66] X. Jin. C. Wang, F. Jiang, *et al.* 'Summary of evidence in lenslet coding", *ISO/IEC JTC1/SC29/WG04*, m56790, Online, April 2021, https://github.com/google/draco.

[67] G. E. Hinton. 'Learning translation invariant recognition in a massively parallel networks'. in *International Conference on Parallel Architectures and Languages Europe*. Springer, Berlin, 1987, pp. 1–13.

[68] F. Rosenblatt. *Principles of Neurodynamics: Perceptrons and the Theory of Brain Mechanisms*. Washingotn, DC: Spartan Books; 1962.

[69] P. Werbos. 'New tools for prediction and analysis in the behavioral sciences'. Ph.D. dissertation, Harvard University, 1974.

[70] D. E. Rumelhart, G. E. Hinton, and R. J. Williams. 'Learning representations by back-propagating errors'. *Nature*, vol. 323, no. 6088, p. 533, 1986.

[71] Y. Le Cun, O. Matan, B. Boser, *et al.* 'Handwritten zip code recognition with multilayer networks'. in *Proceedings 10th International Conference on Pattern Recognition*. IEEE, Piscataway, NJ, 1990, pp. 35–40.

[72] L. Chua and T. Lin. 'A neural network approach to transform image coding'. *International Journal of Circuit Theory and Applications*, vol. 16, no. 3, pp. 317–324, 1988.

[73] M. W. Gardner and S. Dorling. 'Artificial neural networks (the multi-layer perceptron) – a review of applications in the atmospheric sciences'. *Atmospheric Environment*, vol. 32, no. 14–15, pp. 2627–2636, 1998.

[74] R. J. Schalkoff, *Artificial Neural Networks*. McGraw-Hill, New York, 1997, vol. 1.

[75] N. Sonehara, M. Kawato, S. Miyake, and K. Nakane. 'Image data compression using a neural network model'. in *Proc. IJCNN*, vol. 2, 1989, pp. 35–41.

[76] G. Cottrell, P. Munro and D. Zipser. 'Image compression by back propagation: An example of extensional programming'. *Models of Cognition: Rev. of Cognitive Science*, pp. 208–240, 1989.

[77] G. Sicuranza, G. Romponi, and S. Marsi. 'Artificial neural network for image compression'. *Electronics Letters*, vol. 26, no. 7, pp. 477–479, 1990.

[78] R. D. Dony and S. Haykin. 'Neural network approaches to image compression'. *Proceedings of the IEEE*, vol. 83, no. 2, pp. 288–303, 1995.

[79] S. Dianat, N. Nasrabadi, and S. Venkataraman. 'A non-linear predictor for differential pulse-code encoder (DPCM) using artificial neural networks'. in *International Conference on Acoustics, Speech, and Signal Processing*, ICASSP 1991, pp. 2793–2796

[80]   C. Manikopoulos. 'Neural network approach to DPCM system design for image coding'. *IEE Proceedings I (Communications, Speech and Vision)*, vol. 139, no. 5, pp. 501–507, 1992.

[81]   A. Namphol, S. H. Chin, and M. Arozullah. 'Image compression with a hierarchical neural network'. *IEEE Trans. on Aerospace and Electronic Systems*, vol. 32, no. 1, pp. 326–338, 1996.

[82]   J. G. Daugman. 'Complete discrete 2-D Gabor transforms by neural networks for image analysis and compression'. *IEEE Trans. on Acoustics, Speech, and Signal Processing*, vol. 36, no. 7, pp. 1169–1179, 1988.

[83]   H. Abbas and M. Fahmy. 'Neural model for Karhunen–Loeve transform with application to adaptive image compression'. *IEE Proceedings I (Communications, Speech and Vision)*, vol. 140, no. 2, pp. 135–143, 1993.

[84]   E. Gelenbe. 'Random neural networks with negative and positive signals and product form solution'. *Neural Computation*, vol. 1, no. 4, pp. 502–510, 1989.

[85]   E. Gelenbe and M. Sungur. 'Random network learning and image compression'. in *IEEE International Conference on Neural Networks (ICNN)*, vol. 6, 1994, pp. 3996–3999.

[86]   C. Cramer, E. Gelenbe, and I. Bakircioglu. 'Video compression with random neural networks'. in *Neural Networks for Identification, Control, Robotics, and Signal/Image Processing, International Workshop on*. IEEE, Piscataway, NJ, 1996, pp. 476–484.

[87]   F. Hai, K. F. Hussain, E. Gelenbe, and R. K. Guha. 'Video compression with wavelets and random neural network approximations'. in *Applications of Artificial Neural Networks in Image Processing VI*, vol. 4305. International Society for Optics and Photonics, Bellingham, WA, 2001, pp. 57–65.

[88]   Y. LeCun, Y. Bengio, and G. Hinton. 'Deep learning'. *Nature*, vol. 521, no. 7553, p. 436, 2015.

[89]   J. Ballé, V. Laparra, and E. P. Simoncelli. 'End-to-end optimized image compression'. arXiv preprint arXiv:1611.01704, 2016.

[90]   J. Ballé, V. Laparra, and E. Simoncelli. 'End-to-end optimization of non-linear transform codes for perceptual quality'. in *Picture Coding Symposium (PCS)*, 2016, pp. 1–5.

[91]   J. Ballé, D. Minnen, S. Singh, S. J. Hwang, and N. Johnston. 'Variational image compression with a scale hyperprior'. in *International Conference on Learning Representations*, 2018.

[92]   D. Minnen, J. Ballé, and G. D. Toderici. 'Joint autoregressive and hierarchical priors for learned image compression'. in *Advances in Neural Information Processing Systems 31*. Curran Associates, Inc., Red Hook, NY, 2018, pp. 10 771–10 780.

[93]   L. Zhou, C. Cai, Y. Gao, S. Su, and J. Wu. 'Variational autoencoder for low bit-rate image compression'. in *Proceedings of the IEEE Conference on Computer Vision and Pattern Recognition Workshops*, 2018, pp. 2617–2620.

[94]   E. Agustsson, F. Mentzer, M. Tschannen, *et al.* 'Soft-to-hard vector quantization for end-to-end learning compressible representations'. in *Advances in Neural Information Processing Systems*, 2017, pp. 1141–1151.

[95]   L. Theis, W. Shi, A. Cunningham, and F. Huszar. 'Lossy image compression with compressive autoencoders'. arXiv preprint arXiv:1703.00395, 2017.

[96]   E. Ahanonu, M. Marcellin, and A. Bilgin. 'Lossless image compression using reversible integer wavelet transforms and convolutional neural networks'. in *IEEE Data Compression Conference*, 2018.

[97]   S. Hochreiter and J. Schmidhuber. 'Long short-term memory'. *Neural Computation*, vol. 9, no. 8, pp. 1735–1780, 1997.

[98]   K. Cho, B. van Merriënboer, D. Bahdanau, and Y. Bengio. 'On the properties of neural machine translation: Encoder-decoder approaches'. in *Proceedings of SSST-8, Eighth Workshop on Syntax, Semantics and Structure in Statistical Translation*, 2014, pp. 103–111.

[99]   J. Chung, C. Gulcehre, K. Cho, and Y. Bengio. 'Empirical evaluation of gated recurrent neural networks on sequence modeling'. Presented in NIPS 2014 Deep Learning and Representation Learning Workshop, arXiv preprint arXiv:1412.3555, 2014.

[100] G. Toderici, D. Vincent, N. Johnston, *et al.* 'Full resolution image compression with recurrent neural networks'. in *IEEE Conference on Computer Vision and Pattern Recognition (CVPR)*, 2017, pp. 5435–5443.

[101] D. Minnen, G. Toderici, M. Covell, *et al.* 'Spatially adaptive image compression using a tiled deep network'. in *IEEE International Conference on Image Processing (ICIP)*, pp. 2796–2800, 2017.

[102] O. Rippel and L. Bourdev. 'Real-time adaptive image compression'. in *Proceedings of the 34th International Conference on Machine Learning*, vol. 70, pp. 2922–2930, 2017.

[103] C. Jia, X. Zhang, S. Wang, S. Wang, S. Pu, and S. Ma. 'Light field image compression using generative adversarial network-based view synthesis'. *IEEE Journal on Emerging and Selected Topics in Circuits and Systems*, 2018.

[104] K. Gregor, I. Danihelka, A. Graves, D. J. Rezende, and D. Wierstra. 'DRAW: A recurrent neural network for image generation.' in *Proceedings of the 32nd International Conference on Machine Learning*, vol. 37, pp. 1462–1471, 2015.

[105] K. Gregor, F. Besse, D. J. Rezende, I. Danihelka, and D. Wierstra. 'Towards conceptual compression'. in *Advances in Neural Information Processing Systems*, 2016, pp. 3549–3557.

[106] E. Agustsson, M. Tschannen, F. Mentzer, R. Timofte, and L. Van Gool. 'Extreme learned image compression with GANs'. in *Proceedings of the IEEE Conference on Computer Vision and Pattern Recognition Workshops*, 2018, pp. 2587–2590.

[107] J. Li, B. Li, J. Xu, R. Xiong, and W. Gao. 'Fully connected network-based intra prediction for image coding'. *IEEE Trans. on Image Processing*, vol. 27, no. 7, pp. 3236–3247, 2018.

[108]   Y. Li, L. Li, Z. Li, *et al.* 'A hybrid neural network for chroma intra pre-diction'. in *2018 25th IEEE International Conference on Image Processing (ICIP)*. IEEE, Piscataway, NJ, 2018, pp. 1797–1801.

[109]   J. Pfaff, P. Helle, D. Maniry, *et al.* 'Intra prediction modes based on neural networks'. in *JVET-J0037. ISO/IEC JTC/SC 29/WG 11*, Apr. 2018, pp. 1–14.

[110]   Y. Li, D. Liu, H. Li, *et al.* 'Convolutional neural network-based block up-sampling for intra frame coding'. *IEEE Trans. on Circuits and Systems for Video Technology*, vol. 28, no. 9, pp. 2316–2330, 2018.

[111]   J. Lin, D. Liu, H. Yang, H. Li, and F. Wu. 'Convolutional neural network-based block up-sampling for HEVC'. *IEEE Trans. on Circuits and Systems for Video Technology*, 2018.

[112]   R. Molina, A. Katsaggelos, L. Alvarez, and J. Mateos. 'Toward a new video compression scheme using super-resolution'. in *Visual Communications and Image Processing (VCIP)*, vol. 6077. International Society for Optics and Photonics, Bellingham, WA, 2006, p. 607706.

[113]   M. Shen, P. Xue, and C. Wang. 'Down-sampling based video coding using super-resolution technique'. *IEEE Trans. on Circuits and Systems for Video Technology*, vol. 21, no. 6, pp. 755–765, 2011.

[114]   J. Pfaff, P. Helle, D. Maniry, *et al.* 'Neural network based intra prediction for video coding'. in *Proc. SPIE 10752*, Applications of Digital Image Processing XLI, 1075213, 2018. doi: 10.1117/12.2321273.

[115]   D. Marpe, and T. Wiegand. 'Neural network based intra prediction for video coding'. in *Applications of Digital Image Processing XLI*, vol. 10752. International Society for Optics and Photonics, Bellingham, WA, 2018, p. 1075213.

[116]   L. Feng, X. Zhang, X. Zhang, S. Wang, R. Wang, and S. Ma. 'A dual-network based super-resolution for compressed high definition video'. in *Pacific-Rim Conference on Multimedia*. Springer, Berlin, 2018, pp. 600–610.

[117]   Y. Li, D. Liu, H. Li, L. Li, Z. Li, and F. Wu. 'Learning a convolutional neural network for image compact-resolution'. *IEEE Transactions on Image Processing*, vol. 28, no. 3, pp. 1092–1107, 2019.

[118]   Z.-T. Zhang, C.-H. Yeh, L.-W. Kang, and M.-H. Lin. 'Efficient CTU-based intra frame coding for HEVC based on deep learning'. in *Asia-Pacific Signal and Information Processing Association Annual Summit and Conference (APSIPA ASC)*. IEEE, Piscataway, NJ, 2017, pp. 661–664.

[119]   Y. Hu, W. Yang, S. Xia, W.-H. Cheng, and J. Liu. 'Enhanced intra pre-diction with recurrent neural network in video coding'. in *IEEE Data Compression Conference (DCC)*, 2018, pp. 413–413.

[120]   S. Huo, D. Liu, F. Wu, and H. Li. 'Convolutional neural network-based motion compensation refinement for video coding'. in *International Symposium on Circuits and Systems (ISCAS)*. IEEE, Piscataway, NJ, pp. 1–4, 2018.

[121] Y. Dai, D. Liu, and F. Wu. 'A convolutional neural network approach for post-processing in HEVC intra coding'. in *International Conference on Multimedia Modeling*. Springer, Berlin, 2017, pp. 28–39.

[122] J. Liu, S. Xia, W. Yang, M. Li, and D. Liu. 'One-for-all: Grouped variation network-based fractional interpolation in video coding'. *IEEE Transactions on Image Processing*, vol. 28, no. 5, pp. 2140–2151, 2019.

[123] N. Yan, D. Liu, H. Li, B. Li, L. Li, and F. Wu. 'Convolutional neural network-based fractional-pixel motion compensation'. *IEEE Trans. on Circuits and Systems for Video Technology*, 2018.

[124] Y. Vatis, and J. Ostermann. 'Adaptive interpolation filter for H.264/AVC'. *IEEE Trans. on Circuits and Systems for Video Technology*, vol. 19, no. 2, pp. 179–192, 2009.

[125] L. Zhao, S. Wang, X. Zhang, S. Wang, S. Ma, and W. Gao. 'Enhanced CTU-level inter prediction with deep frame rate up-conversion for high efficiency video coding'. in *25th IEEE International Conference on Image Processing (ICIP)*, 2018, pp. 206–210.

[126] L. Zhao, S. Wang, X. Zhang, S. Wang, S. Ma and W. Gao, 'Enhanced motion-compensated video coding with deep virtual reference frame generation'. *IEEE Transactions on Image Processing*, vol. 28, no. 10, pp. 4832-4844, 2019, doi: 10.1109/TIP.2019.2913545.

[127] S. Niklaus, L. Mai, and F. Liu. 'Video frame interpolation via adaptive separable convolution'. IEEE ICCV 2017, arXiv preprint arXiv: 1708.01692, 2017.

[128] J. Chen, E. Alshina, G. J. Sullivan, J.-R. Ohm, and J. Boyce. 'Algorithm description of joint exploration test model 1'. in *JVET-A1001. ISO/IEC JTC/SC 29/WG 11*, Oct. 2015, pp. 1–48.

[129] Z. Zhao, S. Wang, S. Wang, X. Zhang, S. Ma, and J. Yang. 'CNN-based bi-directional motion compensation for high efficiency video coding'. in *International Symposium on Circuits and Systems (ISCAS)*, 2018, pp. 1–4.

[130] Z. Zhao, S. Wang, S. Wang, X. Zhang, S. Ma and J. Yang, 'Enhanced bi-prediction with convolutional neural network for high-efficiency video coding'. *IEEE Trans. on Circuits and Systems for Video Technology*, vol. 29, no. 11, pp. 3291–3301, 2019, doi: 10.1109/TCSVT.2018.2876399.

[131] H. Zhang, L. Song, Z. Luo, and X. Yang. 'Learning a convolutional neural network for fractional interpolation in HEVC inter coding'. *Visual Communications and Image Processing (VCIP)*, 2017, pp. 1–4.

[132] N. Yan, D. Liu, H. Li, T. Xu, F. Wu, and B. Li. 'Convolutional neural network-based invertible half-pixel interpolation filter for video coding'. in *25th IEEE International Conference on Image Processing (ICIP)*. IEEE, Piscataway, NJ, 2018, pp. 201–205.

[133] M. M. Alam, T. D. Nguyen, M. T. Hagan, and D. M. Chandler. 'A perceptual quantization strategy for HEVC based on a convolutional neural network trained on natural images'. in *Applications of Digital Image Processing XXXVIII*, vol. 9599. International Society for Optics and Photonics, Bellingham, WA, 2015, p. 959918.

[134] Z. Wang, A. C. Bovik, H. R. Sheikh, and E. P. Simoncelli. 'Image quality assessment: From error visibility to structural similarity'. *IEEE Trans. on Image Processing*, vol. 13, no. 4, pp. 600–612, 2004.
[135] R. Song, D. Liu, H. Li, and F. Wu. 'Neural network-based arithmetic coding of intra prediction modes in HEVC'. *in* Visual Communications and Image Processing (VCIP), 2017, pp. 1–4.
[136] Y. Le Cun, L. Bottou, Y. Bengio, and P. Haffner. 'Gradient-based learning applied to document recognition'. *Proceedings of the IEEE*, vol. 86, no. 11, pp. 2278–2324, 1998.
[137] S. Puri, S. Lasserre, and P. Le Callet. 'CNN-based transform index prediction in multiple transforms framework to assist entropy coding'. in *European Signal Processing Conference (EUSIPCO)*, 2017, pp. 798–802.
[138] G. Cote, B. Erol, M. Gallant, and F. Kossentini. 'H.263+: Video coding at low bit rates'. *IEEE Trans. on Circuits and Systems for Video Technology*, vol. 8, no. 7, pp. 849–866, 1998.
[139] Y. Zhang, T. Shen, X. Ji, Y. Zhang, R. Xiong, and Q. Dai. 'Residual highway convolutional neural networks for in-loop filtering in HEVC'. *IEEE Trans. on Image Processing*, vol. 27, no. 8, pp. 3827–3841, 2018.
[140] C. Jia, S. Wang, X. Zhang, S. Wang, and S. Ma. 'Spatial-temporal residue network based in-loop filter for video coding'. in *Visual Communications and Image Processing (VCIP)*, 2017, pp. 1–4.
[141] C. Jia, S. Wang, X. Zhang, *et al.* 'Content-aware convolutional neural network for in-loop filtering in high efficiency video coding'. *IEEE Trans. on Image Processing*, vol. 28, no. 7, pp. 3343–3356, 2019.
[142] X. Zhang, S. Wang, K. Gu, W. Lin, S. Ma, and W. Gao. 'Just-noticeable difference-based perceptual optimization for JPEG compression'. *IEEE Signal Processing Letters*, vol. 24, no. 1, pp. 96–100, 2017.
[143] X. Song, J. Yao, L. Zhou, *et al.* 'A practical convolutional neural network as loop filter for intra frame'. arXiv preprint arXiv:1805.06121, 2018.
[144] W.-S. Park, and M. Kim. 'CNN-based in-loop filtering for coding efficiency improvement'. in *Image, Video, and Multidimensional Signal Processing Workshop (IVMSP)*, 2016, pp. 1–5.
[145] J. Kang, S. Kim, and K. M. Lee. 'Multi-modal/multi-scale convolutional neural network based in-loop filter design for next generation video codec'. in *International Conference on Image Processing (ICIP)*, 2017, pp. 26–30.
[146] C. Dong, Y. Deng, C. Change Loy, and X. Tang. 'Compression artifacts reduction by a deep convolutional network'. in *Proceedings of the IEEE International Conference on Computer Vision*, 2015, pp. 576–584.
[147] C. Dong, C. C. Loy, K. He, and X. Tang. 'Learning a deep convolutional network for image super-resolution'. in *European Conference on Computer Vision*. Springer, Berlin, 2014, pp. 184–199.
[148] K. Li, B. Bare, and B. Yan. 'An efficient deep convolutional neural networks model for compressed image deblocking'. in *International Conference on Multimedia and Expo (ICME)*, 2017, pp. 1320–1325.

[149] R. Yang, M. Xu, Z. Wang, and T. Li. 'Multi-frame quality enhancement for compressed video'. in *Proceedings of the IEEE Conference on Computer Vision and Pattern Recognition*, 2018, pp. 6664–6673.

[150] L. Zhu, Y. Zhang, S. Wang, H. Yuan, S. Kwong, and H. H.-S. Ip. 'Convolutional neural network-based synthesized view quality enhancement for 3D video coding'. *IEEE Transactions on Image Processing*, vol. 27, no. 11, pp. 5365–5377, 2018.

[151] L. Cavigelli, P. Hager, and L. Benini. 'CAS-CNN: A deep convolutional neural network for image compression artifact suppression'. in *International Joint Conference on Neural Networks (IJCNN)*. IEEE, Piscataway, NJ, 2017, pp. 752–759.

[152] B. Zheng, R. Sun, X. Tian, and Y. Chen. 'S-Net: A scalable convolutional neural network for JPEG compression artifact reduction'. *Journal of Electronic Imaging*, vol. 27, no. 4, p. 043037, 2018.

[153] T. Chen, H. Liu, Q. Shen, T. Yue, X. Cao, and Z. Ma. 'DeepCoder: A deep neural network-based video compression'. in *Visual Communications and Image Processing (VCIP)*, IEEE, Piscataway, NJ, 2017, pp. 1–4.

[154] Z. Chen, T. He, X. Jin, and F. Wu. 'Learning for video compression'. arXiv preprint arXiv:1804.09869, 2018.

[155] M. Ranzato, A. Szlam, J. Bruna, M. Mathieu, R. Collobert, and S. Chopra. 'Video (language) modeling: A baseline for generative models of natural videos'. arXiv preprint arXiv:1412.6604, 2014.

[156] N. Srivastava, E. Mansimov, and R. Salakhudinov. 'Unsupervised learning of video representations using LSTMS'. in *International Conference on Machine Learning*, 2015, pp. 843–852.

[157] Z. Liu, X. Yu, Y. Gao, S. Chen, X. Ji, and D. Wang. 'CU partition mode decision for HEVC hardwired intra encoder using convolution neural network'. *IEEE Trans. on Image Processing*, vol. 25, no. 11, pp. 5088–5103, 2016.

[158] N. Song, Z. Liu, X. Ji, and D. Wang. 'CNN oriented fast PU mode decision for HEVC hardwired intra encoder'. in *IEEE Global Conference on Signal and Information Processing (GlobalSIP)*, 2017, pp. 239–243.

[159] M. Xu, T. Li, Z. Wang, X. Deng, R. Yang, and Z. Guan. 'Reducing complexity of HEVC: A deep learning approach'. *IEEE Trans. on Image Processing*, vol. 27, no. 10, pp. 5044–5059, 2018.

[160] J. van der Hooft, M. T. Vega, C. Timmerer, A. C. Begen, F. De Turck, and R. Schatz. 'Objective and subjective QoE evaluation for adaptive point cloud streaming'. *Twelfth International Conference on Quality of Multimedia Experience (QoMEX)*, May 2020, doi: 10.1109/QoMEX48832.2020.9123081.

[161] J. Rossignac, A. Safonova, and A. Szymczak. '3D compression made simple: Edgebreaker with ZipandWrap on a corner-table'. in *SMI 2001 International Conference on Shape Modeling and Applications*, 2001.

[162] T. Lewiner, H. Lopes, J. Rossignac, and A. W. Vieira. 'Efficient edge-breaker for surfaces of arbitrary topology". *Proceedings. 17th Brazilian Symposium on Computer Graphics and Image Processing*, Curitiba, Brazil, pp. 218-225, 2004, doi: 10.1109/SIBGRA.2004.1352964.

[163] A. Malgo, G. Lavoue, F. Dupont, and C. Hudelot. '3D mesh compression: Survey, comparisons and emerging trends'. *ACM Computing Surveys*, vol. 9, no. 4, article 39, pp. 39:1–39:40, 2013.

[164] A. Doumanoglou, P. Drakoulis, N. Zioulis, D. Zarpalas, and P. Daras. 'Benchmarking open-source static 3D mesh codecs for immersive media interactive live streaming'. *Journal on Emerging and Selected Topics in Circuits and Systems*, 2019, doi: 10.1109/JETCAS.2019.2898768.

[165] S. Schwarz, M. Preda, V. Baroncini, et al., 'Emerging MPEG standards for point cloud compression'. *IEEE Journal on Emerging and Selected Topics in Circuits and Systems*, vol. 9, no. 1, pp. 133–148, 2019, doi: 10.1109/JETCAS.2018.2885981.

[166] Summary on MPEG-I Visual Activities, Serial Number 20339, ISO/IEC JTC 1/SC 29/WG 04 N 0086, April 2021, Online.

[167] R. Doré. 'Technicolor 3DoF+ test materials'. *Standard ISO/IEC JTC1/SC29/WG11 MPEG/M42349*, San Diego, CA, USA, Apr. 2018.

[168] J. M. Boyce, R. Doré, A. Dziembowski, *et al.* 'MPEG immersive video coding standard'. *Proceedings of the IEEE*, pp. 1–16, March 2021, doi: 10.1109/JPROC.2021.3062590.

[169] Text of ISO/IEC DIS 23090-12(E), Information technology — Coded representation of immersive media — Part 12: Immersive Video, ISO/IEC JTC1/SC29/WG04, 2021.

[170] Text of ISO/IEC DIS 23090-12(E), 'OpenV3C – Multi-platform open-source implementation of the V-PCC'. ISO/IEC JTC 1/SC 29/WG 11/ N19375, April 2020.

[171] V. Zakharchenko. 'Open-source initiative for dynamic point cloud content delivery'. *ISO/IEC JTC1/SC29/WG11 MPEG2020/m53349*, April 2020.

[172] A. T. Hinds, D. Doyen, P. Carballeira, and G. Lafruit, 'Toward the realization of six degrees-of-freedom with compressed light fields'. *IEEE International Conference on Multimedia and Expo (ICME)*, August 2017, pp. 1171–1176, doi: 10.1109/ICME.2017.8019543.

[173] ISO/IEC FDIS 21794-2(E), Information technology — Plenoptic image coding system — Part 2: Light field coding, ISO/IEC JTC1/SC29/WG01, 2021.

[174] JPEG dense light field coding: C. Conti, L. D. Soares, and P. Nunes, 'Dense light field coding: A survey'. *IEEE Access*, vol. 8, pp. 49244–49284, 2020, doi: 10.1109/ACCESS.2020.2977767.

Chapter 16

Conclusion and future perspectives

Throughout the textbook, we have shown that VR/AR/XR technology that will provide 6DoF free navigation experiences within a photo-realistic, immersive environment is about to come ... but is not yet fully mature.

3D graphics technology used in 3D video games simulates the physical world with light equations, kinematics, raytracing, etc., and all this represents too high a compute cost for simple immersive applications where one wants to observe the 3D scene from any viewpoint, for instance on a smartphone, without actively interacting with it. Alternative technology using depth sensing devices or 3D reconstruction software for creating point clouds or 3D meshes are not yet fully mature either, especially not for rendering tiny details such as hair and fur, as in the rightmost example of Figure 16.1.

On the other hand, 360 videos, made of 2D videos out of which a viewport is selected in correspondence to the viewer's head and body pose, can present high levels of detail in the scene, at a relatively low cost, but their huge drawback is that they are limited to three degrees of freedom – that is only head rotations are allowed – resulting in strange visual phenomena with static objects following the viewer, and causing severe cybersickness in VR/AR/XR.

Figure 16.1   Non-Lambertian objects with challenging transparencies, specular reflections and fine details

The perfect middle ground is hence 2.5D immersive video, where some 3D geometrical information is added to the 2D captured videos to allow some freedom in the rendering viewpoint. We believe that this is the way to go for applications that need to see the scene from various viewpoints, without the requirement to touch the objects or displace them. Beyond VR/AR/XR, also 3D light field displays like the ones in Chapter 14 might benefit from this technology. This is the reason why MPEG immersive video (MIV) will go beyond its first standard targeting VR, to be published end of 2021.

Exploration studies are already started to prepare for MIV version 2.0, which will also include means to represent very challenging content with transparency, specular reflections, etc., aka non-Lambertian scenes. Figure 16.1 gives some examples of such content. Note that specular reflections, such as the one in the middle picture, can rapidly change their characteristics with a slight movement of the viewpoint in front of the object. It is therefore believed that tiny multi-camera systems will play an important role to acquire such content correctly. So-called plenoptic cameras are built for such situations, using in front of the sensor a microlens sheet acting as a multitude of tiny objective lenses, replicating the scene hundreds of times on the camera sensor, so creating images with tiny parallax changes. With some post-processing, it is then possible to extract all information corresponding to the highly view-dependent reflections and refractions of the objects in Figure 16.1. We will see what the MPEG-I explorations will deliver and how this may lead to a new standard – MIV version 2.0 – in the 3 or 4 coming years... a challenging world ahead!

Index